Praise for Alejandro Jodorowsky and His Works

"... *The Dance of Reality* [film is] a trippy but bighearted reimagining of the young Alejandro's unhappy childhood in a Chilean town ..."

NEW YORK TIMES MAGAZINE

"The best movie director ever!"

MARILYN MANSON, MUSICIAN, ACTOR,
AND MULTIMEDIA ARTIST

"Jodorowsky is a brilliant, wise, gentle, and cunning wizard with tremendous depth of imagination and crystalline insight into the human condition."

DANIEL PINCHBECK, AUTHOR OF
2012: THE RETURN OF QUETZALCOATL

"Alejandro Jodorowsky seamlessly and effortlessly weaves together the worlds of art, the confined social structure, and things we can only touch with an open heart and mind."

ERYKAH BADU, SINGER-SONGWRITER,
ACTRESS, ACTIVIST, AND ALCHEMIST

"Rather than clarifying the meaning of his imagery, [*The Spiritual Journey of Alejandro Jodorowsky*] only inspires readers to enjoy its 'mystery'. . . . a worthy read, filled with growing pains and crises that end in artistic triumph and achievement of wisdom and compassion."

SCENE4 MAGAZINE

Alejandro Jodorowsky with one of his cats.

The Dance of Reality

A Psychomagical Autobiography

Alejandro Jodorowsky

Translated by Ariel Godwin

Park Street Press
Rochester, Vermont • Toronto, Canada

Park Street Press
One Park Street
Rochester, Vermont 05767
www.ParkStPress.com

Text stock is SFI certified

Park Street Press is a division of Inner Traditions International

Originally published in Spanish under the title *La danza de la realidad: Psicomagia y psicochamanismo* by Ediciones Siruela
First U.S. edition published in 2014 by Park Street Press

Library of Congress Cataloging-in-Publication Data
Jodorowsky, Alejandro, author.
  [Danza de la realidad. Spanish]
  A psychomagical autobiography / Alejandro Jodorowsky ; translated by Ariel Godwin.
     pages cm
  Includes index.
  ISBN 978-1-62055-281-0 (pbk.) — ISBN 978-1-62055-282-7 (e-book)
  1. Jodorowsky, Alejandro. 2. Authors, Chilean—20th century—Biography.
  3. Motion picture producers and directors—Chile—Biography. 4. Theatrical producers and directors—Chile—Biography. 5. Actors—Chile—Biography.
  I. Godwin, Ariel, translator. II. Title.
  PQ7298.2.O3Z46 2014
  868'.6409—dc23
  [B]

                                                              2014004218

Printed and bound in the United States by Lake Book Manufacturing, Inc.
The text stock is SFI certified. The Sustainable Forestry Initiative® program promotes sustainable forest management.

10 9 8 7 6 5 4 3 2 1

Text design and layout by Priscilla Baker
This book was typeset in Garamond Premier Pro with Helvetica Neue and Legacy Sans used as display typefaces

Contents

There are problems that knowledge cannot solve. One day we will come to understand that science is nothing but a type of imagination, a specialized type, with all the advantages and all the dangers that specializing brings with it.

GEORGE GRODDECK, *THE BOOK OF THE IT*

ONE

Childhood

I was born in 1929 in the north of Chile, in a region conquered from Peru and Bolivia. Tocopilla is the name of my birthplace. It is a small port city located, perhaps not by coincidence, on the 22nd parallel. Each of the 22 arcana of the Tarot of Marseilles is drawn in a rectangle composed of two squares. The upper square may symbolize heaven, the spiritual life, while the lower square may symbolize Earth, material life. A third square inscribed at the center of this rectangle symbolizes the human being, the union between light and darkness, receptive to what is above, active in what is below. This symbolism, found in the ancient myths of China and Egypt (the god Shu, the "empty being," separates the earth-father Geb from the sky-mother Nut), also appears in Chilean indigenous Mapuche mythology: "In the beginning, sky and earth were so close together that there was no space in between them, until the arrival of the conscious being, which liberated humankind, raising the sky." In other words, establishing the difference between animals and humans.

In the Andean language of Quechua, *Toco* means "double sacred square" and *Pilla* means "devil." In this case, the devil is not the incarnation of evil but a being of the subterranean dimension who gazes through a window made of both spirit and matter—that is, the body—in order to observe the world and share his knowledge with it. Among the Mapuche *Pillán* means "the soul, the human spirit arrived at its final destination."

At times I have wondered whether it was the influence of having been born at the 22nd parallel, in a place called *Double Sacred Square*—a window through which consciousness emerges—that caused me to be so absorbed by the Tarot for much of my life, or whether I was born already predestined to do what I have done sixty years later: to renew the Tarot of Marseilles and to invent psychomagic. Does destiny really exist? Can our lives be oriented toward purposes that surpass the individual interest?

Was it a coincidence that my good teacher at the public school was called Mr. Toro? There is an obvious similarity between "Toro" and "Tarot." He taught me to read with his own personal method by showing me a deck of cards, each of which had a letter printed on it. He then told me to shuffle them, take a few from the deck at random, and try to form words. The first word I spelled—I was no more than four years old—was OJO (eye). When I spoke the word in my high voice, it was as if something suddenly exploded in my brain; thus, in one fell swoop, I learned to read. Mr. Toro, a great smile dawning on his dark face, congratulated me. "I'm not surprised that you learned to read so quickly. You have a golden eye (*ojo d'oro*) in the middle of your name." And he arranged the cards like so: "alejandr OJO D ORO wsky." This moment marked me forever, first because it broadened my view by introducing me to the Eden that is reading, and second because it set me apart from the rest of the world. I was not like other children. Eventually I was placed in a higher grade with older boys who became my enemies because they could not read with my level of fluency. All these boys, most of them sons of out-of-work miners (the stock market crash of 1929 had reduced 70 percent of Chileans to poverty), had dark brown hair and small noses. But I, descended from Russian-Jewish immigrants, had a large, hooked nose and very light hair. This was all it took for them to dub me "Pinocchio," and with their mockery to dissuade me from wearing shorts: "Milky legs!" Perhaps because I had a golden eye, as well as in order to mitigate my awful lack of friends, I cloistered myself in the recently opened town library. At the time, I paid no heed to the emblem above the door of a compass crossed with a square; the library had been founded by Masons. There, in the quiet shadows, I read for hours from the books that the kind librarian allowed me to take from the shelves: fairy tales, adventure stories, adaptations of classics for children, and dictionaries of symbols. One day while browsing among the shelves I ran across a yellowed volume: *Les Tarots* by Eteilla. All my efforts to read it were in vain. The letters looked strange and the words were incomprehensible. I began to worry that I had forgotten how to read. When I communicated my anguish to the librarian, he began to laugh. "But how could you understand it; it's written in French, my young friend! I can't understand it either!" Oh, how I felt drawn to those mysterious pages! I flipped through them, seeing many numbers, sums, the frequent occurrence of the word *Thot,* some geometric shapes . . . but what fascinated me most was a rectangle inside which a princess, wearing a three-pointed crown and seated on a throne, was caressing a lion that was resting its head on her knees. The animal had an expression of profound intelligence combined with an extreme gentleness. Such a placid creature! I liked the image so much that I committed a transgression that I still have not repented: I tore out the page and brought it home to my room. Concealed beneath a floorboard, the card "STRENGTH" became my secret treasure. In the strength of my innocence, I fell in love with the princess.

I thought of, dreamed of, and imagined this friendship with a peaceable beast so much that reality brought me into contact with a real lion. My father, Jaime, had worked as a circus performer before settling down and opening his shop, Casa Ukrania. Trapeze stunts were his specialty, and later hanging by his hair. In this town of Tocopilla, built up against the mountains of the Tarapacá Desert where it had not rained for three centuries, the warm winters were an irresistible attraction for all manner of spectacles. Among them was the great circus of the Human Eagles. My father took me to this circus, and afterward brought me to visit the performers, who remembered him well. I was six years old on that day when two clowns—one who went by the name of Lettuce, clad in green with a green nose and wig, and another called Carrot, clad similarly in orange—placed a lion cub in my arms that had been born just a few days earlier.

Holding a lion that was small but stronger and heavier than a cat, with its broad paws, large snout, soft fur, and eyes of an incommensurable innocence, was an immense pleasure. I took the little animal to the sawdust-covered ring and played with him. I simply became another lion cub myself. I absorbed his animal essence, his energy. Later, as I sat cross-legged on the floor of the ring, the lion cub stopped running back and forth and came to rest his head on my knee. It seemed to me as if he remained there for an eternity. When he finally left, I burst into disconsolate tears. Neither the clowns, nor the other performers, nor my father could quiet me down. Jaime, now in a bad mood, led me by the hand back to our house. My lamentations continued for at least another couple of hours.

Later, once I calmed down, I felt as if my hands had the strength of the lion cub's large paws. I went down to the beach that was a couple of hundred meters from the main street, and there, feeling infused with the power of the king of beasts, I challenged the ocean. The waves that lapped my feet were small. I began to throw pebbles at the waves in order to make the ocean angry. After about ten minutes of stone throwing, the waves began to grow bigger. I thought I had enraged the blue monster. I continued throwing stones with all my might. The waves started to get violent, some of them very large. Then a rough hand grabbed my arm. "Stop, foolish child!" It was a homeless woman who lived by a dumping site; people called her the Queen of Cups, just like the Tarot card, simply because she was often seen falling down drunk, wearing a corroded brass crown on her head. "A little flame can burn down a forest, and one stone can kill all the fish!"

The house in which I lived during my childhood in Tocopilla.

I, six months old, when actor and spectator were not yet separate.

I struggled free from her grip and shouted scornfully at her from the height of my imagined throne. "Let go of me, you old stinker! Leave me alone or I'll throw stones at you too!" She recoiled, startled. I was about to return to my attacks when the Queen of Cups, uttering a cat-like yowl, pointed toward the sea. An enormous silvery cloud was moving toward the beach, and following above it was a thick dark cloud! In no way do I pretend to claim that my childish actions were the cause of what happened next, and yet it is strange that all these events occurred at the same time, bringing with them a lesson that would never fade from my mind. For some mysterious reason, thousands of sardines began to wash up on the beach. The waves threw them, already dying, onto the dark sand, which gradually became covered by the silver of their scales. This brilliance quickly vanished, for the sky began to turn black, full of voracious seagulls. The drunken mendicant, fleeing toward her shelter, yelled at me. "Murderous child! Torturing the ocean like that, you killed all the fish!"

I felt as if every fish was staring at me accusingly in the agony of its death throes. I filled my arms with sardines and threw them back into the water. The ocean responded by throwing an army of dead fish back at me. I kept throwing them back in. The seagulls snatched them from me, uttering deafening shrieks. I sat down on the sand. The world was offering me two options: I could suffer with the anguish of the sardines or rejoice at the good fortune of the seagulls. The balance tilted toward joy when I saw a crowd of poor people—men, women, children—chasing away the birds and gathering up every last fish with frenetic enthusiasm. The balance tilted toward sadness when I saw the seagulls, deprived of their banquet, pecking dejectedly at the few morsels that remained on the beach.

Naively, I told myself that in this reality—in which I, Pinocchio, felt like an outsider—all things were interconnected in a dense web of suffering and pleasure. There were no small causes; every action produced effects that extended beyond the confines of space and time.

I was so affected by this carpet of beached fish that I began to view the crowd of poor people (who lived in a slum of shacks called La Manchurria, built from rusty corrugated iron, scraps of cardboard, and potato sacks) as the stranded sardines and the upper class of merchants and electric company workers to which I belonged as the greedy seagulls. Thus I discovered charity.

There was a short pole by the door of Casa Ukrania with a handle embedded in it, used for raising and lowering the shop's metal shutters. Sometimes, Gadfly would come and scratch his back on it. He was thus named because he had two stumps in place of arms that, according to those who mocked him, wiggled like the wings of an insect. The poor man was one of the many nitrate miners who had been the victim of a dynamite explosion. The white bosses threw out the injured miners without pity, with empty pockets. One could count by dozens the mutilated men who drank themselves into insanity on methylated spirits in a squalid warehouse by the harbor. I said to Gadfly, "Would you like me to scratch your back?" He looked at me with the eyes of a thrashed angel. "Well . . . if I don't disgust you, young sir." I began scratching with both hands. He let forth hoarse sighs similar to the purrs of a cat. A smile of pleasure and gratitude dawned on his face, which was weathered by the implacable desert sands. I felt liberated from the guilt of having murdered the sardines. Suddenly, my father emerged from the shop and chased off the armless man. "You degenerate *roto*!* Don't come back here again or I'll have you thrown in jail!"

I wanted to explain to Jaime that it was I who had suggested this much-needed remedy for the unfortunate man, but he would not let me speak. "Be quiet, and don't let those abusive bums take advantage of you! Don't ever get near them; they're covered with lice that spread typhus!"

Indeed, the world is a fabric of suffering and pleasure; in every action, good and evil dance together like a pair of lovers.

---

*The Chilean term for an individual from the poorest class, who was usually illiterate.

Today, I still have no idea why I embarked on this folly: one day I got
out of bed saying that I would not go out in the street unless I had red
shoes. My parents, accustomed to having an unusual son, urged me to
be patient. Such footwear was not to be found in the small shoe shop
in Tocopilla. They were more likely to be found in Iquique, a hundred
kilometers away. A traveling salesman agreed to take my mother, Sara
Felicidad, to that large port city in his automobile. She returned smiling, bringing with her a cardboard box containing a fine pair of red
boots with rubber soles.

Putting them on, I felt as if wings were sprouting from my heels. I
ran to school, taking agile leaps along the way. I did not mind the torrent of mockery from my classmates, I was used to that. The only one
who applauded my taste was the good Mr. Toro. (Did my desire for
red shoes come directly from the Tarot? In it, the Fool, the Emperor,
the Hanged Man, and the Lovers all wear red shoes.) Carlitos, my desk
mate, was the poorest of all the children. After school he would sit on
benches in the town square, equipped with a little box, and offer shoe-
shining services. It embarrassed me to have Carlitos kneel at my feet,
brushing my shoes, applying color and polish to make the dirty leather
shine again. But I had him do it every day in order to give him the
opportunity to earn a little money. When I placed my red shoes on his
box, he gave a cry of joy and admiration. "Oh, those are so nice! It's
lucky I have red dye and neutral polish. I'll make them shine like they're
varnished." And for almost an hour he slowly, carefully, profoundly,
caressed what for him were two sacred objects. When I offered him
money, he did not want to accept it. "I've made them so shiny you'll
be able to walk in the night without needing a lantern!" Enthused, I
began to admire my splendid boots while running around the square.
Carlitos furtively wiped away a tear or two, murmuring, "You're lucky,
Pinocchio, I'll never be able to have a pair like that."

I felt a pain inside my chest, and I could not take another step. I took the shoes off and gave them to him. The boy, forgetting my presence, hastily put them on and took off running toward the beach. He forgot not only me, but also his box. I kept it, intending to give it to him the next day at school.

When my father saw me return home barefoot, he was furious. "You say you gave them to a shoe shiner? Are you crazy? Your mother went a hundred kilometers out and a hundred kilometers back to buy them for you! That brat's going to come back to the square looking for his box. Go there, wait for him as long as it takes, and when he shows up, take your shoes back, by force if you need to."

Jaime used intimidation as a method of education. The fear of being clobbered by his trapeze artist's muscles made me break out in a cold sweat. I obeyed. I went to the square and sat down on a bench. Five interminable hours passed. As night was falling, a group of people came running along, surrounding a bicyclist. The man was pedaling slowly, leaning down as if an enormous weight was breaking his back. Bent double over the handlebars, like a marionette with cut strings, was the dead body of Carlitos. Through the rips in his clothing I could see his skin, formerly brown, now as pale as my own. His limp legs swung with each pedal stroke, drawing red arcs in the air with my boots. Behind the bicycle and the curious group of mourners, a rumor was fanning out like a ship's wake. "He was playing on the slippery rocks. The rubber soles on his shoes made him slip. He fell into the sea and was battered against the rocks. That's how the imprudent boy drowned." Imprudent he may have been, but it was my generosity that killed him. The next day, everyone at the school went to lay flowers at the site of the accident. On those precipitous rocks, pious hands had built a miniature chapel out of cement. Inside it was a photograph of Carlitos and the red shoes. My classmate, having departed this world too early, without accomplishing the mission that God gives to every incarnated soul, had become an *animita* (little soul). Trapped in this state, he was now devoted to bringing about the miracles that believers requested of him. Many candles were lit behind the magical shoes that had once brought death but were now dispensers of health and prosperity.

Suffering, consolation; consolation, suffering. The cycle has no end. When I brought the shoe shiner's box to his parents they hastily placed it in the hands of Luciano, the youngest brother. That same afternoon, the boy began shining shoes in the town square.

The fact is that during this era, when I was a child of an unknown race (Jaime did not call himself a Jew, but a Chilean son of Russians), no one ever spoke to me outside of books. My father and mother, at work in the shop from eight in the morning until ten at night, put their faith in my literary abilities and left me to educate myself. And what they saw I could not do for myself, they asked the Rebbe to do.

Jaime knew very well that his father, my grandfather Alejandro, had been expelled from Russia by the Cossacks, arriving in Chile not by his own choice but only because a charitable society shipped him where there was room for him and his family. Completely uprooted, speaking only Yiddish and rudimentary Russian, he descended into madness. In his schizophrenia he invented the character of a Kabbalist sage whose body had been devoured by bears during one of his voyages to another dimension. Laboriously making shoes without the aid of machinery, he conversed constantly with his imaginary friend and master. When he died, Jaime inherited this master. Even though Jaime knew full well that the Rebbe was a hallucination, the effect was contagious. The specter began to visit him each night in his dreams. My father, a fanatical atheist, endured the invasion of this character as a form of torture and did his best to exorcise the phantom—by stuffing my head full of it as if it were real. I was not taken in by this ploy. I always knew that the Rebbe was imaginary but Jaime, perhaps thinking that by naming me Alejandro he had made me as crazy as my grandfather, would tell me, "I don't have time to help you with that homework, go ask the Rebbe," or more often still, "Go play with the Rebbe!" This was convenient for him because in his misinterpretation of Marxist ideas he had decided not to buy me any toys. "Those objects are the products of the evil consumer economy. They teach you to be a soldier, to turn life into a war, to believe that all manufactured things are a source of pleasure through having miniature versions of them. Toys turn a child into a future assassin, an exploiter, not to mention a compulsive buyer." The other boys had toy swords, tanks, lead soldiers, train sets, stuffed animals, but I had nothing. I used the Rebbe as a toy, lending him my voice, imagining his advice, letting him guide my actions. Later, having developed my imagination, I expanded my animated conversations. I endowed the clouds with speech, as well as the rocks, the sea, some of the trees in the town square, the antique cannon outside the city hall, furniture, insects, hills, clocks, and the old people with nothing left to wait for who sat like wax sculptures on the benches in the town square. I could speak with all things, and everything had something to say to me. Assuming the point of view of things outside of myself I felt that all things were conscious, that everything was endowed with life, that things I considered inanimate were slower entities, that things I considered invisible were faster entities. Every consciousness had a different velocity. If I adapted my own consciousness to these speeds, I could initiate rewarding relationships.

The umbrella that lay in a corner, covered with dust, lamented bitterly, "Why did they bring me here, where it never rains? I was made to protect from rain, without it I have no purpose." "You're wrong," I told it. "You still have a purpose; if not at present, at least in the future. Show me patience and faith. One day it will rain, I assure you." After this conversation a storm broke for the first time in many years, and there was a real deluge that lasted for a whole day. As I walked to school with the umbrella finally open, the raindrops came down with such force that its fabric was shredded in no time. A hurricane-force wind tore it from my hands and carried it in tatters off into the sky. I imagined the pleasant murmurings of the umbrella as it became a boat and happily navigated toward the stars after traversing the storm clouds . . .

Yearning hopelessly for some affectionate words from my father, I

My paternal great-grandparents.

dedicated myself to observing him, watching his actions as if I were a visitor from another world. Having lost his father at the age of ten and needing to support his mother, brother, and two sisters, who were all younger than him, he had abandoned his studies and begun hard work. He could barely write, could read with difficulty, and spoke Spanish in a manner that was almost guttural. Actions were his true language. His territory was the street. A fervent admirer of Stalin he wore the same style of mustache, fashioned with his own hands the same kind of stiff-collared coat, and cultivated the same affable mannerisms behind which an infinite aggressiveness was concealed.

Fortunately, my maternal grandmother's husband Moishe, who had lost his fortune in the stock market crash but still kept a little shop as a gold dealer, bore a resemblance to Gandhi due to his bald head, missing teeth, and large ears; this balanced things out. Fleeing the severity of the dictator, I took refuge at the knees of the saint. "Alejandrito, your mouth was not made for saying aggressive things; every hard word dries up your soul a little bit. I shall teach you to sweeten your words," he said. And after painting my tongue with blue vegetable dye, he took a soft-haired brush a centimeter wide, dipped it in honey, and made as if to paint the inside of my mouth. "Now your words will have the color of the blue sky and the sweetness of honey."

In contrast, for Jaime/Stalin life was an implacable struggle. Unable to slaughter his competitors, he ruined them instead. Casa Ukrania was an armored tank. Since the main street (Calle 21 de Mayo, named for a historic naval battle in which the hero Arturo Prat had turned his defeat at the hands of the Peruvians into a moral triumph) was lined with shops selling the same articles he was selling, he employed an aggressive sales tactic. He declared, "Abundance attracts the buyer; if the seller is prosperous that suggests that he is offering the best goods." He filled the shelves of the shop with boxes, a sample of the contents sticking out of each box: the tip of a sock, the fold of a stocking, the cuff of a shirtsleeve, the strap of a brassiere, and so on. The store appeared to be full of merchandise, which was not the case, for each box was empty save for the item that was poking out.

In order to awaken customers' desires he organized items into various lots rather than selling them separately and exhibited collections of things in cardboard boxes. For example, a pair of underwear, six drinking glasses, a clock, a pair of scissors, and a statuette of Our Lady of Mount Carmel; or a wool vest, a piggy bank, some lace garters, a sleeveless shirt, a communist flag, and so forth. All the lots had the same price. Like me, my father had discovered that all things are interrelated.

He hired exotic propagandists to stand in the middle of the sidewalk in front of the door. There was a different one every week. Each one, in his or her own way, would loudly extol the quality and low price of the articles for sale, inviting curious passersby to step inside Casa Ukrania, under no obligation to buy anything. They included, among others, a dwarf in a Tyrolean costume, a skinny man dressed as a nymphomaniacal black woman, a Carmen Miranda on stilts, a wax automaton who beat at the shop windows from the inside with a cane, a ghastly mummy, and a stentorian whose voice was so loud that his shouts could be heard a kilometer away. Hunger created artists; the out-of-work miners invented all sorts of disguises. They would make Dracula or Zorro costumes out of flour sacks from the mill that they had dyed black; masks and warrior's capes from debris found in garbage cans. One of them brought along a mangy dog dressed in Chilean peasant clothes that danced on its hind paws; another brought a baby that cried like a seagull.

In those days, with no television and the cinema open only on Saturdays and Sundays, people were drawn to any kind of novelty. Add to this the beauty of my mother, who was tall, pale-skinned, with enormous breasts, who always spoke in a lilting voice and dressed in Russian peasant clothes, and one can understand how Jaime robbed his snoozing competitors of their customers.

The shop next door, the Cedar of Lebanon, had rough wooden tables instead of glass display cases, there were no windows facing the street, and it was lit entirely by a single 60-watt bulb covered with dead insects. From the back room came a distinct odor of fried food. The owner, Mr. Omar, known to us as the Turk, was a short man; his wife was small like him but had elephantiasis in her legs, which were so swollen that although they were wrapped in black bandages they appeared ready to explode and cover the wood floor, gray from years of dust, with a layer of flesh. An invasion of spiders in their shop made up for the lack of customers.

One day, while sitting in a corner of our little courtyard reading Jules Verne's *In Search of the Castaways,* I heard a heartrending wailing from the Turk's yard, which was separated from ours by a brick wall. These cries, punctuated by long feminine "shhh" sounds, were so devastating that curiosity got the better of me and I climbed the wall. I saw the woman with the huge legs using a straw fan to shoo flies away from the scabs that almost entirely covered the body of a boy.

"What's wrong with your son, señora?"

"Oh, it looks like an infection, little neighbor, but no. What's happened is that he has lost his mind."

"Lost his mind?"

"My husband is very sad because of bad business. My son confused this sadness with the wind. Covering himself with scabs to stop the bad air from touching his skin, he went mad. For him, time does not pass. He lives in seconds as long as the devil's tail."

It made me want to cry. I felt guilty on account of my father. With his Stalinist cruelty, he had ruined and devastated the Turk. And now his son was paying the painful price.

I returned to my room, opened the second floor window over the street, and jumped out. My bones held up under the impact, and I only scraped the skin off my knees. A commotion ensued. Blood ran down my legs. Jaime appeared, angrily pushed his way through the curious crowd, congratulated me for not crying, and carried me into Casa Ukrania to disinfect my wounds. Even though the alcohol burned me, I did not scream. In his role of Marxist warrior Jaime saw a sensitivity in me that he considered feminine, and he decided to teach me to be tough. "Men do not cry, and by their will they conquer pain . . ."

The first exercises were not difficult. He began by tickling my feet with a vulture's feather. "You have to be able to not laugh!" I managed to withstand tickling not only on the soles of my feet, but also on my armpits and, in a total triumph, to remain serious when he stuck a feather in my nostrils. Laughter thus subjugated, my father said to me, "Very good . . . I'm beginning to be proud of you. Mind you, I said 'beginning to be,' not that I *am* proud yet! To win my admiration, you must show that you are not a coward and that you know how to resist pain and humiliation. Now, I'm going to hit you. Turn your cheek toward me. I'll start by hitting you very gently. You tell me to hit harder. I'll do that, more and more, as much as you ask me. I want to see how far you get."

I was thirsty for love. In order to gain Jaime's approval, I asked him to hit me harder and harder each time. As his eyes shone with what I took for admiration, my spirit became more and more inebriated. My father's affection was more important to me than pain. I held out. Finally, I spat out blood and a piece of a tooth. Jaime uttered an exclamation of admiring surprise, took me in his muscular arms, and led me, running, to the dentist.

The nerve of my premolar, coming in contact with saliva and air, was causing me atrocious suffering. Don Julio, the local dentist, prepared a calming injection. Jaime whispered in my ear (I had never heard him speak in such a delicate manner), "You have carried yourself like I do; you are brave, you are a man. You don't have to do what I'm going to ask, but if you do it, I will consider you worthy of being my son. Refuse the injection. Let your tooth be fixed without anesthesia. Conquer pain with your will. You can do it, you are like me!"

Never again in my life have I felt such terrible pain. (On second thought, I have—when the shaman Pachita removed a tumor from my liver with a hunting knife.) Don Julio, persuaded by my father's promise of a gift of half a dozen bottles of *pisco,* did not speak a word. He scraped around, used his little torture device, applied a mercury-based amalgam, and finally put a cap on the gap in my mouth. Grinning like a chimpanzee, he exclaimed, "Brilliant, young fellow, you are a hero!" Oh, what a catastrophe: I, who had endured this torture without a murmur, without budging, without shedding a tear, now interrupted the triumphant gesture of my father, who was spreading his arms out like the wings of a condor—and fainted! Yes, I fainted, just like a little girl!

Jaime, without so much as offering me a hand, led me back home. Humiliated, with swollen cheeks, I shut myself in my room and slept for twenty hours straight.

I do not know whether my father realized I had wanted to commit suicide when I threw myself out of the window. Nor do I know whether he realized that by "accidentally" falling on my knees in front of the Cedar of Lebanon (we lived on the second floor, just above) I had been begging the Turk's forgiveness. All he said was, "You fell, you idiot. This is what comes of always having your nose in a book." It is true. I was always absorbed by books, and with such concentration that when I was reading and someone spoke to me, I did not hear a word. Jaime, for his part, would bury himself in his stamp collection as soon as he got home, as deaf as I was with my books. He would soak the envelopes his clients gave him in lukewarm water, carefully remove the stamps with a pair of tweezers—if so much as a tooth was lost from the edge, the value would be reduced—dry them between sheets of blotting paper, then classify them and keep them in albums that nobody was allowed to open.

Two large, almost circular scabs formed on my knees; my father applied cotton wool soaked in hot water, and when they softened he peeled them away in one piece with his tweezers, exactly as he did with his stamps. Of course, I held back from crying. Satisfied, he applied alcohol to the red, flayed living flesh. New scabs formed by the next morning. My allowing him to peel them away without complaint became a ritual that brought me closer to a distant God. When my knees began to feel better and the pink hue of new skin heralded the end of the treatment, I took Jaime's hand, led him out to the courtyard, asked him to climb the wall with me, showed him the mad child, and pointed to my knees. He understood without any other gesture being necessary. In those days there was no hospital in Tocopilla. The only doctor was an affable, plump man called Ángel Romero. My father dismissed his current salesman—a boxer who was pummeling a mannequin decorated with a large dollar sign—and accompanied by Dr. Romero asked Mr. Omar's permission to enter to visit the sick boy. Jaime paid for the consultation and made the 100-kilometer journey to Iquique to buy medicine with a prescription from the doctor. He returned to the Omars' armed with disinfectants, tweezers, and the basin in which he soaked off his stamps. With infinite gentleness, he soaked and softened the scabs that covered the poor boy, and peeled them off one by one. After two months of such assiduous visits, the younger Turk regained his normal appearance.

It should be understood that all these things took place over a period of ten years. My relating them all together may make it seem as if my childhood was full of bizarre events, but this was not the case. These were small oases in an infinite desert. The climate was hot and dry. During the day an implacable silence descended from the sky, gliding in from the wall of barren mountains that held us against the sea, rising from a terrain made up of small rocks without a speck of fertile soil. When the sun went down there were no birds to sing, no trees for the wind to blow through, no crickets to chirp. There was only the odd vulture, the braying of a distant burro, the howls of a dog sensing death approaching, the seagulls skirmishing, and the constant crashing of the ocean waves whose hypnotic repetition one would eventually cease to hear. And the cold nights were even more silent: a thick mist, the *camanchaca,* gathered on the tops of the mountains to form an impenetrable milky wall. Tocopilla seemed like a prison full of corpses.

One night, when Jaime and Sara were out at the cinema, I awoke in a terrified sweat. The silence, an invisible reptile, had come in through the door and was licking the feet of my bed frame. I knew that I was in danger; the silence wanted to enter me through my nostrils, settle in my lungs, and drain the blood from my veins. To frighten it away, I began to scream. My cries were so intense the windowpanes began to vibrate, buzzing like wasps, which increased my terror. And then the Rebbe arrived. I knew that he was nothing but a simple image, and his apparition was not enough to prevent universal muteness. I needed the presence of friends, but what friends? Pinocchio—large-nosed, pale, circumcised—did not have friends. (In this torrid climate, sexuality came early. The firemen's barracks was near our shop; on an old wall in their big courtyard, hanging like the strings of a gigantic harp, were ropes that served to hold up the hoses when they were cleaned and set out to dry after being used to put out fires. The watchman's sons and their friends, a band of eight young rascals, invited me to climb twenty meters up to the top of the wall. Once there, out of sight of adult eyes, they formed a circle and began to masturbate at an age when the emission of sperm was still something legendary. Wishing to fit in, I did the same. Their immature phalli, covered by foreskins, rose up like brown missiles. Mine, which was pale, showed itself without hiding its wide head. They all noticed the difference and burst out laughing. "He's got a mushroom!" Humiliated, red with embarrassment, I slid down the rope, scorching the palms of my hands. The news spread through the whole school. I was an abnormal boy with a different "wee-wee." "He's missing a piece, they cut it off!" Knowing that I was mutilated, I felt even more separated from other human beings. I was not of this world. I had no place. All I deserved was to be devoured by silence.)

"Do not worry," the Rebbe told me, or rather I told myself using the image of that aged Jew who was dressed as a rabbi. "Loneliness means not knowing how to be with oneself." Of course, I do not mean to imply that a child of seven years can speak in such a fashion. But I understood these things, albeit not in a rational manner. The Rebbe, being an internal image, put things into my mind that were not intellectual. He made me feel something that I swallowed, in the way that a newly hatched eaglet, its eyes still closed, swallows the worm that is placed in its beak.

Much later as an adult I began to find words to translate things that were, at that young age—how can I explain it?—openings into other planes of reality.

"You are not alone. Remember last week when you were surprised to see a sunflower growing in the courtyard? You concluded that the wind had blown a seed there. A seed, though it looks insignificant, contains the future flower. This seed somehow *knew* what plant it was going to be, and this plant was not just in the future: although immaterial, although only a design, the sunflower existed there, in that seed, blowing in the wind over hundreds of kilometers. And not only was the plant there, but also the love of light, the turning in search of the sun, the mysterious union with the pole star, and—why not?—a form of consciousness. You are not different. All that you are going to be, you are. What you will know, you already know. What you will search for, you are already seeking: it is in you. I may not be real, but the old man who you now see, although he has my inconsistent appearance, is real because he is you, which is to say, he is what you will be."

All this I neither thought nor heard, but I felt it. And in front of me, next to the bed, my imagination brought forth the apparition of an elderly gentleman with silver beard and hair, his eyes full of tenderness. It was myself, changed into my older brother, my father, my grandfather, my master. "Do not worry so. I have accompanied you and I always will. Every time you suffered, believing yourself to be alone, I was with you. Would you like an example? All right, remember when you made the elephant of snot?"

I had never felt so abandoned, misunderstood, and unjustly punished as on this occasion. Moishe, with his toothless smile and saintly heart, proposed to my parents that he take me to the capital of Santiago for a month during the summer vacation so that my maternal grandmother might get to know me. The old lady had never met me, being separated from her daughter by two thousand kilometers. I hid my anxiety at being away from home to avoid disappointing Jaime. Exhibiting a false tranquillity I boarded the *Horacio,* a small steamboat that rocked so much that I arrived with an empty stomach at the port of Valparaiso. After rattling for four hours in the third-class section of a coal train I presented myself, timid and green around the gills, to Doña Jashe, who did not know how to smile much less how to deal with children as unhealthily sensitive as myself. Sara's half-brother Isidoro, a fat, effeminate, and sadistic man dressed in a male nurse's uniform, began to harass me, threatening me with an insecticide bomb. "I'm going to give you an injection in your ass!"

At night, in a dark room on a small hard bed fixed to the wall, with no lamp for reading, illuminated by whatever moonlight might filter through the narrow skylight, I stuck my finger up my nose, made balls of snot, and stuck them to the sky-blue wallpaper. During that month, little by little, I drew an elephant with my boogers. No one knew, for they never entered to clean or make my bed. At the end of the month, my pachyderm was just about finished. At the time of my departure, as Moishe was about to go back to Tocopilla with me, my grandmother came into the room to retrieve the sheets she had lent me. She did not see a beautiful elephant floating in the infinite sky; she saw a horrible collection of boogers stuck to her precious wallpaper. Her wrinkles turned a shade of violet, her hunched back straightened up, her amiable voice changed into the roar of a lion, her glassy eyes turned into balls of lightning. "Disgusting boy, pig, ingrate! We'll have to paper the whole room again! You ought to die of shame! I do not want such a grandson as you!"

"But Grandmother, I didn't mean to get anything dirty, I just wanted to make a nice elephant. It just needed a tusk, then it would have been finished." This made her even more furious. She thought I was making fun of her. She grabbed a handful of my hair and began pulling, with the intention of yanking it out. Gandhi intervened, holding her back with gentle firmness. The odious joker Isidoro, behind Jashe, waved his insecticide bomb in my direction, agitating it back and forth like a violating phallus.

I was required to assist in removing the wallpaper, for which they used rubber gloves to protect their hands. Then they put the pieces in the middle of the courtyard shared by the group of small houses, sprayed them with alcohol, and made me throw matches on them until they were entirely burned. I saw my dear elephant consumed by flame. A lot of neighbors appeared at the windows. Jashe rubbed the ashes on my nose and fingers and brought me, thus dirtied, to the train. Once we were far away from Santiago, Moishe moistened his white handkerchief with spit and cleaned my face and hands. He was mystified. "You seem numb, my boy. You don't cry or even complain."

I boarded the *Horacio* for a three-day voyage and disembarked in Tocopilla without ever having said a word. When I saw my mother, I ran to her and began to cry convulsively, buried between her enormous breasts. "You jerk! Why did you make me go?" When I saw my father fifteen minutes later I held back my sobs, dried my eyes, and faked a smile.

"I was there, seeing the mental limitations of these people," the old Alejandro said to me. "They saw the material world, the pieces of snot, but the art, the beauty, the magical elephant, those things were lost to them. And yet, rejoice in this suffering: thanks to it, you have met me. Ecclesiastes says, 'The greater one's wisdom, the greater one's pain.' But I tell you, only he who knows pain can approach wisdom. I cannot tell you that I have achieved wisdom; I am no more than a step along the path of this spirit who is traveling toward the end of time. Who will I be three centuries from now? Or what will I be? What forms will serve as my vessel? In ten million years, will my consciousness still need a body? Will I still have to use sensory organs? After hundreds of millions of years, will I continue dividing the unity of the world into sights, sounds, smells, tastes, tactile images? Will I be an individual? A collective being? Once I have known all of the universe, or universes, when I have arrived at the end of all time, when the expansion of matter stops and with it I begin the journey back toward the point of origin, will

I dissolve in it? Will I become the mystery that surrounds time and space? Will I discover that the Creator is a memory with no present or future? You, a child, I, an old man, will we not have been merely memories, insubstantial images, without having had the least reality? For you, I do not exist yet, for me you do not exist anymore, and when our story is told, he who tells it will be nothing but a string of words escaping out of a pile of ashes."

At night, when I awoke alone in the dark house, it became essential for me to imagine this double of myself from the future. Listening to him I calmed myself little by little, and a deep sleep came, gloriously allowing me to forget myself.

During the day I did not despair, despite the anguish of living unappreciated, a Robinson Crusoe on my inner island. In the library my friends the books, with their heroes and adventures, blocked out the silence for me.

There was someone else who used books to escape from silence: Morgan, the gringo. Like all the English, he worked for the electric company that provided energy to the nitrate company offices and the copper and silver mines. He liked to drink gin. When they forbade him to drink any alcohol, dying of boredom he buried himself in the "esotericism" section in the library. The Freemasons had provided shelves crammed with books in English that dealt with mysterious topics. Jaime claimed that *The Secret Doctrine* by Helena Blavatsky had disturbed Morgan's brain. "He's got bats in the belfry!" he would often say. The gringo believed in a group of invisible Cosmic Masters and began fervently believing in the reincarnation of the soul. In accordance with the author he idolized, he declared to anyone who would listen to him that the veneration and burial of cadavers was a barbaric custom because they infected the planet. They should be burned, as was done in India. He sold all his possessions and with the money thus obtained, plus his savings, opened a funeral parlor called River of Ganges Sacred Crematorium. The place of business was decorated with wreaths of artificial flowers, sweets made of almond paste in the shape of fruits, and plaster models of exotic gods, some of which had elephant heads. It opened onto a long courtyard covered with orange tiles, and at the center was an oven similar to those used for making bread with room enough for a Christian inside. The priest, launching diatribes against this sacrilegious monstrosity, was preaching to the choir. Who among the citizens of Tocopilla would permit their deceased loved ones to be burned in some big stove? No one, for sure, wished to see the carnal remains of their dear departed converted into a pile of gray ashes. Morgan, whom people called the Theosophist, shrugged his shoulders: "It's nothing new, the same thing happened to Madam Blavatsky and her partner Olcott in New York; ancestral customs have deep roots." He changed his strategy: if the priest contended that according to Christian theology animals did not have souls, then it was highly advisable to burn their remains. The oven began its function: first dogs, then, thanks to a discount, cats, followed by the odd white mouse or plucked parrot. The ashes were placed in milk bottles painted black with gilded stoppers. Drawn to the nauseating odor, a multitude of vultures came to land on the orange tiles, covering them with their white excrement. The Theosophist would shoo them away with a broom, but the stubborn birds would fly in circles, which eventually turned into spirals, finally returning to the tiles, squawking and defecating. The fetid odor became insufferable. The Theosophist closed the funeral parlor and began to spend most of his time reclining on a bench in the town square, promising reincarnation to anyone who would accept him as their master. It was there that I struck up a friendship with him, for I was saddened to see him become the laughingstock of the whole town.

To me, he did not seem to be a lunatic, as my father claimed. I liked his ideas. "My boy, all evidence suggests that we were something before being born and we will be something after dying. Can you tell me what?"

I rubbed my hands together, stammered, and then said nothing. He began to laugh. "Come to the beach with me!" I followed him, and when we got to the beach he showed me the towers joined by cables on which steel cars glided, full from the mines. They came from the mountains, ran along the beach, and disappeared between other mountains. I saw a pebble fall from one of them, half gray and half coppery.

"Where do they come from? Where are they going?"

"I don't know, Theosophist."

"There, you don't know where they come from or where they are going, but you can pick up one of their stones and keep it like a treasure. You see, boy, I know what mine they come from and what mill they are going to, but what good would it do to tell you? The numbers of those sites will mean nothing to you because you have never seen them. It's the same for the soul that is transported by the body: we do not know where it comes from or where it is going, but now, here, we want to keep it and do not want to lose it; it is a treasure. A mysterious consciousness, infinitely more vast than our own, knows the origin and the end but cannot reveal it to us because we do not have a sufficiently developed brain to comprehend it."

The gringo put his freckled hand into a pocket and extracted four gold-plated medals. On one was Christ, on the second were two interlaced triangles, on the third a half-moon containing a star, and on the fourth were two drops, one black and one white, nested together forming a circle. "Take these, they are for you. They represent Catholicism, Judaism, Islam, and Taoism. They believe that they symbolize different truths, but if you put them in a little oven and melt them, they will form a single grain of the same metal. The soul is a drop in the divine ocean for which we are, for a very brief time, the humble vessel. It comes from God and travels to return and dissolve into God, which is eternal joy. Take this cord, my young friend, and make yourself a necklace with the four medals. Wear it always to remind yourself that a single thread, immortal consciousness, unites everything."

I returned proudly to Casa Ukrania, showing off my necklace. Jaime, more Stalin than ever, trembled with rage. "That idiot Theosophist, appeasing the fear of death with illusions! Come with me to the bathroom!" He seized the medals from me. One by one he threw them into the toilet. "God does not exist, God does not exist, God does not exist, God does not exist! You die and you rot! After that there is nothing!" And he pulled the chain. The rush of water bore the medals away, and with them my illusions. "Papa never lies! Who do you believe, me or that loony?" Which one was I to choose, I who longed so for my father's admiration? Jaime smiled for a second, then looked at me with his customary severity. "I'm tired of your long hair; you're not a girl!"

Sara's father had died before she was born. Her mother, Jashe, had fallen in love with a Russian dancer—not Jewish, a goy—with a handsome build and golden locks. When she was eight months pregnant, he climbed on top of a barrel full of alcohol to light a lamp. The lid broke, he fell into the flammable liquid, and it began to burn. The family legend was that he ran down the street, enveloped in flames, leaping up in the air as much as two meters high, and died dancing. When I was born I emerged with a full head of curly hair, as abundant and blond as the late idolized dancer. Sara never cuddled me, but she spent hours combing my hair, giving me ringlets, refusing to cut it. I was her father reincarnated. In those days no boys ever had long hair; thus, I was incessantly called "queer boy."

My father, seizing the moment while Sara was napping, brought me to the barber. His name was Osamu, and he was Japanese. In a few minutes, reciting several times over, "Gate, Gate, Paragate, Parasamgate, Bodhi Svaha,"* he cut my hair short and impassively swept away the golden curls. Immediately, I was no longer the burned dead man; I was myself. I could not help shedding a few tears, which brought my father's contempt down on me with renewed force. "You wimp, learn to be a macho revolutionary and stop clinging to your mop of hair like a bourgeois whore!" How wrong Jaime was: losing that mane of hair, the subject of so much mockery, was an enormous relief. But I cried because losing my curls also meant losing the love of my mother.

---

*Mantra of the Heart Sutra.

Back at the shop I threw my coppery pebble into the toilet, pulled the chain, and ran proudly to the town square to make fun of the Theosophist, pressing my index finger to my temple as my sole response to his fervent words.

One might think that during my childhood I was more influenced by Jaime than by Sara. However, this was not the case. She, dazzled by my father's charisma, applauded and repeated everything he said. Severity was the basis of the education I was to receive in order to grow up a man and not a woman; after the Japanese barber cut my hair, my mother applied herself diligently to this process. Tied down to the store all day, she had little or no time to devote to me. My socks had holes, and a circle of flesh was visible on each heel. Because of their round shape and color, the children likened them to peeled potatoes. While playing, if I wanted to run in the yard, my cruel peers would point to my heels and call out snidely, "I can see his potatoes!" This humiliated me and obliged me to stay still, keeping my feet in the shadows. When I asked Sara to buy me new socks, she grumbled, "It's a useless expense, you'll tear them the first day you wear them."

"But mama, everyone in school is making fun of me. If you love me, mend them for me, please."

"All right, if you need me to prove I love you, I'll do it."

She took her sewing box, threaded a needle, repaired the holes with great dedication, and showed me the socks, perfectly mended.

"But mama, you used flesh colored thread! Look, I put them on and it looks like you can still see my potatoes! They'll keep making fun of me!"

"I mended them right away. I proved I love you by doing the useless work you asked me to do. Now you have to show me that you have a warrior spirit. Those children being mean shouldn't affect you. Show off your heels proudly, and be thankful for the teasing because it makes your spirit stronger."

Jaime, my father, and Sara Felicidad, my mother. He is seated to hide the fact that he is much shorter than her.

It is amazing what cultural richness was present in that small city isolated in the arid north of Chile. Before the crash of 1929 and the invention of artificial saltpeter by the Germans, this region, including Antofagasta and Iquique, was considered the land of "white gold." Inexhaustible supplies of potassium nitrate, excellent for making fertilizer but above all, explosives, attracted a multitude of immigrants. In Tocopilla there were Italians, English, North Americans, Chinese, Yugoslavians, Japanese, Greeks, Spaniards, Germans. Each ethnicity lived behind high mental walls. And yet, in bits and pieces, I was able to gain things from these diverse cultures. The Spanish brought little books of Calleja's fairy tales to the library; the English brought Masonic and Rosicrucian treatises; Pampino Brontis, the Greek baker, invited children to come and listen to his verse translation of the *Odyssey* every Sunday morning in order to promote his rose jam–filled pastries. The Japanese practiced archery on the beach, instilling in us a love of the martial arts. From time to time, the American women would show their generosity by offering sausages and refreshments in the city hall to the children of the men whom their husbands plunged into misery. Thanks to them, I became conscious of social injustice.

The day my father announced out of nowhere, "Tomorrow we're leaving here. We're going to live in Santiago," I thought I was going to die. I woke up with a horrible rash. My skin was entirely covered with hives, I was delirious with fever, and the boat was leaving in three hours! Jaime stubbornly refused to postpone the voyage, even when Dr. Romero advised that I should stay in bed for at least a week. Cursing Western medicine, my father ran to the Chinese restaurant and, with his salesman's skills, convinced the owner to give him the name and address of the doctor who treated them. There was not just one, but three aged brothers with a command of the science of the yin and yang. Serene as the mountains, with eyes like cats on the prowl and skin the color of my fever, they heated coarse grains of salt, put them on pieces of cotton cloth, folded these into packets, and rubbed them all over my body, almost burning me, whispering, "You go, but you stay here as well. If your branches grow to fill the whole sky, your roots will never leave the soil where they were born." In half an hour the Chinese cured my skin, my fever, and my sadness, initiating me into Taoism.

Seeing me thus restored, my parents allowed me to say goodbye to my schoolmates. No one at school was surprised when I announced that I was leaving for good. After all, I was the child who could disappear in a second. This legend came from a spectacle at which I had assisted at the local theater. The theater usually showed films (it was there that I had the great pleasure of viewing Charles Laughton in *The Hunchback of Notre Dame,* Boris Karloff in *Frankenstein,* Buster Crabbe in *Flash Gordon Conquers the Universe,* and many other marvels), but sometimes the white screen was rolled back from the stage and visiting troupes would put on shows. So it was that Fu-Manchu, a Mexican magician, came to town. He told the adults to make sure the children kept their eyes closed, and with a great saw, he proceeded to divide a woman in two. When he put her back together and the blood was cleaned up, he permitted the children to watch the rest of the performance. He turned toads into doves, drew an interminable cord out of his mouth on which blinking electric lights were suspended, changed the color of a silk handkerchief ten times, then got down from the stage and, from a large teapot that he had filled with water, filled small clear glasses with whatever liquor the spectators requested. He gave vodka to my grandfather, aguardiente to Jaime, and whiskey, wine, beer, and pisco to others. Finally, he showed us a red armoire with a black interior and asked for a child to help. Moved by an irresistible impulse, I volunteered. At the moment I set foot on the stage, I felt for the first time that I was in my proper place. I was a citizen of the world of miracles. The magician told me solemnly, "My boy, I am going to make you disappear. Swear that you will never tell the secret to anyone."

I swore. I was ecstatic. If I disappeared, I would finally find out what existed beyond this gloomy reality. He had me go inside the armoire, lifted his red satin cape to hide me for a second, then let it drop. I had disappeared! Again, he lifted and dropped his cape. I reappeared! There was great applause. I returned to my seat. When my parents, my grandfather, and several other spectators asked me what the trick was, I answered with great dignity, "I have sworn to keep the secret forever, and so I shall keep it." And I guarded the secret zealously until today, more than sixty years later, when I have decided to reveal it. I did not step into another dimension; while I was hidden in the cape a pair of gloved hands spun me around and shoved me into a corner. There was a person dressed all in black inside that black compartment who could not be seen. All he needed to do was cover me with his body in order for me to disappear. What profound deception! The great beyond did not exist. The miracles were mere illusions. And yet, I learned something more important: a secret, even one of little substance, when kept, gives one power. At school I declared that I had gone to another world, that I knew how to go there, that I had the ability to disappear whenever I wanted to. I also hinted that I had the power to make anyone I wanted disappear without returning. This did not gain me any new friends, but it diminished the teasing. I was given the silent treatment; no one spoke to me anymore. I had transitioned from receiving insults to receiving silence. The former had been less painful.

The boat let forth a hoarse sigh and pulled out of the port. The heart of my childhood remained in Tocopilla. The Rebbe, old Alejandro, and my happiness all left me straight away. I headed straight for a dark corner. I disappeared.

TWO

The Dark Years

Do names seal destinies? Do certain places attract people whose emotional state corresponds to the hidden meaning of their names? Did the plaza of Diego de Almagro, where we came to live in Santiago de Chile, become a terrible place because of its namesake, who was a Spanish conquistador? Or was the place neutral and I felt dark, sad, and abandoned there because I made it the mirror of my sorrow? In Tocopilla I was grateful to my nose, despite my dislike of its curved shape, for bringing me the smell of the Pacific Ocean—an ample fragrance that arose from the icy waters mixed with the subtle perfume of the air of a perpetually blue sky. There, the sight of a cloud was an extraordinary event. The white clouds made me think of caravels transporting colonizing angels to enchanted forests where giant sugar trees grew. Beneath a sallow sky the air of Santiago smelled of electric cables, gasoline, fried food, and cancerous breath. The heady sound of the waves was replaced by the grinding of aging trains, piercing car horns, roaring engines, harsh voices. Diego de Almagro was a frustrated conquistador; following the deceitful advice of his comrade Pizarro he left Cuzco for unexplored lands to the south expecting to find temples with fabulous treasure. Greedy for gold he pushed on for four thousand kilometers, burning the huts of natives who were interested in fighting, not in building pyramids. Finally, he arrived at the desolate Strait of Magellan. The extreme cold and the ferocity of the Mapuche people decimated his troops. He

33

returned in disgrace to Cuzco, where his treacherous comrade Pizarro, not wishing to share the riches stolen from the Incas, had him executed.

Jaime rented two rooms in a bedsit facing the unhappy plaza. It was a gloomy apartment divided up into bedrooms that were like cages. In a somberly furnished dining room we were served the same thing for lunch and dinner: anemic leaves of lettuce, a soup suggestive of chicken, a puree of sandy potatoes, a thin sheet of rubber referred to as steak, and for dessert a crippled biscuit covered with paste. In the morning there was coffee without milk and one piece of bread for each of us. Sheets and towels were changed once every fifteen days. And yet, neither my mother nor my father complained. Not my father because, detaching himself from family concerns, he was devoting himself to finding the right location where he could return to his own form of combat—the name of his new shop was El Combate, and he decorated it with a sign depicting two bulldogs pulling at the leg of a pair of women's draw-ers, one on each side, indicating that the article in question was inde-structible—and not my mother because Jashe, her beloved mother, lived just a few meters off the Almagro plaza. Hoping to enroll me in the public school, they left me a prisoner in these inhospitable surround-ings in the charge of the landlady, a widow as dry as the daily potato purée, who would walk into my room without knocking with the sole aim of sharing her rants about the government of the People's Front with me. While Jaime ate empanadas in the street and Sara sat around drinking maté in her mother's house, I was laboriously swallowing the menu of the Eden of Croesus rooming house. Timid as I was, I hid my face behind the pages of the adventures of John Carter of Mars. Across from me sat an old woman, her back bent double, who had lost all her teeth except one canine on her lower jaw. Every time soup was served she would dig in her shabby handbag, furtively bring out an egg, break it against her single tooth with a trembling hand, and drop it into the insipid liquid, splattering the tablecloth and my book. I pictured her squatting in her room like an enormous plucked chicken, laying an egg

each day in lieu of defecating. At the same time that I learned to conquer sadness, I had to learn to master disgust. At the end of each lunch
and dinner she would bid me goodbye, kissing me on both cheeks. I
forced a smile to my lips.

Finally, school started. I got up at six in the morning and carefully put
my notebooks, pencils, and textbooks in order. Trembling from both
the cold and my nerves, I walked out into the square with an empty
stomach and sat down on a bench to wait until the time came to go to
a place with children my age who did not know that I had been called
Pinocchio, did not know that I had a mushroom, and did not know
that my overalls covered milky-white legs.

Suddenly, sirens rang out and lights flashed. A police car appeared,
followed by an ambulance. The empty plaza filled with curious people.
The policemen dragged a dead beggar toward my bench as if I were an
invisible child. Wild dogs had torn out his throat and devoured part
of one leg, his arms, and his anus. Judging by the empty bottle of pisco
that they found next to him he had passed out drunk, not reckoning
with canine hunger. When I vomited the nurses, policemen, and gawk-
ers appeared to see me for the first time. They began to laugh. One
brute wiggled a stump on the cadaver, and looking at me asked, "Want
a bite to eat, kid?" The taunts echoed in the air, and the air burned my
lungs. I arrived at school with no hope left: the world was cruel. I had
two alternatives: become a killer of dreams like everyone else or shut
myself up in the fortress of my own mind. I chose the latter.

Mildewy rays of sun brought an intolerable heat. Without giving us
time to put down our heavy book bags, the teacher loaded us all onto a
bus that departed from the school. "Tomorrow classes start, today we're
going on a field trip to get some fresh air!"

There was applause and shouts of joy. All the children knew each
other already. I sat in a corner on the back seat and kept my nose glued
to the window. The roads of the capital city looked hostile to me. We

drove along dark streets. I lost my sense of time. Suddenly, I realized that the bus was driving along a dirt road, leaving a cloud of red dust in its wake. My heart beat faster. There were patches of green everywhere! I was used to the opaque sienna of the barren mountains in the north. This was the first time I had seen plantations, trees lining the roads for miles at a stretch, and best of all, an intense chorus of insects and birds. When we arrived at our destination and left the bus, my schoolmates threw off their clothes with a clamor of joy and jumped nude into a crystal clear stream.

I did not know what to do. The teacher and the driver left me sitting on the back seat. It took me half an hour to decide to get out. There were hard-boiled eggs on a flat rock. Feeling myself submerged in the same solitude that surrounded the old woman with the single tooth, I took one and scaled a tree. Although the teacher urged me to get down off the branch and jump in the stream, I remained sitting there, immobile, and did not respond. How could she know? How to tell her that this was the first time I had ever seen a stream of fresh water, the first time I had climbed a myrtle tree, the first time that I had smelled the fragrance of vegetable life, the first time I had seen mosquitoes drawing macramé patterns with their ethereal feet on the surface of the water, the first time I had heard the sacred croaking of toads blessing the world? How could she know that my sex organ, with no foreskin, resembled a white mushroom? The best thing I could think of to do was to remain quiet in this alien, humid, aromatic world in which, not knowing me, no one could yet establish that I was different. It was better to isolate myself before they could reject me, thus denying them the chance to do so!

Murmuring "he's stupid," they left me alone and soon forgot me, absorbed as they were in their aquatic games. I slowly ate the hard-boiled egg and compared myself to it. Removing my exterior shell was in my best interest; it made me strong, but also made me sterile. I had the sensation of being too much in this world. Suddenly, a butterfly with iridescent wings landed on my brow. I do not know what happened to me next, but my vision seemed to extend, penetrating time. I felt as if in the present I was the figurehead on a ship that was all things past. I was not only in this material tree, but also in a genealogical tree. I did not know the term *genealogical* at the time, nor did I know the metaphor of the family tree; and yet, seated in this vegetable being, I imagined humanity as an immense ocean liner, filled with a phantasmal forest, sailing into an inevitable future. Unsettled, I asked the Rebbe to come.

"One day you will understand that couples do not come together by pure chance," he told me. "A superhuman consciousness brings them together according to a set plan. Think of the strange coincidences that led to your arriving in this world. Sara lost her father before she was born. Jaime's father had also died. Your maternal grandmother, Jashe, lost her fourteen-year-old son José after he ate lettuce irrigated with infected water, which left her mentally disturbed for life. Your paternal grandmother, Teresa, lost her favorite son, who drowned in a flood on the Dnieper River when he was also fourteen years old, which drove her mad. Your mother's half-sister Fanny married her cousin José, a gasoline seller. Your father's sister, also called Fanny, married an auto mechanic. Sara's half-brother Isidoro is effeminate, cruel, solitary, and ended up a bachelor living with his mother in a house that he, an architect, designed. Jaime's brother Benjamín, homosexual, cruel, and solitary, lived alone with his mother sharing the same bed until she died, and a year after burying her he died. It would appear that one family is the mirror image of the other. Both Jaime and Sara are abandoned children, forever pursuing the nonexistent love of their parents. What they had to go through, they are now putting you through. Unless you rebel, you will do the same thing to the children you have. Family suffering repeats itself generation after generation, like the links of a chain, until one descendant, in this case perhaps you, becomes conscious and changes his curse into a blessing."

At ten years old, I understood that my family was a trap from which I must free myself or die.

It took me a long time to gather the energy to rebel. When my teacher told Jaime that his son was deeply depressed, might have a brain tumor, or might be showing the effects of intense trauma due to relocation or familial abandonment, my father took offense rather than worrying about my mental state. How could this dumb, skinny, hysterical bourgeois woman accuse him—him!—of being a negligent father and his offspring of being a sissy queer? He immediately forbade me to go to school, and taking advantage of having found a location for his shop moved us out of the Eden of Croesus without paying for the last week.

Sara had wanted the shop to be in the city center in order to be well regarded by her family, but Jaime, driven by his communist ideals, decided to rent a storefront in a working class area. Thus we were immersed in Matucana Street.

The business district was only three blocks long. A swarm of indigents, domestic workers, laborers, and hawkers circulated there every Saturday, which was payday. Next to the railroad gate, people squatted, selling rabbits. The carcasses, skin still on with open abdomens revealing shiny black livers the size of an olive, were hung on the rims of baskets, necklaces of flesh assaulted by flies. Street salesmen announced the availability of soap that would remove all stains; syrups to cure coughs, diarrhea, and impotence; scissors strong enough to cut nails. Thin children with the jaundiced tint of tuberculosis offered to shine shoes. I am not exaggerating. On Saturdays it was difficult for me to breathe so thick was the stench of filthy clothes that arose from the multitudes. All along those four hundred meters, like enormous somnolent spiders, three used clothing shops, a shoe shop, a pharmacy, a large warehouse, an ice cream shop, a garage, and a church all opened their webs to the public. In addition, there were seven bustling pubs that were jammed full of patrons and reeked of vinegar. All activities revolved around alcohol. Chile was a nation of drunkards, from the president, Pedro

Aguirre Cerda, who was known as Don Tinto (Sir Burgundy) due to his heavy drinking and red swollen nose, to the miserable laborer who would drink what remained of his pay each weekend after buying new underwear for his wife and shirts and socks for his children, then plant himself in the middle of the railroad tracks—in Matucana long freight trains ran between the road and the sidewalk—and defy the locomotives, fists raised. The virile pride of drunkards knew no limits. Once, I happened to be walking along the street just after a train had smashed a foolhardy man to pieces. The onlookers, yelling with hilarity, made a game of kicking around the pieces of human flesh.

My father, determined to become the king of the neighborhood, hired more and more extravagant loudmouths to attract customers outside the shop door: a surgeon-clown stitching up a bloody doll with a dollar sign on its forehead ("El Combate forces prices down!"), a guillotine on which a magician decapitated fat men who represented exploitative businessmen, a dwarf with a booming voice dressed as Hitler ("War on high prices!"), and so on. Despite the prevalence of shoplifters he placed all the merchandise in piles on the tables, always wanting to give the impression of abundance. He set up a wooden counter with an opening in the center where he sat in plain view of customers using a sharp knife to cut thick cotton fabric according to patterns copied from American clothes. He hired girls who would sew the pieces of fabric together on the spot, making cheap articles of clothing that went directly from production to the consumer. He installed loudspeakers that played cheerful Spanish songs, always with lewd lyrics, at high volume: "*Garnish the cock with cherries . . . While I put the moves on the hen . . . cinnamon, sugar, and cloves . . .*" Fascinated laborers filled the shop. Many came in carrying baskets. I was forced to go to El Combate after finishing my homework to keep watch on the hordes of customers. If I saw some wretch trying to hide a wool vest, skirt, or some other piece of clothing at the bottom of his basket I would give a sign to my father. Jaime would then leap over the counter in a single bound, fall on the thief, and demolish him with blows. The poor man, feeling culpable, would meekly accept his punishment without defending himself. If the thief was a woman he would deliver huge slaps, rip off her skirt, and push her out into the street with a single kick, her knickers about her ankles.

In no way whatsoever did I approve of my father's violence. My insides tied in knots and my chest burned when I witnessed these bloody faces, accepting their punishment as if they were receiving the wrath of God. It was less serious for a man to have a broken tooth or nose than it was for a woman to have her naked buttocks and torn-off knickers, sometimes full of holes, revealed to the eyes of the mocking public. The poor woman would be paralyzed, overwhelmed by embarrassment, hands covering her crotch, unable to reach for the torn-off underwear to pull it back up. Someone had to come—a friend, a parent—and cover her with a jacket or shawl in order to remove her from the hostile crowd. Every time I signaled a thief with my index finger, a bitter taste invaded my mouth; I did not want to harm these people, who stole because they were hungry, but I wanted to betray my father even less. The boss had given me an order, and I had to obey it, even when I felt that I was the one who was being humiliated and whose flesh was being wounded. After each beating, I shut myself up in the bathroom to vomit.

My body, which contained so much guilt, so many suppressed tears, and so much nostalgia for Tocopilla, began to turn sorrow into fat. At age eleven I weighed a little over 100 kilograms. Overburdened, I had trouble lifting my feet off the ground; my shoes scraped the pavement as I walked, and I breathed with my mouth half open, struggling to draw in the air that resisted me, my formerly wavy hair falling limp and lackluster on my forehead. Having forgotten that above me there was a sky without end, I walked with my head hanging down, my only horizon the rough concrete sidewalk.

Sara appeared to notice my sadness. She came back from her mother's house carrying a black-varnished wood box in her arms. "Alejandro, the holidays are over. In a month you'll be able to go to school and make friends, but now you need something to keep you busy. Jashe gave me her son José's violin, may he rest in peace. It will make her extremely happy if you learn it and do with this sacred instrument what my poor brother was not able to do: play us "The Blue Danube" during family suppers."

I was forced to take lessons at the Musical Academy, which was run by a fanatical socialist in the basement of the Red Cross building. I had to walk all the way across Matucana to get there. Instead of being curved in the shape of a violin, the black box was rectangular like a coffin. Seeing me walk by the shoe shiners would jeer sarcastically, "He's carrying a dead body! Gravedigger!" Blushing with shame, my head hunched over between my shoulders, I was not able to hide the funereal casket. They were correct: the violin that it contained was José's remains. Not wishing to bury him, Jashe had made me into his vehicle. I was an empty vessel used to transport a lost soul. Or better, I was the gravedigger for my own soul. I carried it, dead, in this horrible case. After a month of lessons, during which the black notes seemed to me to be in mourning, I stopped in front of the shoe shiners and looked at them without saying a word. Their jeering grew to a deafening chorus. Slowly, their hilarity was drowned out by the sound of an enormous freight train the color of my violin case. I threw the coffin onto the tracks, where it was reduced to splinters by the oncoming locomotive. The ragged people, smiling, began gathering up the pieces to build a fire, paying no heed to me as I stood before them, shaken by age-old sobs. An old drunk walking out of the bar put a hand on my head and whispered hoarsely, "Don't worry, boy, a naked virgin will light your way with a flaming butterfly." Then he went to urinate, hidden in the shadow of a pole.

This old man, made into a prophet by wine, pulled me out of the abyss with a single sentence. He had shown me that poetry could emerge even at the bottom of the bog where I was buried. Jaime, in the same manner that he mocked all religions, was merciless with poets. "They talk about loving women, like that García Lorca, but they're all queers."

Later on he broadened his contempt to include all the arts, literature, painting, theater, and singing. They were all despicable buffoons, social parasites, perverse narcissists who were starving to death.

A Royal typewriter languished in a corner of our apartment, covered with dust. I painstakingly cleaned it, sat in front of it, and began my struggle against the image of my father that occupied my mind as a gigantic presence. He looked at me with disdain: "Faggot!" Transitioning from submission into revolt, I furiously destroyed the mocking god in my mind and wrote my first poem. I still remember it:

> *The flower sings and disappears.*
> *How can we complain?*
> *Nighttime rain, an empty house,*
> *My footprints on the path*
> *Begin to fade away . . .*

Poetry brought about a radical change in my behavior. I stopped seeing the world through the eyes of my father. I was allowed to attempt to be myself. However, to keep the secret, I burned my poems every day. My soul, naked and virginal, lit my path with a butterfly on fire.

Once I could write without feeling shame and without feeling that I was committing a crime I wanted to keep my poems and find someone to read them to. But my father's power, his worship of strength, his contempt for weakness and cowardice, terrified me. How could I announce to him that he had a poet son? Late one night I awaited his return from El Combate, determined to confront his tiredness and bad mood. As was his custom, he arrived home with a wad of banknotes wrapped in newspaper. The first thing he said to me, bitterly, was, "Bring me alcohol! I have to disinfect this stink!" He threw the wrinkled, foul-smelling, dirty bills on his desk and sprayed a sanitizing cloud over them. Putting on surgeon's gloves, he began to sort and count them. Occasionally, cursing, he flattened out greenish bills that looked to me like the cadavers of marine insects. "Put on some gloves, Alejandro, so you don't catch something from this filth, and help me count them." I got up the courage to begin my confession.

"Papa, I have something important to tell you."

"Something important? You?"

"Yes, me!" In this "me," I tried to embody all of my new independence. "I am not you, I don't see the world the way you do. Respect me!"

But like a banknote encrusted with mud, blood, or vomit, Jaime brushed me aside and, uttering maledictions, began to scrape the crud off the bills with a nail file. I got ready to yell at him for the first time in my life. "Imbecile, notice that I exist! I am not your gay brother Benjamín, I am myself, your son! You have never seen me! This is why I've gotten fat, so that you'll notice me, at least my body if not my spirit! Don't ask me to be a warrior; I'm a boy! No, not a boy, because you've killed the boy! I am a phantom that wants to flee the obese cadaver that makes it sick by imprisoning it in a living body that wants to be free of your concepts and judgments!" But I could not even utter the first syllable, because at that moment a tremendous underground roaring announced the arrival of a tremor threatening to grow into an earthquake. As the floors and walls vibrated, one might have thought a huge truck was passing in the street. But when lamps started swinging like pendulums, chairs slid across the room, a dresser fell over, and a shower of dust fell from the ceiling, we knew that the Earth was angry. This time, her fury seemed to be turning into mortal hatred. We had to grab onto the iron bars in front of a window in order not to fall down. The walls cracked, and the room was like a boat rocking in a tempest. We heard cries of the panicked masses from the street. Jaime grabbed me by the hand and dragged me, stumbling, to the balcony. He began guffawing. "Look at these hypocrites, ha ha, they fall on their knees, they beat their chests with their fists, they piss and shit, they're as cowardly as their dogs!" Indeed the dogs were howling, hair standing on end, voiding their bowels. A utility pole fell. The electric cables wriggled on the ground, throwing off sparks. The crowd ran to take refuge in the church, whose single tower was wobbling from side to side. Jaime, more and more full of joy, kept me next to him on the balcony that threatened to collapse, stopping me from running down to the street.

"Let me go, Papa, the house could fall down! We'll be safer outside!"

He slapped me. "Quiet, you're staying here with me! You've got to trust me! I'll never let you be a coward like the rest of them! Don't take the earthquake's side. Fear makes the damage worse. If you pay attention to the Earth, she'll take your confidence away. Ignore it. Nothing's happening. Your mind is more powerful than a stupid earthquake."

The tremors stopped growing. Then, little by little, the ground returned to its habitual calm. Jaime let me go. Smiling like a hero, he looked at me as if from the top of an inaccessible tower. "What did you want to tell me, Pinocchio?"

"Oh, Papa, it can't have been important; the earthquake made me forget it!"

He sat back down at his desk, plugged his ears, and returned—cursing as usual—to counting the laborers' sullied bills as if I had ceased to exist.

I went to my room feeling like my soul had been run over by a steamroller. My father's bravery was invincible, his authority absolute. He was the master, I the slave. Unable to rebel, all I could do was to remain obedient, cease my creative activities, and not exist except as a guided being: the unavoidable meaning of life was to worship my omnipotent father.

Again I had the urge to jump out of the window, this time to be flattened by one of the trains that passed by at all hours of the night, their whistling penetrating my dreams like a pin impaling a dragonfly. One thought held me back from jumping: "I do not want to die without knowing my father's sex. He must have a penis as large as a donkey's."

I waited until four in the morning when my parents' snores, as powerful as locomotives, filled the house. I walked on tiptoe trying not to think for fear that the vibration of a word in my mind might escape through my skull and cause the walls, floor, or furniture to creak. The minute that I spent opening the door to the bedroom felt like an hour. I was hemmed in by rancid darkness. Fearing that I might trip over a shoe or the chamber pot full of urine that my mother emptied every morning while Jaime and I were eating breakfast, I froze like a statue until my eyes adjusted to the blackness. I was getting close to the bed. I dared to light my torch. Taking care not to let any ray of light fall on their faces, I looked over their bodies.

It was the hottest time of the year. They were both sleeping naked. A few flies, drunk on the penetrating odor, buzzed around their armpits. My mother's white skin still had red marks from the corset she wore from morning to night. Her breasts, like two enormous fruits, lay serenely on her chest. A Rubenesque goddess of abundance, she was sleeping with one small ivory hand lying on the thick mat of my father's pubic hair. My surprise was so great that my swollen tongue began to palpitate as if it had turned into a heart. I wanted to laugh. Not from joy, but from nervousness. What I saw dealt a demolishing blow to the mental tower in which Jaime's authority had imprisoned me. The warmth of Sara's nearby fingers had given him an erection. For sure, the circumcised member was shaped like a mushroom, but—incredible!—it was much smaller than mine. It looked more like a little finger than a phallus.

In a flash I understood Jaime's aggressiveness, his vindictive pride, his constant anger at the world. He had precipitated me into weakness, slyly forming me into a character of cowardice, an impotent victim, in order to make himself feel powerful. He made fun of my long nose because he had something short between his legs. He had to prove his own power to himself by enticing customers, dominating my large mother, bloodying shoplifters. His powerful will compensated for his barely adequate penis.

The giant collapsed before me—and with him, the whole world. None of the beliefs that had been inculcated in me were true. All the powers were artificial. The great theater of the world was an empty shell. God had fallen from his throne. The only true strength I could count on was my own, meager as it was. I felt like someone with no skeleton whose crutches had been taken away. However, a miniscule truth was more valuable than an immense lie.

I was enrolled in the Applied School, a magnificent building with capable teachers and an optimal program of studies, but with an unexpected difficulty: the alumni were Nazi sympathizers. Perhaps due to the influx of German immigrants or the influence of Carlos Ibáñez, the dictator who had emerged from an army trained by Teutonic instructors, during the war more than 50 percent of Chileans were Germanophiles and anti-Semites. The obligatory collective shower after gym class was enough for my mushroom to betray me. With shouts of "Wandering Jew!" I was ejected from all the games that the students organized during breaks. I had the privilege of a whole bench to myself during classes: no one wanted to share the double seat with me. I did not understand this exclusion at first. Jaime had never told me that we belonged to the Jewish *race*. According to him, my grandparents were of pure Russian stock, communists who had fled the irate Tsarists; and the Jews, just like the Christians, Buddhists, Muslims, and other religious people, were a bunch of madmen who believed in fairy tales. Little by little, receiving one insult after another, I understood that my body was formed of a despised material, different from that of my classmates. During the first trimester I took my revenge by becoming the top student. This was not difficult; my parents did not talk with me—one sentence too many would convert their weariness into exasperation—and, submerged in the silence to which my peers had condemned me, the only entertainment left was to study for hours and hours, day and night, not for pleasure or out of duty but as a drug that stopped me from confronting my anguish. In this bottomless swamp, like the flowers on a lotus, a few short poems blossomed.

This feeling rational to the point of boredom
watching the mad carnivals pass

waving obscene banners in the streets
as if all were dead clad in gold
while I make my corner into an empty temple . . .

Tired of living as a victim, I tried to participate in the high jump competition. In the middle of the schoolyard was a rectangular pit filled with sand. A horizontal rod between two pillars measured the height of the jumps. As soon as the bell announcing recess sounded, the boys ran there and formed a long queue. One by one, they tried to outdo each other at high jumping. They did quite well. Sometimes the bar was raised to 170 centimeters. When I tried to join the line they pushed me out, muttering "fat stinker" without even looking at me.

I had accepted humiliation from a young age, viewed my being different as a kind of castration, but now that I knew I was equipped with a larger penis than my father I decided to show my enemies that they could not conquer me. I went to the office of the school president, a sacrosanct place that no student dared enter, explained my problem to him, and asked him to help me survive the endeavor I wanted to undertake. He agreed!

When the bell sounded the students in each grade got into formation in the first and second floor loggias, in front of the classroom doors, awaiting the president's arrival. The square yard, with its sandy jumping area, was at the center of the crowd. For five minutes, the president allowed me to try jumping. Given my excess weight, I was far from being an athlete. I decided to start at a meter and a half. At first, it was impossible for me to jump it. I ran toward the bar amid general mockery— there were at least five hundred students watching—put all my energy into a leap as if my life depended on it, rose into the air, knocked down the bar, and fell sprawling in the sand. Laughter rang out. Paying no attention to the deafening hilarity, I tried again. And so, six times a day for five minutes straight without stopping, again and again, failure after failure, I continued for four months. Little by little I lost weight, from a hundred kilos down to eighty; although I was still obese, my new muscularity enabled me to jump over 160 centimeters. In the last two months I lost another ten kilos, and like the best of the jumpers I passed over the bar at a height of 170 centimeters. My success was crowned by furious silence.

I had finished the school year. Standing in the schoolyard in a compact mass, the students waited for the gate to open so that they could run out to the street in a chaotic stampede into summer. I, who had been relegated to the bottom of the heap, felt that before leaving I should thank the president for the favor he had granted me, so I began to make my way among the students. I had to pass through the entire crowd to get to his office. They moved closer and closer together, forming a human wall. I tried to push them apart. No one cried out or made any violent gesture. It all took place in hypocritical silence, because the teachers were watching from the loggias. Arriving at the center of the schoolyard, raising my left arm to part the shoulders of two opponents, I felt a blow to my bicep. I voiced no complaint. Blood began to drip between my fingers. The sleeve of my white shirt was turning crimson, a tear in the fabric showed where I had been cut by a knife.

The gate opened. The crowd ran shrieking out to the street, and in a couple of minutes I was left standing alone in the middle of the yard. Pale, but not crying or yelling, I showed the wound. "There was an accident. Two boys were playing with a penknife, and I got between them just when one of them was making a quick swipe. Luckily I lifted my arm; if I hadn't the blade would have gone into my heart."

The Red Cross was summoned. The ambulance took me to the clinic. The teachers were anxious to leave for the holidays, so no one accompanied me. The doors of the empty school were shut behind me. A rough nurse disinfected the wound and sewed it up with three stitches. "It's nothing, kid. Go home, swallow these pills, and take a nap." I was used to enduring pain and equally used to others showing little interest in what happened to me. Apart from the imaginary Rebbe and the no less imaginary old Alejandro, no one had ever kept me company. Solitude oppressed my body like the bandages of a mummy. I was in agony inside this cocoon of rotten fabric, a sterile caterpillar. And what if I had not lifted my arm and the knife had pierced my heart? Would someone have died? Who? Someone who was not me! My true being still had not germinated. Only a shadow would have fallen dead in the sandy yard. However, chance had ordained that my dead soul would not yet die. If that mysterious pattern called destiny wanted me to live, then first I had to be born in order to live.

I shut myself in the room they had given me, in the interior of the dark apartment. As there were few very cold days in the winter there were no electric or gas heaters, and we heated with braziers. I gathered all my photographs and watched them turn to ashes on those pieces of carbon lit up like rubies. Now no one would ever be able to identify me with the images of what I had ceased to be. I, a sad boy dressed as Pierrot on a bench in the square in Tocopilla, wearing an old black sock for a cap when Sara had promised to make me a white pointed hat with gauze pompoms. In another photo where rather than my usual mussed hair, rope sandals, and long pants I was dressed in the English style with short gray pants, a salt-and-pepper jacket, black and white shoes, and greased hair, I posed stiffly with a sulky expression with bare legs (no one could make me wear cotton socks) in order to send an image to my grandmother that was not my true self: "What a disgrace. Jashe will despise us!" Later, there I was in a high school group, amidst those cruel boys. Even today I remember the names of two of them with shivers of anger, Squella and Úbeda, large bullies who invented a degrading game: when other boys were distracted they would approach them from behind and assault them in the backside with a pelvic thrust, proclaiming, "Nailed!" I had to keep my buttocks against the wall for my first three years there. Finally, given away by my screams, they were caught trying to rape me in the latrine and expelled from the school. Rather than thanking me for this, my classmates broke the silence they maintained toward me with a single injurious word: "Snitch!"

I kept on burning photographs, believing I had destroyed them all, but no, one remained at the bottom of the shoebox where I kept my collection. In it I was posing next to a girl with full lips and large, light eyes, with an expression of arrogant melancholy. I threw it in the brazier. As I watched it burn, I suddenly realized that I had a sister.

It may seem unreal that from birth someone could live with a sister two years his senior, grow up in the same house, eat at the same table, and still feel like an only child. The dense reality that is constructed by the presence of bodies can become invisible if it is not accompanied by a psychic reality. I did not take the place of my sister; she was not a sacrificial dove. I did not become the center of attention by virtue of being a boy. Very much to the contrary, I was the one who was erased, though I did not realize it until that moment. Generally speaking, the much anticipated son who will ensure the continuation of the paternal name is the favorite child. The daughter is relegated to the world of seduction and service. In my case, the exact inverse was true. When she was born, she was the top priority. I, starting with my first newborn cry, was an intruder. Why? Even today I cannot explain it with certainty. I have various hypotheses, all convincing but none that I find thoroughly satisfactory. I never saw my father use his surname. He signed checks with a succinct *Jaime.* On his Communist Party card, he was identified as Juan Araucano. Now and then he would say to me, "You read a lot; perhaps one day you'll be stupid enough to want to be a writer. If you use the name Jodorowsky you will never succeed. Use a Chilean pseudonym." It seems that my grandfather Alejandro had disappointed him. Holding a secret grudge, he hardly ever mentioned his name or told any stories about him, only letting on that he had been a shoemaker with delusions of holiness. Following the advice of his Rebbe, he donated most of the money he earned—which was minimal, since he did not put a price on his shoes or repairs, allowing customers to pay what their meager good will dictated—as alms to the poor. Having suffered so much on their account, he died relatively young, his heart giving out. "What kind of holy man snatches bread away from his family to put it in strangers' mouths?" He left his widow and four children in poverty when he died. The Jewish community, immigrants preoccupied with their own survival, shut them out. My father sacrificed ambitions of studying in order to become an even better theorist than Marx, then devoted himself to whatever work he could find: selling coal, mining, circuses, trying to give a decent life to his sisters (who, according to him, became prostitutes) and helping Benjamín, the youngest, to become qualified as a dentist. He got no thanks from anyone: his brother, rather than giving him a job as a dental technician—as had been agreed upon, since Jaime, having inherited his father's manual dexterity, could make excellent false teeth—fell in love with a dark-skinned young man and entered into a relationship with him. Teresa, my grandmother, sanctioned Benjamín's love affair and acquiesced to living with him and his disgraceful (from Jaime's point of view) lover.

I believe that my father blamed all this on the shoemaker. When people wanted to get rid of a pharaoh in ancient Egypt, instead of condemning him to death they would set about erasing his name from all the papyruses and seals. By thus extirpating his memory, they condemned him to the true death that is oblivion. When a man hates his father, he avoids reproducing in order to stop the name from being passed on or else changes his name.

I suppose that Jaime saw my sister as an only child. I arrived two years later as a surprise: no one had wanted me to come, I was a usurper in the world; my presence was an abuse. I brought with me the threat that the hated name might survive. A second hypothesis, which does not negate the first, is that I was the screen onto which Jaime projected the anger he held toward Benjamín, whose perversion, treachery, and appropriation of their mother were difficult things to accept. He had to regurgitate this resentment, to take it out on someone. He brought me up to be a coward, a weakling. By mocking my feminine side, he encouraged it to develop; from his violent example I learned to detest machismo. Just like his brother, who lived in a house full of books (mostly romance novels and books on topics related to forbidden sexuality), he taught me to love reading by signing me up at the city library and later, in place of toys, letting me buy whatever books I wanted. I ended up living surrounded by four walls of books, like my uncle. Jaime never liked to use my name, and when he decided not to call me Pinocchio he called me *Benjamincito* as if by mistake. Countless times he would declare, "You are the last Jodorowsky," thus subtly inoculating me with sterility.

Another hypothesis is that he ignored me because of my curved nose. Being Russian bothered him (he had arrived in Chile at the age of five), and being Jewish even more so. He wanted roots. Anti-Semitism raged in Chile like a fire in a straw loft: the Guggenheims had taken over the saltpeter and copper mines, and later the banks, prospering from the workers' destitution. In the slightest dispute over politics, business, or simply in the street, someone would shout at him, "Shit Jew! Outsider!" His nose was straight, and the prominent curve of mine caused him constant shame. Perhaps this is why I have no memories of going for walks with only him, going into a bakery or cinema alone with him. Whenever we all went out he would walk between my mother and sister, one of them on each arm, and I behind . . . I would sit in the darkest corner of the restaurant table . . . and in the circus gallery I would sit far from their box seat, near to the ring. In fact, my family was a triangle— father, mother, daughter—plus an intruder.

It is also possible that Jaime, having lost his father at the age of ten, remained a child due to the trauma, never growing up emotionally just as his penis never grew. No one had ever loved him. Teresa, the ideal mother to whom he aspired once he took over the place of his father, had betrayed him. He could not trust grown women. The proof: after his wedding night with Sara there were no bloodstains on the sheets. He had been duped; the bride was not a virgin. Without a penny in his pockets Jaime left his wife, whom he had gotten pregnant, and went to work as a miner for a nitrate company. A year later, in that stifling place where the salt devoured all color, Sara came to search for him with the keys to a shop in Tocopilla and a baby girl in her arms. Jaime, upon seeing his daughter, saw his own soul. For the first time, he felt loved: those large green eyes were a mirror that improved the depreciated image he had of himself. Raquelita, forever a virgin, only his, no one else's, could see him as valiant, powerful, handsome, triumphant. Sara, with her dowry in the form of the shop keys, was accepted again although never pardoned: she was a traitor like Teresa, married to him by force but still in love with another, some imbecile whose large penis must surely be his only notable quality. My mother submissively accepted her relegation to second place, following Jashe's orders to serve and obey her husband no matter how despicable he might be in order to avoid embarrassment among the Jewish community. On their first night back together Jaime possessed her with the same fury with which he desired to punish Teresa, with the same rancor, the same hatred. I was conceived by a sperm thrown like a gob of spit.

Poor Sara, so white skinned, so humiliated, felt like an intruder in life, just like me. Her father had burned himself alive. In Moisésville, the Argentine village where the immigrants arrived believing they had reached the new Palestine but which in fact was an inhospitable terrain, the people shut their doors and windows when they saw that torch of a man bounding along the street yelling for help. Jashe, six months pregnant, saw her blond husband becoming a black skeleton through a peephole in the side door. Three months later she married Moishe (a traveling necktie salesman), gave birth to Sara, and in the following two years to Fanny and Isidoro.

Fanny was born so dark skinned that they called her La Negra. With her kinky hair, large lower lip, and ears as big as her father's she grew up myopic, ungraceful, and conceitedly ugly. She was cunning, drew attention to herself, and was attracted to power. Little by little she brandished the scepter of modesty, allowing a demure appearance, rabbinic morals, and unctuous reverence to preside in the face of gossip. She wore away at what little virility Isidoro had, making him into her bland lackey, and, occupying the center of the family, expelled Sara to the peripheral zone of derision, sarcasm, and criticism. Sara was unusual, an extreme case; pale as a corpse, she did not know how to handle herself, could not avoid attracting attention, projected an air of embarrassment, and was doomed to end up unhappy. The proof: while Fanny married her first cousin to prevent outsiders from entering the family, Sara fell in love with a communist, a pauper, an assimilated man who was practically a goy.

My mother, accustomed to having to fight to gain her mother's affection since childhood (and always losing the battle) identified Raquel with Fanny, Jaime with Jashe, and became enmeshed in a triangular relationship in which jealousy took the place of love. She delayed her daughter's maturation as long as possible. She forced Raquel to keep her hair cut above her neck until age thirteen and forbade her to wear necklaces, earrings, rings, brooches, nail polish, lipstick, or fine lingerie. One day, hypocritically aided by Jaime, Raquel proclaimed her rebellion by appearing with a short skirt, a daring neckline, silk stockings, red lipstick, and false eyelashes. Sara, mad with rage, threw a hot iron at her head. Luckily, Raquel dodged it, only losing a piece of an earlobe. Seeing the blood flow, Jaime punched my mother in the eye. She collapsed, writhing like an epileptic, screaming for her mother . . .

Thus began a new era that I observed as if from a great distance, from another planet: Raquel's beauty blossomed while Sara shut herself away in deep silence, Jaime became very accepting of my sister's caprices, and she never spoke a word to me, looking through me as if I were invisible. All I was allowed to have was a suit, a pair of shoes, three shirts, three pairs of underpants, four pairs of socks, and a wool vest. My sister accumulated a wardrobe with an impressive array of dresses, dozens of boots, and drawers full of all kinds of clothing. Her hair, rendered lustrous by imported shampoo, grew to her waist. In full makeup she was as beautiful as the Hollywood actresses on whom she modeled herself, and Jaime could hardly hide his lustful glances. When passing by her in the narrow corridor between the counters in the shop, he would repeatedly brush against her breasts or buttocks as if by accident. Raquel would protest, furious. Sara would blush. Drawn to her beauty, young boys began besieging her with telephone calls when she was fourteen. Jaime's delusional jealousy also began at this time. He prohibited her from talking on the telephone (and changed the number), from going to parties, and from having friends. Under the strictest secrecy he tasked me with watching her when she left school, following her when she went shopping, and spying on her at all times. Eager for attention, I became a dogged detective. Raquel, condemned to solitude, could only shut herself in her room—the largest room in our apartment—and read women's magazines amidst her white furniture, which was crackle-painted in the style of some former king of France, or play Chopin on her baby grand piano, also white crackle-painted. Jaime had put her in a gilded cage. Swarms of boys would wait for the girls to come out each day at the school, so my father decided to enroll Raquel in a private five-day boarding school. The students ate and slept there during the week then were released to go home, loaded with assignments for Friday, Saturday, and Sunday. This made my father feel secure that no one would steal his beloved daughter away.

He was wrong. The Gross family, who were Jewish, had dedicated themselves to the business of education since 1915. Isaac, the father, a depressive and suicidal history teacher, was replaced by his eldest son, Samuel, who had been crippled by polio; English classes were taught by Esther, Isaac's widow, who had been lame since birth; the two sisters, Berta and Paulina, hugely obese and also lame due to bone problems, taught the gymnastics and embroidery classes. The only one who could walk normally was the other son, Saúl, a mathematics teacher, half bald, obsessively organized, forty-five years old . . . Raquel, who had just turned fifteen, perhaps to liberate herself from her father's rule, declared that she was in love with Saúl Gross, who was prepared to ask for her hand in marriage. What's more, Raquel revealed that she was pregnant. Sara, to alleviate the scandal—a scandal that would be the death of her mother—insisted that the wedding should take place as soon as possible. Jaime, flabbergasted, agreed to accept him as his future son-in-law.

When Saúl came for his official visit, accompanied by his family, the stairs groaned beneath the sound of crutches and canes. At the meeting, the main topic of conversation was money. The teacher promised to buy an elegant apartment in the center of Santiago and to settle there with Raquel, giving her all the luxury to which she was accustomed. Jaime, for his part, agreed to cover all the expenses of the wedding. The ceremony was to take place in an enormous hall near the plaza of Diego de Almagro, near where Jashe lived. This would make it easier for the old lady to get there. A week before the great event, seamstresses completed a bridal gown for Raquel with a train three meters long. When Jaime met with Saúl for a private talk, having been warped by my detective activities I put my ear to the keyhole and listened to what they were saying. My father, his sharp voice infected by bitter anger, said to the groom, "You will be part of our family. We need to mend our fences. Tell me, how can I have confidence in your decency if you, a grown man, and a teacher no less, dared to fornicate with a student, an underage girl, a virgin, in this case my daughter?"

"But what are you saying to me, Don Jaime? Whence such monstrous accusations? Raquelita is a goddess to me, immaculate, pure! Even today, a week before the wedding, I have not yet known the taste of her lips."

"But . . . then . . . my daughter isn't pregnant?"

"Pregnant? To see Raquel with a swollen belly, waddling like a duck, turned into a vulgar wench? Never! It is not my plan to have children. We have enough cripples between my mother and my sisters and brothers. Do not be afraid, Don Jaime. Raquel will continue being what she always has been. Far be it from me to besmirch such a sacred maiden."

Jaime was quiet a good while. I imagine that his face grew purple. He pushed his future son-in-law out the door, slamming it with a bang and a frenetic yell of "lying bitch!" Then he burst into tears of rage.

The wedding was opulent. They bought me striped trousers, a black jacket, a shirt with a stiff collar, and a gray tie. I felt ridiculous thus

My sister, Raquel, Hollywood style

attired, but none of the three hundred guests noticed me. Sara, putting on a show of fake happiness for every guest, making sure that the roasted chicken was not dry, that the stuffed fish, liver pâté, and egg salad were fresh, testing the quality of the sweet and salty beet soup, and lastly giving advice to the twenty-piece orchestra, had no time to think of me. Jaime, uncomfortable in his rented tuxedo, hid in the smoking lounge sipping one vodka after another. The guests, Jewish merchants not tied to the couple by any sort of true friendship, had cleared out the buffet before the ceremony even began. A hunchbacked rabbi yelled out the Hebrew text rather than sang it. The bride and groom said their "I do's" beneath the ceremonial awning. Saúl, trembling, stomped on a glass that would not break at the first, the second, or the third try. At the fourth attempt he succeeded, finally allowing the orchestra to burst into a *freilaj,* a type of saraband to which young and old alike danced stiffly, all feeling guilty for shaking their legs in view of the baleful immobility of the Gross family. Raquel tossed her bouquet of paper roses at the two sisters, who fought over it like a pair of furious hippopotamuses, tearing it to shreds. (A month later, Berta threw herself naked into the sea near Valparaiso. She was found on the beach with the word "Ugly!" written on her belly, her legs spread apart, her crotch covered with scars from cigarette burns.) Suddenly, while the women and children were devouring huge pieces of cake, the men ran to a corner of the great hall and forming a close group around Jaime took him into the dressing room. I approached them. "What's wrong with my papa?"

"It's nothing, son, it's nothing. Jaime isn't used to drinking, and the alcohol and happiness together have gone to his head."

I could hear snippets of my father's voice. "Let me out of here, I'm going to break that thief's face! He's not worthy!" Then a few grunts; tense hands were covering his mouth. Then silence. The party continued. Sara rose to offer a toast, but instead of speaking uttered theatrical wails. Jashe took her in her arms and comforted her. Fanny gave three cheers and shouted, "That's enough; it's a wedding, not a funeral!" She called for another freilaj and rescued Jashe, pulling her in to dance with her, followed by the three hundred guests, paying no heed to the distress—real or feigned—of her sister. Everyone moved without restraint now, because the group of cripples had gone home, as had Raquel and Saúl. After jumping around for another half hour, the guests, bathed in sweat, began departing. The only ones remaining were Sara, munching on silver sugar balls—the last remnants of the huge wedding cake—at one end of the devastated table . . . and I, at the other end, leaning over, my tie swinging like a pendulum. Jaime's snores accompanied the orchestra's final *paso doble*.

This marriage spelled the ruin of my father. He was furious for months, begging manufacturers for deferments, borrowing money from loan sharks, trimming costs. For a while our principal nourishment was bread and cheese and *café con leche*. Then, as if by a miracle, Jaime's economic problems went away the moment that Raquel returned home. When Saúl came looking for her my father kicked him out the door, using skills learned in his circus career.

The marriage was annulled. Apparently, as I learned from our housekeeper, the new husband had turned out to be even more jealous than Jaime. Raquel had jumped out of the frying pan and into the fire. Saúl's jealousy was so great that he had forced my sister to wear ankle-length skirts, broad-brimmed hats that hid her face, and a corset that hid her breasts. She was allowed to go out into the street only for brief moments, measured by a stopwatch, and only to do the day's shopping. Raquel, forbidden to have a social life, acquired a chick to keep her company. The bird followed her around the apartment, taking her for its mother. One morning, when she returned from the market, she found the chicken hanged with a shoelace. Another day, Saúl, thinking that his wife devoted herself too much to the piano, took advantage of a moment when she had gone out to buy aspirin at the chemist's and sawed a leg off the noble instrument, making it fall on its side. He then explained to Raquel that ants had eaten away the leg. Four months after the wedding, my sister still had her hymen. Saúl's excuse was that he could not attain an erection due to hemorrhoids, and he required his wife to anoint his anus with banana pulp every night.

Jaime got out of his slump, paid his debts, bought delicious food, and resumed hiring criers to attract customers. Sara, for her part, began to degenerate, locking herself in the bathroom to smoke cigarettes in secret all day or spending hours making strawberry-filled pastries to send to her mother. Raquel, entrenched in her room, had decided to devote herself to poetry for evermore.

With so much going on, who could care about me? For Raquel, Sara, and Jaime, I did not exist. I knew, through our maid, that Sara had gotten her tubes tied after my birth, declaring, "The tubes are traps!"

With no photographs left to burn, I took a handful of ash, dissolved it into a glass of wine, and drank the grayish mixture. There was no doubt about it now. I had buried the past inside myself.

Now I understood the abuses to which my family subjected me. I saw the precise structure of the trap. They accused me of being guilty of every wound that was dealt to me. The executioner unceasingly declared himself the victim. In an ingenious system of denial, by depriving me of information—by which I do not mean oral information, but rather life experiences that were largely nonverbal—they stripped me of all my rights and treated me like a beggar, with no possessions of my own, to whom their disdainful magnanimity had granted a fragment of life. Did my parents know what they were doing? Not in the least. Devoid of awareness, they did to me what had been done to them. Thus, as the emotional wrongs were handed down from one generation to the next, the family tree had accumulated a load of suffering that endured for centuries.

I asked the Rebbe, "You, who seem to know everything, tell me what I can expect in this life, what is due to me, what my basic rights are." I imagined the Rebbe answering me as follows:

"First of all, you should have the right to be conceived by a father and mother who loved each other, through a sexual act crowned by mutual orgasm, so that your soul and flesh might have pleasure as their root. You should have the right to be neither an accident nor a burden, but an individual, hoped for and wished for with all the force of love, a fruit to give meaning to the couple, creating a family. You should have the right to be born with the sex that nature intended for you. (It is abusive to say, 'We were hoping for a boy and you were a girl,' or vice versa.) You should have the right to be acknowledged from the first month of gestation. At all times, the pregnant woman should accept that she is two organisms on their way to separation, and not just one organism expanding. Nobody can blame you for the accidents that occur during childbirth. What happens to you in the womb is never your fault. Sometimes, due to anger against the world, the mother does not want to give birth and, through unconscious action, wraps the umbilical cord around the child's neck and aborts it. Sometimes the mother does not want to give birth because the child has become an appendage of power, so she retains it more than nine months, drying up the amniotic fluid and burning the child's skin; or making it turn until the feet, not the head, slide toward the vulva, sending the child feet first into death; or fattening the child until it cannot fit through the vagina, requiring a frigid caesarean birth, no more than the removal of a tumor, in place of a natural birth. Or, refusing to accept the responsibility of creation, the mother might call for the help of a doctor who squeezes the child's brain with forceps; or due to a neurosis of failure, the child might be born blue, half-suffocated, forced to represent the emotional death of the parents . . . You should have the right to a profound collaboration: the mother should want to give birth just as the boy or girl wants to be born. The effort should be mutual and well balanced. From the moment that this universe produces you, it is your right to have a protective parent who is always present while you are growing up. Just as one gives water to a thirsty plant you have the right, when you are interested in some activity, to see before you the great number of possibilities that may develop along the path that you choose. You are not put on Earth to fulfill the personal plans of the adults who have set goals for you that are not your own; the greatest happiness life gives you is to allow you to become yourself. You should have the right to your own space where you can be alone in order to build your imaginary world, to see what you want to see without your eyes being restricted by antiquated morals, to hear what you want to hear even if the ideas are contrary to those of your family. You are not put on Earth to fulfill anyone but yourself, you are not here to take the place of any dead person, you deserve to have a name that is not that of a family member who died before you were born: when you carry the name of a dead person, it means that they have grafted a destiny onto you that is not your own, usurping your true essence. You have full right not to be compared to any sister or brother; they are not worth any more or less than you. Love exists when essential differences are recognized. You should have the right to be excluded from all quarrels between your family members, not to be used as a witness in their disputes, not to be the dumping ground for their economic woes, and to grow in an environment of trust and security. You should have the right to be educated by a father and mother who are ruled by common ideas, their intimacy with one another smoothing their contradictions. If they get divorced, you should have the right not to be required to see men through the resentful eyes of your mother or women through the resentful eyes of your father. You should have the right not to be torn away from the place where your friends, your school, and your favorite teachers are. You should have the right not to be criticized if you choose a path in life that was not part of your parents' plan; to love whomever you want without the need for approval; and when you feel capable of doing so, to leave home and go live your own life; to surpass your parents, to go further than them, to do what they could not, and to live longer than them. Finally, you should have the right to choose the time of your death without anyone prolonging your life against your will."

THREE

First Acts

If Matucana felt like a stifling prison to me, then so did my body. Feeling ill at ease in my flesh, I fled into my intellect. I lived shut away in my mind, levitating a few meters above a walking corpse that felt alien to me. I was conscious of myself as a multitude of disordered thoughts that eventually lost their meaning and became masses of empty words without any roots to nourish my being. I was a dry well in which phrases floated around, accumulating into a fabric of anguish. I knew that I was somewhere in there, behind my face, but I could not tell who or what this self of mine was. I felt cold, heat, hunger, desire, pain, and sorrow, but at a distance, as if they were in an alien body. The only thing that kept me alive was the ability to imagine. I dreamed of adventures in exotic lands, colossal triumphs, virgins sleeping with pearls in their mouths, elixirs that conferred immortality. Everything that I wanted could be summarized in a single word: *change.* The essential quality that I needed in order to love myself was to become what I currently was not. Like the frog awaiting the princess, I waited for the arrival of a superior and compassionate soul who would overcome disgust and approach me to give me the kiss of knowledge. Unfortunately I only had two friends, and they were imaginary: the Rebbe and the aged Alejandro. For what I wanted to achieve, I needed more than a couple of ghosts. I decided to be my own helper.

Even after meditations that seemed eternal, I was not able to dissolve my intellect within my body. Getting out of my own head was as impossible as escaping from a strongbox. It was impossible to get rid of the supremacy of my identification with the flesh. Therefore, I decided to try the opposite: since I could not go down, I would make all my sensations ascend! Beginning as pure intellect I began by considering my physical form, then my needs, desires, and emotions. I examined how I felt, then what it was like to live with this sensation. I realized that so-called "reality" was a mental construct. Was it a total illusion? This was impossible to know, but quite clearly I never perceived what was real in me in its entirety. Intellect always provided me with an incomplete fantasy, distorted by the false consciousness of myself with which my family had imbued me. "I am living inside a madman! My rational ship is sailing on a sea of insanity!" What at first I thought was a nightmare changed, little by little, into hope. Since everything that presented itself to me as part of "my being" consisted of illusory images, nothing more than dreams, I was able to change my sensation of myself.

Thus, a long process began. I focused my attention on my feet. They felt heavy, numb, distant, incapable of balancing properly. I began to imagine them as light, fine-tuned, sensitive, confident, their toes extending intrepidly onto the paths of life. I imagined myself with the feet of Christ, pierced by a single nail that fastened them to the pain of the world, a bleeding wound offering ascendancy to change lamentation into prayer. I imagined that the wounds I endured were not mine but those of humanity, and that through those wounds I absorbed the suffering of others and let it circulate in my blood like a balm, transforming it into happiness.

Next, I focused on my bones, felt them one by one. How forgotten was this humble structure! I had lugged it around as a symbol of death, not realizing its vital power. I recreated my skeleton, giving it a strong and flexible material like that of a steel sword, bones almost weightless, with a core of molten lava, like those on which the eagle soars. Suddenly,

I realized that I had created the skeleton of a dancer—the skeleton of my maternal grandfather. Without the intervention of my own will I then felt long, powerful muscles and indestructible entrails forming around this luminous structure, with abundant golden hair falling around its shoulders like a liquid halo. I realized that during my gestation Sara had unceasingly desired to recreate her father, the legendary dancer turned into a burning torch. Those wishes had infiltrated my cells, a mandate contrary to the natural order of things, causing me to be born giving forth cries of dissatisfaction. I was myself—what a sin!—and not the seven-foot-tall giant, the practically weightless solar Hercules. In order to be loved, I would have had to make myself into that myth. The flaming dead man was my ideal of perfection . . . I wanted to undo all of that and imagine another ideal body for myself. And yet, for all that I tried, I could not get rid of it. I recognized that I carried that model embedded in my genes, that every cell in my body aspired to be him. To keep struggling to change the effigy would be to deceive myself. Perhaps for centuries, from generation to generation, nature had been striving to produce that entity. Why not obey her? And if this meant that in a metaphorical manner, I would become my mother's father, then what of it? She had dreamed of being the daughter of a strong yet sensitive man, an artist. Once, shedding many tears, Sara had told me that when her father, Alejandro Prullansky, was dancing down the street engulfed in a rose of flame he had shouted out poems instead of screaming, until he crumbled to ashes.

Feeling myself living in this graceful imaginary body, I now became capable of movements that I had never known before. Space, which had previously seemed to me a terrifying abyss, enveloped me like a soft coat and showed me where to go; it became a protective carpet and ceiling, stretched to the horizon like an enormous harp, standing before me offering views through infinite windows. For the first time, I felt at ease in the world. The sensation of divergence disappeared. Countless invisible threads tied me to the center of the Earth, to the land, to the sky. With the whole planet licking the soles of my feet, I was moved to dance, to jump higher and higher, to go beyond the stars, into the depths of the sky.

What I am relating may seem absurd. What could be the use of such self-deception? My answer is that as a young man struggling to escape the weight of depression during that time, imagining myself to be strong and weightless offered me a lifeline that saved me from suffocating in the trap that was my family and allowed me to undertake liberating work. But, without any guide, where was I to start? Sometimes in those moments of greatest abandonment when we feel utterly deserted a sign appears where we least expect it and shows us the way. Those who dare to advance into darkness, expecting nothing, will at last find their shining goal. On a page torn from a book, which an autumn wind blew around my feet, I read the words that showed me I was on the right path: "The initiate who sets out in good faith to find the Truth, only to find, on all sides, the inexorable barrier that throws him back into the 'ordinary tumult,' will hear the Master say: 'Watch out, there is a wall.' 'But is this wall temporary?' asks the restless soul, 'can I pass through it or demolish it? Is it an adversary? Is it a friend?' 'I cannot tell you. You must discover it for yourself.'"

Who had written these lines, brought to me on a piece of paper that flitted down the street like a dirty butterfly? Was someone trying to tell me that my own being, which I myself despised, was worthy of attention from magical chance? And that I was not a vacant entity, that inside me there existed the power to cross or demolish the wall, because it was I myself who had built it? By saying, "Watch out, there is a wall!" the Master had stated that the disciple was not seeing due to distraction. Perhaps I was confusing the wall with reality, mistaking my mental limits for the natural boundaries of the world. Here is how I saw myself: since childhood I had been robbed of my freedom, my mind enclosed by a fence that prevented expansion. I closed my eyes. I saw myself submerged in a black sphere. This was the wall. As soon as I shut my eyelids, I found myself compressed within a dark skull. And because I felt blind, the possibility of existing escaped me. To lose sight of the outside world was to lose myself. The solitude became even greater when I plugged my ears with my fingers. Blocked off from light and sound, my wretched condition, my lack of sensation, my nothingness, manifested with implacable cruelty. In fact, I told myself, this blackness is impalpable. And if it is impalpable, then it does not have to be a thick barrier; it can be an infinite space. That's it! When I close my eyes, I will imagine that my consciousness is floating at the center of the cosmos.

I began to feel that I was moving forward. I traveled and traveled for a considerable time, farther and farther, extending without end. Gradually, in the infinite blackness, points of light began to shine. Now I was moving through a starry firmament. After enjoying the vastness that was presented to me, I undertook the same experience in reverse, as if I had eyes in the back of my head, then to the left and right, as if I had eyes in my temples. Then I descended into a well of infinite circumference, never reaching the bottom. The farther I went the more I lost the sensation of falling, and at last the descent reversed and turned into an ascent. Farther and farther, always farther; I returned to my center and made the sphere grow in all directions at once. The space around me was constantly expanding. Then I began to contract it. Forward, backward, left, right, up, down, all directions were concentrated on me. I nourished myself with stars, becoming more and more intense. I had eliminated distance. I was a point of light. Ah, such concentration! Attention, attention, attention is all that I was! My mind turned me into a transparent receptacle in which words arranged into sentences without beginning or end—impersonal herds with no use besides their beauty—paraded like windswept clouds.

I allowed the sensation of my body's presence to manifest itself. I concentrated my attention on all the different parts of the organism. I took stock of what I was feeling. Every organ, every limb, every region of the body had something to say. At first there were complaints, accusations of me abandoning them, not trusting them, but then came euphoric declarations of love. I discovered that my arms, my legs, my ears, skin, muscles, bones, lungs, intestines, the whole body was filled with an immense joy of living. I sank into my brain and entered the pineal gland. I imagined it as a diamond reigning on a throne amid reverent convolutions. I then navigated into the bloodstream. The heat of this thick liquid seemed to come from a distant past. I gave myself over to the ebb and flow, the coming and going from the center to the periphery and from the periphery to the center, as from the explosive central point of creation to the confines of the universe, an incommensurable rose opening and closing for all eternity.

Thanks to these exercises I was able to expand my limited mental space. Whenever an idea appeared, locked in a chain of words, I exploded it into a thousand echoes that transformed themselves like clouds. I never again thought linearly but in complex structures, labyrinths, where the effect sometimes came before the cause. The outer surface of my skull became the interior, and consciousness, like the pulp of a peach around its pit, became an exterior inextricably joined to the sky.

These sensations became my great secret. Neither my parents nor my sister knew about this transformation. In any case they paid very little attention to me, and even if I had revealed this to them they would have kept on seeing me the same way, as something invisible. I returned to the high school with no friends and no loving family. From that moment on I sat in my wooden chair with my feet parallel, firmly on the ground, a shoulder's width apart, hands outstretched over my thighs with palms up, my spine held straight with no support at the back, and with eyes closed, devoted myself for hours to my exercises. My mind was a vast and unknown land, and I dedicated myself to exploring it. Thus I continued until the age of nineteen. I moved forward in stages. At first, to help prevent parasitic thoughts from invading my mind, I repeated an absurd word to myself: "Crocodile!"

Having conquered space, I then decided to alter my sense of time. To this end, I eliminated the idea of death. "One does not die, but is transformed. Into what? I do not know! But I was something before birth, and must be something after my body is dissolved." I imagined myself ten years later, thirty, fifty, one hundred, two hundred. I kept advancing into the future, increasing my age to a dizzying figure. "It will be like this when I am a thousand years old, thirty thousand, fifty thousand . . ." I imagined the changes in my morphology. In a million years I would begin to lose my human form. . . . In two million years I would be transparent. In ten million years I would be an immense angel, traveling with other angels in a euphoric throng, traversing galaxies in a cosmic dance, helping to create new suns and planets. Fifty million years later, I would not have a body; I would be an invisible entity. A billion years later, dissolved into the energies and the totality of all matter, I would be the universe itself. And even farther, deeper and deeper into eternity, I would eventually become the point consciousness, the absolute root of existence, where all is in potential, where matter is nothing but love. Finally, after the explosion and implosion of countless universes, the stars dissolved and my mind froze. I began my journey backward, coming back into myself. Then I turned toward the past, seeing myself as a child, a fetus, imagining a multitude of lives, each one more primordial: dark beasts, insects, mollusks, amoebas, minerals, a rock wandering the cosmos, a sun, a point of continual explosion. Beyond this final stage I immersed myself in the unthinkable, the unimaginable, the infinite, the eternal mystery that, being incapable of defining it, we call God.

When I emerged from meditation and saw myself as a human being once again, all my problems seemed insignificant. I went out into the street, and with an arrogance that barely fell short of being a delusion of grandeur, I saw people immersed in their narrow mental space absurdly accepting the brevity of their lives, much closer to being animals than angels. As I had not been loved I did not know how to love myself, and thus, being unable to love others, I watched them with vindictive cruelty.

I thought that I could make my mind into whatever I wanted. If no one would deign to form me, I would be my own architect. Many paths presented themselves before me. Philosophy was one, art another; between intelligence and imagination, I chose imagination. Before setting myself to developing what I then considered the supreme power of the spirit, I asked myself what my ultimate objective would be. "The power to create a soul for myself!" And the objective of humanity? Not one, but three: to know the totality of the universe, to live as long as the universe lives, and to become the consciousness of the universe.

I realized that the basic (why not call it "primitive"?) imagination corresponded to the four primary mathematical operations: addition, subtraction, multiplication, and division. With addition, which is equivalent to enlargement, I considered how literature and cinema have used this technique to exhaustion. An ape becomes King Kong, a lizard becomes Godzilla, or an insect becomes Mothra, a butterfly so enormous that the movement of its wings brings about hurricanes. Inspired by this, a sugar cube might expand to become a runway for starships to land on. My grandmother could extend one arm, reaching around the entire world in order to scratch her back. A saint's heart swells to the point that his chest bursts open, continuing to grow in volume until it becomes as large as a skyscraper. Poor people by the millions come to live near it. They feed by cutting pieces off the organ, which moans with pleasure as they mutilate it.

The second technique, subtraction, decreasing, could be found in fairy tales, where there is an abundance of dwarves, gnomes, homunculi. Alice eats the cake that makes her shrink. Jonathan Swift sends his hero to the land of Lilliput.

Applying this technique, I imagined the wedding ring of a dissatisfied husband shrinking to cut his finger. Eve, cast out of paradise, searches for it for centuries, asking around among the people for its location, but nobody knows the answer. Desperate, she becomes silent; then paradise, as a tiny spot of vegetation, grows on her tongue. A locomotive, pulling train cars full of Japanese tourists, travels among the cerebral lobes of a famous philosopher.

Another aspect of diminution is the removal of some parts of a whole, eliminating them or making them independent. For example, in a movie the hands of an assassin are detached from his dead body and grafted onto a pianist who has lost those precious appendages in an accident; they then acquire their own will and force the musician to commit murder. In *Alice in Wonderland* a cat becomes invisible except for his grin, which remains floating in the air. Dracula has no reflection in mirrors . . .

The windows of a skyscraper, wishing to see the world, detach themselves from the facade and fly away. Flocks of tiny seagulls come to nest in the empty eye sockets of a blind sailor. A holy man's shadow breaks away and goes off on its own adventures, fornicating with the shadows of all the women it meets . . .

Another basic technique is multiplication: a painting by Breughel shows the invasion of thousands of skeletons. One of the seven plagues is the invasion of locusts. To prove that Rahula is his son, Buddha gives him his ring. He says, "Bring it to me," and multiplies into thousands of beings identical to himself. The son, paying no heed to the false Buddhas, goes directly to his father and gives him the ring.

I imagined a parade through the streets of Rome consisting of a hundred thousand Christs, each one on a cross. In Africa, a rain of albino children falls. The Statue of Liberty appears black one morning, because it is covered in flies. The emperor of Japan cuts out the tongues of his two thousand concubines and serves them as sushi to his victorious army. Millions of rabbis blacken the streets of Israel, protesting against their Messiah because, after being awaited for thousands of years, he has decided to return in the form of a pig.

I concluded my development of these simple techniques by visualizing the simplest one of all: grafting. Some part of a ruminant is joined to part of a lion, and to another part of an eagle, along with a human face, creating a sphinx; stick a woman's torso onto a fish's tail and you get a mermaid; put bird wings onto an androgynous human and you have an angel. And instead of having long hair, why shouldn't an angel have very thin rainbows? The trunk of a man on the body of a horse: a centaur. Why not graft the same human torso onto a snail, onto a stone, as the living figurehead of a ship, as the conscious part of a comet? The Aztecs combined a reptile with an eagle and obtained Quetzalcoatl, the plumed serpent, while an eagle covered with scales lurks in the shadows of the stream. If the god Anubis had the head of a jackal, why couldn't he also have that of an elephant, a crocodile, a fly, or a cash register? And why not think that the mysterious face of Muhammad is a mirror or a clock?

Another primary technique is the transformation of one thing into another: a worm becomes a butterfly, a man becomes a wolf, or else a vampire, a robot becomes an interplanetary spaceship, a good fairy becomes a witch, a demon becomes a god, a frog becomes a princess, a whore becomes a saint. In *Don Quixote,* windmills turn into aggressive giants, an inn becomes a palace, bottles of wine turn into enemies, Dulcinea becomes a noble lady, and so forth.

Walking around the city I imagined houses becoming huge lizard heads, an industrialist's wallet transformed into a raven, the pearls on a diva's necklace suddenly becoming small oysters, groaning like cats in agony. My mother grabbed me first with two, then six, and finally eight arms: now she was a tarantula.

From transformation, I went on to petrification: Lot's daughters became pillars of salt, the daughter of King Midas became a gold statue, the adventurers who looked at the Medusa were turned into stone. Time ceases to pass, planets, rivers, people, all things are paralyzed forever; the universe is a museum that no one visits; swallows, transformed into granite, fall from the sky in a deadly rain.

I applied the idea of union to my imaginary world, conceiving of an invisible bond with infinite extensibility, and saw it pass through the third eye of every human being, linking all the denizens of the planet in a living chain; the poet is joined to a humble stone, discovers that it is his ancestor and that what he recites is nothing more than the reading of love that has been inscribed in matter since the beginning of time; I was united with the sick and the poor, I felt that their pain and hunger were mine; I was united with sporting champions, their triumphs became my own; I was united with all the money in the world, making it mine: this energy invaded me like a whirlwind, giving me health, driving me to stop asking for things and start investing, making me realize that I must change from a harvester into a sower. I identified myself with the unifying chain. I felt like a canal; what I had I was receiving, and in the same instant that I was receiving it I was also giving it; there was nothing for me that was not for everyone else. If a child in the desert grabs a handful of sand, then lets it go, all of the desert may pass through his open hand. I was united with Chilean poetry, the poets faded away as their words melted:

> In the evening when the ghosts crack what little earth
> lingers in my body while I sleep
> my heart could deny its small chrysalis
> and those dreadful wings could sprout from it, out of
> nowhere.
> Who are you? Someone who is not you is singing behind
> the wall.
> The voice that answers comes from somewhere more
> distant than your chest.

> I walked like you, probing the infinite star
> and in my net, at night, I awoke naked
> just a catch, a fish trapped in the wind.

> I walked along all the roads asking for the way
> without route or line, driver or compass
> looking for the lost paths of what never existed
> viewing myself in all the broken mirrors of nothingness.
> Oh abyss of magic, open the sealed doors,
> the eye through which I may return once again to the
> body of the earth
> What would become of us without the unlit labor
> without the double echo toward which we reach out our
> hands?

Humberto Díaz Casanueva, Vicente Huidobro, Pablo Neruda, Pablo de Rokha, Rosamel del Valle

I realized that the desire for union was present in every cell of my body, in every manifestation of my spirit. This was not a matter of imagining bonds, but of realizing that they already existed: I was tied to life and bound to death, tied to time and bound to eternity, tied to my limits and bound to infinity, tied to the Earth and bound to the stars. Joined to my parents, my grandparents, my ancestors, united with my children, my grandchildren, my future descendants, joined to every animal, every plant, every conscious being. United with matter in all its forms, I was mud, diamond, gold, lead, lava, rock, cloud, magnetic field, electric spark, soil, hurricane, ocean, feather. I was anchored in the human and joined to the divine. Rooted in the present, united with the past and the future. Anchored in darkness, united with light. Tied to pain, joined to the delirious euphoria of eternal life.

After joining in this manner I decided to look at what was driving me to separate: the voice of the dead father resonating for years throughout the house; millions of tiny silver eagles rising up from half-dollar coins and flying up into the stratosphere to devour satellites; the tiger's skin, having lost the Buddha who used to meditate on it, tells a murderer to use it as his cloak; in the land of the decapitated, the last hat is publicly burned. When all living things perish, the roads moan, thirsty for footprints.

I had the idea to materialize the abstract. Hatred: a cornucopia inside a chest to which we have lost the key. Love: a road where our footprints go in front of us instead of following behind. Poetry: the luminous excrement of a toad that has swallowed a firefly. Betrayal: a skinless person who jumps into another's skin. Joy: a river full of hippopotamuses, their blue mouths gaping open to offer diamonds that they have taken from the mud. Confidence: a dance without an umbrella in a rain of daggers. Freedom: a horizon that detaches itself from the ocean, flying up to form labyrinths. Certainty: A lone leaf turned into the shelter of a forest. Tenderness: a virgin clad in light, hatching a purple egg.

Thus I devoted myself for a long time to conceiving of techniques to develop my imagination. For example, how to overcome the laws of nature (how to fly, how to be in two or more places at once, how to draw water from rocks); how to reverse qualities (fire that cools, water that burns, salt that sweetens); how to humanize plants (a tree grows lottery tickets), animals (a gorilla becomes faculty chair of the philosophy department), and things (an army tank falls in love with a ballet dancer); how to add what has been taken away onto something else (put an octopus's tentacles on the Venus de Milo, the head of a fly on the Winged Victory of Samothrace, an elephant's eye as the apex of the Pyramid of Giza); how to extend the qualities of one being or thing onto all beings or things (a log on fire, a cloud on fire, a heart on fire, a saxophone on fire, a moral judgment on fire).

One night, seeking to enrich my view, which was usually in the horizontal plane, I threw my head back as far as I could to see what it would be like to see along a vertical line. I was distracted by the sight of a cobweb on a lamp: at its center, the web's weaver crouched, waiting. A fly buzzed around the lamp. Instead of feeling sorry for myself, seeing the neglected state of my room—which Sara grudgingly cleaned once a month to satisfy the critical eye of her mother, who complained of the stench of Matucana when she came to visit us—I imagined the different degrees of a story, organizing them into a scale ranging from the lowest to the highest level of consciousness. At the lowest degree, not conceiving of change, striving always to remain what they think they are, the fly spends its life trying to avoid the spider while the spider spends its life trying to catch the fly. At a higher degree the fly, perceiving the spider's carnivorous desire as an input of energy, loses its fear, accepts that it is food, and sacrifices itself. The spider, meanwhile, learns to put itself in the place of the fly and decides to give up trying to catch it, even to the point of starving itself to death. At a third degree, the fly voluntarily enters into the sticky trap and when it is devoured by the spider invades its cells, its soul, and transforms it into a luminous being.

The two creatures, thus amalgamated, are a new entity: neither fly nor spider but both at the same time. At a fourth degree the spider-fly, realizing that the light that inhabits it is not of its own making, that it is a servant whose master is an impersonal inexhaustible energy, breaks free from the web and, attracted by the light, rises up until it is immersed in the sun. At the fifth degree, similar to the first, the spider waits in its web, hoping to catch a fly. But now the spider is not crouching, it is showing itself openly, without greed, and the fly, without distress or unnecessary buzzing around, flies directly toward the web. Change, transmutation, and adoration have submerged the menacing reality in a bath of joy. The hunt has become a dance in which continuous death is accompanied by continuous birth.

Suddenly, without any movement of the legs announcing it, the spider let out a long thread and made as if to drop down on me. I gave a cry of fear and dodged it, my armchair tipped over, and I fell backward onto the floor. I grabbed my shoes, put them on my hands like gloves, and with a single clap crushed the innocent creature. I felt sorry, not for it but for myself. Thanks to the derelict state my room had fallen into I was able to realize that in spite of these imaginative pleasures I did not feel any better emotionally. The images I created might be jewels, but the chest they were kept in, which is to say myself, was worthless. I was using my imagination in a limited form. I had dedicated myself to creating mental representations. This technique certainly opened up dreamlike paths, showed the way to sublime ideals, and provided elements for making works of art, but it did not change the incomplete manner in which I perceived myself. My body still appeared to me as a ghastly enemy, no more or less than a nest inhabited by death, and I was afraid to use it to its fullest extent. My sex organs were filling themselves with shame in order to dissimulate the fear of creating. My heart was immersing itself in malice and indifference to the world in order to avoid developing sublime feelings. My mind was invoking human weakness in order to ignore its power to change the world. Anything infinite, however well I could imagine it, gave me visceral dread. My animal side wanted a small space, a lair, a short amount of time, "I'll only last as long as my body," an opaque consciousness, relegating me to a life in the shadows avoiding responsibilities, an unvarying life bolstered by rigid habits in which change was considered a hidden aspect of death. I decided to free myself from these images, this mental celebration that concealed an avoidance of my organic nature, and to investigate a form of creation by means of my sensations. I thought, "When I hear sad news, I have no desire to move; I feel heavy, dense. By contrast, when the news is good, I want to dance; I feel light, agile. The facts that I know from words or visual images do not change my body, but they do change my perception of it. It must be possible to transform my perception of myself by my own will!"

I began an intense series of exercises. At night, once the insults and occasional blows between my father and mother had ceased, once my sister had stopped playing Chopin exercises on her white piano and the silence spread like balsam over a wound, I sat naked in my wooden chair and began to relax my muscles in order to concentrate and meditate. Unfortunately, several times during each night, trains passed directly below my window with deafening whistles. This noise, like a lance, left a bloody gash at the center of my spirit. I struggled for several weeks not to defend myself, to let the sound traverse my consciousness without retaining it, to pay it no attention and continue with my exercise. When I achieved this, I was able to immerse myself in my meditations without any apprehension. I conquered the flies, which were even more of a nuisance than the trains, in the same manner. Even though I closed the curtains and plunged myself into darkness, those insects never ceased buzzing and circulating, irritating my skin as they walked on it. Added to this, the apartment where we lived had no heating or air conditioning, and the heat and cold were intolerable at times. All these difficulties sharpened my capacity for concentration.

If I wanted to develop my sensory imagination, before anything else I had to liberate it from the tyranny of weight. The planet, always present in my body through its force of attraction, was telling me, "You are mine, from me you came and to me you will return." I felt that what was heaviest was darkness. I filled myself with it, a dense material, painful, overwhelming. I filled my feet with its blackness, then my legs, and the rest of my body. Having become a skin that was filled with tar, I breathed in as deeply as I could and exhaled the magma from my feet, replacing it with light. I emptied my legs, my arms, my torso, my head; I was a hide filled with glowing energy. I felt lighter and lighter. It seemed to me as if I would jump twenty meters when I took a step. The absence of the sensation of weight filled me with joy, with a desire to live, and made me breathe in deeply. My spirit was no longer invaded by psychological garbage, by gloomy serpents of shadow. I wanted to get dressed and go out for a walk. So I did. It was four in the morning. This working class neighborhood, with its dark streetlights (thieves had stolen the bulbs), was almost completely obscured in darkness. I walked along feeling as luminous as the moon, occasionally taking little jumps. Suddenly I saw three evil-looking men approaching. Prudently, I changed my course. Seeing my defensive movement, they fanned out. One pulled a club, the other a knife, and the third a pistol. I set out running toward San Pablo Street, the central artery of the neighborhood, where trains passed and a bar might still be open. "Stop, dickhead!" they shouted. I let out a cry of distress, sounding like a pig squealing in the slaughterhouse. Not a single window opened! Not a door! There was I, who had just recently been weightless, galloping along, feeling heavier than an elephant under the indifferent sky, the fecal footprint of fear growing in my pants. Feeling the pain of shattered dignity, I set all my hopes on getting to the main street. But it was dark! They were ten meters behind me. Giving up, vanquished, trembling, I stopped and waited for the bandits. They came at me and knocked me to the ground with a punch in the stomach. With agonized calm, I begged them not to kill me, to take everything from me, because I was a poet. They searched my pockets, finding a crumpled banknote and my school papers. After examining the papers meticulously, they returned them to me, along with the money, then saluted and explained that they were police and had mistaken me for a thief. "Young man, next time don't run away, because that makes you look suspicious!" With my body and soul aching, I walked on to San Pablo. There, just around the corner at a café a group of people were playing cards under the light of a gas lamp. A few more steps and I would have been safe! If they really had been muggers, they could have slit my throat like a cow's and left me there, a few steps from salvation. At that moment, I swore that I would always sustain my efforts until I had no drop of energy left and that I would never abandon a task I began until I finished it.

I continued my work after I returned to my room. I had met terror face-to-face, a paralyzing sensation of oppression that turned me into an animal. In that realm, where beings devour each other, fear is the essential element of survival. To ascend from animal to human is to escape fear. Fear of what? Animals have no concept of death because they perceive themselves only as matter. Their essential fear is that of losing the corporeal form. I felt the threats to my body that were present like never before. Flesh was bound to age, sicken, die; it had to be nourished and protected. Along with the fear of losing my body came the need to have a lair. Being descended from the Jews, who had been nomads for centuries, I had no homeland, no roots, no burrow. How could I rid myself of this anguish? Should I imitate Buddha, renouncing earthly life, disassociating myself from my body as well as my "ego," returning to the impersonality of the original energy, liberating myself from the chain of reincarnation? Thanks to the atheism that Jaime had inculcated in me this seemed like a fairytale, a coward's way out. "The sword that cuts everything will not cut you when you become the sword." Thinking thus, I decided to become that which caused my terror.

In my preceding exercises I had begun by imagining myself filled with black magma, which was then expelled so that light could inhabit me. But the mythological dragon, being immortal, cannot be conquered by killing but only by seduction. Thus one must accept being its food. I returned to imagining my feet full of that nefarious tar. Then, instead of identifying with my feet, I made myself one with the black stuff. I was the threat; I was the bringer of death; I was the nothing with its carnivorous cravings. I moved up through my legs, filled my pelvis, my trunk, my arms, my head, and erased all traces of morality, becoming a thick evil. With a phenomenal effort, I abandoned my attachment to my human form and turned loose. Leaving the carnal vessel I grew out in all directions like a voracious mass and began to overtake the building, the city, the country, the planet, the galaxy, finally filling the universe and continuing my infinite expansion. Stars lived within me, space monsters, demons, ambiguous entities, insidious ghosts, demented murderers, rats, vipers, venomous insects . . . Then I imagined the inverse: the infinite menace, the mortal shadow, began to invade space from all points and inundated the cosmos, advancing toward me. It swallowed galaxies, our solar system, the planet, the South American continent, Chile, Santiago, the neighborhood of Matucana, my house, my room, and finally concentrated itself on my body. While I occupied the universe, the universe also accumulated beneath my skin. I felt invincible, I was the evil, and there was nothing that could frighten me, least of all my father.

At that late hour of the night, naked as I was, I began slowly walking around the apartment. I walked crouching forward like a hungry beast. My eyes adjusted to the darkness very quickly, and my sense of hearing became sharper, I could hear the slightest creak, and from far off I could hear the deep breathing of Jaime, Sara, and Raquel. Also, my olfactory sense perceived the different smells that filled the house like never before: the sweet scent of damp sheets, the rancid floorboards, the sulfur in the air, the salty smell of the walls. I went into my sister's room. Because the windows were kept closed for fear of thieves, the heat made it necessary for her to sleep naked, with her legs spread. I put my nose a few inches from her crotch and smelled it . . . Both my pleasure and my disgust were such that the blackness of my heart seemed to transform itself into a tarantula. I imagined myself violating her, then ripping open her belly with my fangs to devour her guts. I savored the sight of this forbidden orifice for a long moment, then slipped into the master bedroom. There was my mother, leaning against my father's back. They were sleeping so deeply that they seemed like wax statues. I was invaded by a gigantic anger. I felt sure that I could rip open their jugulars with a single bite. Sara deserved my hatred because her foolish passivity made her complicit with Jaime. Without lifting a finger, she allowed my father to enjoy terrifying me. It was he who had taken pains to make me into a coward because he felt obliged to assert his dubious manhood and needed to overcome his problems with his gay brother. He who had taken me to the beach and made me stick my legs into pools where he knew octopuses lived, distracting me and keeping me there until one of those viscous animals wrapped its tentacles around my ankle. He who let me scream for a little while, then came to me laughing, pulled the suckers off my skin, bashed the animal against the rocks, then stuck his hand under the root of the tentacles and lifted the monster's hood under my nose, turning it inside out. "They're harmless. Don't scream like a little girl; learn to be brave!" But how can a five-year-old child be brave when an adult forces him to hold onto his back, arms around his neck, as he runs into the raging ocean waves? There, clinging to my father like a limpet, I shut my eyes, wrinkled my nose, clenched my jaw, and endured the ordeal as he, roaring like a lion, threw himself under the giant waves again and again, riding them just as they broke. Despite my young age, I knew that if I let go I would die by drowning. The cold water of the Pacific Ocean seemed to turn my body into ice. My fingers were getting stiff. The force of the waves would tear me off Jaime's powerful back. I began to scream. Jaime, furious, deposited me back on the beach while spitting the word "coward!" over and over again, not noticing that my lips were blue with cold. "Stop shaking, sissy! You have to learn to overcome fear!"

Well, now I had won. The guilty couple was there, defenseless, at the mercy of my hatred. I took a flowerpot full of moist soil in which worms had grown instead of the carnation seeds Sara had planted and with feline delicacy crawled onto the bed. Crouching, I emptied it out between their intertwined legs. I saw the masses of worms squirming

very near to their crotches; the demon who protects the denizens of the
night ensured that they did not awaken. I returned to my room, happy
like never before, and fell asleep knowing that reality would no longer
be the same . . . Neither Jaime nor Sara ever commented on the incident. Why? The event was so strange, so impossible, that their minds
erased it like a bad dream.

Little by little, I understood that the being I perceived myself to be was
not exactly the being I was. Moreover, the consciousness I perceived
was not exactly my true consciousness but a distortion of it, brought
about by my family and my education in school. I saw myself as my
parents and teachers saw me. I saw with the eyes of others. My child's
brain, like a piece of wax, had been sculpted into the shape of the judgment of others. I concentrated on my hooked nose. I thought of the
memories it contained—contempt, ridicule, name-calling, Pinocchio,
Big Nose, Tuna Fish, Vulture, Wandering Jew—and then, the contemptuous stares of Jaime and Raquel, so proud of their straight noses.
And finally, the indifference of my mother, who had erased me from
her soul after they cut off my blond locks and left only some short
dark hair. "Yes, I feel ugly, horrible, this enormous, monstrous bony
nose that is not mine, I do not want it, it has invaded me, it is a vampire stuck to my face." Once I had precisely delineated this feeling of
disgust, I began to change it. The hooked nose that had been imposed
on me must be conquered. I softened its boundaries, made it a ductile
and malleable mass, perfumed it, filled it with love, light, and goodness, and finally I gave it sublime beauty. Little by little, I expanded
this beauty across my face, my hair, my head, and then, like luminous
water, over my entire body, washing away the cruel looks and revealing the beauty I deserved. I turned on the radio and heard a piece by
Berlioz. Letting the accusations of ugliness fall away like tattered rags
I began dancing, allowing my body to make graceful, delicate, beautiful movements. I felt that this beauty of form was inundating my soul.
Something was opening up in my consciousness, and I realized that

this assumed beauty was like a flower, spreading its perfume all over the world.

I did the same thing again, with more strength. My father's gaze had trapped me in a corset of weakness. I chose my testicles as a starting point and filled them with an energy that spread through my body. Once I was completely full of this energy I tried to send it out through my fingers and toes, and with those twenty rays to transfix the world, reshaping its negativity to make it positive; but I encountered locks. In my soul there were prohibitions against being myself, requiring that I retain my conditioning, forcing me to live by the norms I had received through an ossified tradition. "You must not eat pork, you must not marry a Catholic, marriage is for life, money is earned through suffering, if you are not perfect you are worthless, you must be and act like everyone else, if you do not get your diploma you will fail in life . . ." Family guardians appeared at my least attempt to transgress these crazy ideas, brandishing swords to castrate me. "How dare you? What do you take yourself for? Who are you to change the rules? If you do this, you'll die of hunger! We are ashamed of you! You're mad; come to your senses! Everyone will reject and despise you; you are destroying yourself! You'll lose our love!" I felt like a dog covered with fleas. I realized my parents had abused me on all levels. On the intellectual level they had blocked off paths leading to the infinite with scathing, aggressive, sarcastic words, portraying themselves as clairvoyant, omnipotent, forcing me to see the world through their colored lenses. They had abused me emotionally with their cruelty, making me feel that they preferred my sister, creating a sordid trio of dependency, jealousy, and love-hate with her. They had bargained with me: "for us to love you, you have to do this or that, you have to be so and so, you have to buy the affection we give you at a high price." They had abused me sexually, my mother because she hid all manifestations of passion beneath a veil of shame, passing herself off as a saint, and my father because he seduced his customers in front of me, hiding scurrilous insinuations beneath a mask of mirth. They had abused me on the material plane: I do not remember my mother ever cooking a meal, which was always done by a servant. I do not remember any cuddling, ever being taken out for a walk, ever having my birthday celebrated, ever being given a toy, ever being given a nice room. I slept on old stitched-up sheets, had plain curtains in my room dyed a hideous shade of burgundy, never had a nice ceiling light in my room, my bookshelves were made of old boards propped up on bricks, and I was always enrolled in horrible public schools. And what's more every Saturday, when the other boys were relaxing or going to parties, I had to "pay" for what my parents gave me by staying in the shop, protecting the goods from the greed of thieves. And now I, this abused child, was abusing myself, trying every instant to reproduce the things that had traumatized me. Because they made fun of me, I sought out friends who despised me. Because they did not love me, I was forced to enter into relationships with people who could never love me. Because they ridiculed creativity, they made me doubt my values, sinking me into depression. By not giving me material things they made me pathologically shy, preventing me from going into a store to buy what I needed. I had made myself into my own bitter prisoner. "I have been despised, I have been punished, so now I do nothing, I am worth nothing, I do not have the right to exist." Unable to feel at peace, I was being persecuted by a horde of ancient furies. I began to shake myself as if to throw this old pain, this infantile anger, these grudges, these chains, away from my body. Enough! This is not me, this depression is not mine, they have not won, they will not stop me from doing what I want to do! Off, invading fleas! My inner universe belongs to me, I am taking possession of it, I am occupying it, exterminating what is superfluous! I opened myself to mental energies; I received them from the depths of the Earth and projected them into the sky; at the same time I received them from immeasurable space and projected them toward the center of the planet. I was a receiving and transmitting channel! I did the same with emotional, sexual, and physical energy: I plunged them into the bottomless void. Every idea, every feeling, every desire, every need touched my soul saying, "You are me!" These were usurping entities. The empty being, capable of containing the universe, did not know what it was and yet was living, loving, creating.

Around the time of my nineteenth birthday there was a quarrel in my family that, despite its monstrosity, revealed another aspect of my creativity: up until that point I had worked with images and sensations, but had not explored a technique composed of objects and actions. It happened that every day, between one and three in the afternoon, my parents shut El Combate to come back to the apartment for lunch. Jaime would sit at the end of the table, facing away from the window (he had appropriated this location where the light from the sky fell on his back). Beside him, on his right, sat my sister. I was disdainfully granted a seat a little farther down the table, on the left side. My mother would sit at the other end, off on her emotional island, always eating with her eyes directed up toward the ceiling to express the disgust that my father's noisy munching caused her. On this day, enervated by an accumulation of debts, Jaime devoured the food that was served by our faithful maid, sullying his lips and shirt more than was customary. Suddenly, Sara gave a low moan and murmured, "This man looks like a pig; it makes me want to throw up."

On the wall behind my mother hung an oil painting by a commercial artist of the lowest caliber. It was the familiar Andean landscape, illuminated by the red light of a sunset. My mother liked it because her mother had suggested she buy it. My sister and I thought it was ridiculous. Jaime hated it because it had been expensive. Raquel and I were silent with terror upon hearing Sara's unexpected words. Generally, in such cases, Jaime would get up and punch her in one of her pretty eyes. This time it was not so: he turned pale, slowly lifted his plate as a priest might lift a chalice, and threw his fried eggs at my mother's head. She ducked, and they landed right on the painting. The two yolks stuck there in the middle of the sky like twin suns. And oh, what a revelation; for the first time this vulgar painting appeared beautiful to me! In one fell swoop, I had discovered surrealism! Later on, I had no trouble understanding the words of the futurist Marinetti: "Poetry is an act."

FOUR
The Poetic Act

Definitions are only approximations. Whatever the subject may be, its predicate is always the entirety of the universe. In this impermanent reality what we imagine as absolute truth becomes inconceivable to us. Our arrows will never hit the white center of the target, because it is infinite. The concepts used by reason are true for me, here, at this precise time. For someone else, in the same place later on, they may be false. For this reason, despite having been raised with the most tenacious atheism, between two beliefs I decided to choose the one that would be more useful or the one that would help me to live. Before coming into the world I was a form of will that chose who its father and mother should be in order that my spirit might develop through suffering and rebellion in contact with the mental boundaries of these two immigrants. Why was I born in Chile? I have not the least doubt: my encounter with poetry justifies my emergence in that country.

Chile was poetically alive like nowhere else in the world during the 1940s and early 1950s. Poetry permeated everything: education, politics, cultural life, love. At the continuous parties that took place every day, where people drank wine without limitation, there was always some drunk reciting the verses of Neruda, Gabriela Mistral, Vicente Huidobro, and other great poets. Why such lyrical joy? In those years, while humanity was suffering from the effects of World War II, far off Chile—separated from the rest of the planet by the Pacific Ocean and the Andes mountain range—observed the struggle between the Nazis and the Allies as if it were a soccer match. There was a map covered with little flag pins on the wall of every home; the ups and downs of the opposing armies were followed amidst innumerable toasts and bets. Despite its internal problems, for the Chileans their long and narrow country was like an island paradise, protected by distance from the world's ills. While death prevailed in Europe, poetry reigned in Chile. With abundant food (four thousand kilometers of coastline provided delicious mollusks and fish) and an exceptional climate for producing cheap wine (a liter of red cost less than one of milk), the most important thing for all social classes, poor and rich alike, was partying. Most of the bureaucrats would behave themselves properly until six o'clock in the evening, but once they were out of the office they would get drunk and undergo a change, shedding their gray personalities and assuming a magical identity. (A respectable notary made people call him Terrible Black Tits when drinking in the bars after six o'clock, and the way he had dealt with one customer was the subject of much mirth: "Señora, I have also been a woman. Let us speak cow to cow.") The whole country was seized by a collective madness at sunset. The lack of solidity in the world was celebrated. In Chile, the earth trembled every six days! The very soil was, as it were, convulsive. For this reason, all people were subject to existential tremors. We did not live in a solid world governed by a rational being, but in a trembling, ambiguous reality. We lived precariously, both on the material plane and in our relationships with one another. You never knew how a night out on the town would end: a couple married at noon might wake up the next morning in other people's beds, the guests you invited over might throw your furniture out the window, and so on. Poets, night owls by necessity, lived to euphoric excess. Neruda, an obsessive collector, built a house-museum in the form of a castle, gathering a whole village around him. Huidobro was not content with writing "Why do you sing the rose, O poets! Make it blossom in the poem!" but also covered the floors of his house with fertile soil and planted a hundred rose bushes there. Teófilo Cid, the son of some extremely rich

Lebanese, gave up his fortune, although he did keep his subscription to the French newspaper *Le Monde,* and, drunk day and night, began living on a bench in Forestal Park. He was found dead there one morning covered by sheets of that same newspaper. There was another poet who only appeared in public on the occasion of his friends' funerals, in order to jump on the coffin. The exquisite Raúl de Veer did not bathe for two years in order to use his stench to identify those who were truly interested in hearing his verses. They had all begun to emerge from literature to participate in the events of daily life with an aesthetic and rebellious stance. For me, as for many other young people, they were idols showing us a beautiful and insane way to live.

In celebration of Jashe and Moishe's golden wedding anniversary the family decided to throw a party, at the same time inaugurating the new house that Isidoro, the architect, had designed for his mother: a large casket from which another smaller casket rose up, balanced on a pair of columns. The event was attended by close relatives and by some distant ones who came from Argentina. Most of them were chubby retirees, and their dark skin contrasted with their white hair, which they wore proudly, full of viscous satisfaction at being part of this humdrum Sephardic family. Sara, between nervous laughter and sugary tears, went from one relative to another uttering exaggerated elegies motivated by her desire to be liked. Unfortunately, being the beautiful swan among so many ugly ducklings, she drew contempt from all. Particularly envious was Fanny, who let slip some cruel jokes about Sara's weight and the whiteness of her skin, comparing her to a sack of flour. Jaime was also despised for having a store in a working class neighborhood. With great condescension he was invited to play cards, and conspiring among themselves they relieved him of a large sum of money.

No one paid any attention to me. They appeared not to see me. I sat for several hours, without eating, in a corner of the dark courtyard. What use had I for them? Was this a dignified life, being obliged to make a thousand bows like my mother in order to be halfway accepted into this mediocre purgatory or being gouged like my father in order to show that he was not a pauper? Seeing them in a large crowd like this filled me with rage. An ax rested next to a big lime tree, the only one that graced the little garden. Driven by an irresistible urge, I took it and began to ferociously hack away at the trunk. Only many years later did I understand the crime I had committed. At the time, when I did not yet feel connected to the world and did not see families as family trees, this plant was not a sacred being but a dark symbol that catalyzed my despair and hatred. I increased the force of my blows with the ax, losing my awareness of everything around me. I woke up half an hour later; I was dealing blows to a wound that already covered half the trunk. Shoske, my great aunt, was shrieking in horror. "You rascal! Stop him, he's cutting down the lime tree!" Jashe, equipped with a lantern and followed by all her relatives, burst into the small courtyard. They had to hold her up lest she faint. Isidoro rushed toward me. I dropped the ax and punched him in the gut. He fell, crushing a bed of daisies with his large rump. Everyone froze. The guests, frozen like wax statues, stared at me with a look of severe judgment. Among them was Sara, red with embarrassment. Jaime, standing behind the group, was doing his best to look detached. The thick, straight trunk of the lime tree gave forth a crack, threatening to break. Moishe emptied a bottle of mineral water onto the ground, took up handfuls of mud, and on his knees, sobbing, began to fill the huge hole in the trunk while my half-aunt, her black hair bristling, showed me the way out with an avenging index finger. "Go away, you savage, and never come back!" I was seized by intense emotion. I was afraid that I would start crying, like the pseudo-Gandhi. With an increasing satisfaction growing in me, I burst out laughing. I walked out and started running, panting with joy. I knew that this atrocious act had marked the beginning of a new life for me. Or rather, at last, it marked the beginning of my life.

I stopped after a while and heard footsteps coming behind me. The thin air and darkness prevented me from distinguishing who it was.

"If it's Fanny," I said to myself, "I'll punch her too." But it was a distant cousin, Bernardo, an architecture student a few years older than I who was tall, bony, and myopic, with big ears and a monkeylike face but a velvety and romantic voice.

"Alejandro, I'm amazed. That was a rebellious act worthy of a poet. I can only compare it to when Rimbaud painted the walls of a hotel room with his shit. How did you get the idea of doing something like that? You said everything without saying anything. Ah, if only I could be like you! The only things that interest me are painting, literature, and theater, but my family, the family you've just left, prevents me. I have to be an architect like Isidoro to satisfy my mother . . . Anyway, cousin, do you dare to sleep at your house tonight? I've heard that Jaime is a fierce man . . ."

My encounter with Bernardo was providential, and I am indebted to him for my entry into the world of poetry, but later he disappointed me to the core. The admiration he appeared to have for my talent turned out to be banal: he had simply fallen in love with me. After much hesitation—knowing that he would receive a resounding rejection—he decided to confess his love to me in the restroom of the Literary Academy, with reddened eyes showing me his erect penis as if it were a divine curse.

That night, on the pretext of wanting only a pure friendship, he brought me to stay with the Cereceda sisters.

Were they orphans? Millionaires? They had a three-story house all to themselves. I never saw them work, nor did I see their parents. The front door had no locks, so their artist friends could come in at any time, day or night. There were books everywhere, with reproductions of the greatest paintings; there were also records, a piano, photographs, beautiful objects, sculptures. Carmen Cereceda, a painter, was a muscular woman with thick hair, absorbed in a pre-Columbian silence. Her room was decorated with a mural on the walls, floor, and ceiling that was somewhere between the styles of Picasso and Diego Rivera, full of thick-legged women and political symbols. Veronica Cereceda, fragile, hypersensitive, eloquent, her head covered with fine down, was a poet and future actress. Both sisters loved art above all things in life. When I arrived with Bernardo, they received me smiling.

"What do you do, Alejandro?" Veronica asked me.

"I write poems."

"Do you know any from memory?"

"The Self is something that consumes / flames pouring from the dream," I recited, blushing to my fingertips. Veronica gave me a kiss on each cheek.

"Come, brother . . ." And taking my hand, she led me to a room decorated with Mapuche motifs where there was a bed, a table with a typewriter, a ream of paper, and a lamp. "This is where I shut myself away when I want to create my poems. You can borrow this space for as long as you need. If you're hungry, there's the kitchen downstairs: you'll find fruit and chocolate bars there; that's all we eat. Good night."

I stayed there, shut in, for several days without anyone bothering me. Sometimes a shadow would pass in front of the door and some-one would leave a couple of apples there for me. When I overcame my shyness I went out to make the acquaintance of the group, which was no more than twenty people. They were composers, poets, painters, a philosophy student. Beside myself—I was the youngest—the others who resided in the Cereceda house included a lesbian girl, Pancha, who made large rag dolls; Gustavo, a pianist and close friend of Carmen; and Drago, a cartoonist with a stutter. Seeing that money was scarce in that house and the fruit and chocolate were provided by the members of the group, I realized that their acceptance of me was a true sacri-fice. Veronica, being idealistic, shared her vast cultural knowledge with me, as well as the few things she possessed, simply because she loved poetry. She is recorded in my memory as an angel. In this world so full of violence, whenever someone disappoints me I remember those sisters and console myself with the thought that sublime beings do exist. In youth, encounters with others are fundamental: they can change the course of one's life. Some are like meteorites, opaque shards that can hit Earth at some moment and cause massive damage; others are like comets, luminous objects bringing vital elements with them. I had the providential good fortune at this time in my life to find beings that enriched me: beneficial comets. During the same period, I knew others who, although they were just as worthy of a creative destiny as I was, fell prey to bad company that led them into failure and death: meteorites. Well, maybe it was more than just luck, through the distrust I had learned during my wounded childhood I had also developed the ability to dodge. In boxing one wins not only by hitting harder, but also by avoiding more blows. I always shunned negative contacts and sought out friends who could be my teachers.

One day Veronica woke me up at six o'clock in the morning. "Enough working with only your mind. Your hands have a lot to say, just like your words. I'll teach you to make puppets." In the kitchen she showed me how to cut newspaper into thin strips to be boiled, crushed, and shredded, then mixed with flour to make a paste that is very easy to sculpt. I could now sculpt puppet heads on a ball made from an old stocking and a few handfuls of sawdust, which hardened when they dried in the sun. Carmen then showed me how to paint them. Pancha sewed the costumes into which I put my hands as if they were gloves in order to make the characters move and talk. Drago built me a little theater, a kind of folding screen, behind which I could work my puppets. I fell in love with them. It was enchanting for me to see an object I had created breaking free from me. From the moment I reached inside a puppet, the character began to live in an almost autonomous way. I was assisting in the development of an unknown personality, as if the puppet was using my voice and hands to take on an identity that was already its own. I seemed to be filling the role of servant rather than creator. Ultimately, I had the impression of being directed, manipulated by the puppet! Moreover, in a certain way the puppets led me to discover an important aspect of magic: the transfer of a person to an object. Because I had had almost no contact with Jaime, Sara, and the rest of my family, I had become an incomprehensible mutant to all of them, invisible most of the time, despised when visible. However, family contact is necessary for the soul to develop. Determined to establish a profound relationship I sculpted puppets that represented them, in caricature but very accurate. Thus I was able to talk to Don Jaime, Doña Sara, and all the others. My friends, seeing these grotesque representations, laughed themselves silly. But when my hands entered the characters, they began to exist with their own life. As soon as I lent them my voice, they said things I had never thought. Mainly they justified themselves, considered my criticisms unjust, insisted that they loved me, and finally demanded that having disappointed them I should apologize. I realized that my complaints were selfish. I regretted the fact that I did not want to forgive them; that is to say, I did not want to mature, to reach adulthood. And the path to forgiveness required my recognizing that, in their own way, my entire family—my parents, aunts and uncles, grandparents—were my victims. I had not lived up to their aspirations, aspirations that, for all that I found them negative and absurd, were legitimate aspirations for them on their level of consciousness. I sincerely asked for their forgiveness. "Forgive me, Jaime, for not having given you the opportunity to conquer all your social complexes and for not pursuing a university career. My earning a diploma in medicine, law, or architecture was the only chance you had to be respected by the community. Forgive me, Sara, for not being the reincarnation of your father. Forgive me, Raquel, for having been born with the penis that you should have had. Forgive me, grandmother, for cutting down the lime tree, for having renounced the Jewish religion. Forgive me, Aunt Fanny, for finding you so ugly. And especially you, fat Isidoro, forgive me for not understanding your cruelty; you never grew up; you were always a giant baby. When I came to stay with your mother, you treated me as a dangerous rival, not as a child." In turn, all the puppets forgave me. Shedding tears, one by one I too forgave them.

Strangely, perhaps due to the magic of the puppetry, my parents' attitude toward me was more understanding and loving once I decided to

resume relations with them. Also, my grandmother, without ever men-
tioning the tree incident, invited me to have tea with her and, for the
first time ever, gave me a gift: a watch that had an elephant in place of
hands, marking the minutes with its trunk and the hours with its tail. A
miracle! I explained to myself that the image we have of another person
is not that person but a representation. The world that is imposed on us
by our senses depends on our way of seeing it. In many ways, the other
is what we believe it to be. For example, when I made the Jaime puppet I modeled it in the way I saw him, giving him a limited existence.
When I brought him to life in the miniature theater other aspects that
I had not captured came to light, rising up from my obscure memory
and transforming the image. The character, enriched by my creativity,
evolved to reach a higher level of consciousness, changing from fierce
and stubborn into friendly and full of love. Perhaps my individual subconscious was closely linked to the family subconscious. If my reality
was different, then my relatives' reality was also different. In a certain
way, when a being is portrayed a nexus is established between the being
and the object that symbolizes it. Thus, if changes come about in the
object, the being that gave rise to what it represents also changes. Years
later, when studying medieval witchcraft and magic, I saw that this
technique had been used to harm enemies. A necklace made that contained hairs, fingernails, or shreds of clothing from the intended victim
was put on the neck of a dog that was then slaughtered. After engraving
a patient's name in the bark of a tree, incantations were recited in order
to transfer the disease to the tree. This principle has been preserved
in popular witchcraft in the form of pictures or wax figurines that are
impaled with pins. My attention was also drawn to the belief in the
transfer of personality through physical contact. Touching someone or
something means, in a certain way, becoming it. Medieval doctors, in
order to heal knights wounded in tournaments, used to spread their
healing ointments on the sword that had inflicted the wound. I was not
aware of this topic at that time in my life, and yet I applied it intuitively
and in a positive way.

I told myself, if the puppets I make come to life and transmit their essence to me, instead of creating characters I despise or hate why not choose characters who can transmit a knowledge that I do not yet possess? During those years Pablo Neruda was regarded as the greatest poet, but like many young people a spirit of contradiction caused me to refuse to be his ardent follower. Suddenly, there came a new poet, Nicanor Parra, who rebelled against the genius Neruda who was so visceral and politically compromised, writing verses that were intelligent, humorous, and different from all other known poetry; these he dubbed "anti-poems." My enthusiasm for this was delirious. Finally an author had descended from the romantic Olympus to discuss his everyday anxieties, his neuroses, his sentimental failures. One poem above all made an impression on me: "The Viper." Unlike Neruda's sonnets, this poem was not about an ideal woman, but about a real bitch.

> *For many years I was condemned to worship a*
>   *despicable woman,*
> *To sacrifice myself for her, to suffer countless*
>   *humiliations and ridicule,*
> *Working day and night to feed and clothe her,*
> *Perpetrating some crimes, committing some offenses,*
> *Small thefts by the light of the moon*
> *Falsifications of incriminating documents*
> *Under the threat of falling into disgrace in her*
>   *fascinating eyes.*

How great was my envy, having never even made love to any woman, of Nicanor Parra having known such an extraordinary female!

> *For long years I lived as a prisoner of this woman's*
>   *charm*
> *She used to show up in my office completely naked*
> *Performing the most difficult contortions imaginable . . .*

I immediately made some paste and started to model a puppet representing the poet. The newspaper had not published any photos of him, but in contrast to Neruda, who was rather bald, stocky, with a Buddha-like air, I sculpted Parra with hollow cheeks, intelligent eyes, an aquiline nose, and leonine hair. Enclosed in my little theater I manipulated the Nicanor puppet for hours, making him improvise anti-poems and, above all, relate his experiences with women. Stifled by my chastity, having had a mother whose torso was always encased in a corset and who blushed at the slightest sexual reference, women appeared to me the greatest mystery of all . . . but once I was imbued with the spirit of the poet, I felt myself capable of finding a muse, preferably on par with the Viper.

In the city center, Café Iris opened its doors at midnight. There, illuminated by cruel neon tubes, the night owls drank beer on tap or else an extremely cheap wine that made them shudder with every sip. The waiters, all dressed in black uniforms, were older people who walked unhurriedly from table to table, taking small steps.

In this calm place, time seemed to stand still in an eternal instant where there was no room for sorrow or anguish. Nor was there room for any great happiness. They drank in silence, as if in purgatory. Nothing new could happen there. And yet, on the very night that I decided to go to Café Iris to find the woman who would become my ferocious muse, Stella Díaz Varin was there. How to describe her? It was 1949, and we were in the most remote country, where no one wanted to be different from everyone else, where it was almost mandatory to wear shades of gray, where the men had to have closely cropped hair and the women had to have chitinous coiffures sculpted at beauty salons, forty years before the first punks emerged. I had just settled down over a cup of coffee when Stella (who had just been fired from the newspaper *La Hora* for her article about the deforestation brought about by the logging industry, which would later devastate the southern part of the country) appeared before me shaking her amazing head of red hair, a sanguine mass that reached below her waist; it was not hair but a mane. I am not exaggerating, never in my life have I met a woman with such thick hair. Rather than powdering her face, as was customary in Chile at that time, she had painted it pale violet using watercolors. Her lips were blue, her eyelids were covered with green eye shadow, and her ears were shining, painted gold. It was summer, but over her short skirt and a sleeveless shirt that highlighted her arrogant nipples she wore an old fur coat, probably made of dog hair, which came down to her heels. She drank a liter of beer, smoked a pipe, and without paying attention to anyone, locked in her own personal Olympus, she wrote something down on a paper napkin. A drunken man approached her and whispered something in her ear. She opened her coat, lifted her shirt, showed him her opulent breasts, and then quick as lightning dealt him a blow to the chin that sent him sprawling three meters away on the ground, unconscious. One of the old waiters, not greatly perturbed, poured a glass of water on his face. The man got up, offered humble apologies to the poet, and went to sit in a corner of the café. It was as if nothing had happened. She continued writing. I fell in love.

My encounter with Stella was fundamental. Thanks to her I was able to move from the conceptual act of creation, through words and images, to the poetic act with poems resulting from a sum of bodily movements. Stella, defying social prejudices, behaved as if the world were a ductile material that she could model at will. I asked the old bartender if he knew her.

"Of course, young man, who doesn't? She comes here often to write and drink beer. She used to work for the secret police, where she learned karate chops. Then she was a journalist, but they fired her for being too controversial. Now she's a poet. The critic in *El Mercurio* says she's better than Gabriela Mistral. He must have slept with her. Watch out, young man, that beast can break your nose."

Trembling, I watched her finish a second liter of beer, feverishly fill several pages in her notebook, and then walk haughtily out into the street. I followed her as inconspicuously as possible. I noticed that she was walking barefoot, and her feet were painted in watercolors, forming a rainbow from the red nails to the violet ankles. She got on a bus that ran all the way along the Alameda de las Delicias toward the central station. I got on as well and sat in front of her. I felt her eyes on the nape of my neck, piercing me like a stiletto. The night became a dream. To be in the same vehicle with this woman meant moving toward our common soul. Suddenly, as the bus was starting to move again after a stop, she ran to the door and jumped out. Surprised, I begged the driver to stop, which he did two hundred meters farther on. I walked toward the point where Stella had jumped off. I saw with surprise that she was looking at me, motioning to me to stop. With my heart pounding in terror, I stood still. I closed my eyes and waited for the fierce punch. Her hands began to touch my body, without sensuality. Then she opened my fly and examined my penis like a doctor. She sighed.

"Open your eyes, squirt! I can see you're still a virgin! I'm too much for you. An ostrich can't hatch a pigeon's egg. What do you want?"

"I hear you write. So do I. Could I have the honor of reading your poems?"

She smiled. I saw that one of her incisors was broken, giving her a cannibalistic air.

"You're only interested in my poetry? What about my ass and my tits? Hypocrite! Do you have some money?"

I dug in my pockets. I found a five-peso bill and showed it to her. She snatched it.

"There's a café open all night next to the Alameda Theater. Let's go there. I'm hungry. We'll eat a sandwich and drink a beer."

So we did. She opened her notebook and, munching bread with salami, her lips whitened by beer foam, began to read. She recited for an hour, which seemed like ten to me. I had never heard poetry like this. I felt each sentence like a knife. In the instant that I heard them these verses transformed themselves into deep but pleasurable wounds. To listen to this real poet, liberated from rhyme, meter, and morality, was one of the most moving moments of my youth. The café was dirty, ugly, lit by glaring lights, and full of sordid, bestial patrons. And yet, as I heard those sublime words, it became a palace inhabited by angels. There was the proof that poetry was a miracle that could change one's vision of the world. And to change the vision was to change the perceived object as well. The poetic revolution seemed more important than political revolution to me. One part of that reading remains in my memory like treasure from a shipwreck: "The woman who loved doves in a virgin's ecstasy, and fed irises at night with her sleeping nipple, dreamed with her back to the wall, and everything seemed beautiful without being so." She abruptly closed the book and, not wanting to hear my words of admiration, got up, took me by the arm, went out into the street, and led me to the nearest corner by the Pedagogical Institute. A narrow door was the entrance to the boarding house where she rented a small room. With a push, she sat me down on the stone step in front of the door, knelt beside me, and caught my right ear in her sharp teeth. She stayed like this, the way a panther holds its prey in its mouth before crushing it. A thousands thoughts ran through my mind. "Maybe she's crazy, she might be cannibalistic, she's testing me; she wants to see if I'll sacrifice a piece of ear to get her." Well, I decided to sacrifice it, knowing this woman was worth such mutilation. I calmed down, stopped tensing my muscles, and gave myself over to the pleasure of feeling the touch of her moist lips. Time seemed to solidify. She made no move to let go. Instead, she squeezed her teeth a little more. I tried to remember where the nearest open pharmacy was, so that I could run there after losing part of my ear to buy alcohol, disinfect the wound, and stop the bleeding. Miraculously, I was saved by an exhibitionist; he passed by us, face covered with an open newspaper, his fly open to show his bulky phallus. Stella let go of me to drive him away, kicking him. The man, running as fast as his legs could carry him, disappeared into the night. The poet, laughing, sat down beside me, wiped the sweat off one of my palms with her hand, and examined my lines by the light of a match.

"You got talent, kid. We'll get along well. Come and pee."

She led me to a nearby church. Next to the gate was a sculpture of St. Ignatius of Loyola.

"Do it on the saint," she said, rolling up her skirt. "Praying and pissing are both sacred acts."

She wore no panties, and her pubic hair was abundant. Kneeling beside me, she let a thick yellow stream fall onto the monk's stone chest. I, with a stream that was thinner but went farther, bathed the statue's forehead.

"I warmed his heart and you crowned him, boy. Now go to bed. I'll see you tomorrow at midnight at Café Iris."

She gave me a quick but intense kiss on the mouth, walked with me to the central station, and the moment I turned my back on her, kicked me in the rear. Without offering any resistance I let myself be pushed, took four precipitous steps, then regained my normal gait and, with great dignity, walked away from her without looking back.

The next day the hours slipped by without my noticing anything. Immobilized, I moved through flat, gray time as through an empty tunnel, at the end of which the anticipated midnight hour shone like a splendid jewel. I arrived at Café Iris at twelve o'clock sharp, with my Nicanor Parra puppet hidden, clutched to my chest. It was a gift for Stella . . . but my beloved had not yet arrived. I ordered a beer. At 12:30 I asked for another; at 1:00, yet another, and at 1:30 another; another at 2:00, and another at 2:30. Drunk and sad I finally saw her enter, looking smug, accompanied by a man shorter than her with a face like a boxer and wearing that sardonic expression common to those broken offspring of Spanish soldiers and raped Indian women. Glancing at me defiantly, she sat in front of me with, I assumed, her lover. They both smiled, looking satisfied. I was furious. I slipped my hand under my vest, took out the puppet, and threw it on the table. "Let this Nicanor Parra be your teacher! You deserve to be with a poet of this dimension, not to debase yourself with down-and-outs like the one you're with right now. If you read his brilliant poem "The Viper" you will find your portrait. Goodbye forever." And, stumbling, getting caught in the legs of the chairs, I headed for the exit. Stella chased me down and brought me back to the table. I thought the insulted boxer would punch me, but no. With a smile he held out his hand and said, "I appreciate what you said. I am Nicanor Parra and the woman who inspired me to write 'The Viper' is Stella." While it is true that my creation bore no resemblance to the features of the great poet, I felt certain that I had my puppet to thank for my having met him. This miracle came from one of the threads from which the world is woven together. Parra graciously gave me his telephone number, informed me with a single glance he was not Stella's lover and that I had a good chance of being that, and said goodbye to us.

Faced with this extravagant and beautiful woman, I was speechless. My drunkenness had dissipated as if by magic. She looked at me with the intensity of a tiger, inhaled the smoke from her pipe, and blew it in my face. I started coughing. She gave a hoarse cackle that drew the attention of everyone in the café, then turned serious and said in an accusing tone, "Don't deny it; you have a knife. Give it to me!" Embarrassed, not wishing to deny it, I dug in a pocket and pulled out my modest knife. She took it, opened it, looked at the half-rusted blade, and asked what my name was. She spread out her open left hand on the table, and with the knife in her right hand made three cuts on the back of it, forming a bloody A. She licked the blood off the blade and returned it to me, wet with saliva. With dizzying speed, I thought, "The A is formed by three straight lines, which makes the cuts easier. If I cut an S I'll have to make a long curvy wound; I might cut a vein, I don't have oily skin like her. What should I do? I'm being tested. I'm going to look like a stupid coward. I have to find an elegant solution." I took her hand and licked the wound, five, ten, endless minutes, until not a drop of blood was left. I offered her my red-stained mouth. She kissed me passionately.

"Come," she said. "We will never separate again. We will sleep by day and live at night, like vampires. I'm still a virgin. We will do everything but penetration. My hymen is reserved for a god who will come down from the mountains."

Nicanor Parra.

When we went outside, she asked me again for the knife. I handed it to her, trembling; surely my gallant act had not been enough to balance out the cuts on her hand. In a peremptory tone, she told me to put my hand into my left pants pocket and pull out the lining. So I did. She deftly cut the seams at the bottom of the pocket. Then she stuffed the lining back into my pants. She put her right hand inside and, with gentle firmness, gripped my testicles and penis.

"From now on, every time we walk together, I will hold your private parts."

Thus we walked along the Alameda de las Delicias, heading to her room, without saying a word. Dawn began to break. The final cold of the night in its death throes became more intense. But the heat her hand imparted to me, the same hand that had written such wonderful verses, not only invaded my skin but also entered into my very depths, lighting up my soul. The birds began to sing as we reached the door of her boarding house.

"Take off your shoes. Retirees sleep late. When a noise awakens them, they moan like turtles in agony."

The stairway creaked, the steps creaked, the ancient floorboards in the hallways creaked. The door of the room, upon being opened, gave forth a long funereal groan like a chorus of turtles. Then there was silence.

"We're not going to turn on the light," she said. "Orpheus must not see his beloved naked, lying in hell."

I stripped off my clothes in three seconds. She did so slowly. I heard a sticky plop as her dog fur coat fell to the ground, then the whisper of her short skirt sliding down her legs. After that, the oily rubbing of her shirt and then, a marvelous memory, I saw her as if she were lit by a hundred-watt lamp. The whiteness of her skin was so intense that it overcame the dark. She was a marble statue with her red mane and, above all, the russet burst of her pubic hair. We embraced, we fell on the bed, and without caring that the mattress made noises like a sick accordion, we caressed each other for hours. As day arrived, the room filled first with red light, then orange. The noises of the street, footsteps, voices, trains, cars, plus the buzzing of flies, tried to dispel our enchantment. But our desire was stronger. Her vagina, anus, and mouth were off-limits. Only the god of the mountains could enter the Sibyl's interior. We stuck with caresses, which grew longer and longer, without our remembering where we had started and without wanting to reach the end. Stella grew tense, and suddenly, instead of giving a cry of pleasure, she clenched her teeth so that they began to creak. This noise increased to the point that I thought every bone in her body would explode. Thus, as if emerging from a tempest of passion, coming forth from the bottom of an ocean of flesh, her bone structure emerged like an ancient shipwreck. Satisfied, she murmured in my ear, "A skeleton sits in my pupils, chewing my soul between its teeth." Then, before falling asleep with her head on my chest, she whispered, "We have given an orgasm to my death."

Thus our relationship began, and thus it continued. We went to bed at six in the morning, caressed each other for at least three hours, then we slept soundly; I because of the stress that being with such a strong woman caused me, she from the effects of large quantities of beer. We rose at ten in the evening. Since money was an evil symbol that the poet was eliminating from her life, my job was to feed her. So I went out, took the train that went through Matucana, used my key to enter my parents' house, and, reassured by the continuous rhythm of their tremendous snoring, stole food from their pantry, a little money from my mother's purse, and a little more from my father's pockets. Then I returned to her lodgings, where we devoured everything down to the crumbs. What little remained attracted an invasion of ants and cockroaches. Sometimes Stella would purposely leave dirty dishes on the floor, and they were soon visited by dozens of the black bugs. She impaled them with pins and stuck them to the wall. She made a compact field of cockroaches on the wall in the shape of the Virgin Mary. A winged phallus, also made of cockroaches, coming from the mountains, flew toward the saint. "It's the annunciation of Mary," she told me, proud of her work, adding eyes to the face in the form of two green beetles; I never knew where she had found them.

We would arrive at Café Iris around midnight, walking side by side, her hand constantly in my pocket. Our entrance would interrupt the chattering of the drunks there. Stella wore a different form of makeup every day, and it was always spectacular. There was always some impertinent man who would come over, not deigning to acknowledge that I existed, and try to seduce her by means of audacious groping. His mission would be curtailed by a punch to the chin. The waiters would pick up the unconscious fool and return him to his table. When he awoke, cured of his drunkenness, the man would order us a bottle of wine, making discrete apologetic gestures. Once they had learned the lesson of the beast, the men would stop feeling her up with their eyes and dive back into discussions that had nothing to do with reason. There was always someone standing up and reciting a poem, half-singing. Stella stuck cotton wool in my ears, required me to stay still like a model posing for a painter, and with her eyes fixed on mine wrote with dizzying speed, filling page after page without looking down at her notebook.

One night, tired of this immobility, I proposed a game: we would observe strangers and, without saying anything, each write on a sheet of paper what the person did, their characteristics, their social status, their economic status, their degree of intelligence, their sexual capacity, their emotional problems, their family structure, their possible diseases, and the corresponding death that would result. We played this game a great many times. We achieved such a spiritual amalgam that our answers started to be the same. This does not mean we were able to draw a correct portrait of the unknown person, which we would not have been able to verify, but at the very least we knew that there was telepathic communication between the two of us. Eventually, every time we were in someone else's presence, a mere fleeting glance between us was enough for us to know how we should act.

Anything that is different attracts the attention of ordinary citizens and also attracts their aggression. A couple like us was unsettling, a magnet for destructive people who were envious of the happiness of others. The ambiance of Café Iris was becoming insupportable. The clientele were directing more and more jeers, aggressive praise, sarcastic comments, and stares imbued with crude sexuality toward us.

"Enough of Iris," Stella said to me. "Let's find a new place."

"But where will we go? It's the only all night café."

"I've heard there's a bar on San Diego Street, the Dumb Parrot, that stays open until dawn."

"You're crazy Stella, that's an awful place, the worst people go there! They say there's at least one knife fight there every night."

I could not dissuade her. "If Orpheus seduced the beasts, we can make that Dumb Parrot sing a mass!"

After midnight, the wine had plunged the sinister patrons of that grisly, dark place into a bovine stupor. My arrival, with the poet on my arm, wearing her most extravagant makeup ever, caused no reaction. Stella was so different from the worn-out whores who beached themselves there, a being from another planet, that they were simply unable to see her. They kept on drinking as if nothing had happened. Offended in her exhibitionism, she decided to drink standing at the bar. I, in normal attire, gradually began to attract some notice. After half an hour, when Stella, having finished her first liter of beer was ordering a second, four men approached me. I did my best to hide the fear that came over me, forcing my face to become an expressionless mask. I tossed a crumpled bill on the counter and said, in a tone that was natural but loud enough for the four men to hear me, "I'll settle the tab now. This is all I have left." I left the change, a few small coins, on a saucer. The four curious men, all looking cynical, took the coins and dropped them in their pockets.

"And you, young man, where are you from?"

"I'm Chilean, like you. What happened is that my grandparents were immigrants, they came from Russia."

"Russian? Comrade?" Sly muttering. "And where do you work?"

"Well, I don't work. I'm an artist, a poet . . ."

"Ah, a poet, like that pot-bellied Neruda! Come on, have a drink with us and read us a poem!"

Stella still seemed to be invisible to them. Their lewd glances were directed at me. They exuded the sexuality of prison inmates. My youthful white skin turned them on. I drank from a glass of sour wine. I started to improvise a poem. The clientele turned their attention toward me . . .

> *Where there are ears but there is no song*
> *in this world that dissipates*
> *and in which existence is given to those who do*
> *   not deserve it*
> *I am much more my footprints than my steps.*

In the midst of reciting I saw that all eyes were now on Stella, and no one was listening to me. Determined to steal my audience, my friend was impaling her arm with a large hairpin that she had taken from her sequin-covered purse. Without any sign of pain, she slowly pushed the pin through until it emerged on the other side of her arm. I was fascinated as well. I had not known that the poet had the skills of a fakir. Once she was sure she had captured the patrons' attention, she began to recite a poem in an insulting tone while lifting up her shirt, millimeter by millimeter.

> *I am the guardian, you are the punished men*
> *the farmhands with oblique gestures*
> *from whom, as you engender false furrows,*
> *the seed flees in terror!*

She now showed her perfect breasts, accusing the offended drunks with her erect nipples, which she moved in a provocative semicircular motion. If I have ever in my life thought that I was going to defecate out of fear, it was on that occasion. Like a volcano beginning a devastating eruption, these dark men were beginning to stand up, reaching into their pockets for the knives they carried at all times. Their hatred was mixed with bestial desire. We were about to be raped and eviscerated. Stella, who had a deep, masculine voice, took in a deep breath and let out a deafening yell that froze them all for an instant: "Stop, macaques, respect the avenging vagina!" I took advantage of their bewilderment to grab her by the arm and make her jump with me through the open window. We ran toward the well-lit streets of the city center like hares being pursued by a pack of raging predators.

We reached the Alameda de las Delicias. At that hour of the night there was not a soul around. We leaned our backs against the trunk of one of the great trees that lined the avenue, catching our breath. Stella, reeling with laughter, pulled the pin out of her arm. Her laughter was contagious, and I started laughing as well, until I shook. Suddenly, our joy vanished. We realized that a strange shadow was covering us. We looked up. Above our heads, a woman was hanging from a branch. The light of a neon sign tinged the suicide's hair with red. In this I saw a sign . . . There was nothing we could do for the dead woman, and we left quickly so as not to have to deal with the police. At the door of the boarding house, I said goodbye to Stella.

"I need to be alone for a while. I feel like I'm drowning without a lifejacket in your immense ocean. I do not know who I am. I've become a mirror that only reflects your image. I can't keep living in the chaos you create. The woman hanging from the tree, you invented that. Every night you kill yourself because you know that you will be reborn the same as you were. But maybe someday you will wake up as someone else, in a body that you don't deserve. I beg you, let me recover; give me a few days of solitude."

"Well," she said in an unexpectedly childlike voice, "let's meet at midnight on the dot, in twenty-eight days, one lunar cycle, at Café Iris . . . But before you go, come with me to urinate on St. Ignatius of Loyola."

For those twenty-eight days, under the pretext of nervous exhaustion I ate only fruits and chocolate and did not leave the room the Cereceda sisters were loaning me. I felt empty. I could not write, think, or feel. If someone had asked me who I was, my answer would have been, "I am a mirror broken into a thousand pieces." Sleeping very little, I spent hours piecing together the fragments. At the end of this lunar cycle I felt reconstructed. However, I realized I had not rediscovered myself; once again, I was the mirror of that terrible woman.

Like a drug addict needing his fix, I went to Café Iris. I got there right at midnight, even though I knew she might be hours late. But it was not so. She was waiting, standing by a window wearing a sober military coat and no makeup. Without her mascara she was still beautiful, but now the expression on her unadorned face was that of a saint. In a voice so soft that she reminded me of my mother when she sang to me in my crib, she said, "I am a carrier pigeon in your hands. Let me go. The god who was waiting has come down from the mountains. I'm not a virgin. I'm sure that I am carrying in my belly the perfect child that destiny has promised me." She showed me a needle threaded with one of her long hairs. I could not keep from shedding tears while she sewed up my pocket. I closed my eyes. When I opened them, Stella had disappeared. I saw her again fifty years later, a prisoner in another body, a sweet little grandmother with short gray hair.

The world fell away from me. I went back to the house in Matucana. My parents did not ask me any questions. Jaime handed me a few bills. "From now on I'll give you a weekly salary. All you have to do is help in the shop on Saturdays; there are more thieves every day." My mother got a hot bath ready for me then served me a hearty breakfast. I saw in her eyes the anguish of not understanding me. If I, being a part of them, was incomprehensible, then that meant the world they had built so strongly had a fault, an area populated by madness that did not match up with their scheme of "reality." It was absolutely necessary for them to consider my behavior as delusional. To maintain their own equilibrium, they had to force the madman into the straitjacket of "normal life." When they realized they could not break me down, they tried to persuade me by filling me with shame. And they succeeded. After several weeks I felt guilty; I lost my confidence in poetry and promised myself not to frustrate their hopes, to continue my studies at the university until I got a diploma. But one night, in a dream, I saw a high wall on which one sentence was written: "Let go your prey, lion, and take flight!" I packed a few books, my writings, the few clothes I owned, and returned to the Cereceda sisters.

I absorbed myself in making my puppets. Like a hermit, I spent the day locked in my room engaging in dialog with them. Only late at night, when my hosts and their friends were asleep, did I go to the kitchen to eat a piece of chocolate. One morning someone gave a few short, discrete, delicate knocks on my door. I decided to open it. I saw before me a woman of short stature with amber-colored hair and an ingenuous expression that touched me deeply. However, I asked her with false brusqueness what her name was.

"Luz."

"What do you want?"

"They say you make some very nice puppets. Can I see them?" I showed them to her with great pleasure. There were fifty of them. She put them on her hands, made them speak, laughed, "I have a friend who is a painter who will love to see what you do. Please come with me to show him your characters."

What I felt for Luz had nothing to do with love or desire. I knew that for me she was an angel, the polar opposite of the Luciferian Stella; rather than breaking the poisonous world into a thousand pieces, she saw a chaos of sacred fragments that it was her duty to put together in order to reconstruct a pyramid. Luz came to draw me out of my dark retreat, to lead me into the luminous world, and once there, to vanish. And so it was. Luz and Stella were two opposing views of the world. Although they both felt themselves to be foreign to the world, outsiders in it, one saw it as having heavenly ties while the other saw it as having roots in hell. One wanted to show the good things in the world by making herself its mirror, the other, in the same way, wanted to reflect its failures. The two were of a piece, consistent with each other: cobras charming men, one wanting to inoculate them with the venom of the infinite, the other with the elixir of eternity.

Luz's boyfriend, obviously madly in love with her, was an older painter by the name of André Racz, who had a prophet-like appearance, wearing long hair and a beard halfway down his chest. He lived in an old studio, much longer than it was wide, at least three hundred square meters. It was reached via a long, dark passageway with a cement floor with rusty rails in it, giving the place the appearance of an abandoned mine. Racz's paintings and engravings were based on the Gospels. Christ, who bore the artist's face, was shown preaching, performing miracles, and being crucified in the contemporary era amidst cars and trains. The soldiers who tortured him wore German-style uniforms. One of them shot him in his side with a pistol. The Virgin Mary was always a portrait of Luz.

I was pulling my puppets out of my suitcase, one by one. Racz, his attention consumed by the beauty of his girlfriend, was barely looking at them. Luz, without seeming to notice this embarrassing situation, smiled as if waiting for a miracle. And a miracle occurred! One puppet to which I had given the supporting role of a drunken bum, wearing a patched coat, long hair, and abundant beard, revealed his true personality upon emerging in this environment full of religious paintings: he was Christ. And the most surprising thing of all was that his features were very similar to those of André Racz. The painter moved the puppet with the enthusiasm of a child, engaging in dialogue with it. Luz took the puppet's hands and began to waltz with it. Racz followed her like a shadow all around the studio. I saw in his dog-like glances that he wanted my puppet to be his own so that he could give it to her. I immediately told him, "It's a gift. Take it." He answered me with great emotion. "Young man, you are a divine messenger. You did not arrive here by chance. Without knowing me, you made my portrait. I have just bought a plane ticket to go to Europe. I need to put an abysmal distance between Luz and myself. I'm old enough to be her grandfather. I'm chaining her to an old man. I know she will sleep with the puppet as she is remembering me. It will make the breakup easier. This is my studio; we have spent unforgettable moments together in it. I will give it to you. I do not want to abandon it to vulgar hands. Now go, I want to say goodbye alone to my Virgin."

I left the room as if emerging from a dream. It seemed impossible that someone would so suddenly give me a studio in which I could live as I pleased. But it was true. The next day Luz came to get me, accompanied me to the studio, and said rather sadly, "André gave me all his paintings but didn't want to give me his new address." She handed me the keys to the studio and left. I never saw her again.

Thus, overnight I found myself the proprietor of a huge space at 340 Villavicencio Street, perhaps the site of an old factory, which, being at the end of a hundred-meter-long tunnel, was isolated from the neighbors. There I could freely make all the noise I wanted. I believed that the ultimate achievement of an artist was to become a creator of parties. If everyday life seemed like hell, if everything boiled down to two words, *permanent impermanence,* if the future that was promised us was the victory of the persecutors, if God had become a dollar bill, then I had to abide by the words of Ecclesiastes: "There is nothing better for man than to eat, drink, and make his soul merry." My weekly "studio parties" became very well known. People from all walks of life attended. A phrase from Hesse's *Steppenwolf* was written on the door: "Magic Theater. Price of Admission: Your Mind." By the door a former mendicant, Patas de Humo ("Smokey Paws"), who normally slept in the tunnel and whom I had taken on as my assistant, gave out a quarter-liter glass full of vodka to each guest. For those who did not gulp it down, there was no getting in. Those who accepted this hefty drink, which would get them drunk immediately, were admitted by Smokey Paws with an affectionate kick in the rear, whether man or woman, young or old, laborer or legislator. Once inside there was no more drinking, just conversation and dancing, but no popular music, only classical. The biggest hit was *Swan Lake*. In that space, as full as a rush-hour bus, groups of people improvised, imitating the mechanical gestures of the Russian ballet with tremendous grace. The mingling of artists with university professors, boxers, salesmen, produced an explosive mixture. As the drink was limited to that initial quarter liter, there was no violence and the party became a paradisiacal game. Naturally now and then, almost without intending to, someone would climb up on a chair and become the center. These interventions were short, but their intensity made them unforgettable. A young law student once loudly declared that his father, a famous lawyer who lived secluded in his immense library, had never permitted his son to read a single one of his precious volumes, always keeping his library locked.

"Well, before coming to this party, I saw my father asleep at his desk, face down on some papers. I entered into this sacred enclosure for the first time ever, with intense emotion I picked up one of his books, and then . . . look at this!" And the young man produced the spine of a book out of the backpack he wore. "All volumes were false: a collection of spines, nothing more, hiding cabinets filled with bottles of whiskey!" Then he started screaming, "Who are we? Where are we?" and let himself fall, arms outstretched, amidst his audience.

Another time, an older man got a seductive young lady to get up on the chair with him. He said, with tears in his eyes, "I waited all my life. Finally I found her. I would cover her with caresses, but . . ." With his left hand he removed his right hand, which was artificial, and shook it: "I lost it as a child. I got so used to my false hand that I grew up without thinking about how it was missing. Until the day that Margarita offered her body to me. And I, only half-caressing her, wished that I had two, three, four, eight, infinite hands to slide over her skin for eternity."

Twenty men raised their hands and, standing in a compact group behind the man with the missing hand, became one with him. The woman let the two hundred and five fingers run over her body . . .

Another man, of a neat appearance, with a deep voice and measured gestures, giving an unexpected shout, climbed onto the shoulders of a young man and asked for everyone's attention. When he had it, he tore off his tie and cried out, "I've been married twenty years; I have a wife and my two children! I'm tired of lying! I'm gay! And the young man carrying me on his back is my lover!"

Without knowing it, by considering the creation of parties as the supreme expression of art, in 1948 I was discovering the principles of the "ephemeral panic," which artists would later call "happenings."

On one occasion a young man of my age, nineteen years, with an intelligent face, a tall and thin body, an African baritone voice, and the hands of an aristocrat, climbed onto the confessional chair and swaying like a metronome put an oval mirror in front of his face like a mask and began to recite a long poem. This was Enrique Lihn. Even at that young age the genius of poetry dwelt within him. His talent awakened great admiration in me. I obtained his address through some mutual friends and went to look for him at the house in the Providencia neighborhood where he lived with his parents, which in those days was considered a very long distance from the city center. The streets were lined with lush trees, and the houses were small, single story, with porches where fruit trees grew. Nervous, I moved the copper ring that served as a door knocker. The poet opened the door. Frowning, he growled, "Ah, the party planner! What do you want?"

"I want to be your friend."

"Are you a homosexual?"

"No."

"Then why do you want to be my friend?"

"Because I admire your poetry."

"I understand, it's not me, my verses are what interests you. Come in."

His room was small, his bed narrow, his closet tiny. But it had been converted into a palace: Lihn had covered the walls and ceiling with

With Enrique Lihn in our puppet theater, 1949.
Photo: Ferrer.

poems written in small, angular letters; he had also covered the shutters and windowpanes, furniture, door, floorboards, and parchment lamp. In addition to this there were mountains of handwritten pages, verses covering the white spaces in the books, train tickets, movie tickets, paper napkins, all barely containing his poems. I felt immersed in a compact sea of letters. Wherever I rested my gaze, I saw the words of a tortured but beautiful song.

"What a shame, Enrique, all this wonderful work will be lost!"

"It doesn't matter: dreams are also lost, and we ourselves dissolve, little by little. Poetry is the shadow of an eagle flying toward the sun; it cannot leave traces on the ground. The prayer most pleasing to the gods is sacrifice. A poem reaches its perfection when it burns, like a phoenix . . ."

On the verge of vertigo, I began to see the letters walking through the walls like an army of ants. I suggested to Lihn that we take a walk.

The poet took two of his father's Maurice Chevalier–style hats and a couple of sticks, just in case robbers assaulted us, and thus armed and hatted, marching briskly, we descended on the Avenida Providencia. I cannot help thinking that the names chance offers contain a profound message. We came across a robust tree that grew in the middle of the sidewalk. Without discussing the idea, as if it were the most natural thing in the world, we climbed up the trunk and sat side by side on a thick branch. There we sat, chatting and discussing things until dawn. We began by finding out that we both agreed that the language we had been taught carried crazy ideas. Instead of thinking correctly, we thought distortedly. Concepts had to be given their true meaning. We spend a lot of time doing this. I remember a few examples:

Instead of "never": very few times. Instead of "always": often. "Infinite": of unknown extent. "Eternity": with an unthinkable end. "To fail": to change activities. "I was deceived": I imagined wrongly. "I know": I believe. "Beautiful, ugly": I like, I do not like. "You are like this": I perceive you to be like this. "Mine": What I currently possess. "Dying": changing form.

Next, we reviewed definitions and concluded that it was absurd to define things with a positive assertion. Instead, the correct thing was to define by negating. "Happiness": to be less distressed each day. "Generosity": to be less selfish. "Courage": to be less cowardly. "Strength": to be less weak. And so on. We concluded that, because of this twisted language, all of society lived in a world plagued by grotesque situations. The word *grotesque,* beside its definition in the dictionary as meaning ludicrous, prodigious, or outlandish, was also taken to mean unconscious noncommunication. For example, the Pope believed himself to be in direct communication with a god who was actually blind, deaf, and dumb. A citizen, while being beaten by the police, believed that the state was protecting him. Two people remained married for twenty years without realizing that they were speaking to each other in different languages. The worst grotesque situations: believing one knows oneself, believing one knows everything about some topic, believing one has judged with absolute impartiality, believing one will love and be loved forever. In conversation, people think one thing and, in trying to communicate it, say something else. The interlocutor hears one thing, but understands something different. When answering, one does not respond to what the other person initially thought, nor to what the other person said, but to what one has understood. The final result: a conversation between deaf people who do not even know how to listen to themselves.

I proposed the poetic act as a solution to this grotesque communication. A heated discussion followed, which ended with the dawning of the sun's first rays. There were two forms of poetry: written poetry, which ought to be secret, a kind of intimate diary created solely for the benefit of the poet, which should only have a minimal number of readers; and the poetry of action, which should be performed as a social exorcism in front of numerous spectators. Discussing these subjects while sitting on the branch of a tree gave them paramount importance.

From that day on Enrique and I frequently saw each other, and over the course of three or four years performed a large number of poetic acts that, unknown to me at the time, would form the basis of psychomagical therapy.

In that city where many streets are at whimsical twisted angles, the first thing we proposed was to choose a destination point and get there by walking in a straight line, without deviating for any reason. This is not to say that we always succeeded. We sometimes found insurmountable or dangerous obstacles; one example is the time when we used the exit to a parking lot as our route. We paid no heed to the sign reading "Private area, entry prohibited." We were advancing in a poetic ecstasy through the damp gloom when a pack of wild dogs came lunging toward us, barking ferociously. Throwing aside all dignity, we fled, certain that we would leave with our pants ripped off. I do not know what divine inspiration led Lihn to bark more ferociously than the dogs, while also galloping on all fours. Terror lent a prodigious volume to his voice. I quickly began to imitate him. In an instant, we switched from being pursued to being part of the pursuing group. The dogs, confused, made no attempt to bite us. We left the dark underground area shaking with nervous laughter, but with a sense of triumph. This adventure made us realize that by identifying with the difficulties we faced, we could make them into our allies. Rather than resisting or fleeing a problem, by entering it, making oneself part of it, one can use it as an element of liberation.

Sometimes we were attacked because if there were a car in our path we would climb onto it and walk over its roof. One furious owner chased us, throwing stones. However, there were many times that we had the joy of achieving a straight line. At houses we would ring the bell, ask for permission, enter through the door, and leave by whichever way we wanted, even through a narrow window. The important thing was to follow the straight line with the precision of an arrow. Luckily for us, Chile was a poetic country in that era. Saying, "We're young poets in action," would bring a smile to the severest of faces. Many kind ladies would accompany us on the journey through their homes and show us out the back door. We were often offered a glass of wine. This crossing of the city in a straight line was a fundamental experience for us because it taught us to overcome obstacles by getting them to participate in the work of art. It was as if all of reality danced with us once we had decided on the act.

Little by little, we were carrying out acts that involved more participants. One day we put a large quantity of coins in a perforated cookie tin and walked around the city center, letting them fall. It was extraordinary to see well-dressed people forgetting their dignity, bending down feverishly behind us—a whole street of people with their backs bent! We also decided to create our own imaginary city parallel to the real city. To accomplish this we conducted inaugurations by gathering at the foot of some statue or famous monument, covering it partly or entirely with sheets, and conducting an inaugural ceremony according to the dictates of our imagination. We would applaud when we pulled off the fabric and then give the statue a meaning that was different from its real history. For example, we applauded the naval hero Arturo Prat because, in his agony after jumping to board a ship and receiving a machete blow on the head dealt to him by an enemy cook, he had been struck by inspiration and invented the recipe for baked empanadas. On another national hero we bestowed the story that he had conquered the enemy army using love as a weapon by sending in an invading horde of expert prostitutes, which thanks to patriotic idealism included his sisters, mother, and two grandmothers. Thus, with these humorous nighttime inaugurations, fueled by abundant wine, we gave new significance to banks, churches, and government buildings. We changed the names of a large number of streets. Lihn decided to live on "Lovesick Street" at the corner of the "Avenue of the God Who Does Not Believe In Me." When other friends joined in our poetic acts we presented a great exhibition of dogs, replacing any given object with them. For example, a poet walked in dragging a suitcase while claiming, in order to validate his "animal," that it had no legs and so could not get thorns in its paws, which meant fewer vet bills. The parade included the dog-lamp (you can read all night by it without it urinating on you), the dog-long underwear (better than a greyhound), the dog-wastebasket (collects waste instead of producing it), the dog-rifle (a very good guard dog), the dog-banknote (very nice and makes you lots of friends), and so forth. Another time we decided that money could be transformed. Instead of coins, we would use boiled shrimp. When we put these red creatures into the hands of the conductor selling bus tickets, he did not know how to react and let us board without a problem. We paid the cover charge to get into a dance hall with a seashell. Many times we went to the Museum of Fine Arts, stood before the pictures, and imitated the voices of the subjects portrayed, attributing all manner of absurd speeches to them. We attained such perfection in this activity that we were finally able to perform it with abstract paintings as well. Sometimes Lihn and I set ourselves goals that were strange due to their simplicity: when we were fed up with university life, we took the train to Valparaiso and determined not to return until an old lady invited us for a cup of tea. In search of our hostess, whom we likened to the magicians in fairy tales, we walked around the jumbled streets of the port district. Feigning extreme fatigue, we recited poems while walking and bumping into each other. Soon a lady offered us a glass of water. We convinced her that it would be better to give us some tea. Having achieved our goal, we triumphantly returned to the capital.

On another occasion I went to a French restaurant accompanied by four very well-dressed poets. We all ordered steaks with pepper. When the steaks arrived, we rubbed them all over our clothes, soaking ourselves in sauce. Once this was accomplished, we ordered the same thing again, and repeated the act. And so on, six times over, until everyone in the restaurant was trembling, seized by a kind of panic. Then each of us, pulling a rope from his pocket, made a six-steak necklace. We paid and left quietly, as if what we had done was the most natural thing in the world. One year later, when we returned to the same establishment, the headwaiter told us, "If you're planning to do what you did the other day, we can't let you in." The event had made such an impression on him that, despite its having been quite long ago, it seemed to him as if he had seen us last week. Another time we decided to announce the arrival of a Sufi sage, whom we named Assis Namur. We distributed leaflets that read, "Tomorrow at 5:00 p.m., at the feet of the Virgin of San Cristobal Hill, the holy Assis Namur-the-poor, after a supreme effort, will achieve indifference." We took the cable car up the hill and sat at the feet of the enormous statue of the Virgin. Lihn, wrapped in a sheet and in a meditative pose, used an eyebrow pencil to write a bold "No!" on his forehead. We waited for hours. No one showed up. However, the next day there was a brief article in the evening paper, the *Diario de la Tarde,* reporting that the famous sheik Assis Namur had visited Santiago de Chile.

Our intention was to demonstrate the unpredictable quality of reality with these poetic acts. Lihn and I pulled ground meat out of our pockets at a meeting of the Literary Academy, flinging it at the worthy attendees while giving cries of horror. This caused a collective panic. For us, poetry was a convulsion, an earthquake. Appearances were to be denounced, falsehoods unmasked, and conventions challenged. Dressed as beggars, we took up a violin and a guitar in front of the patio of a café, as if we were about to play. Then we broke the musical instruments by smashing them against the sidewalk. We gave a coin to each patron and left. At a lecture by a professor of literature in the central hall of the University of Chile, while dressed as explorers we approached the speaker's table crawling on all fours and with melodramatic moans of thirst fought with each other to drink the water from the official carafe. We lined up to enter a movie theater disguised as blind people and crying loudly. In an act paying homage to mothers, on the tenth of May we dressed in tuxedos and sang a lullaby while pouring several bottles of milk over our heads.

However, our youthful enthusiasm also led us to commit some grave errors. We went to the medical school and, with the complicity of friends who were students there, stole the arms of a corpse. Lihn took one arm and I the other, and we each dressed in an overcoat. Then we went around shaking hands with people, giving them the dead hands. No one dared to comment that our hands were stiff and cold because they did not want to face the reality of those dead limbs. Once finished with this macabre game we threw the arms into the Mapocho River without thinking of the consequences and without paying any respects to the human being who had possessed them.

Our feeling of freedom led us to do evil. On the banks of the Mapocho, a wild area in those days, a colony of ants had built a statuesque city. Enrique and I invited a group of artists to this location, promising an "exemplary comedy." We set folding chairs around the ant mound. We dressed as soldiers. We advanced, goose-stepping in our boots, saluting like Nazis, and trampled the ant nest, carrying out a massacre of thousands of insects. Driven mad, they spread out in a black swarm beneath the feet of the spectators, who, disgusted, began to stomp on them. Although everyone certainly understood the meaning of our message, this did not make us any less cruel murderers of ants. We felt affected by this experience, and it led us to question ourselves seriously.

What is the definition of a poetic act? It should be beautiful, imbued with a dreamlike quality, should be above any justification, and should create another reality within the very heart of ordinary reality. It should allow for transcendence to another plane. It should open the door to a new dimension, achieving a purifying courage. Therefore, if we were proposing to perform an act deviating from ordinary and codified behaviors, it was necessary for us to evaluate the consequences beforehand. The act should be a vital fissure in the petrified order perpetuated by society, not a compulsive manifestation of blind rebellion. It was essential to distrust the negative energies that could lead to a senseless act. We understood why André Breton had apologized after yielding to excitement and declaring that the ultimate surrealist act was to go out into the street brandishing a revolver and killing random strangers. The poetic act should be a gratuitous act that allows creative energies that are normally repressed or latent in us to manifest with goodness and beauty. The irrational act is an open door to vandalism and violence. When a crowd is enraged, when manifestations degenerate and people set fire to cars and break windows, this is also a release of pent-up energies. But it does not deserve to be called a poetic act.

A Japanese haiku gives us a clue. The student shows the teacher his poem:

> *"Here's a butterfly:*
> *Now I will tear off its wings.*
> *I get a pepper!"*

The teacher's response is immediate.
"No, that's not it. Listen:

> *"I have a pepper:*
> *Now I add some wings to it.*
> *Here's a butterfly!"*

The lesson was clear: the poetic act must always be positive, aiming for construction and not destruction.

We reviewed the acts that we had carried out. Many of them had been nothing more than hateful reactions against a society that we considered vulgar, more or less clumsy attempts at an act worthy of being called poetic. We clearly saw that on the day we had gone into my father's shop accompanied by Assis Namur, claiming that Jaime was a holy man because he was selling a beautiful void then opening a box to show that it was empty, we should have arrived in a procession with a bag of socks and filled the box with them in order to realize his dream of becoming a merchant. Instead of putting earthworms between the legs of my parents, I should have filled their bed with chocolate coins. Instead of staring in the dark like a beast at the crotch of my sleeping sister, I should have used immense delicacy to place a pearl between those labia. Instead of cutting off the dead man's arms, we should have painted him gold, dressed him in a purple robe, put long hair and a beard on him, and added a crown of electric lights, making him into Christ. We should have put a plaster Virgin smeared with honey next to the ant mound, so that the ants would cover her, giving her a living skin . . .

After this gaining of awareness, we had no more regrets. Errors are excusable if they are committed only once, in a sincere quest for knowledge. These atrocities had opened up our path to the true poetic act. We decided to create an act for the consecrated Pablo Neruda. It was known that he would return from Europe the following spring on a very precise date. We knew a gentleman whose passion was to cultivate butterflies. He had a thorough knowledge of the habits of these insects, and he knew how to breed their larvae. We made him an accomplice in our act and went to Isla Negra with him to a beach where the poet had built a retreat by joining together several houses with a tower rising from their midst. Lihn, with the air of a magician, inserted an antique key—apparently a memento from his grandmother—into the old lock, and without applying the least force, unlocked it. The door to the sacred lair swung open! Although we knew that no one was living there, we walked on tiptoe, afraid of awakening some unknown and terrible muse. The rooms were full of beautiful and strange objects: collections of bottles of all types, figureheads with faces flushed by delusions, bizarrely shaped rocks, huge seashells, old books, crystal balls, primitive drums, coffee mills, all sorts of spurs, folk dolls, automata, and so forth. It was an enchanting museum formed by the child that inhabited the soul of the poet. Out of religious respect, we touched nothing. We moved as little as possible, gliding rather than walking to dodge the artifacts. The butterfly breeder, carrying his packets, stood stiff as a statue, hardly daring to breathe. All at once, Enrique was seized by an angelic energy that made him suddenly lighter on his feet. He began to jump effortlessly, intoning a song composed of unintelligible words, sounding like something between Arabic and Sanskrit. We saw him dance as if his body had lost its bones; his balance was amazing, his movements more and more daring, closer and closer to the precious objects. When he reached a final paroxysm, he shook so fast that he appeared to have hundreds of limbs. He did not break anything. All items remained in place. After the dance, we knelt meditating while the butterfly breeder placed his caterpillars in strategic corners. After the task was completed, we started back toward Santiago. The cultivator assured us that when Neruda returned to his house, clouds of butterflies would emerge from every corner.

In 1953 I threw my address book into the sea and boarded a boat from Valparaiso, bound for Paris with a fourth-class dormitory cabin ticket and barely a hundred dollars in my pocket. I had decided never to return again, not because I did not love Chile or my friends (it hurt me deeply to cut all my ties), but because I wanted to fundamentally live the idea that the poet must be a tree that converts its branches into celestial roots. Before leaving, I carried out two poetic acts, one in Lihn's company and the other alone, that affected my character profoundly.

In a bookstore that, not merely by chance, was called Daedalus, Enrique and I put on a puppet show of a play by Federico García Lorca with our little theater, which we called the Bululú. Taming my poet friend enough to rehearse, and tearing him out of the arms of Bacchus, was a herculean task but luckily we were encouraged by our girlfriends and their sisters, who patiently sewed all the costumes. On the day of the performance the audience, mostly civil war refugees from Spain, filled the place and did not hold back their applause. Although the price of admission was modest, we took in a good amount of money. Elated by success, after several toasts we decided to rent a *victoria*, one of those open horse-drawn carriages popular among romantic couples and tourists. We asked the driver what route he would take us on in return for the amount that we had earned. He suggested a five-kilometer route past the most beautiful sights in the city center and its surroundings. We accepted, but instead of traveling comfortably seated, we ran behind the victoria. (That is to say, we were pursuing fame.) For the last three hundred meters we got on, sat down, and finished the ride with our arms raised as if we were champions. We had intuitively discovered that the subconscious accepts metaphorical facts as real. This act, seemingly absurd and eccentric, was a contract we made with ourselves: we would invest our energy in our work; we would devote ourselves to pursuing victory; we would not be losers but winners. Enrique Lihn devoted his entire life to art and worked unceasingly to perfect what he did until his death at the age of fifty-nine. He is considered one of the great Chilean poets. While in his sick bed, the last verse he wrote was: "... *he unravels the skein of death with his hands, which they say are those of an angel.*"

As I was preparing to leave the second poetic act took place at a farewell party that my friends threw for me at Café Tango on the Alameda de las Delicias. We heard a rumbling that grew and grew, as if a gigantic wave were approaching. We young artists, living isolated in our idealistic sphere and paying no attention to vulgar politics, had not noticed when the country voted to elect a new president. In an absurd historical phenomenon, the popular candidate in this democratic election was the former military dictator Carlos Ibáñez del Campo. Now, by their own will, the people had put him in command for the second time. The deafening rumble proclaiming triumph originated from a crowd of some hundred thousand people who joined the throng, from homes in the slums around the Central Station to posh neighborhoods. It was as if a dark river of euphoric, drunken ants had invaded the broad avenue. Moved by I do not know what force I jumped up and ran to the avenue, full of uncontainable joy, stood in the middle of it, and waited for the crowd to reach me. When the first line of marchers was a few meters from me I began yelling loudly, without thinking for one second of the dangerous consequences, "Death to Ibáñez!" It was not David versus Goliath; it was a flea against King Kong. How could I have had the idea of confronting a hundred thousand people? In a state of ecstasy, alien to my body and therefore alien to fear, I shouted and shouted until I was hoarse, insulting the new president. The river of people did not react. My act was so foolish that it was unthinkable to them. They simply integrated me into their triumph. I was one of them, one more citizen cheering their new leader. Instead of "death to Ibáñez" they heard "long live Ibáñez." As the human torrent passed all around me and I stood there like a salmon swimming against the current, I realized that I was not doing this because I wanted to die, but on the contrary, because I wanted above all to live, meaning to survive without being swallowed by this prosaic world—a world that is so prosaic, however irrational it may seem, that it has glimmerings of the surreal. The people who were marching along were not shouting "long live Ibáñez" but "long live the Horse." The winning candidate had begun his career as a cavalry officer, and because he spoke little and had abnormally large teeth the people called him the Horse. Perhaps that is why he governed the country by stomping on it.

My friends, who had initially thought I had run to the bathroom to vomit, became concerned about my disappearance and went to look for me in the street. They spotted me standing there, shouting against everything in the middle of the parade. Pale, they made their way to me and got me out of there at top speed. I collapsed on a table in the café, short of breath. My whole body ached as if I had been beaten. Then I was seized by nervous laughter and severe trembling, at which point they calmed me down by throwing water from a jug in my face. The Alejandro they calmed thus would never be the same again. A force had awakened within me that would enable me to overcome a great many adverse currents. Years later, I applied this experience to therapy: you cannot heal someone; you can only teach him how to heal himself.

FIVE

Theater as Religion

Before 1929 northern Chile attracted adventurers from all over the world, the Germans had not yet invented synthetic saltpeter, and natural saltpeter was known as white gold. Foreign vessels came to be loaded with thousands of kilos of this ambiguous, dual-natured, androgynous substance that on the one hand is an ally of life due to its application as a powerful fertilizer and on the other hand is an ally of death due to the application for which it was more coveted: making explosives.

In this world of miners money was made hand over fist. In Iquique, Antofagasta, and Tocopilla the bars, whorehouses, and artists all thrived. Huge theaters were built in the mining villages. All kinds of performers visited this new California. Great opera singers, dancers such as Anna Pavlova, and extravagant variety shows all came to perform. Around the time of my birth not only did the stock market collapse in the United States, but synthetic saltpeter also began to come on the market at a much lower price than what was produced in northern Chile. The mines and the cities that fed on them began their slow death. However, despite the economic crisis there was a kind of inertia that kept some performing companies, albeit the more modest ones, visiting those theaters as they slowly crumbled from lack of upkeep; the Municipal Theater of Tocopilla, which had been converted into a cinema, occasionally rolled the white screen back to reveal the large stage, especially in winter, the best season due to lack of rain. Many shows were put on there. Each one taught me something. This is not to say that my childhood brain translated this knowledge into words. My intuition absorbed it like seeds, which grew slowly over the years, changing my perception of the world, guiding my actions, and finally manifesting itself in psychomagic. Besides Fu-Manchu, the magician described in chapter 1, I marveled at seeing Tinny Griffy, an immense white woman weighing at least three hundred kilos who sang, performed, and danced, tapping her feet, dressed like Shirley Temple. The stage, corroded by the salty environment, could not support such a weight, and the fat lady fell through the floor. A compact group of men dragged her out, like ants carrying a beetle, and deposited her in a taxi that took her to the hospital in Antofagasta, a hundred kilometers away. In order to fit in the backseat Tinny Griffy had to stick her huge legs, which looked like enormous hams, out through a window. I learned that there is a close relationship between our gestures and the world. If we break through the resistance of our medium, then that medium, while being destroyed, destroys us at the same time. What we do to the world, we are also doing to ourselves.

A dog show also came to town. There were a great number of dogs of all breeds dressed like people: the nice young lady, her fiancé, the bad guy, the seductress, the clown, and so on. For an hour and a half I saw a universe in which dogs had supplanted the human race, which, I imagined, might have been decimated by plague. When I left the theater, the street seemed to me to be full of animals clad in human clothes. Not only dogs, but also tigers, ostriches, rats, vultures, frogs. At that early age, the dangerous animal part of every psyche became apparent to me.

The magnificent Leopoldo Frégoli also came to town. He played an entire theater company, changing costumes at a dizzying speed. He could be fat or thin, male or female, sublime or ridiculous. His performance made me realize that I was not one, but many. My soul was like a stage inhabited by countless characters fighting to take command. Personality was a matter of choice. We could choose to be what we wanted to be. An Italian family consisting of a father and mother with fourteen children also came to Tocopilla. The children, as obedient as dogs, danced, did acrobatics, performed balancing acts, juggled, and sang. My favorite was a three-year-old boy dressed as a policeman, whacking the guilty and the innocent alike with his baton. Thanks to them, I understood that the health of a family is maintained by shared labor, that there is not a moat separating the generations, that the rebellion of children against parents should be replaced by the absorption of knowledge, provided, of course, that the previous generation takes the trouble to expand its knowledge and pass on what it has acquired. Moreover, seeing children dressed as adults I realized that the child within us never dies, that every human being who has not done his spiritual work is a child disguised as an adult. It is wonderful to be a child during childhood and terrible when we are forced to be like adults at an early age. It is also terrible to be a child during adulthood. To grow up is to put the child in its proper place, to let it live within us not as the master but as the disciple. It should bring us everyday wonder, purity of intention, and creative games, but should never rule as a tyrant.

I also believe that my fascination with theater entered my being due to three events that deeply marked my childhood soul: I participated in the burial of a firefighter, I witnessed a seizure, and I heard the prince of China sing.

Since Casa Ukrania was near the fire station, to fight off boredom my father soon enlisted in the First Company. Fires were rare in this small town, at most one per year. Being a firefighter thus became a social activity, with a parade every year on the anniversary of the fire company's founding, as well as charity balls, public exercises to test the equipment, soccer tournaments between the companies (there were three of them), and band performances on Sundays at the gazebo in the town square. When they were raising funds to buy a new fire engine, the firefighters put on their parade uniforms—white pants and red jackets with a star over the heart—and a group photo was taken. My father offered me up as a mascot. The offer was accepted, and at age six I was magically converted into a firefighter.

In this perpetual dance of reality, just as the fireworks inaugurating the company were ignited, a fire erupted in the poor part of town. And so the company headed to the site of the fire, still dressed in their fancy uniforms that covered their fire truck in red and white. Although no one invited me, I tagged along. I did not extinguish any flames, but I was entrusted with the sacred task of keeping an eye on the axes because the indigents of the neighborhood were fully capable of stealing not only those but also the wheels, ladders, hoses, nuts, and bolts off the luxurious vehicle while the firefighters struggled to save them from the fire. Once the fire had been conquered, it was noticed that the company chief was missing. He was pulled from the rubble, entirely black. A vigil was held for the corpse in the firemen's barracks, with a white coffin covered with orange and red flowers symbolizing flames. At midnight he was brought from there to the cemetery in a solemn procession. No spectacle had ever impressed me so much; I felt proud to participate, sorry for the bereaved, and, especially, terrified. It was the first time I had walked the streets at such a late hour of the night. Seeing my world covered in shadows revealed the dark side of life to me. Dangerous aspects were hidden within familiar things. I was terrified of the residents who crowded the sidewalks, the whites of their eyes glittering in their dark silhouettes as they watched us slowly walk by, our feet gliding without our knees bending. First came the band, playing a heartrending funeral march. Then I came, so small, concealing my immeasurable anguish with the face of a warrior. Next came the ostentatious coach carrying the coffin, and finally behind that the three companies in their parade outfits, each fireman holding a torch. By agreement, all the lights in Tocopilla were off. The siren rang constantly. The flames of the torches made shadows that fluttered like giant vultures. I kept going for about three kilometers, but then I stumbled and fell. Jaime, who was in the wagon next to the driver, jumped down and picked me up; I woke up in my bed with a high fever. It seemed to me as if my sheets were covered

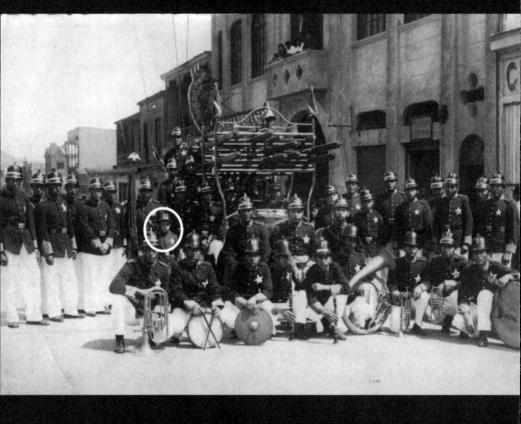

with ashes. The scent of the wreaths of flowers brought from Iquique was stuck in my nostrils. I thought that the shadow vultures nesting in my room would devour me. Jaime could think of no better way to calm me than to say, as he put wet towels on my forehead and belly, "If I'd known you were so impressionable, I wouldn't have brought you to the funeral. Good thing I picked you up just as you fell. Don't worry, no one saw what a coward you are." For a long time I dreamed that the star on my uniform was clinging to my chest like an animal, sucking up my voice to keep me from screaming while I was shut in a white coffin and brought to the graveyard. Later, this harrowing experience taught me to use the metaphorical funeral for psychomagical healing: an impressive ritual in which the sick person is buried.

The Prieto family had built a public spa on the northern edge of Tocopilla. The large swimming pool, carved out of the rocks by the seaside, was filled by the ocean waves. I did not like to swim there because there were fish and octopuses. It was a very popular place. On several occasions I saw people running to a beach nearby because an unemployed bald man known as the Cuckoo was kicking up a cloud of sand, twisting in a fit of epilepsy. The spectators who had been busy bathing or drinking bottles of beer by the dozen would come to watch as the sick man began with hoarse grunts that increased in their intensity until they became deafening screams. Amidst a great deal of nervous excitement the group would carry him to a dark, covered room as he kept on howling, shaking, and foaming at the mouth. The excitement lasted for an hour, which was how long it took for the Cuckoo's seizures to pass over. Proud of having saved him by tying his hands and feet and putting the handle of a feather duster in his mouth, they would then take up a collection and treat him to an empanada and a beer. Looking like a sad dog he would eat and drink, and then leave, hanging his head. I, like many others I suppose, felt very sorry for him.

One Sunday morning, when the spa was full of people, I began to hear the bald man's wheezing before anyone else did. I ran to the beach and saw him comfortably seated on a stone, taking great pains to raise the volume of his lamentations. He did not see me coming. He jumped up when I touched his shoulder, looking at me furiously. He grabbed a rock threateningly and said, "Get out of here, you little shit!" I ran, but as soon as I was hidden behind the rocks, I stopped to watch. When the bathers came running toward him, drawn by his screams, he put a piece of soap in his mouth, lay on the ground, and began to squirm and foam at the mouth. Who would have guessed that the Cuckoo was a rogue actor, as healthy as those who came to save him? When he writhed on the ground, with the soil full of sharp stones, he received painful cuts on his skin; his nervous saviors, lifting him up, would sometimes bang him against rocks; the empanada they bought him was mediocre, and the beer only one. Was it worth doing so much work for so little reward? I realized that what this poor man was after was the attention of others. Later I understood that all illnesses, even the cruelest ones, are a form of entertainment. At the basis of this is a protestation against the lack of love and the prohibition of any word or gesture clarifying this deficiency. That which is not said, not expressed, kept secret, can eventually turn into disease. The child's soul, drowned by this prohibition, eliminates its organic defenses in order to let in the sickness that will give it the opportunity to express its desolation. Disease is a metaphor. It is a child's protest turned into a representation.

There was a large room on the second floor of the firemen's building that no one used. It occurred to Jaime that the company could take advantage of this space by renting it out for parties; time went by and, probably due to the financial crisis, no client rented it. My father said that it was not for lack of money but due to inertia: no one wanted to deviate from the customary ways. Large parties, weddings, and award ceremonies were held in the roller skating rink at the Prieto family's spa, and that was that . . . "We'll show them," Jaime said, and after becoming a regular patron of the Jade Bridge Chinese restaurant in order to convince the owner to be his intermediary, he offered the space

for free to the Chinese community and committed himself to arrang-
ing a lively ball with the bands of the three firemen's companies playing. The Asian families danced tangos to the wind instruments, put
on raffles, ate *churrasco,* and drank wine with peaches and strawberries
spiked with *aguardiente.* This party, exotic for them, was such a hit that
they gave my father a certificate declaring him a friend of the Chinese
community. With the racial ice broken, some Chinese people came to
our house to spend an evening playing mah-jongg.* The most assiduous
player among them was a young man with olive skin tending toward
yellow whose face was perfectly smooth and unblemished. He had long,
manicured nails, black hair trimmed with mathematical precision, and
a face as perfectly sculpted as that of a porcelain figurine. His fine cash-
mere suit, cut to perfection, his wide-collared shirt, his exquisite tie, his
gleaming patent leather shoes, and his silk socks all blended harmoni-
ously with his distinguished gestures. Jaime called him the Prince. I,
who had never seen such masculine beauty, looked at him ecstatically
as if he were a great toy.

He smiled at me with his almond-shaped eyes. Then, with a hypnotic rhythm, he said things to me in Chinese that, though I did not
understand them, made me laugh. One afternoon Sara Felicidad was
very excited and said, "I have wonderful news: tonight the Prince is
going to sing us an opera in the style of his country." I understand why
my mother was so moved: when she was young she had wanted to be an
opera singer, but her stepfather and mother had told her this vocation
was out of the question. The beautiful Chinese singer arrived at ten in
the evening accompanied by two musicians dressed in skirts over satin
trousers. One carried an unusual stringed instrument, the other a drum.
The Prince, carrying a suitcase, requested that they give him an hour to
get dressed and put on his makeup in the bathroom. My parents waited
impatiently, playing dominoes. I, accustomed to going to bed early, fell
asleep. When the Prince came before us a yawn froze in my mouth,

---

*A Chinese game related to dominoes, which uses 144 wooden tiles.

Sara struggled to suppress a nervous cough, and Jaime opened his eyes so wide that I thought he would never be able to close them again. Our Chinese friend had become a beautiful woman. And to say beautiful is an understatement. Taking short and rapid steps to the plaintive sound of the stringed instrument and the metallic rhythm of the drum, he appeared to glide and float. His robe, made of silk and satin, was brightly colored in red, green, yellow, and blue, studded with glass and metal inlays. His small hands, which emerged from wide sleeves, were painted white with lacquered nails and waved an airy handkerchief. On his back were a number of rods with flags on them, by way of wings. His face, also white, had been transformed into the mask of a goddess, and his small lips moved like those of an eel. The Prince, or rather the Princess, was singing. It was not a human voice, but the lament of a millenarian insect. The long, intense, sinuous, otherworldly phrases were interspersed by sudden stops, accentuated by the two instruments . . . I fell into a trance. I forgot I was watching a human; before me was a supernatural being out of a fairy tale bringing us the treasure of his existence. Sara did not seem to feel the same way. With her face red and her breath coming in short bursts, she frowned as if witnessing an insane act. It was obvious that she could not accept the idea of a man playing at transforming himself into a woman. Jaime, after a while, seemed to comprehend the deeper meaning of the performance: he was watching an Oriental clown. The whole thing was a joke that his friend was playing. He began guffawing. The apparition stopped singing, bowed deeply, went into the bathroom, and thirty minutes later the Prince returned, impeccable as always. With haughty dignity, he descended the stairs, followed by his two acolytes, and went out into the street to be lost in the night and never to return.

Thinking again and again about this tense situation, which left an indelible impression on my memory, I realized that every extraordinary act breaks down the walls of reason. It upends the scale of values and refers the spectator to his or her own judgment. It acts as a mirror: each person sees it within his own limitations. But those limitations, when they manifest, can cause an unexpected burst of awareness. "The world is as I think it is. My ills come from my distorted vision. If I want to heal, it is not the world that I should try to change, but the opinion I have of it."

Miracles are like stones: they are everywhere, offering up their beauty, but hardly anyone concedes value to them. We live in a reality where prodigies abound but are seen only by those who have developed their perception of them. Without this perception everything is banal, marvelous events are seen as chance, and one progresses through life without possessing the key that is gratitude. When something extraordinary happens it is seen as a natural phenomenon that we can exploit like parasites, without giving anything in return. But miracles require an exchange; I must make that which is given to me bear fruit for others. If one is not united with oneself, the wonder cannot be captured. Miracles are never performed or provoked: they are discovered. If someone who believes himself to be blind takes off his dark glasses, he will see the light. That darkness is the prison of the rational.

I consider it a great miracle that the choreographer Kurt Joos, fleeing Nazi Germany accompanied by four of his best dancers, arrived in Santiago de Chile. Another miracle was that the Chilean government admitted him and gave him a grant that allowed him to open a school with large rooms where all the expressionist ballets could be re-created. Most of the great foreign performers of that era were hosted by the Municipal Theater, a beautiful and spacious Italianate building in the city center built before the economic crisis. My poet friends and I, having discovered a service door at the rear of the building that was not kept locked, would wait for the performance to begin, slip off our shoes, and sneak through the shadows to the sides of the stage from where we could watch the show. My friends saw *La mesa verde, Pavana,* and *La gran ciudad* only a couple of times. I saw at least a hundred performances. Such was my devotion that I knelt while watching these splendid choreographies. In *La mesa verde* a group of hypocritical diplomats discussed peace around a green table, only to finally declare war. Death appeared dressed as the god Mars, played with great verve by a Russian dancer, showing us the horrors of war. In *Pavana* an innocent girl was crushed by a ritual court; in *La gran ciudad* two idealistic teenagers came to New York and, in their eagerness for success, were destroyed by the vices of the relentless city. For the first time, I saw a technique that astutely used the body to express a wide range of feelings and ideas. The ballet troupes that visited the country had left behind a fastidious legacy: so-called classical dance schools that crammed all bodies into the same mold, deforming them in the quest for a hollow and obsolete beauty. Joos, staging the most urgent political and social problems with sublime technique, planted the seed that later grew in my spirit: the ultimate goal of art is to cure. If art does not heal, it is not true art.

I might have fallen into the trap of limiting myself to an art preoccupied solely with asserting political doctrines, but fortunately, another miracle occurred. The lead dancer, Ernst Uthoff, came into conflict with the brilliant choreographer and decided to form his own ballet, drawing on elements of classical dance. Setting aside the problems of the material world, perhaps wanting to forget the suffering of war, he staged a fantastic tale: *Copelia*. I still remember the name of the dancer who played the puppet whose creator wished to make her human by stealing the soul of a young man in love: Virginia Roncal, a woman who devoted her life to dance. She was not exceptionally beautiful and was short in stature, but her talent was outstanding. The first time I saw her rise up from the table where the inanimate body of the young man whose soul had been stolen lay—first making the rigid movements of an automaton, then little by little feeling life invade her, then finally shaking off the mechanical movements in a sort of frenzy and dancing like a real woman, but then, upon discovering the lifeless young man and realizing that this soul was not her own, returning the life that did not belong to her in a kiss with a supreme effort of honesty and love, then finally resuming her automatic movements—I was moved to tears. I realized that art should not only heal the body but also the soul. All objectives are summarized into one: realizing human potentialities in order to transcend them. Sacrificing the personal in order to achieve the impersonal means nothing is for me that is not for others.

Copelia awoke such admiration in me that I approached Uthoff's school to seek admission. While there I was smitten with a dancer with thick curly hair, strong as an oak tree and tall as a magical horse. Fortunately for me, she liked me; I became absorbed by her. I learned to dance through her movements in love. One night when the electricity was out we embraced on the desk where André Racz had done his drawings. A sticky wetness covered both our bodies. Inflamed with pleasure as we were, we were not concerned. Suddenly, the light came back on, and we found that all our skin was stained black. In our enthusiastic movements we had overturned a large bottle of Chinese ink. Nora saw this as a sign: my enjoyment of her movements had made me forget my talent as a dancer. She did not want to be guilty of destroying a vocation that was sacred to her, so she ended our relationship and introduced me to the Yugoslav Yerca Lucsic, a passionate teacher of modern dance. Her courses were intense, the creation in them unceasing. I learned to move according to the nine characters of Gurdjieff's enneagram, to imitate all kinds of animals; also to give birth and breastfeed, experiencing what it is to be a mother, analogous to women who danced imitating penile erection and ejaculation. We investigated the expression of the wounds of Christ. I had to dance the spear into my side, the crown of thorns onto my head, and the nails into my feet and hands. Dancing became an activity that allowed me to know what I was, but also what I was not.

Yerca wanted to push beyond limits. And because of this, she died. With her savings she had bought a house on an ocean beach near the capital and spent her weekends there. She entered into a relationship with a fisherman. He was a handsome but uneducated man. Rather than educating him, she encouraged him to affirm himself. She dressed him as a traditional fisherman, in a starched white calico suit with bare feet and a red bandanna around his neck, and introduced him to her friends who came to visit on the weekends who were dancers, artists, professors, university alumni, and people of high society. The couple was very popular. She talked incessantly while he mutely served the drinks. One day we waited, but Yerca did not come to class. Not that day, nor the whole week. We learned from newspapers that the fisherman had murdered her, cutting her body into little bits with a pair of pliers and a knife. By the time they took him to prison, denounced by his comrades, he had already used half of my teacher's body as bait.

Criminal acts, despite their horror, sometimes cause the same fascination as poetic acts. For this reason, apprentices in psychomagic must be very cautious. Every act must be creative and must end with a detail that affirms life and not death. The fisherman destroyed the body of the dancer. Yerca destroyed the spirit of the fisherman. If, instead, she had made an effort to involve him in her creative world while at the same time she learned to fish, then he might not have murdered her, and perhaps she would have created a beautiful ballet with fishing as its theme.

Lihn, seeing me frustrated by my lack of classes, suggested that we put on a dance recital. "How, where, with what music?" I asked. He replied, "Naked, with only loincloths so that they don't put us in prison, next to the embassy's electric station, the generators will be our music."

The United States Embassy, which was across from Forestal Park, produced its own electricity with powerful generators so that the frequent tremors would not plunge it into darkness when they affected the central power plant. These generators echoed with a regular rhythm for an hour every day beginning at around ten o'clock at night. We invited our friends, and when the rough rhythm began we undressed and began dancing like madmen. The audience soon followed suit. I realized that everything could be danced and that artistic achievement was the result of passionate choices. Once offered the cake, we had only to see it; we grabbed a slice and ate. It was Alice's cake: when she ate it, she grew or shrank. Such was life, and such was art, a matter of vision and choice. And I finally understood that it was the same for negative aspects. The spirit of self-destruction presents an individual with a menu of all sorts of diseases, physical and mental. The individual chooses his own illness. In order to cure an illness it is necessary to investigate what has led the sick person to select this particular illness and not some other one.

While it is true that reality gives us cake, this does not mean that we should wait motionless with our mouths open. To bring ourselves to fruition, instead of just asking for opportunities to be given to us, we artists, though seemingly insignificant, can offer opportunities to powerful people. This is how I presented myself, carrying a basket full of my puppets, to the offices of the prosperous Teatro Experimental de la Universidad de Chile (TEUCH), the government agency that put on grand shows and ran a theater school. I was received by Domingo Piga and Agustín Siré, who were the general directors, and I said at once, "I want to direct the TEUCH Puppet Theatre!" They responded that TEUCH did not have a puppet theater. I opened my basket and I dumped the puppets out on the desk: "Now you have one!" They immediately gave me the abandoned room behind the clock that adorned the facade of the central building. The poets and their friends helped me to clean away the dust that had accumulated over half a century, and there we began to build the Bululú. This was an activity in which artistic pleasures were mixed with amorous pleasures. The administration provided us with an old bus, and we joined forces with the university chorus and together—the chorus numbering sixty people and we puppeteers consisting of six men and six women—toured throughout northern Chile giving performances. It was a very beautiful, essentially anonymous activity. Hidden, with our arms raised manipulating these heroes, we learned to sacrifice individual exhibitionism. We knew how to put ourselves at the service of the puppets and the audience. What difference was there between puppeteers who were hidden in the shadows, giving energy to the characters that evolved above us, and a congregation of monks concentrating their prayers on exalting God? After putting on a show for the children of miners one of the best puppeteers, Eduardo Mattei, told me, "I feel like a toad full of love, getting glimpses of the full moon." I hid a wry smile, for his words seemed corny. But I realized how sincere he was when, at the end of the tour, he bade us adieu and became a Benedictine monk. The puppeteers all attended the ceremony at the monastery of Las Condes in which the abbot washed Eduardo's feet and gave him his new name, Frater Maurus. Thanks to his work with the puppets, Eduardo had found his faith.

Some time later, I went to visit him. Frater Maurus, dressed in his beautiful Benedictine habit, looked happy. I told him that I was thinking of leaving Chile to study in Europe. He responded, "They will teach you a science of voids; they will show you where there is nothing. They are experts in this: like vultures, they detect cadavers perfectly, but are incapable of finding where the living bodies are. There is only one way to make a chalice, but a thousand ways of breaking it!" I respected his sentiments. It was a position opposite to mine: I wanted to cut my roots in order to span the entire world. He had decided to confine himself there at the monastery, at the foot of the mountains, and sing Gregorian chants for the rest of his life. It was all the more heroic a decision because, as I knew, he had been in love with one of our actresses. For his devotion to God, was it necessary to eliminate women and family from his life? Eduardo's profound vocation revealed the sacred character of theater to me. How could I, who had been raised as an atheist, aspire to holiness? Every religion has its holy men, and Frater Maurus quickly became a Catholic holy man; there are also Muslim holy men, Jewish holy men known as the "righteous," enlightened Buddhist holy men, and so on. Religions have appropriated holiness. To be holy means to respect dogmas. What remains for those of us who are not theological standard bearers, those of us whose animal nature makes us want to be united with a wife? It is impossible to believe that God created women as an evil, just to tempt good men. If women are as sacred as men, intercourse is also sacred, and if this act leads to orgasm, it should be accepted and enjoyed as a divine gift.

I decided that I could become a civil holy man: holiness did not necessarily have to be contingent on chastity or on the renunciation of sexual pleasure, the basis of the family. A civil holy man need not ever enter a church, nor does he need to worship a god with any defined name or image. Such a man, having risen above purely personal interests—not only socially and globally conscious but also cosmically conscious—is able to act for the benefit of the world. In knowing that he is united with others he understands that their suffering is his suffering, but their joy is also his joy. He is able to sympathize and help the needy, but also to applaud those who are triumphant, as long as they are not exploitative. The civil holy man makes himself the owner of the Earth: the air, the land, the animals, the water, the fundamental energies, are all his, and he acts as their possessor, taking great care not to damage this property. The civil holy man is capable of generous anonymous acts. Loving humanity, he has learned to love himself. He knows that the future of the human race depends on partners capable of achieving a relationship in equilibrium. The civil holy man struggles to ensure that not only children are well treated, but also fetuses, which must be protected from neurotic couples who have conceived them as well as from the toxic industry of childbirth. He also struggles to liberate the field of medicine from large industrial companies, makers of drugs that are more damaging than diseases. To achieve civil holiness—to be outside of any sect, sweetly impersonal, capable of accompanying a dying person whose name I did not know with the same devotion as if she had been my daughter, sister, wife, or mother—seemed impossible to me. But, inspired by some initiatory tales in which the heroes are apes, parrots, dogs, all animals capable of imitation, I decided to use this as my technique. By imitating civil holiness over and over, eventually I would authentically achieve it in my actions.

My intent to imitate civil holiness gave me justification for living. However, I committed some grave errors trying to apply what in those years were only theories. An example was the de-virginizing of Consuelo, a young woman I met at Café Iris who had been invited there by her sister, a painter. Consuelo had an ungainly physique but sensuous curves, a wide mouth, deep-set eyes, and protruding ears that gave her a sympathetic simian air. She was introduced to me, and we sat down to talk at a separate table. While combing her hair, which was cut short in a masculine style, she explained that she was a lesbian. Most of her sexual relationships had been with married women who had refused to leave their husbands to go and live with her. Since Consuelo was interested in literature, we began a friendship in which she behaved like a man. Everything was going well, we took great pleasure in getting together to explore bookstores or sit and drink coffee at various popular spots, but my desire to imitate civil holiness came into the mix. I asked if she still had her hymen. "Of course!" she told me proudly. Carried away by the desire to do good in a disinterested way, I replied, "My friend, I know that phallic penetration does not interest you at all, but it would be unfortunate for a future great poet like you to have to grow old as a virgin. As long as you keep this veil, you will never be an adult, nor will you know why you reject the male member: you will be afraid of it; you'll feel it stalking you in the shadows like an implacable enemy. Prove to yourself that you are strong. I propose the following: let's get together in my studio at a precise time. I will borrow an operating table, there's one in the university theater that was used for a play. You will arrive wearing a coat, with hospital pajamas underneath. I will be dressed as surgeon. We will not touch each other at all beforehand, I'll lay you down on the table, pretend to anesthetize you, take off your pants, open your legs, you will pretend to be asleep, and then, with precision and extreme delicacy, I will penetrate you as a purely medicinal act. Once the hymen is torn, I will retreat with the same delicacy with which I entered. There will not be any pleasure; any form of foreplay is excluded. It will be a surgical operation between friends, nothing more. Once this poetic act is finished, you can live your life free of this cumbersome hymen."

She liked my idea. We set the meeting time and performed the operation exactly as planned. Consuelo, happy not to have suffered any trauma, thanked me for the impeccability of my technique, and with her face glowing from having released herself from this troublesome detail, she went out with her friends. However, the following evening, suppressing her drunkenness, she came to me to confess that she had felt a form of pleasure that she wanted to investigate. She literally dragged me to the studio, threw me on the bed, and sucked on me frantically. Although she was not the type of woman who excited me, I responded to her touch due to the energy of my age. After we finished, all I wanted was to be as far away as possible from this impassioned woman. Unfortunately, from that day on, she began a fierce pursuit. Wherever I went, she would show up. If a girl approached me at a party, Consuelo would drive her away with insults and shoving. It did no good to tell her I did not love her, that she was not my type, to remember that she was a lesbian, and finally to leave me alone. She cried, threatened to kill herself, cursed me . . . My life became unbearable. I talked to her sister and begged her to assist with my plan. Understanding the seriousness of Consuelo's delirium, the painter agreed. I locked myself in my studio and did not leave for a week. Enrique Lihn phoned Consuelo and asked to visit her at her home, because he had some serious news to tell her. When he arrived, dressed in black and feigning grief, he told Consuelo that I had been hit by a bus and had died. Her older sister, bursting into fake sobs, told Consuelo that she had been aware of the fatal accident but had not said anything for fear of causing her atrocious pain. Consuelo fell to the floor in a nervous fit. Her sister took her to a vacation house they owned in Isla Negra. She stayed there for three months. When she returned to Santiago and saw me sitting in Café Iris safe and sound she slapped me, burst out laughing, and began passionately kissing a female friend. She never bothered me again. For my part, I decided to stop imitating civil holiness for a long time.

I was drawn to another idea: reality, being amorphous in principle, organizes itself around any given act that is put forward, whatever the nature of that act may be, positive or negative, and adds unexpected details. Thus thinking, I decided to carry out an act in the greatest possible secrecy to see if I received a response. I went to a shop that specialized in manufacturing footwear for artists and asked them to make me a pair of clown shoes forty centimeters long. I asked for them to be made of patent leather with red toes, green heels, and gold edges. I demanded further that whistles be affixed to the soles that, when stepped on, would emit a meow. Dressed in a very proper gray suit with a white shirt and discreet tie, I walked through the streets of the city center at midday when they were filled with people, the time when people would take a coffee break or have a snack. Uttering one meow after another, I moved among them. Nobody seemed to consider the shoes abnormal. They would cast a quick glance down at my feet, then continue on their way. Disappointed, I sat on a terrace having a drink, crossing my legs to raise one shoe, but with little hope of provoking a reaction. I was approached by a well-dressed gentleman of around sixty years old who had a serious face and an amiable voice.

"Will you allow me to ask you a question, young man?"

"Of course, sir."

"Where did you get those shoes?"

"I had them made, sir."

"Why?"

"First of all, to attract attention, to introduce something unusual into reality. And second, because I love the circus, especially clowns."

"I'm glad to hear you say this. Here is my card." The gentleman handed me a business card with his name inscribed on it in small letters, and then in large orange letters: TONI ZANAHORIA (Carrot Clown).

Oh, what an incredible surprise, I had met him in Tocopilla when I was a child! He had placed a lion cub in my arms.

"What's your name, young man?" When I gave my name, he smiled. "Now I understand; you're one of us. I worked with your father. He was the first man to hang by his hair; before that it was only women. The apple doesn't fall far from the tree: these shoes show that you want to return to the world where you belong. And this meeting is no coincidence. We're performing in the Coliseo Theater. There are international artists and a group of comedians: I (the first donkey), Lettuce Clown, Chalupa Clown, and Piripipí Clown. Pacifier Clown walks with the bottle in his mouth, as we say among ourselves. He'll be drunk for a fortnight. We love him, and we're worried that the owners will kick him out. You seem to love the circus so much; if you want to try the experience without anyone knowing, you can wear our friend's costume, wig, and nose, and stand in for him while he's drunk. The routines are easy; it's not that much to do. You stick a fake ax in my head, cluck like a chicken while throwing wooden eggs at Chalupa Clown, and participate in a farting contest where you squirt out clouds of talc from a tube hidden in your pants. If you get there a couple of hours before the first act, we'll teach you the basics and you can improvise the rest."

"I don't think I could do it."

"If you have anything of the child left in your soul, you can. Here's an example: you ask me in a falsetto voice, 'How is a live bull a like a dead bull?' and I answer, 'Easy, mess with a live bull and you're bound for grief.' You say, 'What about the dead bull?' and I say, 'Ground for beef!' And the audience laughs and applauds. It's that easy. Now, have you decided?"

I went to the small apartment that Carrot Clown rented across from the Coliseo to put on Pacifier Clown's costume. It was astonishing to see the ceremony in which the upstanding gentleman I had spoken with on the café terrace was transformed into an orange clown. I had the sensation of seeing the rebirth of an ancient god. This mythical personage then helped me to dress and put on my makeup. In the same way that my friend had designed his costume using the colors of the root vegetable that was his namesake, Pacifier Clown was dressed like a big baby: a ridiculous diaper over long underwear, a hat with bunny ears, and a bottle in his hand; a thick drop of wool representing a booger hung from his false red nose. As soon as I was in the costume, my personality began

A reunion in Chile, forty years later, with Pacifier Clown. This clown, who used to play a baby, is now dressed as his mother.

to fade away. Neither my voice nor my movements were the same. Nor could I think in the same way. The world had returned to its essence: it was a complete joke. With my exterior aspect dissolved into that grotesque baby, I had the freedom to act without repeating the imposed behaviors that had become my identity. How old was Pacifier Clown? No one could know. Mix together the infant, the adult man, and also the adult woman, and here was the ultimate and miserable manifestation of the essential androgyne. When one is young, an immense distress exists beneath one's joy in life. Once transformed into Pacifier Clown only my euphoria remained; my anxiety vanishing along with my personality. I realized once again that what I believed myself to be was an arbitrary deformation, a rational mask floating in the infinite unexplored internal shadows. Later, I understood that diseases do not actually sicken us; they sicken what we believe ourselves to be. Health is achieved by overcoming prohibitions, quitting paths that are not right for us, ceasing to pursue imposed ideals, and becoming ourselves: the impersonal consciousness that does not define itself.

As we crossed the street toward the artists' entrance, Carrot Clown took me by the hand as if I were his child. Although we walked with dignity a group of children followed us, laughing. Once inside the ring, we mingled with the other clowns. Our task was to fill the time necessary for the workers to take down the trapezes and safety nets. The routines were simple, and with my experience as a puppeteer, I had no trouble in performing them. But the circular theater, full of people all around, made an impression on me. In a puppet show, one performs facing forward. Puppetry has a form like the human head, with the eyes facing forward and darkness behind. I realized that since childhood I had been accustomed to seeing the world from the outside: as I watched events happen I sometimes moved toward them, but most of the time they were directed toward me. Being surrounded by the audience immediately makes one into the center, rather than looking in from the outside. For an action to be seen by everyone, it is necessary to turn constantly. This gives us a bond with the planets. We are not outside humanity; we are its heart. We do not come as strangers to the world, the world produces us. We are not migratory birds, but the fruit offered by the tree. Thinking thus, I had an idea for a joke that I told to my friend Carrot Clown. He very kindly decided to premiere it that very evening.

"Hey, clown, tell me what you are."

"I am a foreigner, sir!"

"And what country do you come from?"

"From Foreignia!"

This absurd dialogue caused no laughter. I felt very embarrassed. The clown Piripipí approached me, inviting me to his dressing room. He was different from the others. Outside of the ring, he spoke with a heavy German accent. When performing he answered everything that was said to him without speaking a word by playing various musical instruments. His wife and daughter joined him in the final part of his act, where after having fought to obtain a large sum of money and then being accused of avarice he began to throw his coins onto a rectangle of wood that was lying on the ground in order to show his disinterest in them. As they fell there, each coin emitted a musical note. Piripipí got excited, and threw the coins in such a way as to play a waltz. The two women accompanied him, playing accordions, then the whole circus orchestra joined in.

I went into the dressing room feeling very nervous. His wife served me maté tea in a gourd with a silver straw. She was Argentinean. Piripipí, wearing a well-cut suit, shirt, and tie, still had his makeup on.

"Do not be surprised," he said. "A few years ago I lost my human face. I do not live in disguise. This clown mask is my real face. My old face remained behind in Germany: my family was Jewish, and they brought it with them to the concentration camp. I was a fairly well-known orchestra conductor. Thanks to a few loyal fans, I was able to hide in the hold of a cargo ship in Hamburg that brought me to Argentina. Another time I'll tell you how I became the clown Piripipí. I liked your joke. It's different. It allows for profound interpretations. It should not matter to us that sometimes the audience does not laugh. You've seen it already: when I drop my coins, some people look serious and some even cry. True comedy permits many levels of interpretation. It begins with laughter, and then arrives at the understanding of beauty, which is the brilliance of unthinkable truth. All sacred texts are comic at their first level. Then the priests, who completely lack any sense of humor, erase the laughter of God. In Genesis, when Adam believes he is guilty of disobedience and hides when he feels 'the footsteps of the Lord,' that's something humorous. God doesn't have feet; he is incommensurable energy. If he creates the sound of footsteps, we can't imagine that he wears clown shoes. 'Where are you?' he asks, pretending to be searching. If God knows everything, how can he ask a little human being where he is? This joke turns into an initiatory lesson when the 'Where are you?' is interpreted as, Where are you within yourself? I, not being anywhere, having no homeland, do not exist as a human being. I'm a clown. An imaginary being who lives in a dream world: the circus. But dreams are real as symbols. The spectacle takes place in a circular ring, a mandala, a representation of the world, the universe. The same door is both the entrance and the exit. That's to say that the goal is the origin. Interpret this as you like; you come from nowhere, you go nowhere.

"When we see beautiful horses, elephants, dogs, birds, and all kinds of animals working in the ring, we understand that consciousness can tame our animal nature, not by repressing it but by giving it the opportunity to perform sublime tasks. The animal jumping through a flaming hoop overcomes the fear of divine perfection and jumps into it. The strength of the elephant is put to constructive use. The cats learn to work together. The knife thrower teaches us that his metal blades, symbolizing words, can surround the woman tied to the target, a symbol for the soul, without wounding her. Words are mastered in order to eliminate their aggressiveness and put them in the service of the spirit: the purpose of language is to show the value of the soul, and that value is absolute surrender. The sword swallower shows us that divine will can be obeyed completely, without offering any resistance. The least resistance causes fatal injuries. Obedience and surrender are the basis of faith. The fire breather symbolizes poetry, illuminated language that sets the world ablaze. The contortionists teach us how to free ourselves from our ossified mental forms: one must not aspire to anything permanent. We must bravely build in impermanence, in continual change. The trapeze artists invite us to rise above our needs, desires, and emotions to the ecstasy of pure ideas. They evolve toward the celestial, which is to say the sublime mind. The magicians tell us that life is a marvel: we do not perform the miracles; we learn to see them. The acrobats show us how dangerous distraction is: achieving a balance means being completely in the present. Finally, the jugglers teach us to respect objects, to know them profoundly, to place our interest in them and not in ourselves. It is harmony in coexistence. Thanks to our affection and dedication that which appears inanimate can obey and enrich us."

After twenty days, when I thought I was going to be a clown forever, the real Pacifier Clown appeared. His face was swollen. Chalupa Clown had tracked him down at the bar to cut off his drinking. The performers thanked me for my collaboration, and as a courtesy let me give a final performance during which I cried genuine tears while at the same time squirting out fake tears three meters out. That night, when the artists had gone to dinner at the theater restaurant, Piripipí led me to the center of the empty ring and handed me a pair of scissors.

"Clip your fingernails and toenails and a lock of your hair." He lifted the rug and showed me a crack in the ground. "Leave these parts of yourself here. Then your soul will know that you have a root in the circus."

I did as he said, while Piripipí hummed a song:

> *Among the ten commandments*
> *there's only one for me:*
> *be as free as the wind*
> *while keeping my roots.*

"Now that your nails and hair are part of the ring, you'll always be in the mandala." He took the velvet box in which he kept his coins and placed it in my hands. "Throw them on the floor. If you follow the order they are in and the rhythm that I give you, you'll play the waltz." I did so. The melody did not sound out perfectly, but however ungainly it may have been, it had the power to move me. "My friend, hear this from someone who lost everything he had in one painful moment, then realized that thanks to that he had found himself: don't let yourself be dragged down by a false conception of money. Always earn it with activities that give you pleasure. If you are an artist, live art. If you are not going to be a professor of philosophy, why do you want that diploma? Leave the university; don't waste your time there. Life is composed of different pastimes for each individual. Play your own game. You'll see, when you're an old man and you take your grandchildren to the circus, some clown there will be saying, 'I am a foreigner, I'm from Foreignia.' See? You've left your mark here forever."

I followed Piripipí's teachings to the letter. I withdrew from the Department of Philosophy, where I had endured three years, and enrolled in experimental theater courses at the University of Chile. I did not stay there long as a student, because my handling of puppets had made me a good actor. I was given the opportunity to act in Cervantes' *La guarda cuidadosa,* Tirso de Molina's *Don Gil de las calzas verdes,* and George Kaufman and Moss Hart's *You Can't Take It With You.* From TEUCH I went on to the TEUC (Teatro de Ensayo de la Universidad Católica). There I performed in Giraudoux's *The Madwoman of Chaillot* and Cocteau's *L'Aigle à deux têtes.* I was fairly successful. I was then asked to act in the professional theater alongside the legendary Alejandro Flores, the best known of the Chilean actors. This did not mean performing for the *crème de la crème* on the weekends, but for the general public all through the week, two shows a day and three on Sundays. It was exhausting but exhilarating work. The play was called *El depravado Acuña;* in those years the popular imagination had been ignited by a serial rapist named Acuña. Alejandro Flores

was in his seventies by then, tall and slim, with a noble face, elegant gestures, long pale hands, a warm voice that resonated in his solar plexus,
and a sardonic, intelligent gaze. I am not sure that he was a great actor,
but he had a magnetic personality. In all the roles I saw him in—whatever the style of the play—he did not change. And this is what delighted
his audience so. They went to see him, and he never let them down.
Flores taught them that a man of the people, of the humblest birth,
could carry himself like a prince.

Although he was haughty at our first meeting, looking down at me
from a glorious height, he became my master from the moment he first
spoke to me.

"Young namesake, this is not an amateur theater. Theories are worth
nothing here; Stanislavsky and his cronies are no use to us. Nobody will
tell you how to talk, move, make yourself up, or dress. You have to figure that out on your own. On the stage, the one with the most saliva
swallows the driest bread. We are not working to go down in history,
but to bring home the bacon, not to be admired, but to have fun for a
couple of hours. It is your duty to entertain them, and if you can't make
them laugh you must at least make them smile. We are not seeking perfection, but effectiveness. Understand? Vanity will not do you any good.
All that is required is that you learn the text by heart. There is no such
thing as a bad comedian who knows his lines. If the audience applauds
you, you'll finish the season with us. If they don't like you, we'll replace
you with someone else after seven days. But since I see you're listening
to me with the respect I deserve, let me give you one tip, and only one.
Ask them to let you into the theater in the mornings. At that time no
one is there. The cleaning crew starts after lunch. There is a work light,
so you won't have to be in the dark. Walk around, not only on the stage
but also in the gallery and the auditorium; sit in each seat, take in the
space, the floor, the walls. Stand in the center of the stage, look at all
the angles, so that no detail escapes you. Integrate the room into your
memory. Never forget this: an actor's body starts in his heart, extends
beyond his skin, and ends at the walls of the theater."

TEATRO IMPERIO

Santiago de Chile — Estado 239 y Agustinas 867 — Teléfono 32627

EMPRESA: COMPAÑIA NACIONAL DE TEATROS S. A.

ALEJANDRO FLORES

RAFAEL FRONTAURA

CIA. NACIONAL DE COMEDIAS

FLORES - FRONTAURA

1.er Actor y Director

ALEJANDRO FLORES

Premio Nacional de Arte

Otro 1.er actor y director	1.a actriz
RAFAEL FRONTAURA	**MANOLITA FERNANDEZ**
Premio Nac. de Arte	

Actuación especial de la 1.a actriz   y

MARIA MALUENDA   **JODOROWSKY**

(Gentileza del T. Experimental de la U. de Chile)   Creador del Teatro Mímico

Actor cómico   Actriz de carácter

JORGE SALLORENZO   **DELFINA FUENTES**

Tarde a las 6,45 — **JUNIO 1953** — Noche a las 10

Poster for the comedy El depravado Acuña *by Santiago del Campo, in which Alejandro Flores played the role of Álvaro and I the mute Evaristo.*

I could see Alejandro Flores's effectiveness when the performances began. When speaking with another actor he did so facing the audience, never turning his head, like a cobra hypnotizing a crowd of apes. Every time the spotlight moved, whether or not the script justified it, he would move toward the illuminated area like a moth at night so that his eyes always gleamed. If another actor was speaking quietly, he raised the volume of his voice. If someone spoke too loudly, he would lower his voice to a mutter. He never let anyone else become the center of attention; he was the boss, and he made that clear at every moment. If someone had a long speech, he would fiddle around in order to attract attention, jingling a few coins in his pocket, struggling to adjust the knot in his tie as if his life depended on it, or simply having a coughing fit. He did all this in a pleasant, elegant manner, without any rudeness. It was an indisputable fact that the people came exclusively to see him. Flores liked indisputable facts. I remember one of his quaint phrases, uttered during conversation in the dressing room: "The fool, when he doesn't know, thinks he knows. The wise man, when he doesn't know, knows he doesn't know. But when the wise man knows, he knows that he knows. The fool, on the other hand, when he knows, doesn't know that he knows." Being bald, he wore a toupee. It was not of very good quality. Before going onstage, I noticed that a few locks of hair had fallen off it, leaving a visible patch of bare skull. I drew his attention to it. He, with exemplary self-confidence, did not even make any gesture to touch his head. "Don't worry, boy," he said to me. "All of Chile knows I'm bald." I do not know whether the calm he always exhibited was natural. Every day, before the curtain went up, a heavyset man of about fifty years old, with the face of a former boxer, would arrive carrying a doctor's bag. He and Alejandro Flores shut themselves in the latter's dressing room for a few minutes. "They're my vitamins," the star explained. "It's morphine," the other actors gossiped. Which was the truth? What does it matter! After the injection, even if the theater collapsed, the lead actor would have continued displaying his amiable, handsome smile. I remember on opening day we were all concerned because we could not find certain props that were necessary for staging the play. Flores shrugged. "The theater is a continuous miracle. If a play begins with a group of men in capes and the actors are missing their capes a second before the play begins, then when the curtain rises, the actors will be perfectly caped."

The villain was supposed to shoot Flores from the shadows at the end of the first act. Flores was meant to collapse, making the audience think he had been murdered, only to reappear alive and bandaged in the second act. In one performance, the revolver did not work for lack of blanks. Flores, who was putting on his boots, waited a few moments for the gunshot, and seeing that it was not going to come, exclaimed, "Acuña has poisoned my boot!" Then he collapsed. "Life is a gray road: nothing is ever absolutely bad, nothing is ever absolutely good" was another of his maxims.

Since the audience applauded my performances, Flores granted me the honor of visiting him in his dressing room. The first thing that drew my attention was a toilet seat hanging from a nail on the wall.

"Boy," he said, "however lofty the king may be, he still has to sit his buttocks on the miserable bowl. Hygiene, in most of the theaters where I act, is not very reliable. My faithful seat cover is always with me. In the same way that an actor respects his name, he must respect his ass."

I then noticed that on a tall stool next to this intimate object was a bronze sculpture consisting of fifteen thick letters thirty centimeters high, forming a shiny ALEJANDRO FLORES.

"Do not be surprised, young namesake: although as a sculpture they are a vulgar jumble, those letters deserve my veneration. Today's public is not attracted to the bag of bones that is my body, but to my name. While it is true that in the beginning I invented that name and put my energy into it as a father does with his son, today it has become my father and my mother. Alejandro Flores is a sound amulet that fills theaters. For example, when I go onstage the audience does not hear, 'Good morning,' but 'Alejandro Flores says good morning.' My name is what speaks and what exists. I am merely the anonymous owner of a treasure. I have heard that people in India keep statues of their gods in their homes to which they offer flowers, candied fruits, and incense, making the statues into idols, giving them the power to perform miracles through religious fervor. That is how I treat this set of letters, as an idol. Every day I polish them and perfume them. I offer the flowers people give me to them. When my mind is tired, I touch my forehead to them and recover. If business is bad, I rub them with my hand for a long while, and soon the money flows in. If I wish I had a woman to take away the night's worries, I prop my heart up on them. They never fail me. Choose a name with fifteen letters, because that is the number of the Devil Tarot card, a potent symbol of creativity. The devil is the first actor in the cosmic drama: he imitates God. We actors are not gods, but devils."

It was the first time that someone had told me that if one exalts one's name, it becomes the most powerful of amulets. Jaime, wanting to become assimilated in Chile, to be equal to others, hating exclusion, never signed with his surname. His checks bore a brief *Jaime*. The Polish-Russian name Jodorowsky bothered him. Over the years I grew to understand that one's first and last name contain mental programs that are like seeds; fruit trees or poisonous plants can grow from them. In the family tree, repeated names are the bearers of drama. It is dangerous to be named after a dead sibling; it condemns one to be the other and never oneself. If a girl is named after an old lover of her father's, she is doomed to play the role of his girlfriend for life. An uncle or aunt who has committed suicide turns his or her name, over the generations, into a vehicle of depression. Sometimes it is necessary to change one's name in order to stop these repetitions that create adverse destinies. A new name can offer a new life. This, I understood intuitively, was why most Chilean poets had achieved fame using pseudonyms.

I asked the actor to give me the great honor of polishing his name every morning. He flatly refused.

"No, boy. I know your intentions are good, that you admire me, but in order to be, you have to learn not to want to be anyone else. By polishing my letters, in a way, you would steal my power. Your name is Alejandro, like mine. Your devotion is bound to turn into destruction. One day you will have to cut my throat. In primitive cultures, the disciples always finish by devouring their master. Go and fertilize your own name, learn to love it, exalt it, discover the treasures contained in it. You have nineteen letters. Find the Tarot card called The Sun."

The performances continued. The audience filled the theater. My acting was getting better, causing more laughter and applause every time. On the day when a fan threw a bouquet of flowers to me, the lead actor once again called me into his dressing room.

"I'm sorry, young namesake, you must come here no more. I will give you seven days. I have to replace you."

"But, Don Alejandro, the theater is full for every performance, I receive applause, good reviews, and all my jokes make them laugh."

"That's the trouble. You stand out too much. You think only of yourself and not of the entire work, and I am the only one here who has the right to think of only himself. A wheel holds up an axle, nothing more. It is I who they come to see. Everything must revolve around me. Understand: I am taller than you, and taller than all the other actors. I only hire people shorter than me. And so I stand out. And that's fair. When you enter a game, you must respect its rules or the referee will expel you from the court. You have been increasing the humor of your scenes. Since I have to maintain the overall balance, I have to struggle to outshine you in every performance. If this continues, I will have a heart attack soon. Look, boy, I became an actor mainly out of laziness: I do not like to work or make any great effort. Above all, I do not like fighting to defend what is mine . . . And don't look at me like that, as if you think I'm an immense egotist. I don't have to give you what I got with my own efforts, with no one helping me. The audience that comes to this place, which not by coincidence is called the Empire Theater, is mine and no one else's. You don't get to steal it from me, shielding yourself behind the hypocritical belief that because you are young the old winner should give you his secrets and hand over what he's earned from a life of efforts. In any case, the people who come here correspond to my human and cultural level. They will never understand you: their ordinary taste will limit you. Go create your own world . . . if you can. You will have to shackle your inner child, which is afraid of investing and is constantly asking for things to be given to it."

"But Don Alejandro who will be able to replace me in seven days? In a certain way, of course second to you, I'm holding up the show."

"You're naive, namesake. In my company, all are necessary but none is indispensable, except for me."

I received the lesson of my life: when I attended my replacement's first performance, wearing a sarcastic smile, I saw that he was none other than the ex-boxer and injection assistant, grotesquely dressed in a costume that was a poor imitation of what I had created for my character. This clumsy man, with his disastrous diction, was more of a rock than an actor. Bathed in sweat, badly doing as best he could, he made me feel pity. I thought, "That's it for this play. At the end, people are not going to clap; Flores will finally see what I contributed." But to my surprise, the audience applauded with the same enthusiasm as always. The curtain went up and down seven times or more. The star of the show, with his long arms spread open amidst his modest supporting actors, received the usual ovations. *El depravado Acuña* finished up the season with a full house. I was reminded of a fable from Aesop: a mosquito comes and settles in the ear of an ox. It announces, "Here I am!" The ox continues plowing. After a while, the mosquito decides to leave. It announces, "I'm leaving!" The ox continues plowing.

I tried to form my own theater company, but very soon lost enthusiasm. I realized I did not like theater that imitated reality. To my mind, that kind of art was a vulgar expression: trying to show something real actually recreated the most apparent and also the most vacuous dimension of the world as seen within a limited state of consciousness. This "realist theater" seemed to me to be uninterested in the dreamlike and magical dimension of existence, and I still believe today that generally speaking human behavior is motivated by unconscious forces, whatever the rational explanations they may attribute to them. The world is not homogenous, but is an amalgam of mysterious forces. Viewing reality as nothing more than immediate appearances betrays it. Thus, detesting this limited form of theater, I began to feel repulsion for the notion of authorship. I did not want to see my actors repeating a previously written text like parrots. Making them creators, rather than interpreters, required everything other than speaking: their feelings, desires, needs, and the gestures they made to express those things. I decided to form a silent theater company for which purpose I began studying the body, its relationship with space, and the expression of its emotions.

I found that all emotions began with the fetal position—intense depression, extreme defense, hiding from the world—to arrive at what I called "the euphoric crucifix," joy expressed with the trunk erect and arms spread out as if to embrace the infinite. Between these two positions was the full range of human emotions, just as all human language stood between a firmly closed mouth and a fully open mouth, just as everything from selfishness to generosity, from defense to surrender, existed between a closed fist and an open hand. The body was a living book. On the right side, ties with the father and his ancestors were expressed; on the left side, ties with the mother. In the feet was childhood. In the knees was the charismatic expression of male sexuality; in the hips, the expression of feminine sexual desire; in the neck, the will; in the chin, vanity. In the pelvis, courage or fear. In the solar plexus, joy or sadness . . . This is not the place to describe everything that I discovered during this epoch. To deepen this knowledge, I did what many do: I began teaching what I did not know. I started a silent theater class. And, while teaching, I learned a great deal. (Years later, I became convinced that the healer who is not sick cannot help his patient. In trying to heal another, one heals oneself.)

My best student was an English teacher in a boys' boarding school who had a monstrous but extraordinary physique. He was extremely thin, with a head that looked as if it had been crushed from the sides;

even seen from the front, his face looked like a profile. His name was Daniel Emilfork. He had been an accomplished dancer. For sentimental reasons he had tried to commit suicide by jumping in front of a train; he had survived but lost the heel of one foot. No longer able to dance as he used to, for a few select admirers he would dance to Bach and Vivaldi records in his apartment, balancing on his good foot, moving his trunk, arms, and mutilated leg. Some friends took me to see him. I fell into ecstasy: here was the perfect actor for my silent theater. I suggested he collaborate with me. Daniel, earnestly melodramatic, told me, "I have suffered martyrdom beyond the stage. If you propose that I act in the manner you have described, you come as an angel to transform my life. I shall abandon the boarding school and dedicate myself body and soul to following your instructions. However, you must know that I'm a homosexual. I do not want any misunderstandings between us."

Around that time, the French film *Children of Paradise* had come to Chile. Seeing it, I realized I had invented something that had already existed for a long time: pantomime. I immediately christened the future group Teatro Mímico and started looking for beautiful young women to join the company while at the same time satisfying my sexual needs. At first, everything went very well. But after a while, I was astonished to find that the women stopped coming, one after another. I discovered with dismay that Daniel, apparently in love with me, was driving them away out of jealousy. I asked him to explain why what began as sweet wine should so quickly turn to vinegar; I ended up expelling him from the company. Emilfork, determined to continue his life in the theater, asked the directors of the theater school at the Catholic University to grant him an audition. They agreed to his urgent request, because the fame of his talent had spread across all cultural circles.

The audition took place in the school's small theater. There was a creaky wooden stage with burlap curtains in front of twenty seats. The directors, designers, and actors in this group were amateurs belonging to high society. They wore gray suits, ties, and their severely groomed hair shone. They told Emilfork to lie as if dead, and then, little by little, interpret the birth of life. My former friend, without giving anyone time to stop him, stripped naked and fell to the floor. He remained as he had fallen. Still, like a stone, apparently not breathing. A minute passed, then two, five, ten, fifteen, it seemed as if Daniel would stay there forever as a corpse; the examiners begun to fidget in their seats. After twenty minutes they began whispering among themselves, fearing that the actor had suffered a heart attack. They were about to get up when a slight tremor began in Emilfork's right foot, then grew more and more and spread throughout his body. His breathing, which had been unobservable, was now growing in volume and deepening until it became the gasping of a beast. Now Daniel, as if in an epileptic fit, dragged himself into each corner of the stage, uttering deafening howls. The energy that possessed him kept on increasing, seeming limitless. With flaming eyes and an erect penis, he now began to take huge leaps, climbing up the curtains, which soon broke free of their rods. Emilfork then shook the wooden walls that surrounded the stage. They shattered into pieces. Next, with incredible strength, he began unpinning the floorboards and waving them around as weapons. Then he jumped into the audience. The honorable members of the theater school fled, squeaking like mice, leaving the deranged actor locked inside. His screams were heard throughout the building for an hour. Then they died down. There was a long silence, followed by a few discrete footsteps inside the door. They opened it, trembling. Daniel Emilfork emerged, impeccably dressed, well groomed, calm, with his usual gestures like those of a Russian prince. He looked at the group from the heights of a profound contempt. "You bunch of ninnies, you'll never know what life is, and so you won't know what real theater is. You don't deserve me. I withdraw my application for admission." And he not only left the school, but he left Chile. He moved to France, never spoke Spanish again, and lived unceasingly in the world of theater and film, enduring innumerable privations until he finally achieved fame.

We were all affected by Emilfork's departure to France. Some of us, more than others, felt asphyxiated living in Santiago de Chile. Television was

First reunion. From left to right: Daniel Emilfork, Alejandro Jodorowsky, Jacques Sternberg, the incendiary anarchist Fedorov, Fernando Arrabal, Topor, Lis (Arrabal's wife), and Toyen (surrealist

not yet fully commercialized, and one had the sensation that nothing new could happen in this city so far from Europe that was surrounded by a ring of mountains that felt like prison walls. There were always the same people, always the same streets. I knew that there were great mimes in France: Ettienne Decroux, Jean Louis Barrault, and above all, Marcel Marceau. If I wanted to improve my art I should do as Emilfork, drop everything and leave. But I had some very close ties that kept me there. First of all, there were my friends, girlfriends, and my commitments to the Teatro Mímico, which had already held some successful performances. Then there was my ambition to test the effectiveness of the poetic act on a large scale. Finally, deep down in the shadows, there was my desire to take revenge on my parents, to rub their faces in the suffering they had caused me through their lack of understanding. I discovered that rancor can be as constraining as love and entered into a foggy period during which I was unable to make decisions; a deep inertia had taken possession of my soul. I spent the days locked in my studio, reading. I excused this manner of killing time by telling myself that in order to know an author, one had to read all his works. At a forced pace I read everything by Kafka, Dostoyevsky, García Lorca, André Breton, H. G. Wells, Jack London, and oddly enough, Bernard Shaw.

One night my poet friends showed up, almost too drunk to stand, dressed in black and carrying a funeral wreath with my name on it. They lit candles and sat around me, pretending to cry while drinking even more wine. Reality was dancing again: at two in the morning, someone knocked frantically on the door. We opened it. My father walked in barefoot, waving a lamp.

"Alejandro, our house burned down!"

"The Matucana house?"

"Yes, my house, your house, with the furniture, clothes, Raquel's piano, everything!"

"Oh, my writing!"

"Fuck your writing! You're thinking about some filthy sheets of paper and not my money that I kept in the shoe box in the closet, my stamp albums, twenty years' worth of collecting, my cycling shoes, the porcelain your mother kept since we got married, you don't have a heart, you don't have anything, I don't know who you are, we thought we'd come to sleep here, but this is a nest of drunks, we'll go to a hotel!"

And he grunted in exasperation while the poets, elated with the news, danced around. We took up a collection to rent three victorias. We made the journey to Matucana. The weary steps of the horses gave a metallic voice to the dying night. We improvised elegies to the burned house over the rhythm of the horseshoes.

When we arrived, the fire was out. No one was there. Sandwiched between two ugly concrete buildings, my old home slept like a black bird. The poets got out of the carriages and danced in front of the remains, celebrating the end of one world and the rebirth of another. They dug through the rubble in search of the red worm into which the phoenix would have transformed itself. They found nothing but my mother's blackened corset. Ah, poor Sara Felicidad! After all those years without exercise, spending ten hours a day behind the shop counter to the point that her elbows were covered with calluses from so much leaning on that hard surface, and also eating compulsively to compensate for the lack of love in her life, she had grown fat, lost her figure, and felt as if she was drowning beneath a magma of flesh, while my father, under the pretext of door-to-door sales, had become the "neighborhood Casanova," riding his bicycle around, committing adultery left and right with female customers. In order to set herself limits that would reassure her that she was alive, that the world was governed by infallible laws, that she was not open like a river to the thirsty snout of any rapacious beast that might arrive, Sara had donned this corset, constructed of steel rods, which encased her from breasts to midthigh. The first thing she did when she awoke in the morning was to shout for the maid, who came grumbling as usual to help her to tie its laces. She exited her bedroom rigid but with form, her animal nature compressed, a self-confident lady feeling no shyness in front of the scrutinizing gaze of others. At night, returning from the shop with swollen feet and eyes reddened by the neon lights, she would again call the maid to help her out of this instrument of torture. This was done at a time when we should all have been in bed. I always knew that I would not be able to fall asleep immediately. My mother would begin scratching herself with her long fingernails, which were always painted red. Her skin, dry after so many hours of confinement because the canvas fabric of the corset prevented her from sweating, made an insidious, pervasive sound like paper ripping. The concert would last for half an hour. I knew from the maid's gossiping that Sara soothed her itching from her neck to her knees by smearing herself with her own saliva. Her obesity, her elbow calluses, her swollen feet, her itching, were things that I always viewed with a kind of sarcasm, as if my mother were guilty of this ugliness, an ugliness that she had to hide in a corset. Now, watching the poets kicking around this blackened framework and giggling, I felt sad for her—poor woman, naively sacrificing her life simply due to lack of awareness. Her myopic husband, mother, stepfather, half-siblings, and cousins had been unable to see her glorious whiteness of body and soul. Punished as a child, considered an intruder even before her birth, given birth to apathetically, received into a cold cradle, she was a swan among proud ducks . . .

Dawn was breaking. Reality resumed its dance. A man passed by selling red heart-shaped balloons. With a harsh shout, I stopped the poets' soccer game. With my remaining money I paid the three carriage drivers and bought all the man's red balloons. I tied the corset to the volatile bunch and released it. It rose up until it was just a small black spot in the middle of the rosy dawn sky. I compared this ascent to the Assumption of the Virgin Mary. I started coughing and had to take a long drink. Perhaps it was then that I understood the close union that the subconscious forms between people and their intimate objects. For me, releasing my mother's corset, sending it high into the sky carried by heart-shaped balloons, was like setting her free from her daily imprisonment, her lackluster life as a shopkeeper's wife, her sexual misery, the blinders of an unwanted fatherless child, and her absolute lack of love.

I had spent all those years complaining about her lack of attention and tenderness to me, but I had been unable to give her the slightest bit of affection, blinded as I was by my own spite. As for her, a prisoner of her narrow consciousness, there was little I could give her. I offered my love to her corset, making it into an angel.

The burned house seemed to send us a message that one world was ending and another was about to be born from the ruins. This event coincided with the end of winter and the beginning of spring. Realizing that no carnival had been held in Chile for more than twenty years, we set out to revive the Spring Festival. There were three of us who had this idea: Enrique Lihn; José Donoso, later well known as a novelist (*The Obscene Bird of Night*); and I. Every day at six in the evening, the time at which people left work and filled the streets, we went out in costumes in order to create collective enthusiasm. Lihn dressed as a thin, electric devil, wiggling like a scarlet noodle, waving his hard arrow-tipped tail, questioning passersby about their intimate depravities with an underhanded canniness. Donoso, dressed as a nymphomaniac, wearing black with two soccer balls as breasts, went around sensually assaulting men who escaped from his attacks amidst collective laughter. And I, dressed as Pierrot, in white from head to toe, exuding a universal loving sadness, would nestle in the arms of women in order that they might cradle me like a wounded child . . . Other poets and a group of college students followed our example, and soon a euphoric costume show was there for passersby to see every day in the city center. Some astute shopkeepers made the most of the idea and organized a dance at the National Stadium. It was an unprecedented success. The seats all filled up, and also the stands, and then the exterior grounds and adjacent streets. One million people danced, got drunk, and loved one another that night. We, the initial performers, had to pay admission like everyone else. Nobody thanked us. We had turned into part of the general anonymity. Disgusted, knowing that a bunch of businessmen had robbed us blind, we went to drown our sorrows at a bar near the Mapocho station, where we drank under the spell of the strident noise of the trains. We no longer had the wisdom of the Bhagavad Gita: "Think of the work and not of the fruit." We were annoyed that we had not been recognized. I learned years later from certain bodhisattvas to secretly bless everything within my view. That night we wanted to be congratulated: "Thanks to you, a marvelous celebration has been reborn. You deserve an award, a cup, a diploma, or at least a hug or free entry to all the festivities." We got nothing, not even a smile. We decided to celebrate in the Mapuche style: we put the chairs on the table and sat on the floor with our legs crossed, forming a circle. We stopped talking, and each one of us drank with a funereal rhythm from his own bottle of rum until it was finished: one liter of alcohol per head. My friends crumpled in silence. I felt like I was dying. I was drowning in the excess of alcohol. I ran out into the street, threw up next to a street lamp, walked with my arms open to the sky, and finally sat down in the ditch at a solitary corner. The sadness of Pierrot began to invade me. Who was I? What was my purpose in life?

Thus I sat, ruminating on my ideas, pierced by the cold of dawn, when I heard the tapping of velvety paws. I raised my head, which I had buried in my chest, and saw the dog approaching. I do not say simply *a* dog, I say *the* dog for I have seen this dog again and again in my memory so many times that it has become an archetypal example of something marked by the divine. He was of medium size, with a shaggy coat that might have been white had not the vicissitudes of life turned it gray and crusty. He had a limp in his right front leg. In short, a miserable dog, with that look of doleful pride mixed with humility that is common to dogs without masters. He approached me with an intense need for companionship. His heart was beating so hard that I could hear it pounding. His tail, scarred from bites, was wagging happily. When he came up to me, he let a white stone fall from his mouth with great delicacy. His eyes revealed a love so profound, I had never before received such a sign of affection, and it made me suddenly see how little I had been loved in my life. Aided by drunkenness, which brought down the walls of my shame, I began to cry. The animal gave a couple of feeble jumps, ran a few yards away, stopped, came back, and licked the stone. I understood. He wanted to play. He was asking me to throw the stone so he could chase it, pick it up in his mouth, and bring it back to me. I did so, many times, at least twenty. A cyclist passed by. The dog ran off after him. Both disappeared around a corner. They did not return. I was alone with the white stone. That stone was my ancestor. Millions of years old, it had dreamed of speaking, and there I was, Pierrot, as white as the stone, becoming its voice. What did it want to say? I waited to receive the most beautiful of poems, dictated by this stone dropped from the muzzle of a dog. In my mind I received something that I can only compare to a blow from a hammer! This stone was going to last longer than me! I understood with a hallucinatory lucidity that I was a mortal being. My body, with which I so deeply identified, was going to age, rot, and disintegrate. My memory was going to dissolve into nothing. My words, my consciousness, everything, would fall into the black well of oblivion. The houses and streets would also disappear, and all living beings—the planet, the sun, the moon, the stars, the entire universe.

I flung the white stone away, as if it were a witch: it had injected an anguish that would last for all of the short life that indifferent fate had granted me. I had not received any metaphysical bromides from my father. He had never inculcated any idea of an afterlife in my youthful mind: reincarnation, the hope of a merciful God, an eternal soul, or all those myths that the religions so effectively proclaim in order to comfort the mortals . . . I set off running through the streets, howling. No one was surprised to see this clown, thinking I was a last remnant of the carnival ball. I arrived at my studio, fell on the floor, and slept like a piece of inanimate matter.

This fear of dying would haunt me for the next forty years. It was an anguish that drove me to travel the world studying religions, magic, esotericism, alchemy, and the Kabbalah. It drove me to frequent initiatory groups, to meditate in the style of numerous schools, to seek out teachers, and in short wherever I went to search without limits for something that might console me in light of my transient existence. If I did not conquer death how could I live, create, love, prosper? I felt separated not only from the world but also from life. Those who thought they knew me only knew the makeup on a corpse. During those excruciating years, all the works I accomplished, as well as all my love affairs, were anesthetics to help me bear the anguish that gnawed at my soul. But in the depths of my being, in a hazy kind of way, I knew that this state of permanent agony was a disease that I had to cure by becoming my own therapist. At its heart, this was not about finding a magic potion to keep me from dying, but above all about learning to die with happiness.

By a thousand ingenious methods (including selling myself for a couple of nights to an elderly millionairess), I earned the money to buy passage on an Italian ship, the *Andrea Doria*—fourth class, in a dormitory with twenty beds, living on dried scallops, wine made from water and powder, and flavorless tomatoes—bound for France. I gave away everything I had: books, puppets, drawings, notebooks full of poems, sets and costumes from the Teatro Mímico, a few pieces of furniture, and my clothes. With nothing but a suit, a coat, a pair of socks, a pair of underpants, and a nylon shirt that I washed every night; with no suitcase and a mere hundred dollars in my pocket; after throwing my address book into the sea I began a five-week journey up the Pacific coast to the Panama Canal, and from there to Cannes, where I landed in France without knowing a word of the language.

The act of throwing away my address book was a fundamental necessity for me. Those pages were my connection to the past; the connection was all the stronger for having been pleasant. I did not leave my country as a political exile, a failure in life, or someone hated by society. I was leaving a country that had accepted me as an artist. I was leaving a company of twenty mimes that already had a solid repertoire. I was leaving kind friends, many of whom were great poets, and impassioned young women, one of whom I could have married. I was also leaving my family for good; I never saw them again. Nor did I ever again see my friends: forty years later when I returned to Chile I found that they had all died, succumbing to tobacco, alcohol, or Pinochet.* It was a form of suicide for me to disappear. To rid myself of emotional knots, to stop being someone born of painful roots, to change myself into someone else, a virgin ego, permitting me—by being my own mother and my own father—to eventually become what I wanted to be and not what family, society, and my country imposed on me. On that third day of March, 1953, at the age of twenty-four, as I threw my address book into the sea, I died. Forty-two years later, in 1995, also on the third of March, my beloved son Teo died suddenly, also at the age of twenty-four, in the midst of a party. With him, I died once again.

To arrive in Paris without speaking French, with barely enough money to survive for a month, without any friends, and wishing to be successful in the theater, was madness. The painter Roberto Matta once said with humor, "It's very easy to succeed in Paris, only the first fifty years are difficult." I believed with ingenuous self-confidence that I was coming to Europe as a savior. The first thing I did after I got off the train at two o'clock in the morning was to call André Breton, whose telephone number I knew by heart. (In Santiago, the fervent surrealist group La Mandrágora maintained relations with the poet, who was married to a Chilean pianist, Elisa; he had nailed down the lid of her piano out of hatred for music.) He replied thickly, "Yes?"

"Do you speak Spanish?"

"Yes."

"Are you André Breton?"

"Yes. Who are you?"

"I'm Alejandro Jodorowsky and I come from Chile to save surrealism."

---

*[Dictator of Chile from 1973 to 1990 —Ed.]

"Ah, well. You want to see me?"

"Immediately!"

"Not now, it's late, I'm in bed. Come to my apartment tomorrow at noon."

"No, not tomorrow, now!"

"I repeat. This is not the time for visiting. Come tomorrow and I'll gladly talk with you."

"A true surrealist is not guided by the clock. Now!"

"Tomorrow!"

"Then never!"

He hung up. Only seven years later did I have the pleasure of meeting him, in the company of Fernando Arrabal and Topor, at one of the meetings held at the café La Promenade de Venus.

During those first months in Paris, I saw my illusions crumble. I made a living doing all kinds of miserable work: collecting old newspapers from apartment buildings in order to sell them by the kilo to an Armenian man who ran a paper mill, selling my drawings on café terraces, sticking stamps on mountains of envelopes, packaging suppositories for a flu epidemic, and so on. Through hard work, I earned enough money to study for three months with Ettienne Decroux. Pantomime had become a religion for me. I was ready to devote my life to it. I believed that my collection of laudatory newspaper articles and photographs showing my creations would secure me the master's admiration. After all, we were both struggling to establish the same art form, generally considered a decadent historical curiosity. I had never imagined that this legendary creator of modern mime, a man with a broad frame, large hands, and a nondescript face, would be so cruel, so bitter, and so envious of the success of others. I knew he had performed with his students in London that year at the same time as Marcel Marceau. Marceau's show was declared the best of the year; Decroux's was declared the worst. His implacable, inhuman technique, which required incredible effort to make each movement, bored the spectators. By contrast Marceau's finesse, his ingenuity, his airy gestures that conveyed everything so effortlessly, were enchanting to the audience. Decroux shuffled through my photos with ostentatious contempt, asked me to undress, and calling his son Pepé to act as a witness, proceeded to examine my body, classifying its defects with medical coldness. "Early stage scoliosis, Semitic body type with protruding buttocks, atrophy of the abdominal muscles: in a few years he will have a pot belly." He asked me to move. I tried to make some beautiful gestures. He concluded, "He pulls his elbows when he moves. Bad expressionist style." Then, dismissing me to oblivion, he left the meager room where he received his students. Pepé, with a cruel smile, handed me a receipt for three months of lessons paid for in advance . . . As I was leaving, I picked up a program. There I read that the teacher, in the company of his wife and son, had been giving a performance in this small apartment every night for the last two years for an audience of only four people.

The first lesson with Decroux was a paradox, like a koan: "Pantomime is the art of not moving." To explain this, he told us, "The turtle is a cat inside its shell," "The greatest force is the force that is not used," "If the mime is not weak, he is not a mime," and "The essence of life is the struggle against gravity." For endless hours, we studied the mechanism of marching, the expression of hunger, thirst, heat, cold, overly bright light, darkness, the various attitudes of a thinker, and finally, all the ranges of physical suffering: pain caused by diseases, broken bones, wounds (in the back, chest, side, extremities), burns, acid, asphyxiation, and so on.

We met in a large school gymnasium once a week. With an old man's lewdness Decroux declared, "Men do not interest me," and had us stand in the back. (I was reminded of the old pain of knowing that Jaime had eyes only for Raquel.) When he gave his demonstrations he rolled up his baggy trousers and, often, as if unaware of doing so, exposed his testicles. I hated his Chaplinesque imitations. He made mime into an art as strict as classical ballet. The only thing that was different was the awareness of weight: "Only idiots stand on their tiptoes." We analyzed the laws of equilibrium, the mechanisms of loads, pulling and pushing, we studied the manipulation of imaginary objects, we learned to create different spaces with our flat hands . . . The knowledge he transmitted to us was conveyed slowly, drop by drop, as if he were reluctant. Despite charging a very high price for his classes, he gave us the feeling that we were robbing him. He quoted a phrase from Breton to justify this attitude: "'A bad writer is like a water stain on paper; it spreads quickly but soon evaporates. A good writer is like a drop of oil: when it falls it makes a small spot, but as time goes on it extends to fill the entire sheet.' The lessons I'm giving you now will last you ten years." He was right. His surgical cruelty, which eliminated any sort of warm relationship, forced me to be the judge of myself without expecting any external confirmation. In order to resist contempt and deconstruction I had to seek and find my own values, like a fisherman who dives into the dark ocean and comes up carrying a pearl. I learned that creativity cannot be effective if it is not accompanied by good technique and also that technique, without art, destroys life.

When Marcel Marceau arrived six months later, my theatrical destiny took off. The mime accepted me into his company after a minute examination, giving me a very minimal role to show me that even if I had been somebody in my country, I was still nobody in France. Little by little I gained his appreciation and eventually rose to the highest role he granted to a collaborator: holding the signs announcing his pantomimes. Thus I accompanied him on his tours through several countries. While my friend slept late, exhausted from the previous night's performance, I would get up early and visit whatever teacher or sacred place I could find. Since I did not have the opportunity to realize my ideas, I decided to give them to Marceau. I wrote *The Mask Maker, The Cage, The Heart Eater, The Samurai's Sword,* and *Bip the China Salesman* for him, pantomimes that would bring new energy to his career. Having decided that I did not want to grow old making mute gestures with makeup covering my wrinkles, I bade adieu to Marceau. Unemployed again and with a young wife to support, I had to take a job as a house painter.

In this dance of reality it happened that Julien, the head of the company, was a member of a group organized by Gurdjieff and his collaborator, the philosopher Amir Sufi. Painting an entire house with them on the outskirts of Paris became a mystical experience. The owner of the mansion, an obviously incapable pseudoaristocrat, claimed to be an abstract painter and sculptor. He made striking splotches on large canvases using a whip dipped in paint. As a sculptor, he made imprints of his buttocks in a mold and used them to manufacture plastic chairs. We dubbed him the Furious. His wife had beautiful green eyes, and Julien loved her. One night, as an exotic spectacle, the Furious invited us to dinner with him and his friends in a pavilion that was painted in gold, blue, and red—colors that, according to them, were worn by the kings of France. We drank a lot of wine. Possessed by a poetic furor, I improvised verses composed exclusively of insults. The guests were terrified and began to leave. When only we three painters remained, an out-of-control "workers' trio," our trembling hosts placed three bottles of wine in front of us and went upstairs to the mezzanine to sleep. After a while, filled with the euphoria of breaking down limits, I went into their bedroom and lay down between them, not even taking off my shoes. Before falling asleep, I penetrated the Furious's wife, very briefly, as a way of saying good night.

Early in the morning, I left my snoring employers and went to work. The Furious arrived at noon, smiled at me, and set about painting his canvases with his whip as if nothing had happened. Julien, however, did not conceal his bad mood. He pointed to my abundant hair and growled, "With that artist's mane, you're not real to them. They take you for a fool. If you want to break down conventions, make yourself into a normal man, like us, so that you'll learn to savor the consequences of your actions. These people are dangerous, the power is on their side;

our lives are practically in their hands." And straight away, brandishing a pair of scissors, he cut my hair almost down to the scalp. Then he sent me to clean up a ceiling covered with spider webs, knowing that I had a phobia of those creatures: "Neither the poor, nor any sentient beings, have the right to have phobias." When I went to the bakery splattered with plaster and paint, my new look drew the attention of several well-dressed ladies. They desired me, taking me for a socially inferior man, while making a show of rejecting me. I realized that the world was composed not only of artists, who are a tiny minority, but also of millions of anonymous people, destined for oblivion. In those people beliefs, feelings, and desires took on strange forms. Something was wrong. My view of life was lamentable. I was not yet ready to accept life for what it was. I needed to take refuge in a theater, sleep and eat on stage, not read newspapers . . . and grow my hair back.

Just then, I was surprised to see a luxury car arrive, its seats covered in leopard skin. The chauffeur, wearing a blue Hollywood-style uniform, entered the house and inquired after me. I presented myself, covered in flecks of paint. "Monsieur Maurice Chevalier wants to speak with you." I followed the chauffeur, stepped into the Rolls Royce, and found myself face-to-face with the famous singer, who at that time was already over seventy years old. "The impresario of your trio, Mr. Canetti, who is also my impresario, recommended you highly to me." (While working with Marceau, I had made a foray into the music hall, directing a group of singers called the Three Horatios.) "I would like you to help me improve the gestures in my songs and put on a couple of comic pantomimes. I am returning to the stage after a long break, and I want to surprise the audience with new things. If you are a true artist and not a house painter, come with me." I took a moment to say goodbye to Julien, Amir, and the owners of the house, who, open-mouthed, watched me depart for good.

For a month, the old celebrity came three times a week to my staff quarters, two meters wide by three meters long, where we rehearsed with great discipline. Canetti, for his part, told me a secret: "Chevalier is already passé. His success does not interest me; I believe it impossible. Instead, I know a great young musician, Michel Legrand: I'm going to take advantage of the show to launch him. I'm hiring a one-hundred-piece orchestra, something never seen before. It will be an absolute triumph. He'll fill the Alhambra Theater. I'm asking you to accentuate his presence with your staging."

I set up the hundred musicians on a wide staircase, forming a wall at the bottom, each wearing a suit of a different color in order to reproduce a painting by Paul Klee. Legrand was dressed in white. His arrangements of popular melodies were truly outstanding. But he, his hundred musicians, and the monumental sound of the instruments, were all overshadowed when the old man entered, dressed as a vagrant, with a red nose and a bottle of wine in hand, singing "Ma pomme." It was a delirious success! So much so that the show, which had been expected to stay in theaters for a month, kept running for a year. The theater was renamed the Maurice Chevalier Alhambra. The singer rented an apartment across the street, so that every day he could look at the huge illuminated letters of his name.

From that moment on, I never ceased my theatrical and poetic activities. To relate everything I experienced during those years would be a subject for another book. Because Marceau's sign holder had fallen ill he asked me, as a special favor, to replace him for the tour of Mexico. I did so. I fell in love with the country and stayed there, founding the Teatro de Vanguardia and putting on more than a hundred shows over the course of ten years. We worked with the greatest actresses and actors of the day; we premiered works by Strindberg, Samuel Beckett, Ionesco, Arrabal, Tardieu, Jarry, and Leonora Carrington, among many others, as well as the works of Mexican playwrights and my own works. We adapted Gogol, Nietzsche, Kafka, Wilhelm Reich, and a book by Eric Berne, *Games People Play,* which is still being performed today, thirty years later, and for which I had to assert myself, fight against censorship, and at one point even spend three days in jail. Some of my performances

The cast of my theatrical work Zaratustra (Mexico, 1976). From left to right, back row: Henry West (musician); Héctor Bonilla (actor); Mickey Salas (musician), with his son; Carlos Áncira (actor); Isela Vega (actress); Jorge Luque (actor); and Álvaro Carcaño (actor), with his son. Front row: Luis Urías (musician); Brontis Jodorowsky; Valérie Trumblay (in her womb, Teo Jodorowsky); El Greñas (seller of programs for the play); Alejandro Jodorowsky with Axel Cristóbal Jodorowsky; and Susana Camini (actress), with her son.

were shut down; at others, members of the extreme right wing stormed the theater, throwing bottles of acid. I had to flee in the dark, hidden in the back of a car, to avoid being lynched when my first film, *Fando y Lis,* premiered at the Acapulco Film Festival. Gradually, between successes, failures, scandals, and catastrophes, a profound moral crisis was demolishing the fanatical admiration I held for the theater. Theater, as a profession, is characterized by a display of those vices of character that people who are not artists do their absolute best to conceal. The egos of the actors are displayed in full view, without shame, without self-censorship, in their exaggerated narcissism. They are ambiguous, they are weak, they are heroic, they are traitors, they are faithful, they are stingy, they are generous. They fight for recognition; they want their name to be bigger than everyone else's and to be at the top of the poster, over the title of the work. If they all earn the same salary, they demand that an envelope be slid into their pocket containing a few more dollars. They greet each other with great embraces but say horrible things about one another behind each other's backs. They try desperately to get more lines; they steal the scene by stealthily calling attention to themselves. They are full of pride and vanity but also have no security in themselves, they want to be the center of attention, and they never stop competing, demanding to be seen, heard, and applauded at all times, even if they have to prostitute themselves in commercial advertisements. They only know how to talk about themselves, or about humanitarian problems such as a famine, epidemic, or genocide if they happen to be the lead promoters of some superficial solution. To increase their popularity they pass themselves off as devotees, tagging along with the pope or the Dalai Lama. All in all, they are adorable and disgusting, because they show in full daylight what their audience keeps hidden in darkness.

I wondered, Would it be possible for the theater to dispense with the actors? And, Why not the audience? The theater building seemed limited, useless, outdated. A show could be created anywhere, on a bus, in a cemetery, in a tree. It was useless to interpret a character. The person acting—not an actor—should not be putting on a spectacle to

During the performance of Zaratustra *in Mexico, with Fernando Arrabal and the Zen master Ejo Takata. Photo: Hermanos Mayo.*

escape from himself, but to reestablish contact with the mystery within. The theater ceased to be a distraction and became an instrument of self-knowledge. I replaced the creation of written works with what I called the "ephemeral."

During a performance an actor should completely melt into the "character," fooling himself and others with such mastery as to misplace his own "person" and become another, a character with concise limits, made from sheer imagination. In the ephemeral, the acting person should eliminate the personality and attempt to be the person he is playing. In everyday life so-called normal people walk around in disguise, playing a character that has been inculcated by family, by society, or that they themselves have fabricated: a mask of pretense and bluster. The mission of the ephemeral was to make the individual cease to play a character in front of other characters, and ultimately to eliminate that character and suddenly become closer to the true person. This "other" who awakes amidst the euphoria of free action is not a puppet made of lies, but a being with minor limitations. The ephemeral act leads to the whole, to the release of higher forces, to a state of grace.

Without my realizing it, this exploration of the intimate mystery was the beginning of a therapeutic theater that ultimately led me to the creation of psychomagic. If I did not imagine this at the time, it was because I thought that what I was doing was a development of theatrical art. Before happenings began in the United States, I put on spectacles that could take place only once; I introduced perishable things like smoke, fruit, gelatin, the destruction of objects, baths of blood, explosions, burns, and so on. Once we performed in a place where two thousand chickens were clucking; another time we sawed through a double bass and two violins. I proceeded by searching for a place that someone would let me use, any sort of place, as long as it was not a theater: a painting academy, an asylum for the mentally ill, a hospital. Then I persuaded a group of people I knew, preferably not actors, to participate in a public presentation. Many people have an act in their soul that ordinary conditions do not allow them to carry out, but under favorable circumstances they rarely hesitate when offered the opportunity to express what sleeps within them. For me, an ephemeral had to be free to attend, like a party: when we staged them, we did not charge the guests for food or drinks. All the money I could save was invested in these presentations. I would ask the participant what he wanted to expose, then give him the means to do so. The painter Manuel Felguérez decided to slaughter a hen in front of the spectators and do an abstract painting on the spot using its guts, while at his side wearing a Nazi soldier's uniform was his wife Lilia Carrillo, also a painter, who devoured a grilled chicken. A young actress who later became famous, Meche Carreño, wanted to dance naked to the sound of an African rhythm while a bearded man covered her body with shaving cream. Another woman wanted to appear as a classical dancer in a tutu without underwear and urinate while interpreting the death of a swan. An architecture student decided to appear with a man-nequin and beat it violently, then pull several feet of linked sausages out from the crushed pubic area. One student came dressed as a university professor carrying a basket full of eggs and proceeded to smash one egg after another on his forehead while reciting algebraic formulas. Another, dressed as a cowboy, arrived with a large copper basin and several liters of milk. Lying in the container in a fetal position he recited an incestuous poem dedicated to his mother as he emptied the milk bottles, drinking the contents. A woman with long blond hair arrived walking on crutches and screaming at the top of her lungs, "My father is innocent, I am not!" At the same time she took pieces of raw meat from between her breasts and threw them at the audience. Then she sat down on a child's chair and had her head shaved by a black barber. In front of her was a crib full of doll heads without eyes or hair. With her skull bare, she threw the heads at the audience, screaming, "It's me!" A man dressed as a bride-groom pushed a bathtub full of blood onto the platform. A beautiful woman dressed as a bride followed him. He began to fondle her breasts, crotch, and legs, and finally, getting more and more excited, submerged her in the blood along with her ample white dress. He then rubbed her with a large octopus while she sang an aria from an opera. A woman

Smashing a piano on Mexican television, in 1969.

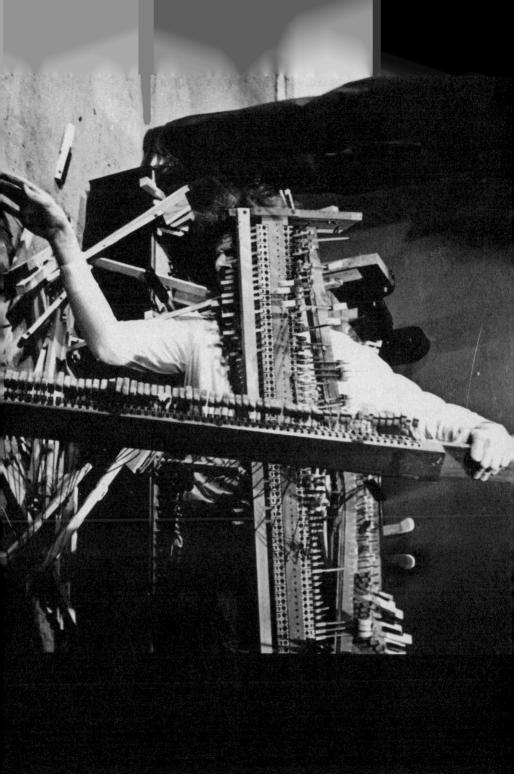

Destruction and restoration of a piano

with a great deal of red hair, pale skin, and a gold dress that clung close to her body appeared with a pair of shears in her hands. Several brown-skinned boys crept toward her, each one offering her a banana, which she sliced while laughing out loud.

All of these acts, these true delusions, were conceived and realized by persons considered normal in real life. The destructive energies that eat away at us from the inside when they are left stagnant can be released through channeled and transformative expression. Once the alchemy of the act is accomplished, the anguish is transmuted into euphoria.

The ephemeral panics were conducted without publicity, with the place and time given out at the last minute. On average about four hundred people would attend through this system of word of mouth. Thankfully, no articles about them were published in the newspapers. The government's office of performances, headed by an infamous bureaucrat named Peredo, exerted an imbecilic form of censorship. In one theatrical work I was forced to hide a character's belly button. In another, the actor Carlos Ancira wore a cape with two balls about the size of soccer balls hanging at the bottom; the troublesome civil servant considered them too suggestive of testicles and made us remove them. Thanks to the discrete and free nature of our ephemerals, we were able to express ourselves without any problem. The reaction was very different when I was invited to perform one on national television.

My work in the Teatro de Vanguardia had drawn the admiration of Juan López Moctezuma, a writer and journalist who was the host of a cultural television program. He had been given an hour of airtime without any commercials because an American TV series that attracted the majority of viewers was on at the same time on a different channel. Juan asked me to do whatever I wanted during those sixty minutes. I concentrated deeply, then knew precisely what ephemeral act I wanted to perform: what I had hated most, back in my dark days, was my sister's piano. That instrument, smiling sarcastically with its black and white teeth, showed me that Raquel was my parents' favorite child. Everything was for her, nothing for me. I decided to destroy a grand piano on camera. The explanation I gave to the public on this occasion was the following: "In Mexico, as in Spain, bullfighting is considered an art. The bullfighter uses a bull for performing his work of art. At the end of the fight, when he has expressed his creativity by means of the bull, he kills it. That is to say, he destroys his instrument. I want to do the same thing. I will put on a rock concert, then I will kill my piano."

I found an old grand piano in the newspaper classifieds that was within my price range and had it sent directly to the studio where the cultural program was filmed. I also hired a group of young amateur rock musicians. When the broadcast began, after reciting my text I gave the order for the group to start playing, pulled a sledge hammer out of a suitcase and began to demolish the piano with great blows. I had to use all my energy, which was augmented by the rage that I had built up over so many years. Smashing a grand piano to pieces is not easy. I progressed slowly but incessantly in the demolition. The few spectators called their family and friends. The news spread like an uncontainable flood: a madman is smashing a grand piano with a hammer on channel 3! After half an hour, most Mexican viewers had switched from their favorite programs to see what this strange man was doing. The phone calls rose in quantity from one hundred to a thousand, two thousand, five thousand. Parents' groups, the Lions Club, the minister of education, and many other notable entities protested. How dare this man destroy such a precious instrument before the eyes of so many poor children? (At that hour, the children were asleep.) Who had allowed this scandalous act of violence to be shown? (The American program being aired at the same time was a bloody war show.)

By the time I finished my work, lying amidst the rubble with a couple of pieces on top of me in the shape of a cross from which I extracted a few plaintive notes, the scandal had reached national proportions. The next day, all the newspapers mentioned the ephemeral. I had stripped Mexican art of its virginity in a brutal manner. I was admired for my audacity while also considered a cursed artist. Satisfied with the enormous notoriety I had achieved, I declared that on the next program

Ephemeral Panic (Paris, 1974). Bathing the father (dressed as an enormous old rabbi) with a liter of milk before castrating him.

Juan López Moctezuma would interview a cow to show that she knew more about architecture than university professors. The television station declared that this program would not take place, because "no cows are allowed in the studio." I answered, "That is not true, many cows perform in the soap operas." There was a fresh scandal in the press. The students of the School of Architecture offered me their department's amphitheater in which to interview the cow. I arrived there, in front of an audience of two thousand students, along with my cow, which a veterinarian had previously injected with a tranquilizer. I presented the animal with its rear, which I compared to a Gothic cathedral, facing the public. The interview lasted two hours with the laughter growing and growing, until a group of burly employees arrived to tell me, and my bovine companion, to leave that honorable place and never return.

These ephemerals showed me the enormous impact that they could produce, much greater than conventional theater. In those formative years I believed that in order to change the collective mentality I had to attack the fossilized concepts of society; it did not occur to me that a sick person needs to be healed, not assaulted. I had not yet conceived of the social therapeutic act.

After returning to Paris I met with Arrabal and Topor, and for three years we attended meetings of the surrealist group. Breton, a few years before his death, old and tired, was already a supreme pontiff surrounded by untalented acolytes who were more concerned with politics than with art. It was then that we founded the panic group. We opened it with a four-hour ephemeral that I have described in another book. This show ended a stage in my life. In it, I was symbolically castrated, had my head shaved, was whipped, opened the belly of a huge rabbi from which I extracted pork offal, and was born through a huge vulva into a river of live turtles . . . I came out of it sick, exhausted, and anemic. Despite its success—*Plexus* magazine called it "the best happening Paris has seen," and the beatnik poets Allen Ginsberg, Lawrence Ferlinghetti, and Gregory Corso praised it and included it in their *City Lights Journal*—I was not satisfied. I saw the specter of dark destruction prowling about

Ephemeral Panic (Paris, 1974). The " furies" use scissors to cut me a suit made of raw beef. The meat was later fried and served to the audience. Photo: Jacques Prayer.

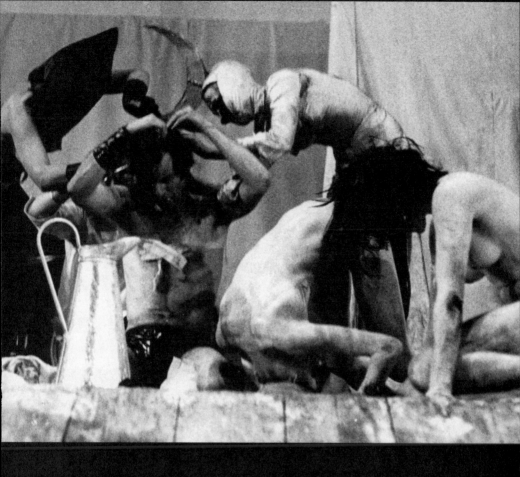

Ephemeral Panic *(Paris, 1974). One woman dressed as the moon and another dressed as an executioner shave my head on stage. There is a viper on my chest. Photo: Jacques Prayer.*

Ephemeral Panic *(Paris, 1974). I submit to torture in order to rid myself of my physical narcissism. The executioner whips me until I bleed. Photo: Jacques Prayer.*

me and felt more than ever that theater must go in the direction of light. In search of positive action I abandoned all exhibitionist theatrical activity, with its desire for recognition, awards, reviews, and mention in the media, and began the practice of theatrical advising.

If someone wanted to express his psychic residue, the serpents of shadow that gnaw at him from within, I would communicate the following theory to him: "The theater is a magical force, a personal and nontransmissible experience. It belongs to everyone. If you simply decide to act in a different way from how you act in everyday life, this force will transform your life. Now is the time to break away from conditioned reflexes, hypnotic cycles, and erroneous concepts of the self. The literature devotes a great deal of space to the theme of the 'double,' someone identical to you who gradually expels you from your own life, takes over your territory, your friendships, your family, your work, until you become an outcast, and even tries to kill you . . . I am here to tell you that in fact you are the 'double' and not the original. The identity that you think is your own, your ego, is no more than a pale imitation, an approximation of your essential being. If you identify with this double, as ridiculous as it is illusory, then your authentic self will suddenly appear. The master of the place will be restored to its rightful position. At that moment, your limited 'I' will feel persecuted, in danger of death, which indeed it is—because the authentic being appears by dissolving the double. Nothing belongs to you. Your only possibility of being is by appearing as the other, your profound nature, and eliminating yourself. This is a holy sacrifice in which you will give yourself entirely to the master, without fear. Since you live as a prisoner of your crazy ideas, your confused feelings, your artificial desires, and your useless needs, why not adopt a completely different point of view? For example, tomorrow you will be immortal. As an immortal, you get up and brush your teeth, as an immortal you get dressed and think, as an immortal you walk around the city . . . For a week, twenty-four hours a day, and with no spectator observing it other than yourself, be the man who will never die, acting as another person with your friends and acquaintances, without giving them any explanation. You will become an author-actor-spectator, presenting yourself not in a theater but in life."

Although I devoted most of my time to filming, creating movies such as *Fando y Lis, El Topo, The Holy Mountain,* and *Santa Sangre*—an activity that gave me experiences that would require a whole book—I also continued developing the art of theatrical advice. I established a series of acts to perform in a given time: five hours, twelve hours, twenty-four . . . It was a program developed as a function of the problem brought in by the patient, aimed at breaking the character with which he had identified in order to help him restore ties with his profound nature. "Whoever is depressed, delusional, or failing, that is not you." To an atheist, I assigned the task of taking on the personality of a saint for some weeks. To a woman who suffered from a hatred of her children, I assigned the duty—in a written contract, signed with a drop of her blood—of imitating motherly love for a hundred years. To a judge, concerned with the power he held to punish in the name of a law and a morality that he doubted, I assigned the task of dressing up as a vagrant to go begging in front of the terrace of a restaurant while taking handfuls of dolls' eyes out of his pockets. To an unhealthily jealous man of questionable virility I assigned the task of showing up at a family reunion dressed as a woman.

In this manner I created, overlaid on the personality, a person intended to visit everyday life and make it better. At this point my theatrical quest was acquiring a therapeutic dimension. I transformed myself from writer and director into an adviser, instructing people in order that they might free themselves from their personalities and conduct themselves as authentic beings in the comedy that is existence. The route I offered them was that of imitation. Gone was the inexpert youth who, believing himself to be imitating civil holiness, had sexually exploited a poor young woman. Now the process was based on a real desire to change.

Converted into a film actor in El Topo.
The character transforms violence into (musical) art.

If a good Catholic practiced the imitation of Christ, why shouldn't an atheist who is tired of his disbelief begin to imitate a priest? Why shouldn't a weak man, feeling impotent, imitate virile strength by painting his testicles red? Why shouldn't a woman, raised as a boy by her family, overcome her sterility by sticking a pillow under her dress to imitate pregnancy? I myself, imitating what I needed most—faith—realized how far I was from believing in God, in human beings, or in anything at all. I doubted art. What was it for? If it was to entertain people who were afraid of waking up, I was not interested in it. If it was a means of succeeding economically, I was not interested. If it was an activity taken on by my ego to exalt itself, I was not interested. If I had to be the jester for those in power, those who poison the planet and leave millions of people starving, I was not interested. What then was the purpose of art? After a crisis so profound that it led me to think of suicide, I arrived at the conclusion that the purpose of art was to heal. "If art does not heal, it is not art," I told myself, and I decided to unite my artistic and therapeutic activities. I do not wish to be misunderstood: the only therapy I had known was carried out by scientific minds, confronting the chaotic subconscious and trying to bring order to it, extracting a rational message from dreams. I approached therapy not as science, but as art. My goal was to teach reason to speak the language of dreams. I was not interested in art turned into therapy, but in therapy converted into art.

I owe this profound entry into the expression of the unconscious force—which, if we listen to it, is not our enemy but our ally—to Ejo Takata, who was my Zen master for a period of five years. Without really knowing what I was getting into, I agreed to be part of a group that meditated for seven full days, sleeping only twenty minutes each night. Full of courage, I knelt with my buttocks supported on a cushion, crossed my hands, put my thumbs together with minimal precision as if I were holding a cigarette paper between them, stretched out my spine, felt myself anchored in the ground and united to the center of

the Earth while my skull reached up toward the sky, relaxed my face
and then the rest of my muscles, eliminated all words and feelings from
my mind, and, believing my technique to be perfect, prepared to remain
there motionless, like Buddha, for a week. After barely two hours, the
torture began. My knees, legs, back, and entire body hurt. If I moved
just a little, the giant Mexican patrolling with his baton would give me
a hiding on the shoulders. If I winced when flies walked on my face,
the master would yell demonically. My imagination flared up, and so
did my anger. What was I doing here, suffering needlessly in the midst
of these enlightened shaved heads? I saw my shoes in a corner, like open
mouths, inviting me to fill them and leave this hell . . . At the sound of
a gong, we had to run to the dining room and gobble down a bowl of
rice, almost boiling hot, in two minutes, without leaving a single grain
in the bowl. We returned to meditate with bloated bellies. A concert of
belches and continuous farting began. With anger and shame I noticed
that the others, especially the women, were holding it in better than I.
At midnight we lay down like dogs to sleep on the floor for those divine
twenty minutes. We awoke to screams and insults and had to run to
sit and continue our meditation. We were allowed to go and defecate
once a day in a communal latrine, where a row of holes over an arte-
sian well invited men and women alike to completely give up privacy. I
resisted and resisted, out of pride rather than mysticism. Takata began
playing the drum, singing the Heart Sutra. Luz María, a chunky lesbian
in front of him who also was playing the drum, flew into a rage and
threw her instrument at his head. The monk made a minimal movement, ducking by a few centimeters so that the heavy instrument passed
millimeters from his ear and smashed into the wall, leaving a hole. Ejo,
not in the least perturbed, kept chanting the Sutra. No comment was
made about this assault.

By the fifth day I had become a scarecrow. My knees were swollen
and bloody, my belly was full of gas, my eyes were tear filled, and there
was a pain in my chest. At three in the morning, I was dragged by two
aggressive students to a room where the master was going to give me a

riddle, a koan. I was forced to fight and defend myself as the fanatical pair rained blows on me. I crept down the stairs and sat in front of the curtain hiding the sacred room.

"My chest hurts," I said. "I think I'm going to have a heart attack."

"Break yourself!" they replied, and left.

A gong sounded, indicating that I should go in. And so I did. There was Ejo, transfigured, dressed in a ceremonial robe that made him look like a saint. He looked at me with an objectivity that I construed as contempt and said to me as I knelt before him with my forehead touching the floor, "It does not begin, it does not end. What is it?"

I had been prepared to respond to a classic riddle, "This is the sound of two hands clapping, what is the sound of one hand clapping?" to which I would have raised my open right hand, answering with a broad smile, "Do you hear?" Or, "Does a dog have Buddha nature?" to which I would have responded by screaming, "Mu!" But when asked this question, so simple, so ingenuous, so obvious, I could only stammer, "Ejo, what do you want me to say? God? The universe? Me? You? All of this?" The monk took up a hammer and hit the gong, signaling for all the zendo* to hear that I had failed. I bowed, humbled, and began to leave. Then Ejo yelled, "Intellectual, learn to die!" These words, spoken in an atrocious Japanese accent, changed my life. Suddenly, I realized that all my searching up to that point, everything that I had done, had been carried out by a cowardly intellect that, afraid to die, was clinging to the iron bars of reason . . . Existence began when the actor-self stopped identifying with the observer-self. In a flash, I entered the world of dreams.

---

*Premises or room where zazen, Zen Buddhist meditation, is practiced.

SIX

The Endless Dream

I had my first lucid dream at the age of seventeen without realizing it. As I was not prepared for such an important event, I felt a profound terror and thought I was immersed in an anomaly. In the first part of the dream I was in a cinema in which an animated film was being shown. There was a landscape of large rocks in the film that gradually became softer and softer until they became dark rivulets that seeped out of the screen and into the room. I then saw that I was sitting in the middle of the vast cinema as the only spectator. I knew beyond doubt that I was dreaming, which is to say that I woke up in the dream. This knowledge that everything I saw was unreal, that my own flesh did not exist, that this lava of molten rocks swallowing row after row of seats was pure illusion, was distressing to me. Despite the fact that it was a dream, the danger frightened me. I wanted to run but I thought, "If I go through that door, I will go into another world and will never be able to return to my own; perhaps I will die." Then I panicked! My only hope of salvation was to wake up. I found it impossible. As impossible as if at this moment you were to lift your eyes from this book and tell yourself, "I'm dreaming, I must wake up." I felt trapped in a monstrous world that was trying not to let me go. I made an immense effort to get out of the dream, I felt paralyzed, I could not move my arms or legs, and the lava was coming toward my seat. It would soon bury me. I continued desperately trying to wake myself up. I ascended from the depths to my real body, which was sleeping stretched out on the surface like an ocean liner. I reintegrated myself into my body and woke up drenched in sweat, my heart beating rapidly. I felt that this dream was a sickness, though in reality it was a gift. Thereafter, I felt threatened every night when I went to bed. I was afraid that the dream world would swallow me forever.

This fear prompted me to read books about dreams, their mechanisms, their qualities, and how to interpret them. There are different kinds of dreams: sexual, harrowing, pleasant, and also therapeutic. In ancient times the sick would visit the temple hoping to dream with a goddess who would cure them. Dreams were considered prophetic. Freud gave them the role of revealing our psychic residue, our frustrated desires, our amoral impulses, systematically attributing symbolic meaning to certain images. According to Jung explaining the events in dreams was not important; the focus should be on continuing to live through them in a waking state by means of analysis in order to see where they would lead us, what message they were giving us. However, all these interpretative methods consider the dream as something we receive with the goal of getting it to act in the rational world. They are symbols, not realities. A patient says often enough, "I had a dream," but never, "I visited a dream." The next stage, situated beyond rational interpretation, is to enter the lucid dream in which we know we are dreaming; this knowledge gives us the ability to work not only with the content of the dream but also with our own mysterious identity.

When André Breton recommended that I read *Les rêves et les moyens de les diriger,* written by Hervey de Saint-Denys in 1867, I understood the essential part of the question: we all act as victims of dreams, as passive dreamers, believing that we cannot intervene in them. We often see hints that we are dreaming, but out of fear or ignorance we immediately flee from this sensation and remain trapped in the dream world. Hervey de Saint-Denys explained his method for controlling dreams: he did not have a very extraordinary goal, he did not suggest delving into the deep mysteries of being, he simply wished to "drive away unpleasant images and encourage happy illusions."

After reading this book I put my fear aside and leapt into the adventure of taming my nightmares as a first step in the conquest of the dream world. A lucid dream is not achieved by will. One must start by hunting for it. To do this one must prepare by not drinking alcohol or other stimulants such as tea, coffee, or drugs; by eating lightly; by not exposing oneself to a barrage of images on film or TV; and by convincing oneself that it is possible in the midst of a dream to realize that one is dreaming and search for an element, a gesture, something that indicates that one is not acting in the world we call "real." At first, when I could not distinguish well between the two worlds, in order to ask myself, "Am I awake or dreaming?" I would lean forward with both hands in the air, as if placing them on an invisible table, and give a shove. If I floated up, it was because I was dreaming. I would turn around in the air and try, until I succeeded, not to *see* myself fly but to *feel* myself fly. Then I would start to work on my dream. This is not to say that this is the only method; every lucid dreamer must find his own method. It is my belief that, given the vast number of neurons that make up our brain, we know everything but do not realize that we do. We need something to reveal it to us. I am reminded of the tale of the lion that having lost his parents was adopted by a sheep that raised him as part of the herd. He grew up peaceful, timid, communicating in little meows. One day an old lion hunted down one of the sheep and began devouring it while keeping the terrified young lion trapped underneath one of his paws.

"Stop shaking, my little friend, and eat a tasty meal with me."

The young lion vomited at the idea of devouring raw meat, yet he felt himself seized by a strange anxiety. He could not stop trembling, but not from fear. An unknown energy was shaking his body. The old lion brought him to the edge of a gently flowing stream.

"Look at your reflection and tell me, Do you see a sheep?" The young lion shook his head. "What do you see?"

"I see a lion."

"That's what you are!"

The young lion gave a thunderous roar for the first time in his life, and then began to devour the herbivore's remains.

Such an activity does not occur to us until we know we can have lucid dreams. But once the idea is revealed we can begin, first slowly and then with greater and greater frequency, to think about it during the day and to prepare for the night. The dreamer has a memory, he can remember what he decided to do while awake, and success is very likely. I proceeded slowly for years, with inexhaustible patience, until I conquered the world of dreams. I do not use the word *conquer* in the sense of winning a battle or a territory. For me, conquering means to live in the fullness of the dream world, which has no limits. In this conquest there are difficulties and also traps into which one can fall, remaining without progress for years. Drought periods may occur, during which the subconscious refuses to provide us with dream lucidity. We can dream unceasingly, all night long, and awake without remembering any of it. Patience. Faith. Suddenly, like a flower opening up, we will once again find ourselves lucid, living in this other world. These dreams teach us, they show us at what level of consciousness we have arrived, and they give us the joy of living.

I had to first overcome the nightmares: my dreams were populated by menaces, shadows, murderous persecutions, disgusting events and objects, ambiguous sexual relations that excited me while also making me feel guilty. Here, I was a character inferior to my level of consciousness in the real world, capable of misdeeds that I would never have allowed myself to perpetrate while awake. I repeated many times, like a litany, "It is I who dream, just as it is I who am awake, and not a perverse and vulnerable child. The dreams happen in me; they are part of me. All that appears is myself. These monsters are aspects of me that have not been resolved. They are not my enemies. The subconscious is my ally. I must confront the terrible images and transform them." I often had the same nightmare: I was in a desert, and a psychic entity determined to destroy me would come from the horizon as a huge cloud of negativity. I would wake up screaming and soaked in sweat. Now, tired of this undignified flight, I decided to offer myself in sacrifice. At the climax of the dream, in a state of lucid terror, I said, "Enough, I will stop wanting to wake up! Abomination, destroy me!" The entity approached threateningly. I stood still, calm. Then, the immense threat dissolved. I woke up for a few seconds, then peacefully went back to sleep. I realized it was I myself who had fed my terrors. I now knew that what terrifies us loses all its power in the moment that we stop fighting it. I began a long period during which whenever I had dreams, instead of running I would face my enemies and ask them what they wanted to tell me. Gradually, the images transformed before me and began to offer me presents: sometimes a ring, other times a golden sphere or a pair of keys. I now understood that just as every devil is a fallen angel, every angel is also a demon that has risen.

Once I became used to not being afraid, to turning threats into useful messages and monsters into allies, I was able to embark on further quests. Finding myself in unknown places I would rise up in the air in order to see that I was dreaming, then explore those places in search of spiritual treasures. Sometimes I met with obstacles such as a large wall, an insurmountable mountain, or a stormy sea. I had to give up a few times, but then I achieved the power of passing through matter. No obstacle could stop me then. For example, I jumped into the raging sea, ready to drown. I sank, but soon, down in the water, I found a tunnel that led me to the beach. I traveled through the inside of a mountain to its top; once there, I threw myself into the air, fell down, crashed on the ground, and immediately found myself standing looking at the broken body of someone who was not me. I realized that for the brain, death does not exist. Every time I killed myself or an enemy killed me, there was an immediate reincarnation.

Once I had conquered matter I began to encounter mysterious, threatening, mocking characters that I did not dare to approach, like gods who held secrets that I was unworthy of knowing. I said, "Just as

I challenged the nightmares, I must also confront the sublime beings, speak to them without being disturbed by their mockery, establish contact with them, learn those secrets that I think are forbidden to me. But in order to achieve that, I must first convince myself that I am strong, that I rule this dimension, that I am the master, that I am a magician." When I woke up within a dream I asked for things. For example, I want a thousand lions parading on the street. My desire was not realized immediately. A short time passed, then I saw the lions parading. "I want to go to Africa and see elephants." I went to Africa and saw elephants, and from there moved to the North Pole, among polar bears and penguins. Other times there were circus shows, operas, visits to cities full of baroque skyscrapers. I visited enormous battles from olden times and museums where I saw hundreds of paintings and sculptures. Once I acquired this power of transformation I was tempted to create erotic experiences. I created sensual women, half human and half beast, organized orgies, became a woman to let myself be possessed, grew a colossal phallus, visited an oriental harem, gave lashes with a whip, tied up schoolgirls . . . But when I surrendered to pleasure, the dream inevitably absorbed me and turned into a nightmare. Once desire seized hold of me, it made me lose the lucidity, and events escaped my control. I would forget that I was dreaming. The same was true for wealth. Once I became entrapped by a fascination with money, my dream ceased to be lucid. Every time I tried to satisfy my passions, I forgot that I was dreaming. Finally, I realized that in life, just as in dreams, it is necessary to distance oneself and control identification in order to stay lucid. I discovered that in addition to my sexual and monetary fascinations I was drawn like a magnet by the desire to acquire fame, be applauded, dominate the multitudes. I banished these temptations from my dreams.

I returned to working on my levitation and realized that every time I rose up in the air I became proud and vain: I was performing a feat that others could not achieve; I was worthy of admiration. I overcame this problem. I transformed it into something normal, useful, that was of service to me not only for traveling the world but also for leaving it.

I began by ascending. I felt enormous terror. It was the same feeling I had experienced in my first lucid dream, in which I did not dare to leave the cinema in which I was shut. I felt that a vital link tied me to planet Earth. I woke up with my heart hammering. Many times during the day I imagined my body floating up through the stratosphere into the depths of the cosmos. At night, dreaming, I achieved what I had desired. I overcame the fear of death, the sensation of weight and of drowning, and I began to travel between the stars with the speed of a comet.

It was an unforgettable experience to move through that calm vastness, where the great masses of planets and the incandescent stars move in an orderly dance, knowing that I was invulnerable, discarnate, a pure and conscious form. It is difficult to explain in words: the cosmos somehow enclosed me, like an oyster with its pearl, as if I were a precious thing; it cared for me as if I were a flame that must not go out; I represented the consciousness that matter had taken millions of years to create. The cosmos was my mother, singing a lullaby to make me grow. The words that I could utter were not mine, but were the voices of those stars. The feeling of floating in infinite space, surrounded by their complete love, made me awaken filled with happiness.

I do not pretend to claim that this initiatory process of lucid dreaming can take place in a short amount of time. In my case, these dreams did not depend on my will; they presented themselves to me amidst the multitude of ordinary dreams as genuine gifts. Sometimes I spent a whole year without having these sorts of experiences. Nor did they happen in the order in which I have described them; sometimes I investigated one type of dream reality, sometimes another, to then return and continue with the first. No rational order exists in the world of dreams, and cause and effect are abolished. Sometimes an effect appears first, and this effect is followed by its cause. Suddenly, everything exists simultaneously, and time acquires a single dimension that is not necessarily the present as reason conceives it. There is no world, but simultaneity of dimensions. What reason calls life here has another meaning there. I determined, as I wandered awake among my dreams, to enter the dimension of the dead.

After crossing a furious ocean in a small boat, I landed on the island where the door to the realm of the dead is to be found. There were lines of applicants, eager to enter. A gloomy doorman palpated them and decided who did or did not deserve to cross the final threshold. Those he refused were devastated at having to continue living. The doorman touched me and declared me dead. As soon as I passed through the door, I found myself in a landscape of green hills. The dead people—relatives, friends, celebrities—did not approach me, but looked at me kindly, as if expecting me to do something that would show them my good intentions. I threw empty envelopes in the air, which came down filled with treats and precious objects. It was a gift to the deceased . . . I woke up very happy, saying to myself, "Now I know that in my next lucid dream, I can converse with them. They have accepted me."

I can affirm to all who have not had these experiences that in some region of the brain, if it really is the abode of the spirit, a dimension exists where the dead people we have loved—as well as those we are concerned with but did not know, and for that reason cannot love—are alive, continue to develop, and take immense pleasure in communicating with us. One might respond that this survival is pure illusion and that only I exist in my psychic world. This is true, and yet not true. On the one hand human brains can be interconnected, and on the other hand they can be connected to the universe, which in turn may be connected to other universes. My memory is not only my own; it also forms part of the cosmic memory. And somewhere in that memory, the dead continue to live.

I dreamed of Bernadette Landru, the mother of my son Brontis: she loved me; I never loved her. She went with the newborn to Africa, and from there when he was six years old she sent him to me. I took care of him from then on. Her love for me turned into hate; she followed her own path. Her great intelligence led her into politics, to the most extreme communism. She was a leader. In 1983 the plane departing from Spain that was meant to take her to a revolutionary congress in

Colombia, along with other distinguished Marxist intellectuals such as Jorge Ibargüengoitia, Manuel Scorza, and others, exploded during take-off. Even today, I believe it was not an accident but a crime perpetrated by the CIA. I lamented that she perished so violently without having had the opportunity to engage in a confrontation, which for the sake of Brontis might have led us to a friendly reconciliation. Thanks to a lucid dream, I was able to meet with her in the dimension of the dead. It was in a small village similar to those in the north of France. We sat on a bench in a public square and began to talk. For the first time, I saw her calm, amiable, and full of friendship. We finally clarified that loving someone passionately does not make it obligatory for that person to reciprocate. We also clarified that although Brontis had had an absent, irresponsible father for the first six years of his life, I had settled that debt by taking care of him for the rest of his childhood and adolescence. Finally, we embraced as friends. She said to me, "Politically, I always considered you useless because you lived in your mental island, separate from the misery of the world. Now that you have decided that only art is worthwhile for healing others, I can help you. Politics is my specialty. Consult with me whenever you want." Today, before taking a position on world events that seem serious to me, I consult with Bernadette.

In that same dimension I find myself in the company of Teresa, my paternal grandmother, whom I never had the opportunity to know due to family quarrels. She is a small woman, thickset, with a wide forehead. In the dream I know that in reality we do not know each other, that we have not been together even once. I ask her, "How is it possible that you, my grandmother, never held me in your arms?" I realize this is an immoderate thing to say and rectify it with, "Rather, how is it, Grandmother, that I, your grandson, never gave you a kiss?" I suggest that I kiss her now and she accepts. We hug and kiss. I wake up with a clear memory of the dream, happy to have recovered this family archetype.

Thanks to these lucid dreams I can meet again with Denisse, my first wife, a delicate, intelligent woman, affected by madness. When I settled her in a home for the mentally ill in Canada, her home country, she began to build a table with twenty legs. She also watered a dry plant in a flowerpot by the window of her room. One day, a green leaf grew on the dry stalk. To Denisse it seemed that this plant, which had appeared dead, wanted to thank her for her care. "I finally understood what love is: being grateful to someone else for existing . . ." Along with her I also saw Enrique Lihn, who was still writing and giving lectures; Topor, who having passed through this mystery of death that had prevented him from appreciating life was now drawing images full of happiness; and my son Teo, on July 14, 2000, who would have been thirty, in the midst of his incomparable vital euphoria, having left this world at age twenty-four. In this dimension, he knew his grandmother, Sara Felicidad . . .

When I threw my address book into the sea, I cut off my family tree at the roots. I never saw my mother again. One night, shortly after I turned fifty, she appeared in my dream. I first heard her voice, which I thought I had forgotten, singing lightly. "Come in, do not be afraid." I realized that I was in a hospital. I opened the door and saw her, very tranquil, reclining in her bed. I sat by her, and we talked for a long time, trying to resolve our problems. She explained to me why she had been so locked up in herself, and I explained my silence for all those years. Finally, we hugged like we never had before. Then she stretched, closed her eyes, and murmured, "Now I can die in peace." I woke up sad, convinced that this meeting was prophetic: my mother was dying. I immediately wrote a letter to my sister, whose address I had thanks to the poet Allen Ginsberg, whom I had chanced to meet in Paris (he had been expelled from Cuba for saying in a radio interview that he had dreamed of making love to Che Guevara), and mailed it to Peru, where Raquel lived with my mother. I wrote, "Raquel, I do not know if Sara Felicidad is still in a condition to read my letter. However, even if it seems that she cannot hear, read the words I write to her. Her soul will capture them." The letter arrived two days after my mother's death. I kept a copy of it:

Cast of my Opéra Panique, ou l'éloge de la quotidienneté *(Paris, 2001). From left to right, back row: Edwin Gerard, Jade Jodorowsky, Adan J., Brontis J., Valérie Crouzet, Marianne Costa, Kazán, Cristobal J., and Marie Riva; front row: Damián J., Rebeca J., Alma J., Alejandro J., Dante J., and Iris J. Photo: Alberto García Alix.*

Dear Sara Felicidad:

I regret not being beside you in these difficult moments. If fate so wills, we will see each other once again before the great final voyage. We were born in tragic circumstances and remain marked for life. The pain we felt and the mistakes we made mostly originated from the world that other human beings created around us. It took me years to realize that the pain we had in this family that you tried to build was the result of our lack of roots, of our race that, having been so much persecuted, is foreign in all places. If there was anything negative between us, I have forgiven it. And if I committed the sin of ingratitude toward you, I beg you to forgive me. We did what we could in order to survive. But I want you to be assured: your essential being, your great strength, your unbreakable will, your fighting spirit, your royal pride, your sense of justice, your overflowing emotion, your appreciation for the written word, all these things have been a valuable legacy for me and have become part of my being, for which I am infinitely grateful. I remember from those days the importance you gave to the shape of the eyes, hands, and ears; how you hated canned food and artificial light; your love of flowers, your generosity in sharing food, your fundamental desire for order and cleanliness, your moral sense, your ability to work for hours and hours, your heart full of ideals. Yes, you suffered a great deal in this world, and I understand why. A few days ago, I had a dream about you. You were ill. But you looked calm. We talked as we have never done. We decided to stay in contact, you and I. I understood that you had received very little love during your time on Earth. I expressed my love as your son and blessed you that you might cease to suffer. You were exactly the mother I needed in order to set me on the path of spiritual development that was necessary for me. The truth is that without you, I would have gotten lost along the way. And now I want to tell you that I am by your side,

that I am accompanying you, and that I know you will finally
know the happiness that your name indicates. Trust in the will of
the Mystery, surrender to its designs. Miracles exist. All this is a
dream, and the awakening will be magnificent . . .

Your son forever.

In the dimension of the dead, they live by the energy of memory. Those whom we are forgetting pass like faded silhouettes, almost transparent; they appear in more distant places each time. Those whom we remember appear clearly, close to us, they speak, there is a grateful joy in them. But in the dark there are silhouettes of ancestors who lived centuries ago. It is because we did not know them that they fade away. If we merely move toward the areas where they are, they will appear more clearly and will speak to us in languages that we may not know, always with great affection. Those not familiar with this experience may have noticed that relatives and friends consider it very important for us to prove to them that they are not forgotten by celebrating birthdays, sending postcards while on a trip, calling them on the telephone. We know that, to the extent that others remember us, we are alive. If they forget us, we feel that we die. It is exactly the same in the world of dreams. If the unconscious is collective and time is eternal, one can say that every being who has been born and died is engraved in this cosmic memory that every individual carries. I would dare to say that every dead person waits in the dream dimension for an infinite consciousness to finally remember him or her. At the end of time, when our spirit achieves its maximum development and spans the entirety of Time, no being, no matter how insignificant it may seem, will be forgotten.

I also explored the dimension of the myths, where ancient gods live along with magical animals, heroes, saints, cosmic virgins, powerful archetypes. Before being accepted by them we must overcome a series of obstacles that are, in fact, initiatory trials. They present themselves in malignant form, attacking us, mocking us, or seeming insensitive, asleep, indifferent. Jung, in his autobiography, writes that he had a dream in which he found a sleeping Buddha in a cave, his inner god. He did not dare to wake him up. However, if we keep calm, if we do not run away, if we act with faith, if we are brave and dare to face them or awaken them, the monsters turn into angels, abysses become palaces, flames become caresses, the Buddha does not reduce us to ashes with his gaze when he opens his eyes. On the contrary, the Buddha communicates all the love in the world to us; we obtain allies who can be invoked in any sort of danger. Lucid dreaming teaches us that we are never alone at any moment; that individual action is illusory. Thought, trapped in the net of rationality, tries to reject the treasures of the dream world. But it is constantly besieged by forces coming from the depths of the collective memory; in real life, the dethroned gods have become clowns, film stars, football legends, political heroes, mysterious multimillionaires. We want to make them into powerful allies, but they have no consistency: they disintegrate very quickly into oblivion. In the dream dimension we encounter real entities with ancient roots. I could often see the arcana of the Tarot there, embodied in persons, animals, objects, or heavenly bodies; the symbols are living entities that speak and convey their wisdom. At first, when I tried to contact the divine beings without being prepared for it, I had a dream:

I had set up a round table in the living room of my house to dine with the gods and converse with them as equals. The first to arrive, despite his not being a deity, was Confucius, an imposing and enigmatic Chinese man, tranquil and immutable. As soon as we sat down, a young Hindu man with blue skin appeared wearing brilliant clothes and jewelry, elegant and powerful: he was Maitreya. Then, right in front of me sat Jesus Christ, a giant three meters high, so powerful that I began to get nervous. Another being emerged behind him: Moses, even taller, even stronger, with a severity that truly terrified me. I felt that behind the prophet, the incommensurable figure of Jehovah began to take shape. The room filled with such incomprehensible energy that I panicked. How did I, so weak and ignorant, dare to try to converse with these gods as equals? I tried to wake up. Confucius slowly disintegrated. As Moses and Jehovah dissolved into a grim shadow that started to fill the room, imprisoned in the dream world I begged Maitreya and Jesus for forgiveness. They smiled and amalgamated into one being, a gentleman in a leisure suit, like a wise grandfather. Smiling, he offered me a cup of tea. The dark liquid glowed. I awoke with my hair standing on end.

Encounters with divine archetypes are very dangerous if we do not prepare for them in advance. I would not exclude cardiac arrest from the list of possible dangers. I searched in alchemical texts to prepare myself for such a risky encounter. One treatise, the *Rosarium philosophorum,* written in Latin in the first half of the fourteenth century, inspired me with its enigmatic passages. "The contemplation of the authentic thing that perfects all things is the contemplation by the elect of the pure substance of mercury." Before attempting to unite the individual self to the universal force, it is necessary to contemplate, feel, and identify with that source, to accept it as one's essence, to disappear in its infinite extent. This force must act in our intellect as a dissolving agent. When the kind god in my dream offered me some tea, it was to tell me that I am the sugar cube that is to be dissolved in the hot liquid: love. "The work, very natural and perfect, consists of engendering a being similar to what one is oneself." I understood that for the majority of the time we are not ourselves; we live manipulating ourselves like puppets, presenting a limited caricature to others. We must create the being that resembles who we really are in ourselves like a model, discovering the pattern, the designs and order that it carries like a seed. A tree, in its formation, endeavors to grow in order to become the plant pattern that guides it. The engendering of the similar is not a doubling but a transformation: in order for the natural work to be realized, the self must transform itself into the impersonal pattern "I," the highest level of perfection. Thus we become the guides of ourselves. "Euclid has advised us not to carry out any operation if the sun and mercury are not united." The individual I and the impersonal I, the intellect and the subconscious, must act together at all times. It is for this reason that Maitreya and Jesus became one in my dream.

In Paris, I had the opportunity to meet the alchemist Eugène Canseliet, who published the works of the mysterious Fulcanelli. I remember him telling me, "The athanor is the body. The heart is the flask. The blood is the light. The flesh is the shadow. The blood comes from the heart, which is active, and goes to the flesh, which is passive. The heart is the sun, the body the moon. The positive is in the center. The negative is around the center. The two form unity." If we think that the universe has a creative center then the individual, who is a miniuniverse, should also have one. After reaching the age of fifty I decided to attempt the highest encounter through lucid dreaming: to see my inner god.

I am at a family dinner with my wife and children. We are eating on the terrace, around a rectangular table. It is nighttime, and the stars are sparkling in the sky. Cristina, the servant who took care of me so well during my childhood, serves us a roast goat kid on a cross-shaped plate.

"I'm dreaming."

I put my hands out flat in the air, support myself on them, and levitate. I speak from above to my loved ones.

"I am leaving this world."

They smile knowingly and begin to disappear. A profound grief fills me. This piercing sadness forces me to stay, but Cristina appears waving a pair of pruning shears, with which she snips at the air. "Go! If you rise you are an angel; if you sink you are a demon!"

Relieved, free, I begin to ascend. I see myself floating in the cosmos. The stars shine brighter than ever. I want to exit the cosmic dimension to enter the dimension where my consciousness reigns. Suddenly, all the stars disappear: I find myself in a space that appears to extend into the infinite. This dark void is intermittently traversed with the rhythm of a human heartbeat by circular waves of light, like the ripples that occur in a lake when a stone falls on calm waters. I see the center in the distance. It is a mass of light, like a sun without flames, vibrating, beating, producing iridescent undulations. Its colossal size compared to me, smaller than an atom, fills me with dread. I want to wake up, but I restrain myself.

"This is a dream. Nothing can happen to me."

"You're wrong, if the experience is too intense it could cause your death in real life; you might never awaken!"

"Dare to try it! Remember what Ejo Takata said: 'Intellectual, learn to die!'"

I decide to take the risk, fly speedily toward this tremendous being of light, and throw myself into it. At the moment of sinking into this matter I experience the immeasurable vastness of its power, for the glare is so dense that I can feel it in my skin . . .

In order to make myself better understood at this point, I should recall a crucial moment that the actors and I experienced during the filming of *The Holy Mountain*. We had already lost our link to reality after two months of preparation due to having been locked in a house without going outside, sleeping only four hours a night while doing initiatory exercises the rest of the time, plus four months of intense film shooting and traveling all over Mexico. The cinematographic world had taken its place. Possessed by the character of the Master, a sort of hybrid of Gurdjieff and the magician Merlin, I had become a tyrant. I wanted the actors to become enlightened at all costs; we were not making a movie we were filming a sacred experience. And who were these comedians who, also entrapped by illusion, consented to be my disciples? One was a transsexual I had met in a bar in New York; another was a soap opera hunk; then there was my wife, with her neurosis of failure; an American admirer of Hitler; a dishonest millionaire who had been expelled from the stock exchange; a gay man who believed he could converse with birds in Sanskrit; a lesbian dancer; a cabaret comedian; and an African-American woman who, ashamed of her slave ancestors, claimed to be Native American. I was inspired by alchemy in hiring this bunch: the first state of matter is the mud, the magma, the "nigredo." From this, through successive purifications the philosopher's stone is born, which transforms base metals into gold.

These people, drawn from the masses and not theatrical artists by any stretch, were supposed to become enlightened monks by the end of the film. Searching for magical sites, we had climbed all the Aztec and Mayan pyramids that had been largely rebuilt for the tourism industry. Thus we arrived at Isla Mujeres and contemplated the magnificent blue and turquoise waters of the Caribbean Sea—at last, something authentic. There, I decided to arrange a fundamental experience: after having all of us shaved, myself included, we went out on a small shrimp boat. After an hour, we were on the high seas. A resplendent blue-green circle surrounded us. The beautiful ocean, with its gigantic but gentle waves, stretched all the way to the horizon. I gathered the actors around me and, in a state of trance, said, "Let us jump and submerge ourselves in the ocean. The individual soul must learn to dissolve in that which has no limits." I do not know what happened at that moment. They looked at me with childlike eyes, offering me a faith that in fact I did not deserve. I then gave a karate-style scream and jumped, pushing the group into the sea. As soon as we fell, I received an enormous lesson of humility. We had jumped in wearing the costumes of Sufi pilgrims. We had on heavy boots, baggy trousers, sashes at the waist, roomy shirts, and long coats, as well as broad-brimmed hats. The hats were not a problem, they just floated; but the costumes became dangerously heavy as soon as they filled with water. I felt myself sinking into the depths of the sea like a stone, a descent that seemed to last for an eternity. Suddenly the whole sea was pressed against my body, with its incommensurable power, its unfathomable mystery, its monstrous presence. I was trapped in its superhuman belly, feeling smaller than a microbe. Who was I in the midst of this colossal being? I moved as well as I could, not sure that I would be able to save my life; perhaps I would continue sinking into the dark depths. I never thought to pray or beg for help; I had no time. Then the enormous mass of water threw me up to the surface. The dive had lasted only a few seconds, but we came up about fifteen meters from the boat. On land fifteen meters are barely anything, but offshore, such a distance is like kilometers. I had not considered that sharks and other carnivorous creatures might live there. On the boat the fishermen, taking us for crazy gringos, set about improvising a rescue. For our part, trained by those months of initiatory exercises, we waited calmly. The individuals bobbing on the waves became a collective being. The Native American, slapping gently at the water, said that she did not know how to swim. The Nazi, who turned into a champion swimmer, held her by the chin and helped her float. Corkidi, the photographer, completely forgetting that his task was to film transcendental moments such as this, cursed while helping to throw us a lifesaver attached to a long rope. The millionaire, who was closest to the boat, threw the lifesaver to the nearest person, the bird communicator, who reciting a mantra threw it to another, and so on until we were all joined, clinging to the rope. Without this tranquillity, we might all have drowned.

We boarded the ship in religious silence. We undressed and wrapped ourselves in towels. We began to shiver. When they recovered the use of their jaws, the actors, as well as the photographer, his assistants, and the shrimpers, began to insult me. Only two remained silent. The comedian, who in the film had the role of a thief, a symbol of the primitive and egotistic Self, had behaved as such in the water: without any concern for the group, he had simply emerged from the depths and swum with all the strength of his well-developed muscles toward the boat. The other silent person was my wife, the only one of the group who had not jumped. She had remained on the deck, watching us, paralyzed or simply disbelieving. Because of this, something between the two of us was cut off forever. In that moment, we realized that our paths were going in different directions. I realized that in order to become my true self I had to cleanse myself of this leprosy that was the fear of abandonment and accept my solitude in order to one day achieve genuine connections with others.

The actors, however, declared that they did not give a damn about becoming enlightened monks and that all they had wanted was to become film stars. The dip in the Caribbean Sea was a mistake that had taught them a lesson: they would never again obey my follies as a director. To begin with, they demanded a good breakfast with orange juice, eggs, toast, cereal, butter, and jam, plus no more improvisation beyond what was in the script. Otherwise they would quit. For me, this was an essential experience. I knew that from then on I would have the courage to face the subconscious without letting myself be invaded by terror, knowing that the ship of my reason would always throw a rope out to save me.

But let us return to the lucid dream. I had just thrown myself into that gigantic being of light, and just like in the Caribbean Sea, I experienced the immensity of its power. But this time, prepared as I was by the previous experience, I did not struggle to come to the surface as if escaping from the jaws of a monster, but let myself slide toward the bottom. I had the sensation of falling slowly while dissolving, as if the light was an acid. Finally, shouting with a mixture of euphoria and peace, I let go of my last crumb of individual consciousness. I was integrated into the center. I exploded into a succession of inconceivable shapes, thousands of them, millions, and they formed worlds that evaporated, oceans of color, words, phrases, conversations in countless languages intermixed like colossal labyrinths, and as time became an eternal instant, palpitating, opening itself into endless possible of futures, I was the creating nucleus, detonating unceasingly, never stopping, never silent, in countless metamorphoses. I was shaken by a kind of violent earthquake, and eight gates opened at my inconceivable extremities, or eight bridges, eight tunnels, eight mouths—what can I call them? And from them, other universes began, also exploding with delirious creations, joining in turn with the other universes until they formed an astral mass like a colossal hive.

How long did this dream last? I do not know. The concept of duration had been abolished. I was lucky, or unlucky, that a torrential rain accompanied by gale force winds assaulted the city that night. The blinds on my windows started banging, making a racket. I woke up thinking that I was still in the dream. It took me a long time to recover my reason. The wall that separated me from the subconscious had partly crumbled. Although I knew I was an individual, in my brain I could still feel the incessant creation of images.

My brain continued to produce worlds; it was an immense hurricane of creative madness. The "I" lived within a multifaceted demented god. Reason was a small boat sailing an infinite ocean, rocked by every storm, traversed by every entity, angelic or demonic, there was no distinction; by every language, living, dead, or as yet uncreated; by the inconceivable multitude of forms; by the absolute dismembering of unity.

After this extreme vision, which in certain ways I used to create my *Incal* books, I did not dream again for a long time. Lucid dreams started to become a popular topic, first in the United States, then worldwide. There was even an American who tried to sell machines that could produce them. Several books were published, some of them serious, others less so, as in the case of one author who claimed to have magical powers. I read the books avidly. They helped me to understand something fundamental: people who describe their lucid dreams describe things that correspond to their level of consciousness and to their beliefs. If they are Catholic, for example, they see Christ with great emotion. If they have some form of morality, the messages in their dreams will corroborate it. I remembered having a conversation with a psychoanalyst friend who gave me examples of dreams: the patients of Freudian analysts had dreams with sexual symbols in them, Jungians had mandalas and shape shifting, Lacanians had word games, and so on. That is to say, they dream in accordance with their analysts' theories, which for them have the power of dogma. I realized that something similar happened with lucid dreaming: a pretentious writer will direct her consciousness within the dream like a pretentious person; a mythomaniacal ethnologist will create adventures in his dream world in which he holds the nontransmissible secrets of indigenous magic. I examined my vision of the creative center. When I became one with it, I had eight gates. That is, a double square.

Tocopilla! Toco: double square. Pilla: devil consciousness. Was it a coincidence? Had the Quechuas dreamed my same dream? Does the eternal creator, Pillán, communicate with other creators through his eight bridges? Either that or the name of my hometown had influenced my images. Why not nine gates, or ten, or a thousand?

I decided to proceed with the greatest of caution. I had reached the peak of the mountain: I had blended myself into mad universal creation. What more could I want? For what purpose was I trying to modify my dreams? If I wanted to achieve something useful, I would do better to modify the dreamer, the being who is awake, who introduces himself into the dream world in order to try to control it. To do this, I had to undertake some other experiences, following a different path in the dream.

I observed that remaining conscious during the lucid dream required a considerable effort. Ultimately, the great lesson I learned was less about the extraordinary world I was able to create than about this requirement of lucidity. Without lucidity, nothing was possible. From the moment that I let myself be drawn into events, feeling the emotions they aroused in me, the dream absorbed me, and I lost the clarity. The magic only worked at a distance; what made the game possible was the clarity of the witness, while fusion with events narrowed the field of possibilities. I told myself, "Dreams have a reason for being. As products of universal creation, they are perfect; there is nothing to remove from them or add to them. The spider in itself is not terrible; it is only so to the fly. If I have overcome fear, the dream world does not have to affect me. And if I have conquered vanity and I see sublime images, they should not alter me either. In fact, the person who wakes up in the dream is not a superior being endowed with fabulous powers, it is a consciousness whose role is to become an impassive witness. If one intervenes in dreams, in the beginning one does so to experience an unknown reality, but later vanity can lead one into a trap. The microbe that is conscious of the Caribbean is not the Caribbean. Divinity can be me and continue being itself; I cannot be divinity and continue being myself." I decided then to set aside my will and surrender to the lucid dream as an observer. I should mention that being the observer does not mean removing oneself from the action, it means to live through it indifferently; if a beast attacks me, I defend myself without fear. If it wins, I let it devour me and observe what it means to be mauled. At the beginning of these new experiences, I found myself in situations where I could kill. I did not. While awake I am not a criminal, so why should I be in the dream? As a result of my work, which extended over several years, many things in my primitive personality were vanquished. By deciding not to intervene in the events in my dreams, I ceased having nightmares altogether. The distressing, disgusting, and perverse images also stopped. It seems that the subconscious, knowing that I was open to all its messages without wishing to defend myself or adulterate it, became my partner.

Whether or not to wake up within a dream becomes a secondary consideration. One reaches a level of consciousness where one knows that one is dreaming in all the dreams that occur. The dream images are experiences that transform us just like events in real life. Indeed, sleep and wakefulness go hand in hand so much that when speaking of them we refer to a single world. One stops searching for detachment, for lucidity, and humbly accepts the blessing. Lucid dreams become happy dreams. But this cannot be achieved all at once; one must pass through different stages. In my case, once I stopped playing the magician and had tamed my nightmares, turning every menace into an ally, into a gift, into positive energy, I began to dream of transforming myself into my own therapist. I healed emotional wounds and alleviated deficiencies. For example:

I am lying naked in my bedroom, just as it is in reality: a room with white walls and curtains. A bed made of boards, a hard mattress, a bedside table, a chair, and a small wardrobe, nothing more. No decorations. My father appears, the same age as me. He is on his bicycle, with a box full of merchandise on the rear fender: women's underwear, ties, trinkets. He is dressed in a suit copied from a photograph of Stalin. He asks me, with an intense expression of surprise, what I am doing here. I reply, "I am your son, you're not in Matucana. Now you live in my level of consciousness. Leave that bike behind; you're not a merchant, you're a human being. Forget your communist uniform and recognize that you're worshiping a false hero."

As I speak, the bicycle disappears, as does his suit. He is naked. I approach him with open arms. He draws back in fear or disgust.

"Calm down, stop being ashamed of your penis. I've known it's small for ages; it doesn't matter. Filial love exists, and so does paternal love. You were so afraid of turning out gay like your brother you eliminated all physical contact between us. Men don't touch each other, you said. And throughout my childhood, you never gave me a hug, never kissed me. You made me fear you, nothing more. At the slightest fault, you hit me or yelled at me in rage. It is a mistake to build paternity on a foundation of fear. I want love, not terror, to be what binds me to you. I was a victim as a child, but now that I'm grown I will hold you in my arms and you'll do the same." And without fear, I take him in my arms, kiss him, and then rock him like a toddler. And as he quiets down, I feel the surprising strength of his back.

Now he is a hundred years old, and so am I! We are two old men, tough, full of energy. "Love extends life, my father!" I still rock him, boldly, tenderly. "Because you never communicated with me through touch, I also refused all physical contact with my son, Axel Cristóbal." And now my son appears, the same age as I am in the dream, twenty-six years old. I caress him with great tenderness and ask him to cradle me as I have just cradled my father. He takes me in his arms, weeping with happiness, as do I . . .

Then I woke up. My son telephoned me and suggested that we have breakfast together. I told him to come and see me. As soon as I opened the door, I embraced him. He was not surprised and returned equal affection, as if we had communicated physically all his life. I explained the dream and asked him if he felt that he could give nurture as well as receiving it.

"Hold me like a child and rock me, whispering a lullaby."

At first Cristóbal did so timidly, but little by little, he was touched, and we established a contact in which filial and paternal love intermingled indivisibly. Finally, there is prosperity and peace in our relationship.

Naturally, without intending to, I transitioned from these dreams in which I healed myself to some in which I cared for others:

I am flying over the Champs-Élysées Avenue in Paris. Below me, thousands of people are marching, demanding world peace. They carry a cardboard dove a kilometer long with its wings and chest stained with blood. I begin to circle around them to get their attention. The people, astonished, point up at me, seeing me levitate. Then I ask them to join hands and form a chain so that they can fly with me. I gently take one hand and lift. The others, still holding hands, also rise up. I fly through the air, drawing beautiful figures with this human chain. The cardboard dove follows us. Its bloodstains have vanished. I wake up with the feeling of peace and joy that comes from good dreams.

Three days later, while walking with my children along the Champs-Élysées Avenue, I saw an elderly gentleman under the trees near the obelisk whose entire body was covered by sparrows. He was sitting completely still on one of the metal benches put there by the city council with his hand outstretched, holding out a piece of cake. There were birds flitting around tearing off crumbs while others waited their turn, lovingly perched on his head, his shoulders, his legs. There were hundreds of birds. I was surprised to see tourists passing by without paying much attention to what I considered a miracle. Unable to contain my curiosity, I approached the old man. As soon as I got within a couple of meters of him, all the sparrows flew away to take refuge in the tree branches.

"Excuse me," I said, "how does this happen?"

The gentleman answered me amiably.

"I come here every year at this time of the season. The birds know me. They pass on the memory of my person through their generations. I make the cake that I offer. I know what they like and what ingredients to use. The arm and hand must be still and the wrist tilted so that they can clearly see the food. And then, when they come, stop thinking and love them very much. Would you like to try?"

I asked my children to sit and wait on a nearby bench. I took the piece of cake, reached my hand out, and stood still. No sparrow dared approach. The kind old man stood beside me and took my hand. Immediately, some of the birds came and landed on my head, shoulders, and arm, while others pecked at the treat. The gentleman let go of me. Immediately the birds fled. He took my hand and asked me to take my son's hand, and he another hand, so that my children formed a chain. We did. The birds returned and perched fearlessly on our bodies. Every time the old man let go of us, the sparrows fled. I realized that for the birds when their benefactor, full of goodness, took us by the hand, we became part of him. When he let go of us, we went back to being ourselves, frightening humans. I did not want to disrupt the work of this saintly man any longer. I offered him money. He absolutely would not accept. I never saw him again. Thanks to him, I understood certain passages of the Gospels: Jesus blesses children without uttering any prayer, just by putting his hands on them (Matthew 19:13–15). In Mark 16:18, the Messiah commands his apostles, "They shall lay hands on the sick, and they shall recover." St. John the Apostle says mysteriously in his first epistle, 1.1, "That which was from the beginning, which we have heard, which we have seen with our eyes, which we have looked upon, and our hands have handled, of the Word of life."

There was an amazing coincidence between my lucid dreams and the bird man. In a certain way, the same laws operate in the waking world as in the world of dreams. Someone who has achieved conscious detachment through humility and love in order to be useful to others, communicating his level to them, must not only unite with them spiritually but also physically. The soul can be transmitted through physical contact. This was the beginning of the development of what I later called "initiatory massage." I told myself, the method by which Jesus touched the children, placing his hands on them and conveying his doctrine without saying a word, was not the method of a doctor. The doctor listens to a biological machine and discovers an illness there; this is not a communication from soul to soul but from body to body. Nor did Jesus act as a soldier, a guard, a warrior, or a master, people who command our bodies by imposing their rules, beating us, terrorizing us, humiliating us, and limiting our freedom. Nor did he act as a seducer, giving the body a purely sexual or emotional significance. He considered those things secondary and made his hands the continuation of his spirit; he transmitted consciousness through physical contact. Was this possible? To do this, he had to defeat the intellectual center that brings about the doctor's attitude, the sexual center that produces lasciviousness, and the physical center with its animal nature engendering abuses of power.

I concentrated on my hands and felt the power of evolution in them, those millions of years it took for them to become human, emerging from hooves and paws, evolving from the prehensile fingers to the opposable thumb, developing into extremities that not only manipulate instruments and seek food, shelter, and touch, but that can also transmit spiritual energy . . . Desiring to awaken this sensibility, I had the idea of putting my hands in contact with sacred symbols or beneficent idols. I stood before the Aztec solar calendar in the Museum of Anthropology in Mexico City. This great granite wheel on which the mysterious wisdom of an ancient civilization is engraved is a mandala with a face in the center surrounded by an inner circle of twenty symbols, with another circle on the edge formed by two serpents with their tails joined together at the top and their human faces forehead to forehead at the bottom. This mandala, today a symbol of the Mexican nation, drew me like a magnet. In the inexplicable dance of reality the room in which the monument was exhibited among other sculptures, also of immense value, was momentarily empty of visitors and the guard was absent, perhaps having gone to relieve himself. I was alone with the calendar. I stepped over the barrier and put my hands on the center, right on the bas-relief face that looks out at the viewer (the faces of the two snakes are presented in profile). As soon as I placed my hands on that surface, a chill ran through my body. I do not claim that the mandala produced it; it may have been a psychological reaction, not caused by the stone. However, wherever it came from, a tremendous energy filled my cells. My vision changed, and I no longer saw this monument as a disc, but as a cone. The apex was the face that was under my hands and the base, a hundred meters distant, was composed of the two serpents that formed the outer circle. That is to say, the stone began at the animal level and rose in twenty rings, each one formed by an encircling symbol, until reaching the angelic/demonic consciousness represented by the forward-facing face. I felt that this face, bright as a sun, looked at me as if I were its mirror. I felt that the body of a serpent was growing behind it. And if I was its reflection, my spirit also had the body of a serpent: two snakes in profile forming a circle, and now two snakes facing forward, this face and I forming another circle because in addition to this union at the top our animal natures were also intermingling at the roots, far down below. This intense experience lasted about five minutes. Then I heard the footsteps of the guard and also a large group of tourists. The room filled with people. I left the museum feeling like a different person.

A statue of the Black Virgin, an idol of the Roma people, is preserved in a small church in the town of Saintes-Maries-de-la-Mer in the Camargue region of France. Once a year during the summer thousands of Roma, coming from all corners of Europe, gather there to pay homage. The saint is paraded, sung to, and prayed to in an impressive public ceremony. After these celebrations, the nomadic people leave and the little church stands empty again. When I visited in the winter, the doors were unlocked. No priest was guarding the place. I approached the Black Virgin, who despite her great importance appeared abandoned. Impressed by her legend, I knelt before her. My first impulse was to ask for something, as all others do. But I held back. I approached her and started to massage her back. One might say that this is a subjective projection—that a piece of carved wood cannot have feelings— but through my hands I perceived the effort this idol made to bear the weight of so many requests. I stroked her back as if she were my mother, filled with a painful tenderness that was gradually transmuted into joy.

When I felt that she was restored I joined my hands, which despite the cold winter were full of warmth, and prayed, "Teach me to transmit consciousness through my hands." Her sweet voice resonated in my mind, "Give life to the stone." I did not understand the meaning of this sentence. I attributed it to a folly of my imagination . . .

Months later, during the holiday period, I was invited to give seminars on the Tarot in the south of France. The architect Anti Lovacs had a beautiful property on the slopes of the mountains in Tourrettes-sur-Loup with a sphere-shaped house in which I stayed for two months. On a long mountain road, from which one could see the valley extending to the coast, I found a rock that was almost oval in form and approximately six feet tall. Here was this mineral, simple, humble, anonymous, beautiful, a witness to the passage of millions of years. I understood the message I had received from the depths of my subconscious in Saintes-Maries-de-la-Mer. The Aztec solar calendar, with its symbolic system very similar to the Tarot, had placed its energy in my hands, entering through the intellectual portal. The Black Virgin, a powerful idol, had done the same, but had entered through the emotional portal. Now I had to face matter in its original state, without any human sculptors having intervened in its form. This was the body-to-body method. There was nothing significant about this stone other than itself. It was not part of a cathedral, a wailing wall, or the tomb of a demigod; it was itself, living with a rhythm infinitely slower than mine but also with a colossal capital of life. I remembered the five mottoes that appear on the engraving adorning the Rosarium philosophorum: *Lapis noster habet spiritum, corpus et animam* (Our stone has a spirit, a body, and a soul). And then *Coquite . . . et quod quaeris invenies.* The word *coquite*, being ambiguous—likely "sew"—I translated as "massage," which gave me "Massage . . . and find what you seek." *Solve, coagula* (Dissolve, coagulate) indicated to me that I should feel that I was dissolving the stone into its own consciousness, in order then to reintegrate it into its body again, this time as an illuminated material. *Solvite corpora in aquas*

(Dissolve the bodies in water) told me that in the action of massaging the stone, I should dissolve both my body and the rock in an absolute communion, feeling the love of the mysterious alchemical elixir that dissolves everything, that transforms all things into unity. And finally: *Wer unseren maysterlichen Steyn will bauwen / Der soll der naehren Anfang schauwen* (He who wants to realize our perfect stone / should first contemplate the nearest beginning). In order to surpass the individual "I" it was necessary that I let myself be possessed by the impersonal "I," the universal consciousness (the impersonal is closer to the truth than the personal), and thus, in a trance, reach the living heart of the stone. I decided to massage it for two hours every morning, from six to eight, before having breakfast with my students.

The first day, in a morning mist that submerged us in an abstract space, I saw the rock as an immense egg, insensible to my presence. It seemed clear that whatever I did, no contact would ever be established between us. But I thought of the fable of the hunter who wants to shoot the moon. He tries for years. His arrows never reach it, but he becomes the best archer in the world . . . I realized that this was not a matter of making the stone a living thing, but of trying to do so. The alchemist must attempt the impossible. The truth is not at the end of the road, but is the sum of all the actions we perform to get there. I felt that I should be naked while performing the massage. Patiently, with water, soap, and a sponge, I washed the stone. Then, aided by lavender oil, I began to caress it. The sun had not yet shone its brightest rays. Although I never ceased fondling the stone, its surface remained cold, impenetrable . . . True to my decision, I continued my massages every morning. Slowly, I began to love it as one loves an animal. I learned to forget the idea of an exchange, to give with no hope of receiving. I learned to love the existence of this stone without preoccupying myself with the question of whether it was conscious of my existence. The more insensible its body was, the more profound my massages. I remembered the words of Antonio Porchia: "The stone that I take in my hands absorbs a bit of my blood, and palpitates." Those two months passed by without my knowing it. On the last day, concentrating on massaging as always, I do not know why I raised my eyes but a black raven with a white spot on its chest was there, quietly perched on the rock. It locked eyes with me, squawked, and flew away.

The workshops were coming to a close. A student confessed to having spied on me one morning, and requested a massage. I agreed. I asked her to undress, to lie on a table. I started to massage her without anything in mind. My hands moved by themselves. Accustomed to the apparent insensibility and hardness of the stone, they felt not only the skin and flesh but also the viscera and bones. This body appeared to me to be divided by horizontal barriers, and I dedicated myself to establishing vertical connections from head to toe. The next day, my student gathered up her savings and set off on a trip around the world.

In the series of dreams in which the central character, the self, gives more importance to the realization of others than to its own realization, there was one dream that marked me deeply and that may have been the result of my experience massaging the rock:

I am sitting, meditating before the gates of a temple. I know that they will not let me into the temple because I am carrying a huge bag with me, seemingly full of garbage. I believe that this bag is part of me and that therefore I have the right to attend the ceremonies that are performed inside the temple accompanied by my burden. A group of men and women approach, each one sadly carrying a bag similar to mine. I rise, full of joy, and say, "If you have to see it to believe it, then take a look!" I open my bag and empty it out. A thick stream of black ink flows out of it, forming a puddle at my feet. The poor people follow my example and begin to empty out their bags, which are also full of thick black ink. We have created a dark lagoon . . .

I remove a thin column from the facade of the temple with which I stir this goo. As the stone rod rotates, long stems emerge from the pool, rising up many meters. Enormous sunflowers open up at their ends. These flowers attract light, and soon the place is pervaded by a golden glow. The towers on the temple also open like flowers. The people's joy is so intense that it infects me. I awake in a state of joyous excitement. Sunlight comes pouring in through the window of my bedroom.

In the Bible it is said in Exodus that Moses found a bitter pool while leading his thirsty people through the desert. God indicated a bush to him. Moses stirred the water with the bush, and it became sweet. Thus he slaked the thirst of two or three million throats (Exodus 15:22–25).

When Moses did not reject the bitter water, that is to say, did not reject the apparent nightmare and took action using the branches above him, making the plant into an extension of himself, the water was converted into his sweet ally. The conscious, when it recognizes the subconscious and surrenders to it with love, leads the subconscious to reveal itself with all its positivity. (This is the opposite of what was described by Robert Louis Stevenson in *The Strange Case of Dr. Jekyll and Mr. Hyde.*) In the world of lucid dreams we begin by acting, giving, creating. Then we have to learn to receive. Accepting the favor that the other person or thing can perform for us is a form of generosity. Knowing how to give must be accompanied by knowing how to receive. All the characters and objects in our dreams have something to offer us. All the beings that we see in real life, animate or inanimate, can teach us something. For this reason, little by little I set aside voluntary acts and obeyed the will of the dream more and more. At last, I felt very comfortable being what I was in this dream world: a serene old man, surrendering to events, knowing that by virtue of their manifestation, they are a celebration. The following are some happy dreams. I used to write them down. Today I no longer do. That which has a natural tendency to fade should be allowed to do so.

I am exploring the slopes of a mysterious mountain without any concern for the legend of it being inhabited by ferocious golden warriors. In an ice cave I discover a hot spring. I plunge my hands into the water, knowing that after healing all my diseases it will give me the power to cure the ills of others.

I am a child. I go into a school run by a family of fat people. The gym teacher is an elephant. During the exercises I become very fond of the animal. I grow two extra arms from my shoulders. I receive a diploma giving me the title of Rising Demon.

A Mandarin Chinese man lies comatose. A group of elderly priests apply a hot iron to his side to see if the pain makes him react. "You're wasting your time," I say. "He's definitely dead." The old men stop burning him, and the cadaver looks at me. Puzzled, I wonder, "What am I doing here in China? Who am I?" The dead man answers, "You are me. Worship the one who burns you!"

I have gone up a very high mountain in search of my dead son. I arrive in a valley by automobile. The snow has covered all the roads, but I drive with enthusiasm, despite the danger of falling off a precipice, because I am taking Teo to a huge party. He laughs. We enter a city. On the streets there are carnival parades, led by his brothers.

When we achieve the role of the lucid witness, when we submit our will to that of the dream world, when we realize that we are not ourselves dreaming, nor the person who is asleep, nor the person who is awake in the dream, but the collective self, the cosmic being, who uses us as a channel to make human consciousness evolve, then the barrier between waking and sleep, if it does not disappear, will at least be transparent. We realize that in the shadow of the rational world, the mysterious laws of the dream world thrive . . .

I suggest that my clients treat reality as a dream, initially as a personal and nonlucid dream, in order to analyze the events as if they were symbols of the subconscious. For example, instead of lamenting because thieves have ransacked the house or because a lover has left, I suggest that they ask, "Why have I dreamed that I was robbed or that I was deserted? What am I trying to say with this?" During my interviews I realized that events tend to arrange themselves, seemingly "by chance," into series in the dream that correspond to the metamorphosis of a single message. It is common for people to suffer from a breakup with a partner, lose money, or be robbed. In other cases, people who are caught up in conflicts that give rise to irrational anger may dream that they are suddenly in the middle of a hurricane, an earthquake, or a flood.

One client's mother, with whom he had had a love/hate relationship, had just committed suicide. After the cremation ceremony, his apartment caught fire. In this type of chain of events, reality presents itself to us as a dream inhabited by distressing shadows in which we are victims, passive beings to whom things happen. If we stop identifying with the individual self through conscious effort, if we are able to "let go" and become impassive witnesses to what seems to happen to us by accident, and even more, if we stop suffering from what happens to us and begin to suffer from suffering from what happens to us, then we can get past the stage that corresponds to the lucid dream and introduce unexpected events into reality that cause it to evolve. The past is not immovable; it is possible to change it, enrich it, strip it of trouble, give it joy. It is evident that memory has the same quality as dreams. The memory consists of images as immaterial as dreams. Whenever we remember we recreate, giving a different interpretation to the events remembered. The facts can be analyzed from multiple points of view. The meaning of something in a child's consciousness changes when we pass on to the adult level of consciousness. In memory, as in dreams, we can amalgamate different images. I spent three months during a harsh winter stuck in a hotel room in Montreal, Canada, waiting for a visa to enter the United States as an assistant to Marceau. The room was gray and depressing, the bed narrow and hard, the sink constantly emitted grunts like a pig, and the window invaded by arrows of neon light from a nearby pizzeria. Not wanting to remember those months as a time of such painful loneliness, in my mind I started painting the walls of the room in brilliant colors. I gave it a large bed with silk sheets and feather pillows, converted the grunts of the sink into gentle trumpet notes, and replaced the arrows in the window depicting a bleeding pizza with a blue lunar landscape in which luminous entities danced. I changed my nasty room into an enchanted place, as if retouching a bad photograph. Eventually, the real room was forever joined to the imaginary room. Then I started to dig up other unpleasant recollections in order to add details to brighten them. I turned egotists into generous teachers, deserts into lush forests, failures into triumphs.

I used a different technique with the closest memories, those I had experienced during that same day: I got in the habit of reviewing them before going to sleep, first from start to finish, then the other way around, following the advice of an old book on magic. This practice of "walking backward" had the effect of allowing me to place myself at some distance from events. After having analyzed, judged, and reprimanded or praised myself upon first examination, I went back over the day again in reverse and found myself to be distanced. Reality, thus captured, presented the same characteristics as a lucid dream. What this made me realize, more than ever, was that like everyone, I was to a large extent immersed in a dreamlike reality. The act of reviewing the day in the evening was equivalent to the practice of recalling my dreams in the morning. But to merely recall a dream is to organize it rationally. We do not see the complete dream, but the parts that we have selected depending on our level of consciousness. We reduce it to fit within the limitations of the individual "I." We do the same with reality: when reviewing the last twenty-four hours, we do not have access to all the events of the day, but only to those we have captured and retained, which is to say a limited interpretation; we transform reality into what we think it is. This selective interpretation is the largely artificial foundation on which we then base our judgments and evaluations. To be more conscious, we can begin by distinguishing our subjective perception of the day from what constitutes that day's objective reality. Once we stop confusing the two, we can view the events of the day as spectators, without letting ourselves be influenced by judgments, evaluations, and juvenile emotions. From this point of view, life can be interpreted as a dream is interpreted.

One client did not know how to get some young and unscrupulous tenants to vacate a house he owned. Something kept him from going to the police, even though the law was on his side. I said, "This situation is fitting for you. Thanks to it, you are expressing an old anxiety. Try to interpret it like a dream from last night. Do you have a younger brother?" He said yes, and I asked him if he had felt neglected when this intruder robbed him of his parents' attention. He answered that it was so. Next, I asked him about his current relationship with his brother. As I had expected, he told me that it was not a good relationship, considering that they never saw each other. I explained that it was he himself who encouraged the invasion of his tenants (who were younger than he) in order to externalize the anguish he had felt in his childhood due to the presence of his younger brother. I added that if he wanted to resolve the situation, it was necessary to forgive his brother, treat him well, and become friends with him. "You should bring him a big bouquet of flowers and have lunch with him, so as to establish a fraternal relationship and set aside the past, in which you felt displaced by him. If you do this, you will put an end to your problem with the tenants." He looked at me oddly. How could solving an old problem resolve a present difficulty? And yet, he followed my advice to the letter. He later sent me a short note: "I brought flowers to my brother and spoke with him on Friday at midday. On Friday night, the tenants left, taking all my furniture with them. But at least they left and I could get my house back. Could the loss of furniture mean that I have broken away from a painful part of my past?" This question revealed that my client was learning to decipher real situations as if they were dreams.

If we realize that we are dreaming in the dream world, then in the waking world, trapped in the limited conception of ourselves, we must jettison preconceived ideas and sentiments in order to immerse ourselves in the Essence with a naked spirit. Once this lucidity is gained, we have the freedom to act on reality, knowing that if we only try to satisfy our egotistic desires we will be swept away in the whirlwind of emotions, lose our equanimity and control, and thus lose the ability to be our own selves acting on the level of consciousness that corresponds to us. In the lucid dream, one learns that everything one desires with true intensity—with faith—will be realized after patient waiting. Knowing this, we must stop living like children, always demanding, and live like adults, investing our vital capital.

Two monks pray continuously. One is worried, the other smiling. The first asks, "How is it that I am anxious and you are happy, if both pray for the same number of hours?" The other replies, "It is because you always pray to ask, while I only pray to give thanks." To achieve peace, both in the nighttime dream and in the daytime dream that we call waking, we must become less and less implicated in the world and in our image of ourselves. Life and death are only a game. And the ultimate game is to stop dreaming, that is, to disappear from this dream world and integrate oneself into the one who is dreaming.

There is a dimension with which I have not yet been lucky enough to experiment: shared therapeutic dreams. It is said that María Sabina, the mushroom priestess, received a man who had a terrible pain in his leg. Neither the most sophisticated remedies, nor acupuncture, nor massage had been able to relieve it. The old woman divided a portion of mushrooms into two equal parts to share with her patient. She lay down beside him. They fell asleep embracing. In her dreams, she saw the patient as a wizard, devouring a lamb. The shepherd of the herd struck it with his staff, injuring a leg. María took the animal and, laying her hands on it, healed the injured limb. The healer and her patient awoke at the same time. The pain in his leg had vanished. He never again experienced such suffering.

SEVEN

Magicians, Masters, Shamans, and Charlatans

My first encounter with magic and madness combined into art was during my childhood. I was about five or six years old when Cristina came to work as our maid. With my childish eyes I saw her as an old lady, though in fact she was only forty years old; the air, doubly salt-laden from the sea and from the nitrate dust of the desert, had made furrows in her forehead and cheeks. All her clothes were brown, like the habits of Carmelite nuns. Her hair, stretched and tied back to form a bun, looked like a helmet. It was she, clean, quiet, and friendly, with large but sensitive hands, who gave me the touches that my mother withheld, who rubbed my feet when I had a fever, who dressed me in the morning to go to school, who baked my favorite pastries filled with dark caramel that we called *manjar blanco*. How I loved Cristina! My need for my mother was very affective and painful, I was united to her absence, but Cristina, with her rustic humbleness, was balsam for my wounded heart.

I was surprised when my father, seeing me in the arms of my beloved maid, said in front of her with a cynical, self-satisfied smile, as if she were deaf: "I'm the only one who will give work to a madwoman." Those words pierced my soul like a knife. I blushed, struggling to hold back my tears. Jaime shrugged his shoulders with a look of contempt,

236

and left. Cristina began to rock me in her arms until I fell asleep. At about three o'clock in the morning, I woke up in my bed. I heard my father's loud snoring and my mother's breathing, which sounded like grumbling. I had gone to bed without my supper. Hungry, and with a dry mouth, I got up to get a glass of water and a fruit. The rooms were dark, but from the kitchen came the faint glow of a candle flame. At first, Cristina seemed not to notice my arrival. With strange concentration, she was sitting on a stool before the bare table, gently and precisely moving her hands in the air. She seemed to be shaping something, creating forms, smoothing invisible matter, going over and over imaginary surfaces with her fingers. A long time passed, maybe an hour. I stood there, mesmerized, transfixed, watching something that I could not understand and that corresponded to nothing I had known. At last, tired, hungry, and thirsty, I could hold back no longer.

"What are you doing, Christina?"

She slowly turned her head and, still stroking the air, looking at me with glazed eyes, said anxiously, "Do you see? I'm finishing. When God took my son, the Virgin of Carmen came to me and told me, 'Make me a sculpture of me from the air. When it's finished and everyone can see it, your child will rise from his grave, alive again.' You see it, right? Tell me!"

What could I say? I did not know how to lie. It was the first time I had been in contact with madness, the first time I had seen a person acting as a unit without observing herself, without a social mask. Terrified, I felt frozen to the spot. The cold night wind, blowing down from the mountains, started sighing. Cristina embraced her invisible sculpture, distraught. "No, I don't want you to take him, damn you!" She seemed to be struggling against a hurricane, then, sobbing, put her face on the table with her arms dangling as if her hands were empty. After some seconds, she returned to being the person I knew. She gave me a glass of water, peeled an apple for me, and took me to bed. She stayed by me until I dissolved into sleep.

My second encounter with magic was in Santiago. Our group of young poets attracted many older homosexual intellectuals. Sometimes they were painters, sometimes writers, sometimes university professors. They had a unique culture, spoke several languages with French being the preferred one, and were very generous. Knowing us to be heterosexual they fell in love platonically, revered us in silence, and in order to enjoy our youthful presence often invited us to the German pub to drink beer, eat sausages, and listen to a string trio accompanied on the piano by Pirulí (Lollipop), a lanky effeminate man with hair dyed a violent yellow who played Viennese waltzes. Among these men was Chico Molina, about fifty, short in stature with a broad chest, slender legs, and tiny feet, who seduced our minds with his encyclopedic knowledge. He was a polyglot, could read Sanskrit, and knew every author or artist that one could name. One day, apparently more drunk than usual, he revealed to us that his intimate millionaire friend, Lora Aldunate, owned a magic mirror made in the fourteenth century. He had apparently bought it in Italy, in Turin, a city consecrated to the devil. If certain secret rituals were performed in front of it, the mirror would stop reflecting reality and would show old reflections. Molina swore to us that he had seen, more clearly than on film, a night scene in a forest in which naked women kissed the anus of a billy goat beneath the light of the full moon. Excited by such revelations, we rushed him out of the German restaurant and took him to the home of Lora Aldunate, which was very close by. We started yelling, asking him to let us in, demanding to see the magic mirror. A tall, distinguished, deathly pale man opened the blinds on the second floor and emptied his bedpan full of urine onto our heads. "You indecent drunks, don't play with magic! You will never see my mirror! When I die, I'll take it to the grave, locked in my coffin with me!" Molina looked at us with a wide smile on his simian face. "See? It's true. I never lie. As Neruda said, 'God forbid me from making things up when I'm singing!'"

Some time later, we learned that he was a pathological liar and fraudster. For months he had sparked our admiration by reading us chapters from his magnificent novel *The Swimmer without a Family* in

exchange for invitations to dinner, until one of our friends, a philosophy professor, discovered that it was a translation of Herman Hesse's
The Glass Bead Game, which had not yet been published in Spanish.
Well then, did the magic mirror exist, or was it a lie made up with Lora
Aldunate's complicity? His anger had seemed sincere when he opened
the blinds, but Lihn raised a doubt: no one fills a chamber pot with
urine in a single night; it was hard to believe that such a distinguished
man would accumulate so much of the yellow liquid just for the pleasure of collecting it. But countless depravities exist . . .

I have encountered this kind of certainty exhibited by Chico
Molina, claiming something reason cannot accept is the truth, in almost
all people who say they have had contact with higher planes. It was after
this that I began to consider that lying, apart from its despicable quality, also has a mystical utility. In the Bible, in Genesis, Jacob cheats his
brother Esau by persuading him to sell his birthright for a meal of lentil
stew. He then takes advantage of his father's blindness to impersonate
his brother and get his blessing. Later, it became clear to me that lying,
or "sacred trickery," as I called it, is a technique used by all masters and
shamans.

Thanks to Marie Lefevre, in 1950 I had my first encounter with the
optical language that is the Tarot. At what age had Marie arrived in
Chile? She never wanted to tell us. When we knew her, she was over
sixty years old. A small woman made up and dressed like Dracula's
daughter with her long gray hair dyed with a blue rinse, she lived in a
basement with her lover Nene who was an unemployed and uneducated
youth of eighteen years, but of an angelic beauty. After having heated
metaphysical discussions at Café Iris, we poets would arrive drunk
around three in the morning at her basement, knowing that a pot full
of tasty soup would be waiting for us there, heating up on a slow fire.
Nene, naked as usual, with a pink silk ribbon tied in the shape of a butterfly around his penis, slept soundly. She, who never slept, got up to
serve us cups of the delicious soup made from all the leftovers that the

nearby restaurant gave her in exchange for reading the Tarot to customers. Lefevre had drawn her own deck of seventy-eight cards. Instead of cups, swords, wands, and coins, she shuffled *sopaipillas* (coins), gourds of maté (cups), Shivalingams, male and female genitalia forming a unit (wands), and eyes above a triangle (swords). I remember some of her major arcana: she had a cowboy and a beautiful cowgirl in place of the Emperor and Empress. The Priestess was a Mapuche machi. The World was a map of Chile. Despite the ingenuousness of this deck, she gave readings of a surprising psychological accuracy, her very Chilean language contrasting with her strong French accent. I had removed money from my life without feeling poor, surviving on adventure, caught up in the present without ever thinking about tomorrow; for me, she predicted hundreds, thousands of trips all around the world. It was hard for me to believe her, and yet her prediction came true. To Carlos Faz, an exceptionally talented painter, she said, "Never travel by sea!" A year later on his way to America at a stop in Ecuador where the passengers were forbidden to disembark Carlos, drunk as usual, jumped from the ship toward the dock, misjudged the distance, fell into the water, and drowned. He was twenty-two. For me, this lady was an example of generosity, freedom, and subtlety. She did not tell Faz that he was going to drown, which would have become an order to commit suicide (the mind tends to fulfill predictions), but warned him of danger, leaving him the possibility of either confronting it or not. She also taught me that one can create miracles for others: somewhere in this world, there was a well-intentioned woman who would receive you at any hour with a humble smile on her lips, give you a bowl of soup, and read the cards for you, for free, just out of love for human beings.

Another teacher who changed my worldview was Nicanor Parra. When I met him I was a teenager, he a grown man, a mathematics professor at the School of Engineering. As a revolutionary reaction against the emotional poetry of Neruda, Pablo de Rokha, García Lorca, and Vicente Huidobro, he had declared himself an anti-poet. For us young people, his emergence in the literary world was akin to that of a messiah. After my awkward encounter with him at Café Iris, my pathological shyness kept me from visiting him. Stella Díaz had to help me. Making what for her was an immense concession, she covered the flames of her hair with a beret. "Nica doesn't want me to show up with my hair uncovered. He says that redheads drive the students mad." And she took me into the territory of the great anti-poet. Parra was an unassuming man, and the admiration of young poets encouraged him. We met many times, also with Enrique Lihn present. We talked in a small bar near the National Library, over that wonderful drink that is sweet chicha. One day Nicanor handed me a large envelope full of typewritten sheets of paper of different sizes. "They're various writings, a sort of literary journal. Can you organize them for me? I've reread them so many times that I can't see their value. I labeled them 'Notes on the edge of the abyss.'" To receive such a gesture of confidence from a consecrated poet was like a spiritual explosion for me. I spent many nights locked away, reverently reviewing these unpublished texts, sorting them by subject, eliminating repetitions. In a concise style—"I want a clinical-photographic art"— the poet described his inner life in prose. After fifteen days I returned the notes to him, copied onto regular size sheets of paper, in an order that seemed perfect to me. Parra never published them, nor did he ever speak of them again.

With a university education far superior to that of his predecessors, who were all self-taught, Parra had specialized in the study of the Vienna Circle and the work of Ludwig Wittgenstein. Galileo interested him just as much as Kafka, whose diary he admired above all else. He had his own interpretation of the famous phrase from the *Tractatus,* "What one cannot speak about, one must be silent about." For him metaphysics, like religion, was forbidden territory; likewise the expression of personal feelings. "The poet should not exhibit himself: the strings must be pulled from outside." Neruda and his followers presented themselves as great justices, great lovers, great humanists, with sublime anxieties and hopes—in short, as inflated romantic egos. Parra hid behind his intellect, then assumed one mask, then several. The poet was a professor with his tongue eaten away by cancer, a little man crushed by society, by women, a tragic clown; later he spoke through an ingenuous character who believed in Christ; then an old skeptic; and finally, he became a translator and took on the personality of Shakespeare. Lyricism was replaced by acerbic humor. "Knowledge and laughter become confounded." Ultimately, he invented himself. As I write these lines, Parra must now be eighty-six years old, and like Castaneda—"the warrior leaves no footprints"—I am sure that no one can boast of knowing him intimately. The anti-poet has made his heart into an impenetrable fortress. The words of Jesus, "By their works ye shall know them," cannot be applied to him.

The memories I have of Nicanor Parra, over a bottle of chicha, date from half a century ago. At the age of twenty, I had his theories burned into my mind as if by a red-hot iron. But this concealment of the ego, this veiling of personal emotions, this impersonality of the creator, led me toward magic rather than distancing me from it. In magic, the same principles apply, but go further: the magician accepts the cutting of the ties that bind him to external influences, but knows how to receive, from the inside, the essential, impersonal being that has its origin beyond our solar system.

Parra was present in one of my happy dreams in 1998: in the helicopter I am piloting circling around the mouth of an erupting volcano Nicanor, as a young man, gives a lesson in poetry to a group of elderly poets. "Do not describe your experiences; the poem should be experience. Do not show what you are, but what you are going to be. Do not show your feelings; create a new feeling with the poem. Do not reveal what you know, but what you suspect. Do not seek what you desire, but what you do not desire. So, now that you are a dream, stop dreaming." Then I woke up.

When I got to Paris, not having been able to establish the immediate contact I so much desired with André Breton and being always in search of metaphysical aspirin that would comfort me for being mortal, I found two teachers in books. One was Gurdjieff; I read everything he had written or dictated, as well as the works about him written by his disciples. The other was Gaston Bachelard, whose book *La philosophie du non* endeared me to philosophy and proposed new visions of reality that overwhelmed me. I gradually came to know excellent artists who, although they enriched me aesthetically, never suggested the idea of entering into the territory of magic or therapy. Quite the contrary, their quest was to escape from the Essential Being in order to exalt the power of the personal "I." I do not mean to imply that I despise this; unlike some extemporaneous gurus, I believe that the part of our spirit with which we often identify ourselves—the ego—should not be destroyed or neglected. When well-managed, the egotistic personality can become an admirable servant. It is for this reason that the Buddha is depicted meditating on a sleeping tiger, Jesus Christ riding a donkey, Isis stroking a cat. The gods have steeds, and these represent the ego. The personal "I" is admirable if it is surrendered to the cosmic will. If it disobeys the Law, it becomes a nefarious monster that devours consciousness.

The Canadian sculptor Jean Benoit, a fervent surrealist, invited me to spend a few days of vacation in Saint-Cirq-Lapopie, a small town in southern France. Across from his house was that of André Breton, built of wood and carved stones. My friend laughed at my shyness and dragged me over to the home of the poet. His wife received us, saying she did not know where André was but that he would return soon and that we could wait while she was in the kitchen. I waited there with Benoit, who, joyously anticipating the future encounter and certain that it would be "electric," began emptying a bottle of wine. I trembled from head to toe. The idea of seeing the mythological creator of surrealism in his private home caused me a nervous excitement, a mixture of panic and euphoria. After ten minutes I had an irresistible need to urinate. Benoit, enjoying the wine, made a vague gesture toward the stairs leading to another floor. "It's on the left." I climbed the stairs looking for the bathroom, feeling like an intruder but at the same time possessed by an extreme curiosity. On the second floor, I saw a small wooden door to the left. My pressing need to relieve myself caused me to open the door immediately. There I was, face to face with the master, sitting on the toilet, pants down below his knees, defecating. Breton, his face contorted and deep red, gave a tremendous yell as if his throat were being cut. His cry must have been heard not only throughout the house but also in the surrounding houses, because several dogs started barking. I slammed the door instantly and flew down the stairs, fled to the station, and got on a bus that was going to Paris. The scene had lasted only a few seconds, but I had committed sacrilege by seeing the exquisite poet shitting. Would it be forgiven someday? Doubting so, I decided to emigrate to Mexico.

The National Institute of Fine Arts, led by the poet Salvador Novo, hired me to teach pantomime in its theater school. My arrival in Mexico's capital aroused much enthusiasm, and I had hundreds of students. My goal was to move from pantomime into theater—why not talk?—and thence into film, for which I had to train capable actors. I set up a laboratory for the study of bodily expressions at a private site, freeing myself from the stereotypes of pantomime. I was surprised to see the arrival of a group of doctors, all disciples of Erich Fromm. This renowned psychiatrist and essayist, suffering from heart disease, lived very near the capital in the pleasant city of Cuernavaca, which at that time was not yet sullied by pollution, enjoying the mild climate, lush vegetation, and low altitude close to sea level. A group of Mexican psychiatrists and two Colombians, drawn to his radical humanism, had asked Fromm to accept them as disciples. I suppose that Fromm found them to be caught in the traps of intellect, and in keeping with his atheist mysticism—"God is not a thing, and therefore cannot be represented by a name or an image"—invited them to free themselves from all mental chains, all "idolatries," and to lose their individual limits in order to surrender peacefully to a happy relationship with nature. Of course,

Performing in a pantomime (Santiago de Chile, 1950). (Was I a precursor to Iggy Pop?)

the body was the nature that was nearest, and for this reason, having learned of my courses in bodily expression, he recommended them to all. These psychiatrists, extraordinarily well educated after many years of intensive study, were skillful at handling theories but awkward when moving their bodies. Stiff, tense, and inexpressive, they identified with words and did not control their gestures. The first thing I did was to have them visit different spaces to feel how their attitudes changed depending on the dimensions of the place and the location of their bodies. They saw that they felt better or worse in certain places than in others; they understood that communication is not only oral but also spatial; they learned that their brains functioned on the basis of a territory, real or imagined. They noticed how rigid their spines were and how unbalanced their gait. They took the work very seriously and made great progress. I was asked by Dr. Millán to accompany them to the Tlalpam Sanatorium to help them investigate the body language of mental patients. I did so. Pleased with the results, they finally decided to invite me to Cuernavaca to meet their teacher.

Fromm received us in a beautiful bungalow with bougainvillea-covered walls. He had white hair and gentle blue eyes, a voice free of aggression, often quoting the Torah to affirm his atheism, and wore white pants and a light blue jacket so brightly colored that it gave him the appearance of an orchestral musician in the style of Tommy Dorsey. This kind Jewish man seemed to bear no resemblance to the stern father image that he projected to his Mexican students. As his wife served an appetizer, Fromm asked me to describe the techniques of pantomime, especially those related to the expression of weight. "The man who has not realized his freedom, that is to say who has not cut his incestuous ties to his mother and the ties connecting him to his family and his homeland, experiences all these as a burden without knowing that he carries that weight," he said to me. As our conversation continued, Fromm suggested that we go to lunch at a restaurant on one of the hills on the outskirts of Cuernavaca. "I will go by car with the mime," he announced to his students. "My heart does not allow me to take the pleasure of that delightful climb. But I advise you to go on foot, in complete harmony with nature and one another. All love is based on knowledge of the other; all knowledge of the other is based on shared experience." When we arrived at the restaurant Fromm asked for a jug of tamarind water and said to me with a blissful smile, "Let's drink this healthy liquid in tranquillity. My collaborators, talking to each other and enjoying the beautiful scenery, will take at least an hour to get here."

The master was wrong: his disciples arrived in less than twenty minutes, perspiring, pale, and short of breath. One of them fell down half-conscious in a chair, another vomited, and the others ran to the cold drinks, imbibing them in large and desperate gulps. After a short time, ashamed, they confessed their mistake. They had started out completely calm on the road that led to the mountain restaurant. By common agreement, in order to better commune with Mother Nature, they had decided to march in silence. After a few minutes, they had noticed that the two Colombians, subtly speeding up their pace, were walking ten meters ahead. The rest of them hurried to catch up. A competition of long strides began, each one trying to prove that he was stronger than the other. This degenerated into a race. The last hundred meters were taken at a sprint, leaving them almost totally exhausted. Fromm burst into laughter, tinged with sadness and compassion. He said, "The beginning of freedom lies in the capacity of man to suffer. And man suffers if he is oppressed, physically or spiritually. Suffering moves him to act against his oppressor, seeking to end the oppression rather than seek a freedom of which he knows nothing. Your greatest oppressor, my friends, is the individual 'I.' No therapist can cure it on your behalf. Remember what Hindu medicine tells us: the physician prescribes, God heals . . . It seems essential that you continue meditating with the Zen monk." I was surprised, a Zen monk in Mexico? I had not heard any news of it. I knew that Erich Fromm had invited Daisetz Teitaro Suzuki to Mexico and had published a book with him, *Zen Buddhism and Psychoanalysis,* but I was excited to hear of the existence of this monk, whose name was Ejo Takata. I had read every book on the topic that I could get my hands on, but direct contact with a Zen master bore more weight than a ton of printed pages.

On the return bus trip, I asked them where I could find the monk. Some minutes of embarrassed silence passed before they answered me: "It's a secret. Apart from us, no one knows he is here. We cannot communicate his address. The only one who can give an answer is Dr. F., our treasurer." Dr. F received me in his large office and said, "Ejo Takata works exclusively for us. We have built a small zendo on the outskirts of the city. If you wish to go there to meditate with us every day at six o'clock (except for Saturdays and Sundays, of course), you must first offer a donation, for example . . ." (and without finishing the sentence, he wrote a large sum on a piece of paper. It may not have been so large for him, but for me, it was equal to all my savings.) Without a second of doubt, I signed a check. He gave me a card with Ejo Takata's address and a map showing how to get there.

At six o'clock the next morning I walked on a path alongside a ravine, the bottom of which was filled with garbage and rats, and came to a modest one-story house surrounded by a garden. With my heart pounding fast, I gave a few timid knocks on the door. It was instantly opened by a Japanese man in monastic clothes: he had a shaven head, a face of indefinable age, a smile showing teeth mounted on steel frames, and small bright eyes. He gave a bow then embraced me with affection as if he had known me for years. He led me to the small meditation room and showed me a box of red cloth with a white circle in the center containing a Japanese word. He translated: "Happiness." How could I have realized that in that moment, Ejo Takata had transmitted the essence of Zen to me? He searched my face and saw that I had not understood the message. He clicked his tongue a few times, tilting his head from one side to the other. In his Japanese accent he muttered, "Need much zazen." He handed me a black cushion—a zafu—showed me how to place it under my buttocks and meditate on my knees, corrected the position of my hands and my spine, and sat to meditate in

Ejo Takata around 1980.

front of me, as still as a wax sculpture. Half an hour passed. My legs hurt atrociously. The psychiatrists began to arrive. Without apologizing for the delay they sat down and, with profound and extraordinary concentration, remained still for an hour and a half. Then, smiling, they made quick bows and left. My body was numb, and I could barely walk. For three months I suffered martyrdom, all my muscles and joints hurt, my legs fell asleep, and my neck sunk into my back, making me feel like a sick turtle. Ejo would give me hard blows on the shoulder blades with his wooden cane to make me regain energy. The doctors, by contrast, were always smiling and could spend hours without moving. Once I conquered the bodily aches, I had difficulties with my mind. Because sitting still was excruciatingly boring, I started imagining poems, stories, sensual images, solutions to all kinds of problems. But I realized that it was foolish to seek the Master's admiration by imitating the appearance of a Buddha: I had to overcome my mental chaos. I realized that at every moment my mind was invaded by endless dialogues, monologues, judgments, and images that, by giving them names, I compared to other images. I called this "mental chatter." I started trying not to let words into my mind. I struggled for three years until I was finally able to keep my mind empty of words whenever I wanted to. I was very glad of this victory. However, I realized that in order to keep language out of my mind I had to devote my attention to doing so, making a continuous effort. This is not the correct way to stop the internal dialogue. What I had to do was to stop identifying myself with my thoughts. They were mine, but they were not me. As I meditated, I let the words go through my mind like clouds blown by the wind. The phrases came, nobody would take control of them, they would leave. I arrived at the zendo one misty morning ready to start this new struggle. I found Ejo carrying his few possessions in a cloth sack.

"Doctors cheat: take pills before meditating. They want to appear, not be. I am leaving." He walked next to me, very calm, carrying his bag down toward the city.

"Do you have money, Ejo?"

"No."

"Do you have a place to sleep?"

"No."

"Do you have friends in the city?"

"No."

"What will you do?" He shrugged his shoulders and replied quietly, with a big smile, "Happiness."

He declined my offer to host him, and while I took a taxi to the capital he started walking toward the mountains.

Two years passed before I saw him again. He had been in the mountains teaching the indigenous people to cultivate soybeans. He also taught them how to build hygienic huts with outdoor kitchens, facing the sunrise, and how to make methane gas from their excrement. Because his teaching was free, the local officials at first thought he was a dangerous communist. Many times they threatened to shoot him. Without worrying about losing his life, Ejo continued his work, saving countless families from misery. When he returned to the capital, he and his new students set about healing illnesses with herbs and acupuncture. One day, while I was filming *The Holy Mountain* on the snowy peaks of Ixtaxihuatl, suffering from the cold and an enormous number of technical difficulties, the monk came to visit me. In desperation I asked him, "When will the mountain stop being white?" He concentrated on his belly for a moment, then answered, laughing, "When it is white, it is white, and when it is not white, it is not white!" I knew that I had to stop setting my hopes on the future and accept the present situation with happiness. Until his death Ejo Takata always lived in borrowed accommodations, subsisting on scant donations.

When I finished writing the script for *The Holy Mountain* and gave myself the role of the alchemist, a Gurdjieff-style master, I realized that I knew perfectly well the motives of the student, but lacked the miraculous, superhuman experiences that I assumed the gurus had. In this dance of reality, while I was preparing the music and sets for the film, a New Yorker contacted me, wanting to be my secretary. Because his exaggerated insistence bothered me, I hung up the phone in the middle of one of his imperative sentences. He got on a plane and came to visit me the next day. Upon seeing him, so fanatical and brutal, I realized that I had found Axon, the military tyrant who cuts off testicles in my film. When I told him that I did not want to hire him as a technician, but as an actor, he told me, "That's what I wanted, but since I've never acted, I asked for a position as an assistant. But if I have come here and succeeded in joining the cast, it's because I developed my psychic abilities with just a month and a half of study in Arica Training, founded by a Bolivian master, Óscar Ichazo, who knows all the secrets of Gurdjieff." I asked him what this teaching had consisted of, and he said, "Óscar says it does not hold any new ideas. What he proposes is a mixture of different techniques, Taoist, Sufi, Kabbalistic, alchemical, and others, which allow one to obtain enlightenment in forty days. If you're looking for a guru, he's the one. He currently has 240,000 students." In fact, contact with a Hindu or East Asian guru—the sort of holy men for which ads abounded in *The Village Voice*—would not have suited my needs. My character was a Western alchemist. I was won over by the fact that Ichazo was South American and had named his technique after a Chilean port city, Arica, where my father had built a mattress factory. Axon told me that Ichazo had brought a group of fifty-seven American truth seekers, including Lilly and Claudio Naranjo, into the Tarapacá desert to teach them a method that would allow them to levitate in ten months.

I traveled to New York, obtained an interview with Ichazo, and suggested that he come to Mexico to initiate me (three days would suffice) and bring two of his assistants to initiate my actors (this would take six weeks of continuous work for twenty hours a day). We reached an agreement: first class travel for him and his Chilean secretary, a haughty aristocratic lady, two connected apartments in a five-star hotel, plus $17,000.

Óscar Ichazo and his companion landed in Mexico. As soon as they arrived at the hotel she asked me, "Where's the weed?" Very surprised, I told her that since I did not smoke, I had not thought about that. The lady, furious, began to shout, "It's stupid and unforgivable to have us come to Mexico without at least a kilo of herb waiting for us! Go now and get some, or you won't get anything from the Master!" The lady's despotic tone filled me with rage. I would have liked to take the wind out of her sails, but I held back because I believed the meeting with Ichazo to be essential for the success of my film. In less than an hour, my assistants arrived with a kilo of top-quality marijuana, wrapped in sheets of newspaper. The Chilean calmed down. So did I. A Tibetan sacred text says, "Do not be concerned with the defects of the master: if you need to cross a river, it does not matter if the boat that takes you to the other side is badly painted." Ejo Takata, for example, smoked cigarette after cigarette, but that did not stop him from showing me the heart of Zen.

We scheduled the private meeting with Ichazo for the following day at six o'clock in the afternoon at my house. There, on the third floor, I had a large study with the walls lined with books and the window looking out onto Río de Janeiro Plaza. The previous night when we dined together the master had told me where his powers came from:

"I was born in 1931 in Bolivia. The son of a Bolivian soldier, I was educated in La Paz, at a Jesuit school. One night when I was six years old I was in bed reading a fairy tale when I was seized by a strange attack, like epilepsy. I passed out immediately and left my body in the astral state. I saw myself dead, lying on the bed. Thus dematerialized, I learned the mysteries of the hereafter. When I returned to my child's body, I had the mind of an adult, of one who knows truth. When the priest who was my teacher described hell I thought, 'I've been to hell and it was not like that.' I abandoned my children's stories and started reading, fully understanding all kinds of scientific, philosophical, and sacred books like the Bhagavad-Gîta, the Tao Te Ching, the Zohar, the Upanishads, the

Diamond Sutra, and many others. I was also interested in the writings of Gurdjieff and his disciples. When I was nine years old I was already taking classes in hatha yoga, hypnotism, and martial arts with a real samurai. At age thirteen some Bolivian healers initiated me in their magical rites, giving me ayahuasca to drink. At nineteen, I met an old man who was interested in my great spiritual development. In 1950 he invited me to Buenos Aires, where I got in touch with a group of old sages, many of whom were eighty or older. They had come from all over the world, especially from Europe and the Orient, to exchange their spiritual techniques. I arranged to work for them, cleaning the rooms, doing the shopping, cooking, and serving them in everything they needed. That way, they could devote themselves unhindered to discussing techniques, yoga, Hindu and Tibetan tantra, the Kabbalah, the Tarot, alchemy, and so forth. I would get up at four in the morning to prepare their breakfast, and would discreetly remain among them. Little by little, they got used to my presence and began to use me as a guinea pig to test the effectiveness of their knowledge, such as a particular kind of meditation or a recitation of mantras. After two years, possessing all of the techniques, I knew more than any of them. Proud of my synthesis, they gave me valuable contacts with Eastern brotherhoods. They opened the doors of the most secret sites to me, places very difficult to enter, almost impossible. I started traveling. Everywhere I went, I was received not as a student but as a master. I visited India, Tibet (places where I corroborated my knowledge of tantra), Japan (where I solved all the koans), Hong Kong (where the secrets of the I Ching were revealed to me), Iran (where the Sufis showed me the true meaning of the enneagon and the secret name of God). I returned to La Paz to live with my father and digest this knowledge. After meditating for a year, I fell into a divine coma that lasted seven days. Ecstasy kept me motionless, as if dead. Thus I knew how the universe was created, the mathematical relationships between things, the sickness of the current civilization, and how to cure it. When I was able to move again, I knew I was enlightened. I realized that instead of helping myself, I must try to help God.

Óscar Ichazo. Photo: Peter Schlessinger

Ichazo told me all this with the same conviction with which Chico Molina claimed to have seen a magic mirror at work. It was the same conviction with which Carlos Castaneda had told me that, while walking with Don Juan along the Paseo de la Reforma in Mexico City, he had become distracted looking at a passing woman and stopped listening to the old man, who had then given him a slap that sent him fifty kilometers away in less than a second. It was the same conviction with which Ichazo later told me that he had been by Jesus's side at the moment when he "suffered" his transfiguration. Did he want to tell me that he could travel through time or that he had memories of previous incarnations? The latter possibility is consistent with the fact that Ichazo claimed to possess a prodigious memory: he claimed to remember all his experiences with total clarity starting at one year of age.

At six o'clock that evening, Ichazo knocked on the door of my house. As if he had been there many times, he went ahead of me up the stairs to the third floor and sat in the comfortable chair that I had bought for him that very morning. He smiled with satisfaction at smelling the new leather.

"Bravo . . . this furniture has no past. It's like me. I am the root of a new tradition. Forget all the Christs, forget all the Buddhas; personal fulfillment does not exist. Now, I myself will teach you how to tame the ego. I'll show you the path to return to the impersonal power that breathes us, the force that exists beyond the level of our conscious mind." And without more ado, from his pocket he pulled a packet of caramel sweets, a tube of vitamin C tablets, a lighter, a joint, and a mysterious little piece of paper. He asked me to bring him a glass of water. He opened the slip of paper; it contained an orange powder. He poured it into the water.

"It's pure LSD. Drink it."

Although it was fashionable, I had never wanted to undertake psychedelic experiences. In my interviews, I stated that I did not need them because my films gave me such powerful images. I gulped and, overcoming my fear, drank the brew. We waited in heavy silence. An hour passed. There was no effect. He lit the joint.

"Smoke it. It will speed the process."

We shared the joint. A few minutes later I started to have my first hallucinations. I was overcome with a childlike joy. Through the large window of the study I saw the Río de Janeiro Plaza, with its trees and its bronze copy of Michelangelo's *David,* change appearance as if it were a collection of paintings by artists I liked—Bonnard, Seurat, Van Gogh, Picasso, and so on. Suddenly I heard a cracking that seemed to split the house in two, and I exclaimed, "This isn't any use, it's like watching a Walt Disney movie. Also, I've lost control of my movements. If someone attacked me now, I couldn't defend myself."

"Stop criticizing and have confidence in me. Enough paranoia. Wherever you go, you can come back from there. Also know that in the state you're in, you can handle yourself perfectly well in everyday reality."

At that moment, the phone rang. "Answer it," he ordered. As if descending from another galaxy, I approached the phone and took it off the hook. It was one of my actors asking for certain information. Without any great difficulty, I answered his questions.

"See?" Ichazo said, satisfied. "Now that your fears have calmed down, let's see if your images are as childish as you say."

He told me to go to the bathroom and observe my face in the mirror. So I did. I saw myself a thousand different ways, in continuous change. One after another of my personalities appeared: the ambitious, the egotistical, the lazy, the choleric, the murderer, the saint, the vain genius, the abandoned child, the indolent, the melancholy, the resentful, the usurping jester, the fake madman, the coward, the proud, the envious, the complex-ridden Jew, the erotomaniac, the jealous, and many others. My flesh cracked, my features swelled, my skin was covered with sores. I saw my mind and matter rot. I was disgusted with myself. I started to vomit . . . Ichazo gave me candy, then a vitamin C pill. A wave of warmth, carried by my blood, inundated my body. I felt better.

"If you have ever felt compassion, true compassion for someone, remember it."

I began to cry like a three-year-old child. I held Pepe, my gray cat, in my arms, dying: my father had poisoned him. His glassy eyes and dangling tongue broke my heart. I would have given my life to save him.

"Make that emotion grow, compassion for all animals, for the world, for humanity. There. Now look at yourself in the mirror again, but with mercy . . . That being with so many dark sides is your poor ego, dying. If you can now reach this high level of consciousness, it is thanks to it, its incessant suffering in search of unity. Its monstrousness engendered you; its defects were the roots that have nourished your essence. Have compassion for it; give your hand to your ego. The butterfly is not disgusted with the caterpillar that gave birth to it."

I pressed my face to the silver surface, absorbed my image through my skin. When I drew back, the mirror reflected everything in the room except for me. Despite realizing that this invisibility was a hallucination, I knew I would never again live criticizing every one of my steps. The harsh inner judge had melted away. For the first time, I felt at peace with myself.

"Don't just stand there!" Ichazo exclaimed. "Keep going!" He made me take out all the photographs and play programs that I kept in my desk drawers and scatter them on the floor. "Those were your plays, your couple of films, your actors, your friends, yourself, wrapped up in the comedy of fame. In the state you're in now, how do you see it all?"

I saw everything with an extraterrestrial mind, without desires, without ties; the anguish of separation was present in every detail, the truth could be felt, but it was far away, like an irreparable mystery, a painful hope. There, where life was suffering, ignorance became pride, and the "I" was in a prison without doors or windows.

"Do you understand? You've lived searching in the distance for what was inside you, for what was you." I lay down on those pictures, those newspaper clippings that mentioned me, those programs and recordings, as if they were all an old skin that I was shedding from my body. Óscar said, "There are three centers in the human animal: the intellectual, the emotional, and the vital. My teachers called them the *Path,* the *Oth,* and the *Kath.* As long as the ego is false and the consciousness distorted, they sleep without performing their task of relating us to the immediate world, surpassing the obstacles that are illusory but deadly. Let's wake them up!"

First, I had to concentrate on a point in my belly about four inches below my navel. I perceived an immense force there.

"Don't observe it from the outside. Don't define what you feel. Enter the *Kath,* become this center." Ichazo's voice sounded distant. I dissolved into—how can I describe it?—a dimension of inexhaustible energy, like an opening in a rock where a torrential stream flows out. "You can send this energy, in the form of invisible tentacles, as far away as you want. You can use it to enter other people's bodies and give them life or death." He gestured to the people outside walking across the plaza. "Launch the *Kath.* Penetrate them."

I gave a push and felt as if a stream of energy was coming from my belly, invisible and long, which would tie itself to the bodies of the pedestrians. I immediately felt united to them; I understood their minds, grasped their emotions, and knew—or imagined?—much of their past. After following them for a hundred meters they became friends for whom I felt an immense pity, such was the pain that filled them.

"They suffer because they are not conscious. Don't stay there. Look for the union that best suits you, without giving yourself limits."

I climbed up to the roof and lay naked on the concrete surface.

Night had fallen, and the sky was full of stars. I sent out a long tentacle and joined myself to the brightest star. I did not feel it to be indifferent. This celestial body was a being that recognized our link and sent me a form of energy that enriched my soul. I decided to tie myself to other stars. My invisible beam split into innumerable branches. I noted with surprise and fascination that each star had a different "personality." They were all distinct, each one with its own type of benevolent consciousness. This seemed natural to me: creation never repeats itself.

I had always lived with cats and had never known one with the same character as another. Similar yes, but not the same. Every snowflake that falls is unique. And so are the stars. Up there was a mass of individual beings like the countless facets of a single diamond, sending me their energies. At the same time, I received the strength that the Earth sent to me. My center of gravity was joined to the center of the planet and from there went back up to the *Kath* of every living being. I was afraid. The temptation of power was compelling. Just then, Ichazo asked me, "What will you do with that power?"

"Help my neighbors!" I said, and the fear vanished.

"How does your heart feel?"

"Like an enemy, an unrelenting muscle, an indifferent clock marking the running out of my time, an executioner threatening at every moment to stop and end my life," I answered.

"You're wrong. Enter it. There you will find the *Oth*."

In the state I was in, thinking of something meant doing it immediately. Right away, I found myself immersed in my heart! The beats rumbled like thunder, the sound of rain determined to penetrate everything, to demolish any illusion of personal existence. I remembered an afternoon when, alone on the terrace of my hotel in Bangalore, India, I had watched the cloudy sky agitated by a strong storm. Every rumble seemed to speak the sacred syllable *Ram*. In the same way, those beats shaking my heart and then agitating my body, the room, the city, the world, the entire cosmos, seemed to be the voice of God the creator. It was the repeated echo of the first word: *Ram, Ram, Ram.* There I was, innocent as a newborn, in the middle of a gigantic golden temple that throbbed with devotion, repeating the divine name. And that thunderous rhythm, once my fear and mistrust had disappeared, became a constant explosion of love, organized in waves spreading out from the center to the infinite edges and from the infinite edges back to the center. That nucleus was my consciousness, transparent as a diamond, protected by the golden temple, a metaphor for the universe. I began to feel the immeasurable love that the heart felt for me. I finally knew what it was to be loved.

There was no longer an executioner residing in my chest, but a wonderful friend, mother, and father at the same time, a bridge between this material world into which the spirit is born and the spiritual world that produces matter. In that immense golden cradle, floating in an ocean of infinite joy, lulled by the waves of love, like a happy child who had found his family and his rightful home, I began to fall asleep. I woke to Ichazo's fierce order, "Don't be self-indulgent. Happiness is a beautiful trick. Go further away. Sail the sea of crazy ideas. Submerge yourself in the mental energy. Find the *Path*."

We returned to the terrace. There was a large neon Coca-Cola advertisement with a luminous circle revolving around a vertical axis.

"We do not need Tibetan mandalas or esoteric symbols. This sign, if you concentrate your attention by removing the words from your mind and not taking your eyes off it, will become the portal."

I watched as the rotating sign transformed into an oval, into a line, back into an oval, into a circle, and so on. It was swallowing my rational borders, my will to exist, and . . . suddenly, without intending to, as if I had taken an immeasurable leap, I felt myself outside the world of sensations. How to explain this? The strength of the *Kath* and the happiness of the *Oth* were thrown into an immutable transparency, the *Path*. I had lived in a world of compact gray clouds, and now I rose up to float in a translucent sky. Without desires, without definitions, in pure continuation, free from any beginning or end, exempt from time and space, I immersed myself in bliss. How many hours did I lie there motionless? When I recovered my body, my name, my rational island, I was alone in front of the flashing Coca-Cola circle. I felt ridiculous, but also euphoric. I had not imagined what I remembered; I had experienced it. That experience became my guide. I had been shown the goal, now it was up to my perseverance to actually reach it. Ejo Takata, when I asked what the Buddha was, had replied, "The mind is the Buddha."

The following morning I received a phone call from Óscar's lofty partner, who told me it was urgent that I find someone to inject the Master with a dose of morphine for he was suffering excruciating pain. I was speechless and considered refusing. She shouted, "Idiot, do what I ask!" I needed to continue my experience, and Ichazo had promised me two sessions: I swallowed my anger and ran to the house of Dr. Toledano, a friend who had acted in *Fando y Lis,* extracting a vial of blood from the actress's arm and drinking it greedily in front of the camera.

We arrived at the hotel. The ogress, fearing that the doctor would leave with me if she expelled me from the room, accepted my presence with a smoldering glare. Ichazo lay in bed, writhing, curled up. His muscles, bones, guts, everything hurt. Toledano quickly injected him with a dose of morphine, and the affliction died down. Rising from the bed in full possession of his faculties, he explained, "I am intimately attached to my school. We form a collective body and spirit. Because of my absence, serious disputes and problems have erupted back in New York. The students are not yet ready to manage themselves alone. For this reason, I felt the catastrophe in my body. I'm very sorry, I have to return immediately to New York!" The woman had already packed their bags. They coldly took their leave and, without more ado, took a taxi to the airport.

The end of the encounter with Ichazo resembles the end of my meeting with Carlos Castaneda. The writer, surrounded by an aura of sulfur, was impossible to track down. During the time that he was most famous, hundreds of North Americans went to Mexico in search of him, greedily desiring that he introduce them to Don Juan, the mythological peyote master. I did not have to look for him. He came over to my table at El Rincón Gaucho, the restaurant that the former wrestler Wolf Rubinsky had opened on Avenida Insurgentes in the capital, where I was eating an Argentinean beefsteak in the company of a television actress who, after taking a training course at a church of Scientology,* had decided to change her Mexican name to Troika. "In the Russian valleys, covered

---

*Sectarian movement founded by the author Lafayette Ronald Hubbard.

by a blanket of snow which is a symbol of purity, a troika glides without effort or obstacle: as my mind does now." I was not interested in her mind, but in her lush curves. At first, when Castaneda approached, I thought he was a waiter. In Mexico, it is easy to determine the social class to which an individual belongs merely by seeing his or her physique. He was short and solidly built, with curly hair, a flat nose, and slightly pockmarked skin—in short, a humble native. But when he spoke, I knew from the relaxed tone of his voice, his delicate pronunciation, and the luminous vibration of his intellect that he was a man of high culture. His personal charm made me instantly consider him a friend.

"Excuse me, Alejandro, for interrupting. I have seen your film *El Topo* several times, so I am happy to greet you. I am Carlos Castaneda."

He could have been a con man—nobody knew the face of the writer—but I believed him. Later I found through a drawing in a book and a photo published by his ex-wife that it was indeed he. Troika also believed him. Although she had never read his works, she seemed intoxicated by his fame. With an offhand gesture, as if the heat was bothering her, she opened her neckline, showing the tip of one of her two magnificent promontories, and inflated her lips as if kissing an invisible phallus to whisper, "How interesting!" Castaneda, after casting a falcon's eye on the living flesh that was being displayed above a bloody beefsteak, smiled: "If we have met, it must be for some reason. I would like to talk to you in a quieter place." I suggested to Castaneda that we go to his hotel, but he insisted on coming to mine. I, being a successful producer, was staying at the luxurious Camino Real. What better place to meet with Castaneda than a *Camino Real* (Royal Path)! We agreed that he would come the next day at noon.

I waited impatiently. At five minutes to twelve, the phone rang in my room. I said, "He must surely be calling to tell me he can't come." I answered. In a respectful tone, he asked me if it would bother me to receive him slightly before the scheduled time. Such tact was touching to me. As soon as he entered, I offered him a chair. We sat face-to-face and locked eyes, scrutinizing one another like two warriors, but certainly without any aggression and of course with much hope of finding a pleasant interlocutor. How long did this last? An eternity. He was the first to speak. Soon I arrived at the question we were interested in:

"In your books you have revealed a way of seeing the world differently, you have revived the concept of the spiritual warrior, you have made the topic of lucid dreams current again, and yet I do not know whether you are a madman, a genius, or a liar."

"Everything I tell is true. I have not invented anything," he replied with a bright smile.

"Reading your works I have the impression that, based on actual experiences in Mexico, you have developed and introduced concepts drawing on the universal esoteric tradition. In your books one can find Zen, the Upanishads, the Tarot, Hervey de Saint-Denys's work on dreams, and so forth. However, I am sure of one thing: it's evident that you have traveled all around this country to do your research. It seems likely that, bringing together all your findings, you have created the figure of Don Juan."

"Absolutely not. I assure you, he exists . . ."

And as he continued he told me how the shaman (with whom he had been walking on the Paseo de la Reforma, the central artery of Mexico City) had, with a simple slap on the back, projected him several kilometers away because he had been distracted by a woman passing by. Then he talked about the sexual life of Don Juan, who was capable of ejaculating fifteen times in a row. I remember he also told me that his master despised those human beings who "manufactured" children, sacrificing their magical abilities. "Every child steals a piece of the soul." He introduced the topic of Saturnine cannibalism. But, perhaps seeing my look of horror, he changed the subject:

"Why have circumstances brought us together? Could it be for us to make a film? Hollywood has offered me several million dollars to bring my first book to the screen, but I don't want Don Juan to be played by Anthony Quinn."

We were starting to agree on the possibilities of filming at the real sites, showing true miracles, real shamans, without using special effects and stunts that would turn all those teachings into banal fairy tales, when Castaneda began to have stomach pains, something that he said, between moans, never happened to him. In the mountains he drank water from streams without any ill effect, but in the city, where the water was ostensibly potable, he suffered from diarrhea. He began to squirm more and more. I called a taxi and accompanied him to his hotel, the Holiday Inn. Due to the usual traffic congestion, it took us almost an hour to get there. As soon as we had shaken hands, he ran off. I never saw him again. At the same time that he suffered those stomach cramps I had been struck by a violent pain in my liver that kept me in bed for three days. Once recovered, I called the hotel. He was gone and had left no address. When I stopped by there, the porter I questioned told me that the gentleman had been accompanied by an attractive woman, and his description matched the appearance of Troika. For a long time, Castaneda's diarrhea caused me no suspicion. This malady, which the Mexicans call "Moctezuma's revenge," attacks a great many tourists, but little by little, recalling the details of our meeting, I began to have some doubts. Diarrhea requires speedy evacuation. Why hadn't Castaneda used my bathroom? That would have brought him quick relief. If he needed to shit, how did he resist the urge in the taxi for over an hour? Moreover, this obnoxious illness tends to make people curl into a knot around the abdomen, rather than squirming, which can bring on an attack of nausea. Besides his stomach, intestines, and viscera hurting, he also seemed to be feeling pain in his muscles and bones. Perhaps some spirit sent by other sorcerers attacked both of us at the same time in order to prevent us from realizing the project, which would have meant revealing certain secrets to the entire world . . . or else his body, running out of its usual drug, needed a morphine injection, like Ichazo. I have never solved this mystery. Troika disappeared from the soap operas. Someone told me that she had signed a contract to work for five thousand years on L. Ron Hubbard's ship.

Óscar Ichazo's withdrawal had left me frustrated. I felt that I had lost the opportunity to have an essential experience. However, the dance of reality granted me that opportunity . . . Francisco Fierro, a painter and friend of mine, came back from Huautla, where he had gone to eat mushrooms with the famous Mazatec curandera María Sabina. He came looking for me at the house where I had already been holed up for a month with my group of "actors," preparing to film *The Holy Mountain*. Ichazo had left us two instructors, Max and Lydia, who, certain that they possessed the supreme secrets, managed us like tyrants. She was an American of short stature, nearsighted and fat, and he a thin and gangly man, his face invaded by pimples. We were allowed to sleep only four hours a night, from midnight to four, and the rest of the time we had to spend on all manner of pseudo-Sufi, pseudo-Buddhist, pseudo-Egyptian, pseudo-Hindu, pseudo-shamanic, pseudo-tantric, pseudo-yogic, and pseudo-Taoist exercises. These exercises ultimately were no use to us whatsoever. Francisco Fierro brought me a jar full of honey in which there were six pairs of fungi.

"It's a gift from María Sabina. She saw you in her dreams. It seems that you are going to accomplish something that will help our country. When? What? She didn't say. What she did say was that she, and others like her, want to help you. Eat them all. They are males and females. Those that aren't of use to you, your body will reject and vomit up. She said to eat them at night, so that you will advance toward the light and see the dawn for the first time."

While my actors went to sleep, awaiting the gong that would sound four hours later to invite them to take their cold shower, I lay on the roof, naked in a sleeping bag, and ingested the mushrooms. The hallucinations were not just visual this time. The ensemble of all my senses acquired fantastic characteristics. I began to realize that what I considered to be "myself" was merely a mental construct obtained on the basis of sensations. "I only feel how I think I am." The toxins in the mushrooms then began to show me other possibilities. I understood that I constructed myself from the intellect: "this is a hand," "this is my face," "I am a man," "here are my limits." Now something was telling me, "When you speak of limits, you actually mean unknown infinities. You can be something more than a human."

I squatted, and little by little I became a lion. "This is not a hand; it is a paw." "This is not my face; it is the savage countenance of a feline." "I am not a man; I am a powerful beast." My animal strength had awakened. It was a bodily sensation; every muscle acquired the strength of steel and an intoxicating elasticity. Like a folded fan that quietly opens, my senses extended themselves. I could distinguish the different scents carried by the air, listen to a countless array of noises, see unsuspected details, feel the power of my jaws. Before this, I had been almost blind, deaf, and mute with no sense of smell. The *Kath* seemed to boil in my belly: I was a predator, a thousand prey were calling to me to offer me their vital energy, but something stopped me. The pure mental strength, which I perceived as penetrating, subtle, delicate like a woman, was confronting the beast with intense love. I now understood the deeper meaning of card XI of the Tarot, Strength, which shows a woman with a hat in the form of a figure eight lying sideways—an infinity symbol—opening or closing the muzzle of a lion. Until this moment I had lived repressing my animal nature with contempt and fear, while at the same time my rationality limited the infinite extent of my mind, making it into a logical island. In the *Oth,* the heart, I was a human; in the *Path,* the spirit, I was an angel; and in the *Kath,* the body and sex, I was a beast. I stayed there, lying in wait, not for some small prey but for all of life. The stars shone brighter than ever, bestowing inexhaustible energy on me, and the Earth was manifested first in the form of a limited territory, the rooftop I was on, and then spread out like a woman giving herself, over the city, the country, the continent, the entire planet. I squatted down, clinging with my claws to the terrestrial globe, traveling through the cosmos. Dawn began to break. I felt the movement of the planet, turning to offer its surface, little by little, to the caress of the sun. I felt the Earth's pleasure at receiving this light and vital warmth, the sun's euphoria at giving its unceasing and engendering gift, and all around, the joy of the other planets and stars, crossing the firmament like iridescent ships. Everything was alive, everything was aware, everything from explosions to births to catastrophes was dancing, enthralled by the marvel of this moment. These were the mysterious alchemical weddings: the union of heaven and Earth, the fusion of the animal-vegetable-mineral with the intangible spirit in the human heart, the spring from which divine love flows forth in torrents.

These two experiences of LSD and mushrooms changed my perception of myself, and reality, forever. I felt that my mind had opened up like a flower bud. These events coincided with a gift that Ejo Takata's teacher Yamada Mumon, who had come to visit from Japan after Takata left Fromm's disciples, sent me via one of his students in gratitude for my having offered Takata my house for founding his new zendo. The student, of typical Mexican appearance, dressed like a Japanese monk, his forehead and cheeks invaded by the pimples common to all aspiring students of the Buddha, handed me a folded handkerchief. "Sit down and open it," he exclaimed, standing beside my chair with his back bent, the palms of his hands together at chest height, and his eyes narrowed as if trying to look oriental. I opened the handkerchief. It was folded in such a way as to reject symmetry. There were multiple folds, all beautiful, large and small, diagonal, horizontal, vertical, each one ironed with devotion. It had clearly taken the teacher a long time to achieve this effect. Opening this true work of art, which required me to use my fingers respectfully, brought me deep aesthetic enjoyment. Once the handkerchief was spread open, I saw that in the center, in black ink, a sentence was written in Japanese. The student, in the manner of a samurai, solemnly read what he seemed to know by heart: "When a flower opens, it is spring in the whole world." He turned and left without saying goodbye. I tried unsuccessfully to refold the scarf, but I could not. The experience of life is irreversible.

Reality, in its constant dance, now decided that I was ready to enter the world of operational magic. My neighbor Guillermo Lauder, an agent for popular artists, lived in an apartment building fifty meters away on my same street and invited me to attend a session with the healer Pachita. The lady went there every Friday to "operate" on the sick. I had heard of her. It was said that she opened up bodies with a rusty knife, that she replaced diseased organs with healthy ones, that she could materialize objects, and many other things. All this made me apprehensive, for it sounded like naive inventions, a crude imitation of real surgery. My first contact with folk magic had been at the home of F. S., an Education Ministry official, who hosted a cocktail party in my honor to celebrate my arrival in Mexico to teach pantomime courses. He lived in a luxurious mansion, the walls covered in modern Mexican paintings. These artists were impressively powerful—their works blended muralist expressionism, surrealism, and the abstract schools— but I felt that something was missing. F. S., a very intuitive homosexual who never took his eyes off my face and body for an instant, said, with- out my having voiced this sentiment, "What our painters lack is the magical root. Searching for the chimera of international acclaim, they have forgotten that the sacred basis of Mexican life is witchcraft. Come with me, I'll show you a real creation."

I followed him down a long corridor lined with cabinets lit by greenish lights, full of pre-Columbian pottery and sculptures. We came to his bedroom. Next to the metal bed (the headboard depicted the tree of good and evil, and the ceiling was covered by a large paint- ing by Juan Soriano that showed a gigantic hand stroking the penis of a headless naked Adonis), there was a chest inlaid with black ivory. When he opened it, the inside of the box lit up. I felt a lump form in my throat. He told me to look inside if I dared. There, on velvet-cov- ered trays, lay all kinds of wax figurines. I immediately felt a sharp pain in my head. Those figurines, the color of rotting flesh, were impaled by multiple needles in their eyes, sex organs, anuses, breasts, and all extremities; the expressions on their putrid faces showed unspeakable suffering. Their open mouths, with some of the teeth pierced by pins, gave forth mute howls. These objects, so full of evil energy, affected my body. I wanted to cry. How could there be beings in the world capable of expressing such evil? F. S. closed the lid, offered me a drink of tequila, and laughed, seeing my astonishment.

"Welcome to Mexico, mime. If this is the land of light, then it is also the land of shadow. Do you understand? All the paintings in my rooms together do not have the power of a single one of those wax figures. They are authentic objects of witchcraft, intended to harm someone. I obtained them thanks to certain dangerous contacts I have. I hope that one day the government authorities will allow me to organize an exhibition of this great art."

A couple of years later, F. S. was found murdered in his bed. After castrating him, the killer had stuffed his bleeding penis into his mouth.

This was why, until this moment, I had avoided all contact with folk magic. However, the temptation to see Pachita operate made me decide to face the danger. Urban legends told that black magicians could surreptitiously introduce themselves into the subconscious of a visitor and put a curse on him or her with a delayed effect that, after three to six months, would consume the victim to the point of death. For this reason, before visiting the old woman I protected myself as best I could. In a certain way, without my realizing it, this was my first act of psychomagic. I felt that I had to hide my identity so that her curses would be misdirected by my anonymity. So I dressed in new clothes and shoes. In order that I might not be judged by my tastes, it was important for these clothes not to be chosen by me. I gave my measurements to a friend and asked him to buy all the clothes. I also created a document of identification under a false name (in this case, Martin Arenas) with a different place and date of birth and a photograph of someone else (the face of a dead actor). I bought a pork chop, wrapped it in foil, and put it in my pocket. Every time I put my hand there, the unaccustomed contact with the meat would remind me that I was in a special situation and at all costs must not let myself become captivated. Before heading out the door, I took a shower and rubbed lemon juice all over my body in order to remove as much of my personal scent as possible. Trembling,

Pachita.

I walked the fifty meters between my residence and Guillermo Lauder's apartment.

It must be noted that it was a privilege to be received there by Pachita. When the witch went to operate in other cities, thousands of people would attend. One time they had to pull her out of a pestering crowd using a helicopter. On the other days of the week, she worked on the outskirts of the capital city, serving the poor. On Fridays she healed well-to-do people at Lauder's residence, including powerful politicians, famous artists, sick people who came from far-off countries, and urgent cases.

The door was ajar. I did not hear any voices or footsteps. The place seemed empty. Trying to walk silently, I slipped inside. Everything was dark. The windows had been covered with blankets. Trying not to trip over any furniture, I made my way to the meeting room. Three candles granted a little light to the darkness. Several bodies lay on the floor, wrapped in bloody sheets. Women and men knelt next to them, reciting prayers. Comfortably seated in an armchair was the old woman, wiping blood from her hands. Despite the half-darkness and some distance, I seemed to see her in full light due to the intense magnetism that emanated from her body. She was small, plump, with a long sloping forehead and one eye lower than the other, as if it had fallen down, veiled by a white membrane. I tried to blend in among her acolytes. It was useless. Like a cobra hypnotizing a monkey, she fixed her flashing eye right on my silhouette and, boring into me, said with a voice of great sweetness, "Come, dear child. Why are you afraid of this poor old woman? Come sit next to me." Slowly, I moved toward her, stupefied. This woman had found the right words and tone to direct toward me. Although I was nearly forty years old, I had not matured emotionally. When I fell in love, I behaved like a nine-year-old child (corresponding to the age at which I had been abruptly uprooted from Tocopilla; the loss of the place I loved had dammed up my heart, preventing me from growing up emotionally). For all that I held my pork chop, still I fell into full fascination. I approached Pachita feeling like a son who had finally found his lost mother. She smiled at me with the universal love with which I had always hoped a woman would smile at me. "What do you want, *muchachito*?" The response came from my lips before I could think about it.

"I would like to see your hands."

To general surprise—everyone wondered why she was treating me so preferentially—she put her left hand in mine. The palm of that hand had the softness and purity of a fifteen-year-old virgin! I was invaded by a sensation that is difficult to describe. Before this old woman with her disfigured face, I had the impression of being in the presence of the ideal woman whom the adolescent in me had always sought. She laughed. She withdrew her hand from mine and raised it to the level of my eyes, leaving it there, extended and still. A murmur arose from the attendees: "Accept the gift."

"What gift?" I thought at full speed. "She's making the gesture of giving me something, invisible of course. I'll play along. I'll act as if I'm taking an invisible gift . . ."

I stretched out my fingers and brought them close to her palm as if to grab something. To my surprise, a very small metallic object glinted between the base of her middle and ring fingers. The unthinkable was happening. I had just been holding her hand, it was not possible that she had held anything hidden there, and yet here was the gift. I took it. It was a triangle with one eye inside it. That made an impression on me, because an eye within a triangle was the symbol of my film *El Topo*. (At this moment, believing that the old woman was thinking of me as a cinematographer, I missed a more profound message. On dollar bills, beside the pyramid crowned by a triangle with an eye, is the motto "In God we trust." Perhaps Pachita, in a nonverbal language, was saying to me, "I'll help you find what you need: your inner God.")

I began to draw conclusions from this amazing experience. "This woman is an exceptional prestidigitator. How did she manage to make that triangle appear out of nowhere? And as a villager without any background in film, how could she tell that this was the symbol of my movie? Is Guillermo Lauder her dishonest accomplice? Whatever the case, I want to see how she heals people." I then asked her if she would permit me to view her operations. "Of course, darling child of the soul. Come next Friday. But it is not I who operate, it is Brother."

The following Friday I arrived on time. Pachita was waiting for me. The small apartment looked like a full bus: there were at least forty patients, some on crutches, others in wheelchairs. She asked me to follow her to a small room where there was nothing but a chromolithograph depicting Cuauhtémoc, the deified hero.

"Today, my boy, I want you to be the one who reads the poem that my Lord loves so much."

She put on a yellow robe that was saturated with blood clots in between the gemstones and Indian designs that adorned it. She sat on a wooden bench and handed me a handwritten sheet of paper. She appeared to fall asleep. I read the verses:

> *You were King on this earth*
> *you were great Majesty*
> *and now you are Eternal Light*
> *in the celestial throne.*
> *Come quickly Blessed Child*
> *come to comfort us*
> *come to give us your counsel*
> *and rid us of all evil.*

The poem was long. Pachita occasionally yawned. Then she twisted around as if her body were receiving a being. And suddenly, what had looked like a tired old woman gave forth a raucous cry, raised her right arm, and began to speak with a man's voice: "Dear brothers, I thank the Father for allowing me to be with you again! Bring me the first sick one!"

Patients began to file in, each with an egg in one hand. After rubbing the egg all over the patient's body, the witch cracked it into a glass of water, then examined the white and yolk to discover the evil. If she found nothing very serious, she recommended infusions of olive, mallow, or sometimes a variety of strange things such as coffee enemas, papaya poultices, termite eggs, stewed potatoes, or human excrement. She also prescribed the tongues of certain birds, a glass of water in which rusty nails had been soaked, and remedies that were actions: one sick person was advised to find a stream, put a red flower into it, and observe how the water carried it, then put a bowl of water under the bed to absorb evil thoughts. When the problem seemed serious, she proposed an "operation."

That first Friday, Brother Cuauhtémoc carried out ten operations. I witnessed incredible things. Dressed in my new clothes, I wanted to grip my pork chop. Pachita's assistants, half a dozen of them, immediately ordered me to keep my hand out of my pocket. They also forbade me to cross my legs or arms, requiring me to look at Brother without turning my head. It was astounding to see this possessed woman wielding her great knife and plunging it into the flesh of the patients, making the blood spurt out. Although something in me was saying that this was all theater, an act of prestidigitation designed to impress using terror as the principal healing element, the woman's personality dominated me. Lauder told me that one day the wife of the president of Mexico, having heard so much about her, invited her to an evening reception in the courtyard of the Governor's Palace, where there were many cages containing different varieties of birds. When Pachita arrived, those hundreds of birds awoke and began chirping as if they were greeting the dawn. The medicine woman did not use her charisma alone. Several assistants would also contribute by giving their energy to the operation. These persons were not complicit in a hoax; they all had immense faith in the existence of Brother. In the eyes of these good people, what mattered was the action of the discarnate being. They saw Pachita only as its "flesh." She was a "channel," an instrument used by the god. When not in a trance, she was respected but not worshiped. For them, the discarnate being was more real than the person through which it manifested. This faith that enveloped Pachita generated a sacred atmosphere that contributed to convincing the sick that they had the possibility of being cured.

The patients, sitting in the darkened room, waited for their turn to enter the "operating room." The aides spoke in whispers as if they were in a temple. Sometimes one of them would leave the operating room, hiding a mysterious package in his hands. He would go into the bathroom, and through the door, left ajar, one could see the glare of fire consuming the object. An assistant advised in a whisper, "Do not go until the harm has been consumed. It is dangerous to approach it while it is active. You could catch it . . ." What was this "harm," really? The patients ignored it, but the mere fact of having to refrain from urinating while one of those immolations took place produced a strange impression: they were gradually leaving habitual reality to immerse themselves in a totally irrational parallel world.

Suddenly, four assistants emerged from the operating room carrying a lifeless body wrapped in a bloodied canvas, depositing it on the floor as if it were a corpse. Once the operation was finished and the bandages were in place, Pachita required the patient to be absolutely still for half an hour, under penalty of instant death. The surgical patients, afraid of being killed by magical forces, did not make the slightest move. Needless to say, this clever arrangement served as preparation for the next patient. When Pachita called them in her low voice, always using the same formula, "It's your turn, child of my soul," the patient would start trembling from head to toe and reverting to childhood. I remember that on this day she gave a caramel candy to a minister while asking him in her low and tender voice, "What hurts, little one?" The man replied in a child's voice, "For weeks I have not slept. I have to get up to urinate every half hour."

"Do not worry; I will change your bladder."

Pachita, after turning into Brother and always with her eyes closed, called the men first, stating that since they were weaker than the women, their pains had to be soothed first. There was nothing but a narrow bed with a plastic-covered mattress in the operating room. Each patient had to bring a sheet, a liter of alcohol, a pack of six rolls of cotton, and bandages. The assistants would remove his shirt, and if necessary—for example, for an operation on the testicles—his pants. All manipulations took place in half-darkness, by the light of a single candle, because according to Pachita electric light could damage the internal organs. The patient would cover the bed with his sheet and then lie down. An assistant would ceremoniously hand the healer a long hunting knife. The handle was wrapped in black electrical tape, and the blunt blade bore an Indian engraving with a plume. At Brother's indication of which place on the body was to be opened, an assistant surrounded the area with cotton and liberally poured on alcohol. The smell of the substance filled the room, creating a hospital-like environment.

The first patient was the minister. Brother asked, "Enrique, have you prepared the bladder?" Pachita's son produced a flask containing something resembling organic tissue. The man lay trembling, frozen with fear. I took his hand. The healer made an incision in his belly about fifteen centimeters long. I struggled not to pass out as I saw the blood flow. The old woman palpated the abdomen, raised her hand, made a gesture, and a pair of scissors materialized. She cut something that produced an unbearable stench. She pulled out a mass of stinking flesh, which Enrique wrapped in black paper. Then she took the new bladder from the flask. She placed it next to the wound, and to my great surprise, I saw it absorbed, without anyone pushing it, into the interior of the body. She placed the alcohol-soaked cotton wool over the incision. She pressed down for a moment, then she cleaned away the blood, and the wound disappeared without leaving a scar. "My dear child, you are cured." Her assistants blindfolded the man, wrapped him in his sheet, and carried him out to lay him down in the waiting room. Another assistant ran to the bathroom to burn the black packet.

Despite my disbelief, this act had seemed so real that my reason

278 Magicians, Masters, Shamans, and Charlatans

began to falter. Was she a brilliant prestidigitator or a saint who performed miracles? I was ashamed of myself. How could I not believe that this old woman was a trickster? By light of a single candle, one can hide a myriad of fraudulent manipulations. And if she could perform miracles, why did she need a knife? Did she want us to believe it was a magical instrument? To prove that there was no trickery, she had an assistant hand it to her—but—did she use the same knife that was handed to her? Perhaps, in the darkness, she switched it for another knife with a rubber handle, concealed by the electrical tape, full of dog or chicken blood. It was said that she took in stray dogs out of good will, but what if instead of being a saint she was an impostor who killed these animals in order to extract their vital fluid? And why did she put cotton around the wound? The knife was never disinfected . . . so what was the alcohol for? Pachita, although it was said that she never ate, looked fat, with a large paunch. She always wore an apron over her clothes. What if this belly were false? Was it full of plastic bags containing blood and objects that appeared "magically"? Was she a madwoman? A pathological liar? Like Ichazo, like Castaneda, she told of things that no person of average intelligence could believe. "I know who will die here, and when. I know how many days everyone who comes to visit me has left to live." "Do not worry about the drought. Tomorrow I will make it rain." "I just give a push and I leave my body. Sometimes I visit places, Siberia, Mont Blanc, Mars, the moon, Jupiter." "A cyclone was approaching the Cora Indian Territory, so I went to ask the Father for protection for them, and I got it: the cyclone was blown off course." "When I fall into a trance, I live in the astral world. If someone destroys my body, Brother reconstructs it." Pachita also claimed to travel in time, predicting future events or going back into the past to retrieve some object or other.

Standing at her side, I saw her pour an egg white over the eye of a blind man, then stick her index finger, with its long red-painted nail, into the eye. I saw her change a patient's heart, seeming to open the chest with a single blow, letting loose a stream of blood that stained my face. Pachita made me put my hand into the wound to feel the torn flesh. (When I told Guillermo that it felt cold like a raw steak, he said it was because Brother performed this work in an astral dimension, distinct from our own.) I felt the new heart arrive in the hole; it had allegedly been previously purchased by Enrique; I did not know where or from whom, perhaps from a corrupt morgue employee. The muscle mass was implanted in the patient in a magical manner. This phenomenon was repeated in each operation. Pachita took up a piece of intestine that, as soon as she placed it on the "surgical patient," disappeared into his insides. I saw her open up a skull, remove cancerous pieces of brain, and put in new gray matter. These tactile and optical illusions, if that is what they were, were accompanied by olfactory effects—the smell of blood, the stench of cancers and wounds—as well as auditory effects: the aqueous sound of viscera, the clatter of bones being cut by a carpenter's saw. By the third operation, everything began to seem natural to me. We were in another world, a world in which natural laws were abolished. If a transfusion was needed because the patient had lost too much blood, Brother put one end of a tube in her own mouth and the other end into a hole in the patient's arm, and began to spit out liters of reddish liquid. On two occasions I saw the illness transformed into a kind of animal that seemed to snort and moved excrescences that were like limbs. I returned to my home at midnight, astounded and covered in blood. The world would never be the same to me. I had finally seen a superior being performing miracles, whether true or false.

I decided to attend the operations every Friday. The healer's work had gained my deep admiration. She was not getting rich with this activity. Upon leaving, the patients deposited however much money they wanted to give in a saucepan. Most left only coins, and the richest ones, those who had come from other countries, showed a strange stinginess. One man, whom she had supposedly cured of paralysis, said, "I have no money to pay you." She replied, "Very well, pay me nothing now. When you are healed, you will return to work. Then you will pay me what you want to." Lauder told me that Pachita lived in a modest house on the outskirts of the city surrounded by dogs, parrots, monkeys, and an eagle. Apart from supporting her children, the little money she could save went to a small school in her neighborhood. "In the poor settlements of Mexico people see nothing but nastiness. It's almost impossible to straighten up a jerk once he's grown big. They have to be taught good things while they're still little." Obviously, healing was Pachita's vocation. If she was performing trickery, it was sacred trickery. Deception with a charitable purpose is accepted in all religions. The mystic Jacob deceived his brother and his father. In Islamic tradition, lying is forbidden, but clever solutions are accepted. A fugitive passes along a road where a sage is sitting on a stream bank. "Please," he says, "do not tell my pursuers that I went this way." The sage waits until the fugitive disappears from his sight, then goes and sits on the opposite bank. When the persecutors come and ask him if he saw anyone pass, he responds, "I haven't seen anyone pass the whole time I've been sitting here." For a miracle to occur, faith is necessary. Shamans know this. They perform false miracles in their ceremonies with neophytes so that the students' rational vision will rupture and thus, convinced that there are other dimensions beside their rigid reality, they will begin to have faith. Thanks to this new vision, exceptional events can occur. Was Pachita a great creator of sacred tricks?

I attended countless surgeries over the course of three years. Many were healed. Others died. For example, two people suffering from incurable diseases came from Paris. One, a prominent journalist, had cancer of the hip. The other, who had serious heart disease, was the public relations manager of a film company. Both of them were accompanied by a Dominican priest, Maurice Cocagnac (who later wrote a book about these experiences), and were operated on by Brother. One had his heart changed; the other had a new bone inserted into his hip. Before they returned to France, Pachita said, "Dear children, you are healed. Stop taking medicines, and whatever you do, do not consult a physician before six months have passed." As soon as he returned to Paris, the journalist assembled a meeting of doctors. The results were clear: the cancer was still there. He died a month later. The other man, however, stopped taking his pills and saw no doctors for six months. Then, when they examined him, they were speechless: the heart was healthy, working like that of a young man . . . I realized that in the magical world, not only faith but also obedience played a vital role. Even if one did not believe in the witch's power, it was desirable to give that power every chance to act by following her instructions to the letter.

I later applied this idea in psychomagic. A psychomagical act must be performed to the letter, as a contract. The client must promise to obey. If he does not, or if he deviates from the instructions, out of prejudice, fear, or desire for comfort, then the subconscious realizes it can disobey, and the healing will not be achieved. When I was shooting *Tusk* near Bangalore, India, one of the acting elephants, perhaps unnerved by the heat, destroyed a set. Its mahout* (or cornac) began to punish it with an iron bar. It was impressive to see this elephant, trembling like a child, urinating on itself with fear of its vulnerable master. The man beat it until it bled. I protested. It seemed inconceivable to me that one should punish an animal with such intense cruelty. The official who was in charge of the elephant colony said, "Please do not intervene. The trainer knows what he is doing. If you let your elephant disobey, even in something small, it will feel free to do what it wants, and later will end up killing humans." The subconscious behaves in the same way. The trainer has to teach it to obey. This is difficult; in fact, people fall ill because they have a painful problem that they cannot solve or become conscious of. They want to be treated—that is, they want their symptoms eliminated—but not cured. Although they ask for help, they then struggle to stop that help from being effective.

Brother required unconditional collaboration between the patient and all the assistants for these operations. Sometimes the work seemed to become complicated; at those times, the surgeon and the patient himself would request the help of all those present. I remember operations during which Cuauhtémoc suddenly exclaimed through Pachita's

---

*Elephant trainer.

mouth, "The child is getting cold; warm the air quickly or we will lose him!" We all ran around hysterically in search of an electric heater. Upon plugging it in, we discovered that the electricity had been cut off. "Do something, you wretches, or the child will go into agony," growled Brother, while the sick man, frozen with terror and on the verge of cardiac arrest, no doubt from seeing his belly opened up and his guts in the air, moaned, "Brothers, I beg you, help me." We all brought our mouths close to his body and anxiously breathed on him, forgetting ourselves, trying desperately to warm him with our breath. "Well done, dear children," said Brother suddenly. "The temperature is rising, the danger is over, I can continue now." I realized that all healing is collective, tribal. The shaman does not act alone—he or she is always surrounded by invisible allies—and the sick person is not alone either. When I had the opportunity to interview the principal machi at a *machitún** in Temuco, Chile, I asked what methods he used to heal the sick. He replied, "The first thing I do is to ask them who is their owner."

"Their owner?"

"That's right, all sick people belong to someone: their spouse, their family, their employer. Those who have no owner cannot be cured. Once that is known, I discuss the price. To cure, one must organize a meal and invite friends who will help to drive away the devils with noises, drumbeats, or gunshots. Once the place is clean, I can operate accompanied by beneficent spirits. We work for the sick person here on Earth while they do the same in heaven."

Since my meeting with Castaneda I had continued to feel a sharp pain in my liver. So, armed with an egg, I went to see Pachita. She rubbed the painful region and said, "Dear child of the soul, you have a tumor there. I will operate on you to remove it." Seeing the pallor on my face, she laughed. "Fear not, little boy, I have been operating for over seventy years, thousands of people have been opened by the knife of Brother. If an accident had happened to any one of his patients, I would

---

*Sacred Mapuche festival.

have been put in prison long ago. Listen: when I was ten years old, I saw a commotion near the tent at a circus because the pregnant elephant could not bear her baby, which was positioned sideways. There she was, in agony, lying on a carpet of sawdust. The poor performers were weeping. That elephant was the star of their show, and if she died, they too would die, from hunger. The elephant suddenly began to scream deafeningly. I do not know what happened to me then. I fell asleep, and when I woke up I was covered with blood. They told me that I had taken one of the knife thrower's knives, opened the animal's belly, removed her child, and then closed the wound, laying on my hands, without leaving a scar. Since then, I have never ceased to operate on both humans and animals."

I considered what she was telling me to be a therapeutic story, completely untrue. But, seized by an irresistible curiosity, I decided to undergo the experience to see what it felt like to be in such unusual circumstances. I removed my shirt as if I were doing something funny. But once I was lying on the bed, with Pachita brandishing her knife before me dressed as an Aztec hero and surrounded by praying fanatics, I began to feel afraid. Maybe they were all crazy. Panicking, I exclaimed, "My pain is gone, Brother. It is not necessary to operate." I tried to get up. The possessed woman, with irresistible authority, obliged me to remain lying down, placed the tip of the knife behind my left ear, and slowly lowering it said, "If you do not want me to operate on the liver, I'll begin by opening you from here, I'll take your heart out"—she continued lowering the knife—"then I'll cut through your stomach, and finally, I'll remove that bothersome devil from your liver!"

It was incredible psychological subtlety: she was forcing me to choose the less atrocious of two atrocious possibilities. Forgetting the third possibility, which was to jump up and run away, I said that she should only operate on the liver, please! A pair of scissors appeared in her hand; she pulled up a roll of my skin, and she made an incision. I heard the noise of the two steel blades. The horror began. This was not theater. I felt the pain of someone whose flesh is being cut with scissors! The blood flowed, and I thought I was going to die. Then she gave me a cut in the belly with the knife, and I had the sensation of my guts being exposed to the open air. It was horrible! I have never felt such pain. For minutes that seemed eternal, I suffered terribly and turned white. Pachita gave me a transfusion. As she spat the strange red liquid through the plastic tube that she had pushed into my wrist, I gradually felt a pleasant warmth come over me. Then she lifted my bleeding liver (mine or a calf's, what do I know?) and started pulling an excrescence from it. "We will pull it out at the roots," Brother said. And I endured, in addition to the odor of the blood and the horrifying sight of my crimson viscera, the greatest pain I had ever felt in my life. I squealed shamelessly. She gave one final pull. She showed me a piece of matter that seemed to move like a toad, had her assistant wrap it in black paper, put my liver back in place, ran her hands over my belly closing the wound, and at that moment the pain disappeared. If it was an illusion, it was executed perfectly: not only I, but all who were present, among them the film producer Michel Seydoux, saw the blood flow and the belly being opened. I was blindfolded, wrapped in a sheet, carried to the waiting room, and laid down among the other surgical patients. I lay there perfectly still for half an hour, glad to be alive. Then Pachita, wiping off blood, knelt beside me, took my hands, and asked me what my name was. She embraced me in her arms, and I surrendered to my thirst for mothering. The more I asked for, the more she gave; I wanted infinite tenderness, I received infinite tenderness. This woman was a mountain, as impressive as a mythical Tibetan master. I never felt so much gratitude as at the moment when she told me I was cured and that I could and should leave. Indeed, Pachita knew the human soul and knew very well how to use a therapy that mixed love and terror. In this regard, I am reminded of the words of Maimonides at the beginning of the Treatise Berachot in the Talmud: "Gather, sages, and wait in your seats. I will give you a beautiful gift: I will teach you the fear of God."

It is necessary to collaborate with the healer in order to free oneself from disease. Despite believing in the power of Brother, some people may very well not have wanted to recover their health. I remember a brilliant phytotherapist named Henriette, a patient of my doctor friend Jean Claude, who had been told she had no more than two years left to live. Henriette had cancer, and both her breasts had been removed. At the request of Jean Claude, who wanted to try everything, she traveled to Mexico. She stayed with us in our house. Although very depressed, she declared that she was ready to let Pachita operate on her. Pachita proposed replacing all her blood and injecting two liters of plasma from another dimension, materialized by Brother. The day came, and after the usual ceremony, Henriette lay on the bed. Brother cut her arm, and we heard her blood trickling into a brass bucket. It was a thick and foul-smelling stream. Then, as in other operations I had seen, Brother inserted the end of a plastic tube into the wound, this time raising the other end up in the air to connect it to the invisible. We heard the sound of a liquid slowly emanating from who knows where, and Brother said, "Receive the holy plasma, daughter; do not reject it."

The day after the operation Henriette was sad, downhearted. We tried to bring her around, but to no avail. She was like a child, surly and selfish. She tried to make us feel guilty for wanting to save her from her ordeal. Two days later, a large purulent abscess appeared on her arm. Very scared, I called Enrique, who, after consulting with his mother, said, "Your friend has faith in medicine, but she rejects it. She wants to rid herself of the holy plasma. Tonight she should relieve herself in a basin and apply the excrement to her arm tomorrow morning." I conveyed the message to Henriette, who shut herself in her room. I do not know if she followed the advice or not, but what I do know is that the abscess burst, leaving a huge hole, so deep that one could see the bone. We immediately brought her to the house of Pachita, who, as Brother, said in her masculine voice, "I have been waiting for you, my child, I will give you what you want. Come . . ." The healer took her by the hand like a child, led her to the bed, and surprisingly, began to hum an old French song as she moved the knife back and forth before the patient's wide eyes. It seemed to me that she had hypnotized her. Then she asked, "Tell me, my dear, why did you want them to cut off your breasts?"

To which Henriette, who spoke Spanish, answered in a childlike voice, "To not be a mother."

"And then, my dear child, what do you want them to cut out?"

"The ganglia that swell up in my neck."

"What for?"

"So that I won't have to talk to people."

"And what next, my child?"

"I would like them to cut out the ganglia that will swell under my arms."

"What for?"

"So that I won't have to work."

"And what next?"

"I would like them to cut out the ganglia that swell around my crotch, so that I can be alone with myself."

"And what next?"

"The ganglia in my legs, so that I won't have to go anywhere."

"And what do you want after that?"

"To die . . ."

"Very well, my child, now I know the path of your illness. Choose: either you advance on this path, or you heal."

Pachita put a plaster on her arm, and after three days the abscess had healed. Henriette decided to return to Paris and died two weeks later in the arms of Jean Claude. The last gesture she made was to put a wedding ring onto her doctor's ring finger. When I told the sad news to Pachita, she told me, "Brother comes not only to heal. He also helps those who want to die. Cancer and other serious diseases present themselves like armies of warriors, following a precise plan of conquest. When you reveal to a patient who wishes to destroy herself the path that her illness is taking, she will quickly follow that path.

This is why the Frenchwoman stopped fighting instead of suffering for two years. She surrendered to the disease and let it carry out its plan in two weeks."

It was a great lesson: before this, I had believed that it was sufficient to make a person aware of their self-destructive urges to save them. Pachita made me understand that this discovery could also hasten death.

The first thing Pachita did with anyone who came to see her was to touch them affectionately. From the moment they felt this old woman's warm hands she became the Universal Mother. Pachita knew that in all adults a child sleeps, eager for love—even those most secure in themselves—and that physical contact is more effective than words for establishing trust and putting the subject into a receptive state. This contact also seemed to allow her to make the diagnosis. I remember the day I brought a French friend, Jean Paul G., to her. He had been feeling pain for some time, and it had taken the French doctors six months to find a polyp in his intestine. Pachita ran her hands over his body and immediately exclaimed, "My boy, you have a bad lump in your insides."

My friend was stunned! But apart from showing these almost divinatory abilities, the sorceress also gave advice that seemed to me like acts of psychomagic: one day she received a man who was on the verge of suicide because he could not bear the idea of going bald at age thirty. He had tried all possible treatments without success and could not accept that he was bald. Brother asked him, through the old woman's mouth, "Do you believe in me?"

The man replied in the affirmative, and indeed he did have faith in Pachita. The spirit then gave these instructions: "Gather a kilo of rat excrement, including the urine, and mix it well into a paste that you will apply to your head. That will make you grow hair."

The man protested weakly, but Pachita insisted, saying that if he wanted to avoid baldness, he had no choice. Three months later, he came back to see the old woman and said, "It is very difficult to find rat droppings, but I finally found a laboratory where they breed white rats. I persuaded one of the workers to save the droppings for me. Once I had a kilo, including urine, I made the paste, and then I realized that I did not mind having no hair. So I did not apply the ointment and decided to be content with my fate."

Pachita had asked him to pay a price that he was not willing to pay. When he found himself confronting the act, he realized that he could accept his lot perfectly well. Faced by the reality of the difficult act that was required, he discovered that he preferred to remain bald. He left his imaginary world and stared the real world in the face. These instructions, initially seeming absurd, gave him cause to mature, putting him through a process that finally made it possible for him to accept himself as he was.

I remember one person for whom money posed a serious problem: he was unable to make a living. The old woman prescribed a strange ceremony.

"You should urinate in a pot every night until it is full. Then leave the full container under your bed for thirty days and sleep above your pee."

I witnessed the consultation, and of course, I wondered what her intent could be. Slowly, I began to make sense of it: if a person who does not suffer any physical or intellectual disability cannot earn a living, it is because he does not want to. Some part of him could not tolerate money. Following Pachita's prescription would expose him to some real torture; it does not take long for a pot of urine, kept under a bed, to start smelling terrible. The patient, forced to sleep above the pot, steeped in his own vapors, would unconsciously establish a symbiotic relationship: urine is yellow, like gold. But at the same time, it is waste. Producing waste is a physiological need, and the need to urinate and defecate is itself a consequence of another necessity, eating and drinking. To provide for this, one must earn money. Money, insofar as it represents energy, needs to circulate. This person was not earning a living because he felt repulsed by money, considered it dirty, vile, and did not want to be involved in handling it. He refused to participate in the movement whereby money goes in and out, turning into food. It disgusted him to acknowledge the rightful place of "gold" in the network that constitutes all existence. Pachita forced him to master that repulsion. When he found himself alone with his urine every night, he had the revelation that money is dirty only when it does not circulate. The problems had begun when he refused to look at money and stuck it under the bed. Moreover, the requirement that he continue the exercise until its end forced him to prove his will, an indispensable quality for earning a living normally.

On another occasion, a woman from whom Brother had removed lung cancer in a previous operation came back complaining that she still had severe respiratory distress. Pachita told her with great severity, "Your cancer is cured, and you have not understood that. When one thinks one is sick, the body becomes sick. You are well, but you do not want to cooperate. Do not think that you are sick and you will stop feeling discomfort."

One must live in a world in which superstition becomes reality in order to be a witch or shaman. For my part, I did not have sufficient belief in primitive magic to become a healer. I was sure those bloody tumors that moved and snorted were just animals, lizards, frogs, whatever. Thus, although I did want to learn from Pachita, I never expected to receive her gift of making me a healer, and I realized that in order to learn from Brother I had to assume that all the miracles were faked. If I had started with the assumption that it was all genuine, I soon would have found myself at a dead end, straining to make myself into a magician with no success, or with only partial or mediocre success, because, in my belief, one cannot change one's skin, free oneself from rational culture, and play at being a "primitive." Thus, I found myself mentally disposed to learn something that would later serve me in my own context; for example, how to use symbolic objects in order to produce certain effects in others, or how to address myself directly to the subconscious in its own language, whether through words or actions. Later, thanks to the example of this remarkable woman, I became interested in learning about the role of magic in history. I read a good number of books on the topic, trying to identify universal elements worthy of being used in my own practice in a conscious and nonsuperstitious manner. All ancient cultures believed in the power of incantations, the idea that desires that were expressed in words in the required form would be realized. But the name of the god or the spirit was often reinforced by its association with an image; the ancients also knew intuitively that the subconscious is receptive to forms and objects. They attached great importance to the written word when it was transformed into a talisman. Another universal practice was purification, or ritual ablutions. In healing ceremonies in Babylon the exorcists would order the patients to undress, throw away their old clothes—symbols of the sick "I"—and put on new clothes. The Egyptians considered purification a preliminary prerequisite for the recitation of magical formulas, as this text illustrates: "If a man pronounces the formula for his own use, he should anoint himself with oils and salves, and hold a full censer in his hand; he must have a certain kind of natron behind his ears and a different kind of natron in his mouth; he must put on new garments after washing himself in the waters of the flood, wear white sandals, and have the image of the goddess Maat painted on his tongue with fresh ink." The ancients also attributed the role of ally to numerous objects: magical texts were recited over an insect, a small animal, or even a necklace. Linen bands were used, and wax figurines, feathers, hair, and so forth. The mages engraved the names of their enemies in vessels that were then broken and buried; a similar destruction and disappearance was supposed to happen to their adversaries. Effigies of "evil ones" were painted on the soles of royal sandals so that the king could trample on potential invaders every day. Along similar lines, studying the Hittite witches led me to discover the concepts of substitution and identification: the mage does not destroy the evil but takes control of it, discovers its origins, removes it from the body or spirit of the victim, and returns it to the underworld. According to an ancient text, "An object is tied to the right hand and right foot of the patient, then untied, and a mouse is tied there, while the officiant says: 'I have removed the evil and tied it to this mouse'; then the mouse is released." Pachita extirpated evil and sent it into a plant, a tree, or a cactus, which would then slowly die. She would substitute the sick person with a lamb or a goat; the patient's turban would be put on the head of the goat, then she would cut its throat with a knife that had previously touched the patient's neck. According to Jewish magic it is possible to cheat, deceive, and mislead the forces of evil. Therefore, the person who is attacked by these forces goes in disguise or changes his or her name. If one wishes to purify an object, one buries it in the ground.

Pachita had told me, "I'll visit you in your dreams." It happened that, probably because of an intestinal infection, I had abdominal pains that went on for several days because I wanted to heal myself with herbs and not antibiotics. I slept badly for three nights, but on the fourth night I had a dream: I was in my bed, suffering the same pain that I was having when awake. Pachita came, lay down next to me, and sucked on the right side of my neck, saying, "I will heal you, my boy." With some effort, she slid her left hand between our bodies and put it on my belly. Then she rose in the air without separating from me. We levitated horizontally for a moment, then returned down to the bed. She slowly faded away. I woke up healed, feeling no pain.

When Pachita died, Guillermo Lauder told me that the doctor could not immediately sign the death certificate because the corpse's chest was warm. This warmth lasted for three days. Only then could he declare her dead. Some time later her gift passed to her son Enrique, who, possessed by Brother, began to operate as his mother had done. Claudia, an assistant to the film director François Reichenbach, had been in a car crash during a filming in Belize (known as British Honduras at that

time) in which several nerves in her back were severed and nine vertebrae were broken. She spent three months in a coma. When she regained
consciousness, she was told that she was paralyzed and would not be
able to walk again. As a last resort, she traveled to Mexico and was operated on by Pachita, who, according to Claudia's account, opened her
up from the neck to the tailbone and replaced the damaged vertebrae
with others that she had bought from the morgue. The following week,
she was walking. This "miracle" changed her life and led her to become
interested in Mexican magic. She had a strong desire to help her friends
in France, for which purpose she invited Enrique to come to Paris to
operate. He agreed to come.

At that time, my daughter Eugenia was suffering from an almost
exclusively French disease: spasmophilia, involving very painful invol-
untary stomach muscle contractions. She had lost her appetite and
was skin and bones. No doctor could cure her. Despite her having
a university degree and a rigidly rational education—she had been
raised until age sixteen by her German mother in Düsseldorf—I
proposed that Brother should try to heal her. Although she did not
believe in these "frauds," she agreed out of sheer desperation. When
we arrived at the apartment a Mexican assistant who had come with
Enrique opened the door. Placing his finger on his lips, he indicated
that we should enter in silence. The rooms were dark, the windows
covered with blankets. We groped our way into the living room and
sat down. Our eyes adjusted to the darkness. The silence was impressive. Suddenly, the assistant rushed to the bathroom door and opened
it. A burning object glowed there, and the man murmured, "It's an
evil. Don't go in until it is consumed. Otherwise, it can fall upon
you." And he left. Eugenia, with a contemptuous smile on her lips,
grumbled, "Stories for mental retards."

After a while the back door opened and two people came out carrying a third person who was quite pale, wrapped in a bloody sheet,
apparently asleep or dead. They laid her down on the floor next to us.
Horrified, my daughter asked that we leave immediately, and trembling

from head to toe, she stood up to flee. A strange figure appeared, a man who had stayed hidden in the shadows, and asked Eugenia to come closer. All at once, she calmed down and followed him meekly.

I witnessed the operation. There was only one bed, as before, and the room was barely lit by a candle. A woman was lying on the floor, covered in blood, with a cheerful expression on her face. Brother, wearing an Aztec emperor's robe, was a terrifying site. Although he wielded the hunting knife, the healer never stood up. He remained seated in the shadows. All we saw of him was his hands. The "flesh" had become impersonal. He listened to my daughter's belly, told her that a great anger against her father had accumulated there, and that he was going to cure her of a disease that was not an injury. The knife sank into her flesh, the blood flowed, and he placed his hands in the wound, seeming to put the organs in place. Then he removed his hands, kneaded the skin, and left no trace of a cut. Eugenia never complained. Brother spoke sweetly this time and did not cause pain. As we were leaving, I remarked on this to the assistant, who told me that Brother was progressing from one incarnation to the next and that he had finally learned not to make his patients suffer. Eugenia never had spasms again, returned to her normal weight, and soon after, met the man who would be the love of her life.

After inventing psychomagic and psychoshamanism I went back to Mexico City several times to study the methods of so-called charlatans and *curanderos*. They are very abundant. At the heart of the capital there is a large market for witchcraft. All manner of magical products are sold there: veils, devil fish, pictures of saints, herbs, blessed soaps, Tarot cards, amulets. There are some women in gloomy back rooms with a triangle painted on their foreheads who will "clean" your body and aura. Every neighborhood has its own witch or wizard. Thanks to the faith of their patients, they often achieve a cure. Doctors trained at the universities despise these practices. For sure, this medicine is not scientific, but it is an art. And for the human subconscious, it is easier to understand the language of dreams—from a certain point of view diseases are dreams, messages revealing unresolved problems—than to understand rational language. The charlatans develop very personal techniques with great creativity, I compare them to painters: anyone can paint a landscape, but the style in which an individual does it is inimitable. Some have more imagination or talent than others, but all are useful if faith is placed in them. They speak to the primitive human that still lies inside each and every one of us.

Don Arnulfo Martinez is a soccer player turned sorcerer. I had a hard time finding him. He lives in a poor, chaotic neighborhood. The houses have numbers out of order: eight is next to sixty-two, then thirty-four, and so on. I found him by asking among his neighbors. Don Arnulfo waited for me at the end of a narrow passageway, the walls of which were covered by canary cages. I had to go through a room where his wife, his mother, and his numerous offspring were. Behind plastic curtains shone a little sacred space with shelves full of statuettes representing Christ and the Virgin of Guadalupe, many lighted candles, colored liquids in various types of bottles, and photographs from his soccer-playing days. At the center of the altar reigned a soccer ball, with its black and white pentagons. Rather than hiding the passion of his youth, the healer used it in his magical practices. To diagnose my ailments he first rubbed me all over my body with a bouquet of red and white carnations, then did the same with the soccer ball. He predicted economic problems. He carved my name on a candle with his long fingernails and told me to burn it in my room until it was consumed. By chance, because he wanted it to happen, or by means of some trick, the canaries began to sing when he placed one of his hands on my forehead and the other on my heart to release me from my preoccupations. Nothing is better than a chorus of canaries for calming the soul. Don Arnulfo tells us, "Everyone should be healed with what he loves most, without worrying about what others think. Objects are receptacles for energy, positive or negative. They are not evil or sacred.

It is the hatred or love you place in them that transforms them. A soccer ball can become holy."

Gloria is an energetic woman dressed in shorts and a t-shirt. She is tall, muscular, and the mother of three children. Her loyal assistant is her husband, a small, thin man. Gloria does not appear to have anything extraordinary about her. She lives in an apartment and sells dolls in the likenesses of characters from children's television shows. There is nothing on the bare walls but one large portrait of María Sabina because when Gloria falls into a trance she receives the spirit of this sage of the mushrooms. Her patients then address her as *Abuelita* (Grandma). She does not have a special sacred place. She receives people in her bedroom, which is almost completely filled by a very wide bed and a wardrobe. She sits on a corner of the bed and has the client stand in front of her. She closes her eyes, bends down, and then straightens up transformed into Abuelita, an old woman who speaks broken Spanish mixed with Nahuatl phrases. She examines the person with her hands, after which she begins to dictate a long series of herbs, flowers, and ancient medicines. Her husband religiously writes down these recipes in a school notebook. Finally, "María Sabina" intertwines her fingers and makes a purifying circle with her arms. The patient puts her legs into the circle, draws them back out as if pulling a sword from its sheath, and then does the same with the arms, head, and torso. "You are cleansed, my grandchild." While Abuelita says goodbye and Gloria begins to emerge from the trance, the husband makes photocopies of the handwritten notes on an old machine. Here is one that advises fumigation for purifying a house to expel negative spirits: "Put a little oil and twenty-one chiles de arbol (seeds removed) into a frying pan, fry them, and burn them. As the smoke from the pan passes through the house, say 'I cut, I separate, I remove, I destroy everything that is not in harmony with us and every being of darkness.' Once the pan has passed through the house, leave it in a secure place outside the house for about ten to fifteen minutes. Return to the house and open the windows. Do this on three occasions as close together as possible, but not on the same day."

Éliphas Lévi, in his book *Transcendental Magic: Its Doctrine and Ritual,* summarized this in a few words: "To know, to dare, to will, to keep silence." One could say that Abuelita summarized healing witchcraft in four phrases. *I cut:* the ties are cut that join the patient to negative desires, feelings, and thoughts. *I separate:* the spirit is separated from its material prison. *I remove:* the harm is removed (the disease is seen as a demon sent by envious people or malevolent entities). *I destroy:* the harm is destroyed outside the patient's body. The disease has been assimilated into an object and is still considered alive. Gloria, in a trance, adds a new dimension to the act of possession when Abuelita tells the patient, "Now that you have made contact with me, I am also in you. You go, but I go with you. I will not abandon you. When you want to help your fellow humans call for me and, through you, I will help them." She is telling us that the sublime values of the spirit, once revealed, are irreversible.

Don Ernesto lives in a more affluent neighborhood and has adapted his apartment to use it for his business. The room looks like a little railway station. There are long wooden benches along each side. Clients sit on them, patiently waiting to be cleansed after having previously stopped at the desk by the door and paid his wife the equivalent of three dollars. In the back of the room there is a square on the floor made of white tiles, three by three meters. There Don Ernesto officiates, assisted by his daughter.

The applicant is asked to write what he or she wishes to be rid of on a sheet of paper: illnesses, financial problems, emotional troubles, family tensions, anxieties, and so forth, and to stand at the center of the square. The daughter, squeezing a plastic bottle filled with alcohol, squirts a stream in a circle around the client. Don Ernesto sets light to it. The sheet of paper with the list of evils is consumed in the flames. Once the ring of fire has burned out, he sweeps the client's body with a bouquet of chrysanthemums. Then he extends his open palms in an act of supplication. He stretches his right hand toward the ceiling, makes as if to take some of the air (the divine world), places it in his open left palm, and has the patient grab hold of the invisible gift. Don Ernesto defines this gift with a single word: sometimes *peace,* other times *love, prosperity,* or *health.* The client leaves with clenched hands as if holding a treasure. From Don Ernesto, one understands that in order to give something, it is not necessary to possess it materially.

Don Toño is a Huichol Indian. His clothes are white with beautiful embroideries mixing yellow, sky blue, black, and white. Once a week, an avid promoter picks him up on the mountain and brings him into the capital so that he can practice his medicine in the back room of an esoteric bookstore. The shop owner, equally avid, charges the equivalent of fifty dollars in advance for each consultation. After bowing and uttering an invocation to the four cardinal points in his language, Don Toño asks what the illness is and where the client feels pain. After pressing his fingers on the exact spot he begins to "sweep" the body with a fan made of stiff feathers, from the outermost points to the center of the pain. He gives the impression that he is gathering up the evil that has spread throughout the body. Then, with arms open like the wings of an eagle, he puts his mouth on that center and starts sucking. Next he looks up and spits out a stone of various colors that range from sepia to black, sometimes small, sometimes larger. He has removed the evil. I had a wart on the corner of one eye. After sucking up and spitting out my evil (a greenish pebble), Don Toño put his hands together as if in prayer. He sucked on my fingertips and spat a beautiful crystal into my palm. Then he gave me a beaded necklace with his four sacred colors. From him, one learns that the purpose of medicine is not only to cure, but also for the patient to see his or her own values revealed.

Soledad is a mature woman, brunette, very strong, an actress by profession, who keeps the doors of her apartment open all weekend giving free massages. She is a medium and is possessed by the spirit of Magdalena.

When she saw me coming she recognized me, which did not surprise me since she is part of the world of theater and film. But this was not the reason why she saw me before seeing anyone else. She led me to the small room in which she practices, where there was a small white enameled iron cabinet, like those one sees in hospitals, a black leather massage table, and on the wall a photograph of a woman, looking very Mexican, whose face with strikingly bright eyes was familiar to me.

"She's my lady, Magdalena. She was Don Juan's teacher. You knew her; she told me about you. You went to see her because you had a shortage of energy due to a theatrical failure, right?"

Indeed! I had had so much trouble with the vanity of the actors, the meanness of the press, the little interest shown by the public, and the huge economic loss, that both my energy and my joy of living had deserted me. Someone recommended that I visit Magdalena for an energetic massage. I did so. I found her to be an indefinable woman. On the one hand she was primitive, with simple and direct folk wisdom, and on the other hand at times she revealed an educated mind, using phrases worthy of a university professor. The only way I can define her is to say that she was a like diamond, always showing some new and different facet. She had me undress and lie face down on her rectangular table. She showed me a large jar filled with a paste that looked like Vaseline, and told me that the Mayans of Quintana Roo had taught her how to make this ointment. She smeared it all over my back and also my neck and legs. There was no massage, just a gentle application of the paste. Then she put her hands on my head and prayed in a strange language. I felt lighter, more and more cheerful, and had a fit of the giggles. My depression and fatigue vanished. Before I left, I wanted to pay her. She stopped me. "I did very little. The ointment is what helped you, thank it." I asked what it was made of and, smiling mischievously, she replied, "A few herbs that you wouldn't know and a lot of marijuana ground into a powder and dissolved in hot petroleum jelly. Marijuana awakens joy in the body. The body transmits it to the spirit, and the spirit realizes that beneath all of your troubles, it remains intact, like a bright jewel. Then the weight vanishes because it was just a bad dream."

Soledad confirmed Magdalena's ability to adopt different personalities. On one occasion they had been walking past the Palace of Fine Arts, where a foreign dance troupe was putting on a program, and Soledad had complained sadly that she could not go to see them due to lack of money, because tickets were very expensive. Magdalena had told her to follow her: "They will let us in for free." They were humbly dressed. Soledad felt self-conscious but followed her teacher. Magdalena changed her attitude, and in a few seconds she looked like a princess. One might have said that she was wearing an invisible evening gown. The doormen bowed to her and let the two women pass through. The ushers, with looks of fascinated respect, showed them to a box. They were able to watch the ballet in complete tranquillity, without anyone bothering them.

The recipe for the ointment was a secret. Soledad did not know that Magdalena had done me the honor of telling it to me. It is true that Soledad's massages were excellent. Her hands, with the fingertips brought together with the thumb, were like snake heads; her arms like the undulating bodies of the snakes that she made slither over the skin, pressing until she seemed to be massaging the bones, not the flesh. At the same time, for every part of the body on which she lingered, she recited the name of some Nahuatl god and an oration addressed to that god. She divided the body into twenty sections, with twenty gods. At the belly (*Kath*), instead of naming a god, she sang the patient's name, converting him or her into the center of the divine group. Then she spread on the paste and the marijuana took effect. It was a mystical euphoria. Disease and drunkenness were forgotten. The patient, feeling healthy, regained faith. When the effects of the ointment ceased, the deceived subconscious continued to believe that the body was healthy, so the healing was accomplished.

Don Rogelio is known as the Rabid Healer. He is an old man, thin, yellow skinned, toothless, dressed in black with a skull ring on each finger. He says, "People are envious, and they act on it. Jealousy entangles

the spirit; envy causes damage. So they must be found and driven out."
He cites the Gospel of Luke, in which Jesus healed a man possessed
by an unclean spirit, shouting at the demon with compelling authority,
"Come out of him!"

"When the spirit is tangled, I follow the example of our Lord and
liberate it by force." Don Rogelio, standing in front of the patient, whips
the air around the latter's body with a red rooster, uttering thunderous
cries of rage:

"Get out, you fucking bastard! Go! Go! Leave this Christian in
peace!"

From him, one learns that one must proceed with total certainty
and absolute authority. The slightest doubt causes failure. There is a
Zen saying: "One grain of dust in the blue of midday darkens the whole
sky."

I attended the healings performed by Don Carlos Said at various times
throughout the years. Beside Pachita he is one of the most creative healers, in constant development and adding new elements to his sessions.
When I visited him for the first time he received me in a room of his
large apartment in an old building not far from the city center. People
were waiting in the lounge amidst vases of flowers and paintings depicting Christ. Many people told me that Don Carlos had cured them of
dangerous cancers. He had a small altar, similar to those in Catholic
temples. Beside it was an old Spanish-style wooden chair with red velvet
cushions. According to Said, although we did not see her, his teacher,
Doña Paz, was sitting there. This wise old lady saw the patients and
referred to them as "little boxes"—forms containing different elements,
illnesses, pains, and so forth. She dictated the remedies to him that
would cure these evils. Years later, Don Carlos Said converted the second floor of his home into a temple.

Upon entering, the hopeful visitors find themselves among rows of
chairs, arranged as in a church or a theater. There is room for about
fifty people. Before them stands an altar, a platform with twelve steps

leading up to it, at the top of which is a rectangular table with seven large altar candles burning on it. At each corner of the altar is a vase of chrysanthemums. The walls are covered with pictures, truly in good taste, showing the Stations of the Cross. Don Carlos officiates dressed in white, like a Mexican Indian, and is assisted by two women in white robes who wear no makeup, their hair cut short or else tied at the neck forming a bun. They resemble nuns. To the left of the participants is a row of mattresses where the patients lie wrapped in blankets with bouquets of fresh herbs applied to their bodies.

As soon as the prospective patient enters another assistant pours a little of a magical perfume called Seven Machos onto his hands from a black bottle, then rubs it all over the patient's head and body, thus severing the ties that bind him to the outside. He is entering a completely sacred place. Whatever the sick person is wearing, it must all be brought into the temple. Nothing may be left outside in the ordinary world. What is left behind cannot be cured. Devils are waiting, and as soon as the sick person came back out, they would pounce on him again.

The patients are treated in strict order of their arrival. But there are some who have arrived at dawn, selected for special treatment. They are sitting on a bench, their bodies and heads covered by white blankets. Under the bench Said has placed a basin full of burning coals and incense. A dense, perfumed smoke rises from it, enveloping them.

The healer asks the patient to stand barefoot in front of the altar on a triangle of salt that has been dyed black, surrounded by a circle of white salt. The first thing he does is to put a thick piece of rope with a slipknot around the patient's neck. It sends the message, "This sickness is your sickness, your responsibility. You do not come here to give it to me. Let your spirit recognize it and turn away from it." To emphasize this Don Carlos folds his arms tightly around the patient with his large hands closed, making a cross, then shuts invisible latches in the air. He takes three raw eggs with his left hand and begins to rub the body of his patient with them. Suddenly, he wraps the eggs in a Mexican handkerchief, a red scarf. He keeps rubbing. Then he throws

302   Magicians, Masters, Shamans, and Charlatans

the package forcefully into a container and listens as the eggs explode inside the fabric. He has removed and destroyed some of the damage. Now, holding a knife, he begins to make fierce cuts in the air around the patient. He is cutting away mad desires, mad feelings, mad ideas. He sprays alcohol in a triangle and lights it on fire. When the flames subside he takes the rope, soaks handkerchiefs in the Seven Machos perfume, and unfolding them moves them over the patient from head to toe, using the perfume as a blessing. Before leaving, he gives the patient a paper cup with filtered water and a slice of lemon dipped in black seeds. The purification must not only be external but also internal. He ends the ceremony by giving the patient a heart-shaped sugar candy to suck on. During this complex act, which varies, adding new details for each illness, Don Carlos speaks as if in a trance, revealing that someone has stuck a doll full of pins or hired a negative sorcerer to send evil. Healing is a struggle against an external enemy in which the healer, assisted by invisible allies who gather around him, is always in danger from negative entities that may attack him for having removed the evil. All healers claim that if some heal and others do not, it is because magical operations are not enough: it is necessary for a change to occur in the patient's mentality. Those who live in constant request must learn to give.

EIGHT

From Magic
to Psychomagic

When I was fifty years old, my son Adan was born. Also at that time, the producer of my film *Tusk* declared bankruptcy and did not pay me what he owed me. I had been in India during Valérie's pregnancy, filming in miserable conditions with mediocre technicians—for economic reasons, according to the production company. I suspect that much of the money intended to create good quality images went into the pockets of this greedy organizer. Be that as it may, back in Paris I found that I had a tired wife, a newborn, three other sons, and a zero balance in my bank account. What little Valérie had saved in a Mexican candy box was enough to feed us for ten days, no more. I called a millionaire friend of mine in the United States and asked him to lend me ten thousand dollars. He sent five thousand. We left our spacious apartment in a good neighborhood, and under miraculous circumstances found a small house in Joinville le Pont on the outskirts of the city, where I was forced to make a living giving Tarot readings. All this, looking back on it now, was not a misfortune but a blessing.

Jean Claude, always concerned with finding the origins of diseases—since like the shamans he considered illnesses to be the physical symptoms of psychological wounds caused by painful family relationships or social relationships—had sent me to do Tarot readings for his patients on Saturdays and Sundays for two years. I always did it for free, and often with good results. Now that I was living in poverty, with pressing family responsibilities, I was forced to charge for my readings. The first time I held out my hand to receive money for a consultation I thought I would die of shame. That night, while my wife and sons slept, sitting on my heels as Ejo Takata had taught me to do, I knelt and meditated in the solitude of the little room that I had transformed into a temple of the Tarot by means of a rectangular violet rug. The monk had said, "If you want to add more water to a glass that is already full, it must be emptied first. Thus, a mind full of opinions and speculations cannot learn. We must empty it in order to create a condition of openness." Once I calmed down and saw the shame as a passing cloud, realizing that it was pride in disguise, I recognized that I was not a public charity and that the act of reading the Tarot had a noble therapeutic value. But doubts assailed me. Was what I read in the cards useful for the client? Did I have the right to do this professionally? I thought again of Ejo Takata. When the monk lived in Japan, every year he paid a visit to a small island where there was a hospital for people with leprosy—which in those days was incurable—in order to perform a social service. There, he learned a lesson that changed his life. While walking together along a cliff side, the visitors walked in front and the lepers behind so that spouses, parents, relatives, and friends would not have to see the mutilated bodies of their loved ones. At a certain point, Ejo stumbled and was on the point of falling off the cliff. At that moment a sick man hurried to save him but, looking at his own fingerless hand, did not want to touch Ejo for fear of infecting him. Desperate, he began to sob. The monk regained his balance and went to the sick man, thanking him with great emotion for his love. This man, so much in need of compassion and help, had been able to forget his ego, acting not for his own benefit but with the intention of helping someone else. Takata wrote this poem:

He who has only hands
Helps with his hands

And he who has only feet
Helps with his feet
In this great spiritual work.

I also remembered a Chinese story:

A tall mountain cast a shadow, preventing a village at its feet from receiving sunlight. The children grew up stunted. One morning, the villagers saw the oldest man walking down the street with a porcelain spoon in his hands.

"Where are you going?" they asked.

"I am going to the mountain," he replied.

"What for?"

"To move it away from there."

"With what?"

"With this spoon." The villagers laughed.

"You'll never be able to!"

The old man answered, "I know I never will. But someone has to start."

I told myself, "If I want to be useful, I must do so in an honest way, using my true capabilities. I will not in any way act like a clairvoyant. First of all, I cannot read the future, and second, I think it's useless to know it when we don't know who we are here and now. I'll content myself with the present and focus the reading on self-knowledge, based on the principle that we do not have a destiny predetermined by any gods. The path is being created as we walk along it, and every step offers a thousand possibilities. We are constantly choosing. But who is it that makes this choice? It depends on the personality with which we have been shaped in childhood. And so, what we call the future is a repetition of the past."

I began my Tarot reading sessions at the same time that I was writing the comic *The Incal* for Moebius. The more I progressed with the readings, the more I noticed that all problems have their roots in the family tree. To examine a person's difficulties is to enter into the psychological atmosphere of his or her family. I realized that we are marked by the *psychomental* universe of our families. We are marked by their characteristics, but also by their insane ideas, their negative feelings, their inhibited desires, and their destructive acts. The father and mother project all their phantoms onto the expected infant. They want to see him or her do what they themselves could not experience or accomplish. Thus, we assume a personality that is not our own, but comes from one or more members of our emotional environment. To be born into a family is, as it were, to be possessed.

The gestation of a human almost never takes place in a healthy manner because the fetus is influenced by the parents' diseases and neuroses. After a certain time, just seeing a client move and hearing a few spoken phrases was enough for me to tell the manner in which he or she had been born. (Someone who feels compelled to do everything quickly was born in a few minutes, as if with urgency. Someone who, faced with a problem, waits until the last moment to resolve it, using outside help, was born with forceps. Someone who has trouble making decisions was born by caesarean section.) I realized that the way we are born, which is often not the correct way, alters the course of our entire lives. And these bad deliveries result from our parents' emotional problems with their own parents. The damage is transmitted from generation to generation: the possessed become the possessors, projecting onto their children what was projected onto them, unless there is a gaining of consciousness that breaks the vicious circle. We must not be afraid to explore ourselves deeply in order to confront the ill-formed part of our being, the horror of nonachievement, and shatter the genealogical obstacle that rises up against us as a barrier and obstructs the ebb and flow of life. In this barrier we find the bitter psychological sediment of our fathers and mothers, our grandparents and great-grandparents. We must learn to stop identifying ourselves with the family tree and understand that it is not in the past: on the contrary, it is alive, present within every one of us. Every time we have a problem that seems to us to be individual, the whole family is involved. At the moment we become conscious, in one way or another, the family begins to evolve—not only the living members, but also the dead ones. The past is not set in stone. It changes according to our point of view. We have a different understanding of ancestors whom we consider heinously guilty of altering our mentality. After forgiving them, we should honor them, which is to say, know them, analyze them, dissolve them, reshape them, thank them, love them, and finally see the "Buddha" in each and every one of them. Everything that we have achieved spiritually could have been done by any one of our relatives. The responsibility is immense. Any fall drags down the whole family, including future children, for three or four generations. Children do not perceive time in the same way that adults do. What seems to an adult to last an hour, children experience as if it lasts for months, and it marks them for their whole lives. As adults, we tend to reproduce the abuses we suffered during childhood, either on other people or on ourselves. If I was tortured yesterday, then I keep on torturing myself today, becoming my own tormenter. There is a great deal of talk about sexual abuses suffered during childhood, but we tend to overlook intellectual abuses, which imbue the child's mind with insane ideas like perverse prejudices and racism; emotional abuses that include deprivation of love, contempt, sarcasm, verbal aggression; material abuses like lack of space, abusive changes of territory, lack of clothing, and improper nourishment. There are also abuses of the being, which may include not being given the opportunity to develop one's true personality, having one's life planned out as a function of one's family history; being forced into an alien destiny, not being seen for who one is, being made into a mirror of someone else, being desired to be someone else, being born a boy to parents who wanted a girl or vice versa; not being allowed to see what one wants to see; not being allowed to listen to certain things; not being allowed to express oneself; or being given an education consisting of the implantation of limits. As for sexual abuse, the list is long, as long as the list of accusations:

"I married out of obligation because your mother was pregnant with you; you have been a burden to us; I left my career because of you; you are selfish to want to live your life; you have betrayed us; you let yourself surpass us and achieved what we could not." Family history is full of incestuous relationships, repressed or not, as well as homosexual urges, sadomasochism, narcissism, and social neuroses, which are reproduced as a legacy from generation to generation. This can sometimes be seen in names. One client wrote, "You suggested that I clarify my unconscious incestuous urges with my brother. You were right. My brother's name is Fernando, and the father of my children is also called Fernando. But this can also be found in my genealogy; my mother has a brother called Juan Carlos, and she married a Carlos. It was the same for my grand-mother: her brother was named José and she married a José, and her father (my great-grandfather) was also called José."

When did all this begin? I often see people burdened by problems dat-ing back to the First World War because a great-grandfather returned from the front with lung disease caused by toxic gases, which caused him emotional disturbances, an inability to fulfill himself, moral deval-uation. And when the father is weak or absent, the mother becomes dominant, invasive, and is no longer a mother. The absence of a father brings about that of the mother. The children grow up with a thirst for caresses, which translates into repressed anger that extends through several generations. The lack of touch is the greatest abuse suffered by a child. All this garbage affects us, even if it is not conscious. The rela-tionships between our parents and our aunts and uncles trickle down onto us. For example, Jaime hated Benjamín, his younger brother. I was Jaime's younger child. I became a screen onto which his brother was pro-jected. This allowed him to vent his bottled-up hatred onto me. Even if we know nothing of rapes, abortions, suicides, shameful events, incar-cerated relatives, venereal diseases, alcoholism, drug addiction, prostitu-tion, or countless other secrets in our families, we still suffer from all of it, and sometimes we repeat it. A boy is named René, which means "reborn," and feels himself invaded by a vampire-like personality, not knowing that he was born after another sibling died. A father gives his daughter the name of the woman who was his first love, and this dooms her to playing the role of his girlfriend for life. A mother gives her son the name of his maternal grandfather, and the son fruitlessly tries to be like that grandfather in order to satisfy his mother's incestuous desires. Or, in a family with many daughters, one of them in desiring to give the father an heir to carry on his name will have a one-night stand with a strange man, a foreigner who will then return to his home country, leaving her pregnant. Symbolically this child is engendered by God; she is imitating the Virgin Mary. The Virgin was possessed by her father; he introduced himself completely into her womb, changed himself into his own son, then created a man-god pairing. Together forever, the two now reign in heaven, as if in a marriage. If a single mother gives birth to a son who, metaphorically, is the child of her father, and calls him Jesús or Emmanuel or Salvador, or in fact the name of any saint, then that child will live an anguished life, feeling obligated to be perfect. The sacred texts, when misinterpreted, play a nefarious role in this family catastrophe. Extremist religions create sexual frustrations, illnesses, suicides, wars, and unhappiness. Perverse interpretations of the Torah, the New Testament, the Koran, and the Sutras have caused more deaths than the atomic bomb.

The tree, with all its limbs, behaves as an individual, a living being. I dubbed the study of its problems "psychogenealogy" (just as I called the study of the Tarot "tarology"; years later, "tarologists" and "psychogenealogists" became abundant). Some therapists who have conducted studies in genealogy have wanted to reduce it to mathematical formulas, but the tree cannot be contained in a rational cage; the subconscious is not scientific, it is artistic. The study of families must be performed in a different way. A geometric body, with the relationships between its parts completely known, cannot be modified. In an organic body whose relationships are mysterious, you can add or remove a part, but

In a seminar in France, working with the minor arcana of the Tarot.

in its essence it will still be what it is. The internal relationships of the family tree are mysterious. To understand them it is necessary to enter the tree as if in a dream, so it should not be interpreted, it should be experienced.

The patient must make peace with her subconscious, not becoming independent of it but making it an ally. If we learn its language, we can put it to work for us. If the family within us, rooted in childhood memory, is the basis of our subconscious, then we must develop each relative as an archetype. We must ascribe our level of consciousness to it, exalt it, imagine it reaching its highest potential. Everything we give it, we are giving to ourselves. When we deny it, we deny ourselves. As for toxic people, we should transform them by saying, "This is what they did to me, this is what I felt, this is what the abuse causes in me today, this is the reparation I desire." Then, still within ourselves, we must bring all the relatives and ancestors to their fulfillment. A Zen master once said, "Buddha nature is also in a dog." This means that we must imagine the perfection of every person in our family. Does someone have a heart full of bitterness, a brain clouded by prejudice, deviant sexuality due to moral abuses? Like a shepherd with his sheep we must guide them to the good path, cleansing them of their poisonous needs, desires, emotions, and thoughts. A tree is judged by its fruits, so if the fruit is bitter the tree it came from, even if it is majestic, is considered bad. If the fruit is sweet, the crooked tree it comes from is considered good. Our family—past, present, and future—is the tree. We are the fruit that gives it its value.

As my clients increased in number, on some weekends I had to receive them in groups. To heal a family, I organized a dramatization of it. The person whose family was being studied would choose from among the participants, picking those who would represent her parents, grandparents, uncles, aunts, brothers, and sisters. Then she would situate them, standing, seated on chairs, or lying down (for the chronically ill or dead), at various distances from each other, according to the logic of her family tree. Who was the hero of the family, the most powerful person? Which people were absent or despised? Which people were joined together and by what sort of ties? And so forth. Then the patient would situate herself. Where? At the center, on the edge, or removed from all of them? How did she feel there? Then, she had to confront each "actor." Representing the family in this way, as a living sculpture, the seeker discovers that the people she has "randomly" chosen correspond in many aspects to the real people in her family and have important things to say to her. This produces a conversation that generally ends in intense embraces and tears.

These exercises leave us convinced that, having become conscious of these unhealthy relationships, we are now cured. However, once we return from the therapeutic situation into the real world, the painful symptoms are still there as always. Merely identifying a difficulty is not enough to overcome it! A gain in awareness, a theatrical confrontation, and an imagined forgiving end up being fruitless when not followed up by action in daily life. I concluded that I should induce people to act in the midst of what they conceived as their reality. But I was reluctant to do so. What right did I have to intrude in the lives of others, exerting an influence that could easily degenerate into a power grab, establishing dependencies? I was in a difficult position, considering that the people who came to see me were, in a way, asking me to become their father, mother, son, husband, wife . . . I decided to induce them to act in order for the gaining of consciousness to be effective. I did not call these people my patients, but my clients. I prescribed very specific actions, without assuming responsibility or taking on the role of their guide over their entire lives. Thus was born the psychomagical act, combining all the influences I had assimilated during the years described in the preceding chapters.

First, the person would agree to carry out the act exactly as I prescribed it, without one iota of change. To prevent distortions due to failures of memory, the client had to immediately write down the procedure to follow. Once the act was carried out they were to send me a letter that first described the instructions received, then related in full detail the way in which the act was carried out as well as the circumstances and incidents that occurred in the process. Lastly, the results should be described. Some people waited a year to send me the letter. Others argued, not wanting to do exactly what I recommended, bargaining and finding all manner of excuses to avoid following the instructions precisely.

As I observed with Pachita, when you change something, however minimally, and do not respect the indispensable conditions for the achievement of the act, the effects will be null or negative. Indeed, most of the problems we have, we want to have. We are attached to our problems. They form our identity. We define ourselves through them. It is no wonder, then, that some people try to distort the act and try to devise ways to sabotage it: getting free of problems involves radically changing our relationship with ourselves and with the past. People want to stop suffering, but are not willing to pay the price—namely, to change, to not keep living as a function of their beloved problems. For all these reasons, the responsibility of prescribing an act that must be carried out to the letter was immense. In the moment of prescribing it I had to cease identifying with myself so that I could go into a kind of trance, stop talking with my subconscious, and connect directly with the subconscious of my client. I concentrated on the mere act of giving, alleviating pain, prescribing actions that were similar to lucid dreams, without worrying about the personal benefit that would accrue to me. In order to be in a condition to heal someone, you must not expect anything from that person; you must enter all the aspects of his or her inner self without becoming involved or destabilized.

In *The Book of Five Rings* the swordsman Miyamoto Musashi recommends going to the ring early, before a fight, and acquiring a perfect knowledge of it. Likewise, familiarity with the client's psychoaffective terrain seemed to me a fundamental requirement for the recommendation of any act, so before anything else I would ask them to tell me about their problem in as much detail as possible.

Rather than trying to guess what the Tarot might be hiding from me, I would put the person through an intense interrogation. I would ask about his or her birth, parents, uncles and aunts, grandparents, siblings, sex life, relationship with money, social complexes, beliefs, love life, health, guilty feelings. (Often enough, this resembles a church confession.) Terrible secrets would emerge. One man confessed to me that as a child, at the end of the school year, he had waited on top of a wall for a hated teacher to pass and had thrown a large stone at his head. He thought that the teacher had died, but fled without checking. For thirty years, he felt like a murderer. Another time I met with a Belgian father. I perceived that he was gay. "Yes," he confessed, "and I do it with ten men a day, in the saunas, every time I come to Paris. Do you know what my problem is? I'd like to do it with fourteen of them, like a friend of mine does!" From people who seemed normal, I heard the darkest and most outlandish secrets. One woman confessed to me that the father of her daughter was none other than her own father; a Swiss teenager, seduced by his mother, told me all the details. What most disturbed him was her jealousy, because she would not let him have any girlfriends. Because they did not perceive any criticism in me, people vented with confidence. If the therapist judges in the name of some morality, he does not cure. The attitude of the confessor must be amoral. Otherwise, the secrets never come to light. I am reminded of a Buddhist story.

> Two monks are meditating in the midst of nature; several rabbits surround one monk, but none come near the other. The latter asks, "If we both meditate with equal intensity the same number of hours each day, why do the rabbits surround you and not me?"
>
> "Very simple," replies the other, "Because I do not eat rabbit, and you do."

A participant in one of my courses could not bear for her chest to be touched. As soon as a man, even one with whom she wanted to have sexual relations, made a move to touch her breasts, she would start screaming. This situation caused her much suffering, and she longed to be free from this senseless panic. I suggested that she bare her chest. She did so, revealing a nice pair of breasts. I asked, "Do you trust me?"

"Yes," she replied.

"I would like to touch you in a particular way, not like the caress of a desiring man eager to enjoy your body, nor like the touch of a doctor who examines you coldly. I would like to touch you with my spirit. Do you think my spirit could establish an intimate contact with your breasts that does not have anything sexual about it?"

"Maybe . . ."

I raised my hands, three meters away, and said gently, "Look at my hands. I'm going to approach slowly, millimeter by millimeter. As soon as you feel assaulted or uncomfortable, tell me to stop and I will stop approaching."

I then brought my hands closer, extremely slowly. When I was ten centimeters from her breasts, she asked me to stop. I obeyed, and after a long while, slowly, very slowly, I started moving closer, watching for her reaction. Reassured by the quality of the attention I was paying to her and perceiving that I acted with delicacy and detachment, she did not protest. Finally my hands rested on her breasts without her feeling any discomfort, which caused her great amazement. Applying what I had learned from the man who fed the sparrows, I took another participant by the shoulder and, without letting go of him, had him touch her breasts as well. This caused her no suffering. But when I let go of the man, she started screaming . . . This story is an example of the detachment that, in my view, is indispensable for those who really want to help others. I was able to touch and feel the breasts of a woman standing before me while situating myself far away from my sexual center, without thinking of getting pleasure. In that moment I was not a man, but a being. The important thing is to place oneself in an inner state that excludes any temptation to take advantage of the other person, any temptation to abuse the fascination one exerts over the other in order to assert one's power to dominate his or her will. If these things happen, the helping relationship loses its essence and becomes a masquerade.

For a magical act to have good results the popular charlatan must, by obligation, present himself as a superior being who knows all mysteries. The patient, in a superstitious manner, accepts his advice without understanding how or why it affects his or her subconscious. By contrast, the psychomagician presents himself only as a technical expert, as an instructor, and devotes himself to explaining to the patient the symbolic meaning and purpose of every act. The client knows what he or she is doing. All superstition has been eliminated. However, as soon as one begins to perform the prescribed acts, reality begins dancing in a new way. Unexpected things happen that aid in the accomplishment of something that seems impossible. For example, with an elementary school teacher who had been badly abused in childhood and was afflicted by chronic sadness I advised, among other things, learning to balance on a tightrope as circus performers do. "Impossible!" he said. "I live in a small village in the south of France. Where will I find someone to teach me that?" I insisted that he do what I proposed. Upon returning to school, one of his students told him that he was learning to balance on a tightrope from a retired circus performer who lived just a few kilometers away!

On another occasion, with a patient who had suicidal tendencies and felt that his blood was impure because he was the product of incest, I advised that he go to a slaughterhouse with two large thermoses, buy cow's blood to fill them with, go home, and shower in the blood until all his skin was entirely covered in order to make his subconscious think that his blood had been replaced. Then, without washing off the blood, he should get dressed and go walking in the streets, proudly facing the stares of passersby. He also said, "Impossible." However, when he went to the dentist, he found a copy of *The Incal* in the waiting room. He asked the dentist if he had read it. The dentist said no, one of his patients had left it there, a man who owned a slaughterhouse and admired my work. My client got the man's address, went to him with some autographed copies of my works, and the slaughterhouse owner, very pleased, gave him all the liters of cow's blood he needed.

One day I received a visit from a Swiss woman whose father had died in Peru when she was eight years old. Her mother had made all traces of the man disappear, burning letters and photos, so that my client remained an eight-year-old child on the emotional plane. I prescribed an act: she should go to Peru and visit the places where her father had lived, until she found tangible proof of his existence. When she returned to Europe she should bury the mementos in her garden and plant a fruit tree there, then go to her mother's house and slap her. It should be explained here that her mother was an angry and virile woman who had mistreated and insulted her. The woman went to Peru, found the rooming house where her father had lived, and through that synchronicity that I call the dance of reality, found letters and photos. The father had entrusted them to the landlady, confident that one day his daughter would go to look for them. When she read those letters and saw those pictures, she no longer saw her father as a faceless ghost and finally knew that he had been a being of flesh and blood. By burying the documents in her garden, she also buried the eight-year-old child. Then she went to see her mother with the intention of giving her the prescribed slap. But she was surprised to find that for the first time her mother was waiting for her at the train station and, also, for the first time, had prepared a meal for her. Seeing her so kind, she felt very disturbed at having to slap her because, for once, her mother had given her no pretext for doing so. But she knew that the act was an inescapable psychomagical contract that must be respected. Over dessert, my client slapped her mother for no apparent reason, taking her by surprise, and feared a brutal reaction from her. But her mother only asked, "Why did you do that?" Faced with such equanimity, the daughter finally found words to express every complaint she had of her. The mother replied, "You've given me one slap . . . well, you should give me many more!"

A literary critic around fifty years old, married to a philosophy professor her same age but who was a perennial adolescent, called me from Barcelona because she had discovered that her husband had a twenty-three-year-old lover. "We are intellectual, serious, mature people who shun emotional scandals. But I have fallen into a huge depression from holding back my anger. And he doesn't want to give up either her or me. What should I do?"

"I am going to ask you to analyze your life as if it were a dream. Why did you dream that your fifty-year-old husband had a twenty-three-year-old lover?"

"Oh, I remember when I was exactly twenty-three. I had an affair with a fifty-year-old man! It lasted three years. Then I left him for a younger man."

"See? You are experiencing something that is like a recurring dream. In a certain way, you dream yourself into the place of the deceived wife and you realize how, when you were young, you made your lover's wife suffer. If your affair didn't last, it is very possible that your philosopher's adventure will also only last another year, since you've found out that it's already been going on for two years. Then he will come back and cry in your arms."

"But each passing day seems like a century. I can't tolerate this situation. I feel diminished, sick with rage, old."

"I'm not a charlatan, I won't advise you to wrap a dead hummingbird in red ribbon and get him to touch it or sprinkle rose petals on his footprints in the sand so that he will come right back. But I can help you to accept this triangular relationship in your subconscious and calmly wait for the year to pass." I told her to go to a pet store and buy three canaries, a male (symbolizing her husband) and two females: one young and pretty (symbolizing the lover) and one older, ugly, and fat (symbolizing herself). She should put the birds in a cage and hang them in her office, in front of her desk. After ten days, she should go back to the pet store and give the canaries back to the same man who sold them to her. I said, "The bird seller represents God (your father, an absent man). Once you feel good, you should give away this childish problem of abandonment."

The days went by, then suddenly she called me in a state of shock: "Something amazing happened: I put the canaries together and fed them the same food. But bit by bit, the young female was getting fat, losing her feathers, staying still in a corner; the older one became prettier and thinner, and sang with joy. I learned later that a young female dies if she is not fertilized by the male. On the tenth day, today, when I sat down to work, I suddenly looked up at the cage, and at that precise moment the sick bird fell down dead. I'm terrified. She represented my rival. I feel like I've killed her. What should I do?"

"Reality has danced to comfort you. Accept this gift. Put the bird in the bottom of a flowerpot, fill it with soil, and plant a rose bush. Keep the rose alive in your house as long as you can, and go give the bird seller the remaining pair of birds."

After some time, the client called me again to tell me she was glad of the act. It had been a long time since she had felt so good. She had returned to finding the joy in life. Now she did not care what her husband did.

It might seem like an easy surrealist game to give psychomagical advice, but in fact it can only be dispensed by a person who has done a great deal of work on him- or herself. Each act must fit the subtle characteristics of the client like a pair of shoes made to order. No two people are the same, so no two identical acts may be prescribed. A certain individual felt himself authorized to begin his own practice immediately after attending one of my lectures and rounded up a group of women. He asked each of his students to identify themselves with a doll, to discharge into it their childhood pain and rage against their parents, and to place it in a sack, which they would keep for a purification ceremony to be conducted later. They also had to send their mothers a large pair of scissors and the guts of a chicken. Catastrophic! You cannot prescribe acts "wholesale"! The supermarket of psychomagic is an aberration! Of course, the effect was negative. The relatives did not understand the act, and many thought that their daughters had gone mad. This was not so far from the truth: after the workshop, one terrified woman came to see me on the verge of psychosis, convinced that the "psychomagician" now had power over her. To calm her down I recommended that she go retrieve her doll, but the man could not return it because as soon as his students departed he had thrown them all in the trash. In sum, this was a matter of a businessman dedicating himself to making money by exploiting the credulity of a group of women. I am reminded of a story:

> In a factory, a complicated machine breaks down. The best technicians arrive, working for days with all kinds of sophisticated tools, but they fail to make it work. Finally, an old man comes carrying a small case. He takes a simple hammer out of the case, gives a small tap on one gear wheel on the machine, and it starts up. The old man asks to be paid $1,000,001 for his services. The manufacturers complain: "How is this possible? You are asking for $1,000,001 for just one hammer blow!" "No," the old man answers, "the hammer cost a dollar. The studies I had to do in order to do it effectively cost a million." One can only propose an effective psychomagical act after a long apprenticeship.

When it became clear to me that my advice could cause a transformation in the mind of the client, I realized the enormous responsibility that this implied. An error could provoke catastrophes such as the worsening of an illness, a suicide, a divorce, depression, psychosis, or a criminal act. Therefore, as I began practicing psychomagic I took many precautions, the main one of these being to prescribe very small acts that involved no one other than the client.

I recommended buying pieces of honeycomb to a woman who had grown up verbally tormented by her parents and who could not speak without using harsh words. I told her to sweeten her mouth by chewing on these until nothing was left but a blob of wax, to save these remains in a jewelry box, and then after some time to form that wax into the shape of a heart, anoint her tongue with red vegetable dye, lick the heart to stain it red, and finally nail the heart to her bathroom wall in front of the toilet. Thus, her subconscious would receive the message that to speak is an act of love, not of excretion.

Another client asked that I prescribe her an act that would allow her to forgive her dead father and thus overcome the hatred she had toward all men. I asked her to tell me at what point her father had broken ties with her. "Shortly after my first period," she replied. (It is common for a father to distance himself from his daughter once she becomes a woman for fear of arousal. The girl, not understanding why he draws away, suffers from no longer sitting on his knee and finds it painful to renounce this form of intimacy and contact.) I then asked her where her father was buried, and she suggested we go to his grave. "Bury some cotton wool soaked in your menstrual blood, along with a packet of sugar cubes, as close as possible to the coffin. The sugar is to indicate that this is not an aggressive act but a loving approach, a communication signifying that periods are not an impediment to happiness."

When the person who has caused pain is dead, for the subconscious the grave is the representation of that person. If there is no grave a photograph is used, and if there is no photograph, a drawing. Another client was enrolled at the age of four in a school led by her great aunt. This lady bullied her sadistically. In her work with me, the client discovered the deep hatred she felt for this woman. She could not forgive her, but could not take revenge either, since her victim had already left this world. Therefore, I advised her to go to the woman's grave and give vent to her hatred there: kick the grave, scream insults, urinate and defecate, but on condition that she thoroughly analyze the reactions caused by the execution of her revenge. She followed my advice, and after letting off steam on the grave, felt a fundamental desire to clean it and cover it with flowers. The hatred was nothing but the deformed face of unrequited affection.

If the hated person has been cremated and there is no grave, or if he or she is still alive, one can insult a photograph. Then the image must be burned. After this, the client should take some of the ashes, dissolve them in a glass of wine if male or milk if female, and drink it. Thus the evil, finally purified, becomes an antidote.

A young man complained to me of "living in the clouds," explaining that he could not "get grounded in reality" or "advance" toward financial independence. I took his words at face value and suggested that he take two gold coins and glue them to the soles of his shoes, so that every day he might tread on gold. From that moment on, coming down from the clouds, he set foot in reality and moved forward.

Another client, married with no children, did not feel man enough. He had been raised by his widowed mother along with three aunts and a grandmother, all either widows or spinsters. For him, a father was a nonexistent being: a man who had impregnated a woman, then died. Because of this, he was afraid of his wife becoming pregnant. To make him feel that he existed as a man I suggested that he collect thirty thousand francs (he could borrow the money), roll the stack of bills up along its long edge and hold them together with a rubber band; buy a pair of Chinese balls (the kind that people hold and spin in their hands in order to calm down and meditate); and make a holder out of suede, in which he would wear the roll of bills between his legs as a phallus and the Chinese balls as testicles. With that weight in his pants, for three days he should go to work, visit friends, talk with his family, cuddle with his wife, and sleep wearing the apparatus. This advice, seemingly comic, had an unexpected result: in addition to changing his character, the man got his wife pregnant.

For a singer who was always unsuccessful in auditions, who felt that she had no talent, I advised putting ten gold coins inside a condom and inserting it into her vagina. Thus equipped, she should show up for an audition. She sang like never before and got the part.

Sometimes in order to solve problems I do not hesitate to recommend acts that a prejudiced person might consider pornographic. However, if one intends to heal suffering spiritually, it is necessary to understand that the sex organs are sanctuaries where what we call God can be found. The client must also learn to value his or her body, not disdaining its secretions. Feces, saliva, urine, sweat, menstrual blood, or semen can be used as elements that liberate us from inhibited feelings. One client, a lesbian, felt unable to begin the book that she intended to write. As soon as she turned on her computer, she just started playing games. I explained to her that she had remained a child, that is to say sexless, because when she reached adulthood she knew that she was lacking phallic power. I advised her to go to a sex shop, buy a strap-on dildo, put it on, tape up a large white piece of paper at waist level, dip the dildo in ink, and write the first two sentences of her book with it. After this, the rest would be easy to write on the computer.

In Guadalajara, a pathologically shy man came to see me because he could not settle on projects or finish what he started. I advised him to go to the busy Plaza de la Liberación, naked under a big coat, sit on a bench, put a hand through a cut-out pocket and masturbate to the point of ejaculation. He should keep the semen inside an oval medallion with a picture of his mother, wearing it around his neck as a talisman.

A young French woman had never felt any sexual desires. Her father had died of prostate cancer, and she irrationally blamed this on her mother, accumulating fierce anger toward her. I explained to her that she was afraid that experiencing desire and having sexual relations would cause her to become pregnant and transform her into a mother, that is to say, her mother. I advised her to place two ostrich eggs, a symbol of maternal ovaries, on a photograph of her mother. By smashing the eggs with a hammer, she would make her anger come out. Then with another two ostrich eggs, representing her own ovaries, she should make a huge omelet and serve it at dinner to a group of seven friends. "While you watch them eat, allow yourself to imagine what they would be like in bed, and you will see that desires emerge. As for the remains of the eggs you break with a hammer and the picture of your mother, bury them and plant a white flower there. Then go to your father's grave and wash it with water, soap, and a brush."

A married man with two children, who loved his wife, came to see me because he had premature ejaculation. I asked how long the sexual act lasted. "Just twenty seconds," he answered. I advised him to make love to his wife that night with a stopwatch by the bedside, promising her that he would ejaculate more quickly than ever, in exactly ten seconds. He did so. He came back to see me, happy, and told me with a big smile, "I failed. As much as I tried, I could not. I lasted half an hour."

A young man who had no father felt that he had no authority. He asked me for advice on how to develop his ability to give orders. I suggested that he start by giving orders for things that were already happening. If he saw that it was starting to rain, he should say, "I order it to rain!" If his dog was lying down, he should say, "I order you to lie down!" If he saw cars passing, he should say, "I order the cars to pass!" And so on. In this manner he would overcome his timidity and get used to commanding.

A woman who was abandoned by her father at the age of six always got into relationships with men who abandoned her. She did not want to continue living alone like her mother, who used to tell her, "Better alone than in bad company." She wanted to form a stable partnership. I explained, in light of the Tarot, "Because you've had a lack of communication with your father and you've listened only to your mother, you do not know how to accept men. You must learn to hear male words. I advise you to buy a Walkman and for forty days, listen to the voices of male poets and wise men as you walk around and work."

Not wanting to be seen as a charlatan, I gave up trying to cure physical illnesses. However, I made a few exceptions. A scuba diving instructor had suffered for years from sores in his mouth. No doctor had been able to cure these ulcers. I saw in the Tarot that this illness came from the powerlessness that he felt from being unable to speak with his mother, who was deceased. She had been a divorced, narcissistic woman; she had no husband and spent whole days in front of the mirror preoccupied with herself, fighting against wrinkles. I asked him how tall his mother was. "A hundred and sixty centimeters," he replied. I advised him to get a plaster statue of the Virgin Mary a hundred and sixty centimeters tall. Then, he should dive with this idol down into the ocean until he reached the bottom. Once there he should make holes in the ears of the saint with a drill, then he should put his mouth to each ear hole for a moment. Later, back on land, he should yell everything that he could never say to his mother at the sculpture. Finally, he should bury this virgin with a little of his semen in each ear hole, and plant a tree there. The client followed my advice. His sores disappeared.

My Chilean friend Martin Bakero, a psychiatrist and poet, found it painful to walk because a wart had grown between the fourth and fifth toes of his left foot, reaching down to the bone. The dermatologist, seeing that the ointments he had given him were not taking effect, had begun to burn the wart off in layers and said that this treatment could last between one and two years. I asked Bakero how long he had lived in Paris. "Four years," he replied.

"Did you have a good relationship with your parents during childhood?"

"My father was an absent man. My mother treated me like royalty. I was an only child, and in a way I was her partner. I recognize that we have a deep Oedipal relationship."

"What's happening is that you feel guilty for having left her in Chile. Take a picture of your mother and make ten photocopies. Take one every morning, stick it to your afflicted foot with green clay, and walk with it on your foot all day long."

In a letter, the poet told me about his act: "At first, I was reluctant to carry out what you advised: a sick person's symptoms are always accompanied by an unconscious enjoyment. I told you, 'I have no pictures of my mother,' and you answered, 'Draw one.' 'I cannot draw,' I grumbled, and you replied, 'You're resisting the cure.' The next day I summoned all my strength and found a picture of my mother, performed the act, and upon completion of the ten applications, the wart had disappeared, leaving behind new, clean skin. I have not had any more problems."

A woman with a limp, who needed to support herself with a cane, wanted me to help her walk properly. I explained that I did not work miracles. I was not Pachita, who would have put in a new leg bone and stretched out her leg for her, but I could make her better able to accept her limp. I asked her where she had gotten such an ugly stick, unvarnished and made out of ordinary wood. "It belonged to my paternal grandfather," she said.

"And what became of that grandfather?"

"He never communicated with anyone. He lived as a hermit, holed up in his apartment."

I advised her to burn the cane, take a handful of the ashes, and rub them on her short leg. After that, she should buy the most beautiful cane she could find, made of ebony with a silver handle. She did so. She regained her enjoyment of walking. From prescribing this act, I learned that the places where the body is affected, such as a scar or a hump, should be exalted.

I will conclude these examples by sharing this letter:

"I went to see you at the café where you read the Tarot for free every Wednesday, and consulted you: 'eighteen months ago I felt a sharp pain in my neck. Can this pain be the effect of a regression from the spiritual point of view?' I had consulted doctors, acupuncturists, massage therapists, osteopaths, bonesetters, healers, and of course, taken anti-inflammatory drugs, cortisone, infiltration, and so forth. Nothing had taken effect. You prescribed a psychomagical act for me: I should sit on my husband's knees and get him to sing a lullaby to my neck. But what you did not know is that my husband is an opera singer. He sang a song by Schubert. I'm cured, there is no more pain."

Forming an equation between the neck, the past, and the subconscious, I felt that this client's relationship with her father had not developed well. By seating her on his knees, her husband would symbolically play the role of her father and she would return to childhood. Moreover, singing a lullaby at the site of the pain would fulfill a childhood desire that had not been satisfied, namely the desire for her father to rock her to sleep and communicate with her on the affective plane.

I continued this first series of recommendations over a period of four years, most often given at the end of a Tarot reading, without daring to resolve more significant problems. (Having solved my financial difficulties thanks to the warm welcome received by my comics, drawn in collaboration with ten artists, I decided to conduct Tarot readings for free at a café for two-hour periods, after which I would give a lecture commenting on the readings. I called this activity the Mystical Cabaret.) Although I never gave the same advice more than once, I set myself some rules. For example, I always made sure that the act had a positive end, never advising anyone to do something that would finish in anger or destruction. In cases where it was necessary to sacrifice animals, they were always edible ones, which were then cooked and served in a banquet to family or friends. When something was buried in order to be dissolved and purified in the earth, a beautiful plant would be planted at the site. Any virulent confrontation over a grave was followed by an offering of honey, sugar, or flowers, or by cleaning the grave with soap and water, then perfuming it. In cases where the family had implanted a castrating vision in the client, I advised that he or she appear before them in disguise, first as the vision the family imposed, then as the person the family prevented him or her from being. Many women who had disappointed their fathers by not being born as boys and had been forced to masculinize themselves, resulting in subsequent frigidity and sterility, were advised to show themselves to their fathers wearing a fake pregnant belly, erotic female clothing, ample makeup, and a long wig.

A woman who had lived with her widowed father and four brothers, a "harem of men," had been treated as a decorative but worthless being and had always masculinized herself in order to seek acceptance from her father. I suggested, "Go to see him dressed as a man, bringing him a gift of a bottle of mezcal, his favorite type of alcohol. If he wonders why you came dressed like that, tell him, 'Let's drink a glass first, then I'll tell you.' After drinking, go to the bathroom and transform yourself into a seductive woman with a long wig, false eyelashes, scarlet lips, miniskirt, and so forth. Present yourself before him and say, 'Look, this is an aspect of me that you do not know. I have shown you two extremes: the man you want me to be and the exaggerated woman I do not want to be. Now I'll show you who I really am.' Then dress like a decent woman with good taste. Show yourself to your father and tell him, 'Look at me; I'm not a butch or a slut. This is the woman I am. Being a woman does not mean being an idiot. Accept me as your daughter.'"

Regarding the idea of appearing before ones parents, obeying to the letter the images that they have pasted onto us, by common consensus my son Cristóbal and I performed an act that he says changed his life. I must admit when he was born I was still what I call a "psychological barbarian." I was interested only in my own artistic achievement, not caring to heal my own psychological problems or anyone else's. I thought that people were what they were and took a critical stance toward them. I was an insensitive, stern, competitive father. I remember having a fit of jealousy when I saw him sucking milk from the breasts of "my" woman. That is to say, I behaved toward him exactly the way my father had behaved toward me. In the mist of my neurosis, I gave him two names: Axel, so that he would be an exact imitation of me (Alex), and Cristóbal, so that he might discover a new world . . . Axel Cristóbal, subject to this double desire, seemed to grow up with a double personality. Every time he did something "satisfactory" (imitating me), he was Dr. Jekyll. When he did something "bad" (attempting to be himself), he was Mr. Hyde. This conflict caused him to have kleptomania. (Also, I took away his toys to punish him, as Jaime had done to me.) For years he could not overcome his impulses to steal. Although as time went on our relationship emerged from psychological barbarism to become one of conscious love (we both worked to smooth out the roughness of the past through multiple confrontations, which finally resulted in Axel making way for Cristóbal), he continued to feel these urges to steal things. The struggle to restrain the urges distressed him. He asked me for a psychomagical act to cure it. I told him to dirty his hands with mud collected at the foot of a tree. I knelt before him, placed his dirty hands on my face, and asked him for forgiveness. Then, at my bathroom sink, slowly and with concentrated attention, I washed and perfumed his hands. Following this he rubbed his palms on a Mexican postcard that showed Saint Christopher carrying the Christ child. Finally, I recommended that he have some business cards made that read, "I am Axelito, the thief child. I could have stolen this, but I decided not to. Thank me and bless me." Whenever Cristóbal went into a shop, as soon as he felt tempted he would deposit a card there, taking care that no one saw him do so. Sometimes he would leave more than ten cards. He was so good at this that nobody ever caught him at it. His kleptomania disappeared completely, definitively.

Some time afterward, he came to see me, bringing a suitcase. I sat in the living room while he disappeared into a bedroom and dressed as Dr. Jekyll. With superhuman strength, he let loose his anger and tore apart the disguise, kicking it on the floor. Thus naked, he went back to the bedroom and came back out again dressed as Mr. Hyde, with his hat, cape, stick, and long teeth. He lay in my arms and cried, uttering deep and heartbreaking cries. I understood what I had to do. Also weeping, I began to strip him of his disguise. Then we put the clothes, those of Jekyll and those of Hyde, into a package together and walked out to the Seine. There, with our backs to the river, we threw the package in and without looking back went to celebrate his liberation at a good restaurant.

Another piece of advice I gave several times, each time of course with variations, was for people who suffered from having an invasive mother. Even if they did not live with her, she was in their minds all the time, controlling their lives. I proposed that they treat her as an idol. In India, people feed gods who are represented by sculptures. This means that they bring them offerings of flowers, incense, and food. During the time that I was directing for Maurice Chevalier, I was invited to dinner at his mansion. There I saw a bench where the singer knelt to pray. In the place where Christ or the Virgin would normally be, there was the portrait of a woman. It was the singer's mother. He had exalted her to the status of an idol. Inspired by this, I recommended that instead of fighting fruitlessly to expel the invader, who would keep growing the more they attacked her, my clients should give her a precise location in the house. A photo of the mother should be placed on a small altar, but in a steel frame covered by a wire screen so the subconscious can be assured that the "beast" will not escape. Then, in order to feel that she is satisfied, they should honor her by depositing fresh flowers before her, burning incense, keeping a candle bought at a church burning there at all times. In addition, every time they eat they should save a few morsels of food to place in a saucer before the maternal idol. Thus well fed, she will cease to devour them.

Many consultants suffered problems related to self-worth. Drawing inspiration from the shamanic techniques of Don Ernesto, I asked them to take a sheet of nice paper and write down all the things they wanted to be rid of: crippling self-criticism, lack of talent, pathological jealousy, shyness, and so on, to sign the list with a drop of their own blood, and to bury it. I followed my own advice: for twenty years, I had been polishing and editing my first novel, *El loro de siete lenguas* (The Parrot of the Seven Languages), thinking that no one would ever read it. I buried my "failed novelist." Two months later, I received a phone call in Paris from a Chilean publisher, Juan Carlos Sáez, who had heard from a friend of mine that I had written a novel and offered to publish it. It was published.

For some male clients who complained of not being able to find a lover, I recommended that they write in indelible ink on a pink silk ribbon, "I wish with all my heart to find a woman," sign it with a drop of their blood, and then tie it around the penis and keep it there for a day and a night.

Some women asked me for a psychomagical act that would enable them to find a man. To those appearing to be shut away in themselves, who were timid and unable to express anger against their fathers, I advised going to a specialized school for shooting lessons, not only with pistols and rifles but also with machine guns. I received a letter from one client effusively thanking me for my advice, who told me she was now in a relationship with her instructor. Later she came to me asking for a psychomagical act that would allow her to break free of this man.

Abortions made necessary by emotional or economic problems cause deep trauma. The woman, feeling guilty, becomes depressed and cannot come to terms with it. There may be a crisis in the couple's relationship as they move further and further away from each other. To help my clients in these cases, I suggested that they think of a fruit to identify with the fetus—some chose a raspberry, some a mango, others a small tangerine. Having chosen a fruit, the woman should place it on her bare belly and fasten it there with four strips of flesh-colored bandage. A friend, the husband, the lover, or a family member should dress as a surgeon, cut the bandages and take the fruit out, acting as if pulling it out with great difficulty. During this action, the consultant should relive the feelings she experienced during the operation and express them aloud. Then the "fetus" should be placed in a small hardwood box, and she and the man who inseminated her (or her current partner, a friend, or a family member) should go to a beautiful place, dig a hole with their hands, bury the "coffin" there, and plant a sapling on top of it. Once this is done, the man should kiss her on the lips, slipping a honey candy into her mouth.

When people consult me who have pimples on their faces and I see that they have had a lack of attention from their parents, I advise them to get their mother and father to spit into a green clay pot that they hold in their right hand. Then, with the middle and ring fingers of the left, they should stir the clay and saliva to form a paste that is then applied to the pimples or eczema.

In extreme cases where the child abuse has been so cruel that the damage seems incurable, I advise the client to die . . . and then be reborn as someone else. I advise him to choose a beautiful place; dig his grave there aided by a group of friends; read his funeral rites facing the grave; then lie down, naked and wrapped in a sheet. His friends will cover him with dirt (of course leaving his mouth and nose exposed), and he will stay there, mimicking the emptiness of death, for at least forty minutes.

When he says he is ready his friends will disinter him, wash him, put new clothes on him, and baptize him with a new name.

When a child has unconsciously been given an abominable name, such as that of a sibling who died before he or she was born, that of a relative who committed suicide, or other tragedy, I advise changing the name. To prevent the child from feeling dispossessed of her identity, she should be given two small boxes, one gray and one gold. "In this gray box you will keep your old name." On a simple, opaque card, the mother or father writes the child's name and puts it in the gray box. "And from this box"—the golden box is opened and a brightly colored card with cheerful decorations is taken out—"you get a new, better name." And they read the new name on the card. "From now on you will be called by this name. When you want to remember your old name, take it out of the gray box for a moment, greet it, then put it back again."

For divorced women who cannot get over the anger they feel toward their ex-husbands, I have advised sticking a photograph of the man's face onto a soccer ball and kicking it around.

I have advised people who were never cuddled to get their partner or a friend to give them a long massage using acacia honey instead of oil, completing the massage by rubbing them all over their body with a photo of their mother in the left hand and one of their father in the right hand.

Sometimes I have used active poetry as a remedy for people who suppress their feelings. I told a frustrated musician to get up at dawn and listen to the songs of the birds while repeatedly saying, like a litany, "They are happy because I exist." I told a woman who felt nonexistent to stand in the middle of a bridge at midnight in the summertime, repeating many times while looking at the current, "The river passes but the reflection of the stars remains." I advised a man who suffered from thinking that he was fundamentally disagreeable to whisper in the ears of a hundred people (relatives, friends, colleagues, etc.), "A single firefly in the dark night lights up the whole sky."

Little by little, I was daring to propose more complex acts. At the time of writing, every Wednesday, without any advertising and always for free, aided by the Tarot I prescribe psychomagical acts to around twenty people. Fortunately, my partner, Marianne Costa, has taken notes of this advice (which can be found in Appendix I of this book), because I, being in a state of trance, forget it after a few minutes.

I once gave a series of interviews to Gilles Farcet, which was published in the book *Psychomagic*. His readers wrote to me asking for private sessions, which I did for a year in order to confront important problems and to experiment with new directions in this form of therapy. Many psychoanalysts, osteopaths, and doctors of so-called New Medicine (students of Dr. Gérard Athias in the south of France) took my courses and applied them to their disciplines. Later, the SAT Institute (Seekers After Truth), headed by the psychiatrist Claudio Naranjo, a direct disciple of Gestalt therapy founder Frederick Perls, invited me to teach some courses in Spain and Mexico, where three hundred future therapists learned the techniques of tarology, psychogenealogy, and above all, psychomagic. I also formed groups of students of the psychoanalyst Antonio Ferrara in Santiago de Chile, and then in Naples. To convey this art, which I practiced in a state of trance, I had to force myself to find "laws" that would allow scientific minds to delve into its mysteries.

Psychomagic is fundamentally based on the fact that the subconscious accepts the symbol and the metaphor, giving them the same importance as real things, which was also known to the magicians and shamans of ancient cultures. For the subconscious, acting on a photograph, a tomb, a garment, or some intimate object (one detail can symbolize the whole) is the same as acting on the real person.

Once the subconscious decides that something should happen, it is impossible for the individual to inhibit or completely sublimate the impulse. Once the arrow is launched, one cannot make it return to the bow. The only way to free oneself from the impulse is to fulfill it . . . but this can be done metaphorically.

Many children who have been disliked by their parents grow up with the desire to eliminate them. While they do not do this, they remain submerged in a depression that can lead to suicide, addiction, or fatal disease. For these people I recommend hanging a portrait of the mother from the neck of a black hen and a portrait of the father from the neck of a red rooster. Then they should cut the throats of both chickens and bathe in their blood. After plucking them, they should cook them and serve them at a party with a group of friends. The black and red feathers and the other remains of the animals should be buried and a sapling planted above them.

Cases of female frigidity in which I detected a sexual fixation on the father have been cured by the recommendation that the woman print a photograph of her father on a t-shirt and make love with her partner while he wears that shirt. Thus, metaphorically, the incestuous desire is fulfilled and overcome. One woman who came to see me suffered from wounds and burns in her vagina each time she made love. Looking at her family tree, I could see that at age thirteen she had been separated from her Italian father. To conduct the metaphorical incest, I suggested that she cook a package of spaghetti in three liters of water. She should then send the spaghetti in a bag to her father and douche with the cooking water. She was cured.

It is not possible to eliminate an anxiety or an irrational fear by trying to reason with the client to show him that what he fears can never happen. One must push him toward the anxiety in order to bring about, metaphorically, what he fears so much. In this, I was inspired by an anecdote from the American psychiatrist Milton Erickson, who, as a child, saw his father's workers trying to get a stubborn bull into the corral. The bull refused to budge. For all their pushing, they could not move him. Erickson approached them, took the animal's tail, and tugged on it. Feeling that he was being given an order to retreat, the stubborn bovine took off running toward the corral.

When a person feels possessed—by somebody in her family, a witch, or some evil person—it is impossible to convince her that this is not the case by giving reasons. However well she may accept it intellectually, her emotional center will reject it. She must be treated as a possessed person and must submit to an act that resembles an exorcism. To accomplish this, her entire body should be covered by copies of a photograph or a drawing of the invader, stuck on with a mixture of clay, flour, and water. Then these images should be ripped off while yelling furious orders such as, "Out! Leave this person in peace! Go back to yourself!" Once they have all been torn off, the patient should be bathed, perfumed, and dressed in new clothes. The photographs should be buried and a chrysanthemum planted there.

It may also be advisable to make a fake identification document for the patient with a false name, age, and profession, to mislead whoever wants to possess him. In some central European Jewish families, when someone is gravely ill they call the rabbi to change his name. Thus, when death comes to look for him, it will not find him.

The psychoanalyst Chantal Rialland, who studied with me for many years, writes in her book *Cette famille qui vit en nous* (The Family That Lives in Us), "With regard to the child, the parents feel anguish as a function of their own problems, as a consequence of their childhood and adolescence. They feel this with all the more intensity if the father and mother have felt unwanted, rejected, or not conforming to the family's wishes: 'We hope everything will go well and be normal,' 'We hope the birth will be easy.' Perhaps the last birth in the family was difficult, or perhaps one of the women in the family died in childbirth, a mother, grandmother, great-grandmother, or aunt: 'We hope it won't be as bad as it was for Grandma Agatha,' 'We hope she won't be a druggie like our cousin,' 'A whore like our aunt,' 'Unfaithful like Grandmother Ernestine,' 'We hope he won't be an alcoholic like Grandpa Arthur,' 'A homosexual like Uncle Peter,' 'Lazy and womanizing like our paternal grandfather.' Some parents dread the crisis of adolescence: 'We hope he'll find a decent woman,' 'When I think that my daughter will belong to another man . . .' On the affective plane, every child is compared to his or her family, and since this is a mechanism that tends to reproduce itself, the parents' fears act in the background as curses."

Georg Groddeck in *The Book of the It* writes, "Fear is the result derived from the repression of a desire," and "Fear is desire: those who fear rape, desire it." During childhood it is through the psyches of our parents that the family injects its desires into our minds in the form of fears. Arrows that were shot many generations ago arrive to strike us, demanding that we fulfill their self-destructive impulses: "You have to develop the same cancer that your grandfather had," "You have to lose your ovaries like so many of your ancestors did," "Alcoholism is a family tradition," "The son of the tiger must be born with stripes," "If the mother's a whore, the daughter's a whore." Unless they can be fulfilled metaphorically through an act of psychomagic, these family curses will obsess us for our whole lives.

A psychoanalyst could not shake off the fear of losing her patients and ending up on the street, homeless, a beggar. I advised her to disguise herself as an indigent (dirty and worn out clothes, hair encrusted with dirt, red nose) and receive clients thus in her office. She must also have a liter of wine by her side and a few crusts of hard bread.

"And what am I going to tell them?"

"Tell them you're doing an act of psychomagic."

"And for how long do I have to present myself like this?"

"You're thirty years old. You will be a psychoanalyst-beggar for thirty days."

A wife was obsessed with the desire to have many lovers, but due to a high appreciation of fidelity, she contained herself. I suggested that she trick her husband by remaining faithful to him.

"That's what I want, but it's impossible!"

"It is possible, metaphorically. First of all, you should confess these desires to your husband and convince him to collaborate with you. He will rent a hotel room. Then he will call you, imitating someone else's voice, and tell you to come there for a rendezvous. When you arrive at the room, he will be waiting there disguised as someone else, with a false mustache, beard, or wig, and acting with gestures he never uses. Without saying a word, you two should make love. Then he will leave. You will go back home, where your husband, having restored his own personality, will be waiting for you. He will ask you, 'Where were you?' And you'll answer with a lie: 'I was at the dentist's.' This act should be repeated several times, each time disguising your husband as a different person."

The family incessantly makes predictions about us: "If you do not study, you will fail in life," "You don't have a good ear; don't sing," "You are insufferable; no man will want to marry you," "If you keep on like this, you'll end up in jail." The subconscious tends to fulfill the prediction. Anne A. Schutzberger, a professor at the University of Nice, mentions one aspect of this phenomenon: "If one carefully examines the past of a number of patients seriously ill with cancer, one will find that in many cases, they are people who unconsciously developed a 'life script' during their childhood, sometimes even with the date, time, day, or age at which they will die, and then they find themselves actually in this situation of dying. For example, at age thirty-three—the age at which Jesus Christ died—or forty-five—the age at which a father or mother died, and so on. These are all examples of a kind of automatic fulfillment of personal or family predictions."

It has been proven that if a teacher expects a bad student to remain the same, it is most likely that nothing will change, while on the contrary, if the teacher believes that the child is intelligent but shy and predicts that despite this he or she will make progress, the child begins to study well.

The only way to free oneself from an obsessive prediction is to fulfill it, not to try to forget it. A Spanish friend of mine, a skeptic who always made fun of clairvoyants, had me read the Tarot for her out of curiosity. The cards told her, "Someone very close to you will die, and it will cost you a lot of money." From that moment on, she never ceased to be distressed. The more she tried not to believe the prediction, the greater her obsession grew. I recommended, "Close the doors and windows of your home. Pump insecticides into all the rooms. Watch a fly die. Then it will be true that 'someone very close to you will die.' Then take a dollar bill and add six zeros to it in indelible ink. Wrap the fly in it and bury it. Thus it will have 'cost you a lot of money.'" She did it. Her obsession vanished instantly.

A French woman with an exceptional voice who had been told by her father, "You're a dreamer; you'll never earn a living with your throat unless you sing at the opera house," felt obliged to take singing lessons but never went on from being a student to being a professional. Her impossible goal was to sing at the opera. Knowing she was unable to achieve this, she felt like a failure. I offered to fulfill her father's demands. She was to dress humbly, go to the Palace of the Opera at six o'clock in the evening, and start singing next to the gates with a bowl at her feet. Seven friends, one after another, would deposit a bill in the bowl. After the song, they should applaud her. With the money she received, she should buy an article of clothing that emphasized her beauty. Once the paternal requirement of singing at the opera house was fulfilled, her feelings of inferiority disappeared, and very soon after she became successful at singing the popular songs of which she was fond.

In Mexico City, I met with a young man who was afraid of committing suicide. This fear had been instilled by his mother who, when angry with him, had always yelled, "You're going to end up like your father!" He had been told that his father was a bad man who ended up committing suicide with pills. I asked him what color he imagined these barbiturates to be. He said they were blue.

"Where did he die?"

"In a hotel in Buenos Aires, in Argentina."

"Look in the city for a street named after Buenos Aires or Argentina. Rent a hotel room there, or as close to it as you can. Warn your mother that you are going to perform a therapeutic act that is necessary to prevent you from committing suicide and that you need her help. Go to

the hotel room carrying a small bottle of blue sugar pills. Swallow all of
them and lie in bed, completely still. An hour later, your mother should
arrive and find you like that, 'dead.' She should cry, embracing your
'corpse,' uttering great lamentations and asking for forgiveness. Then
she should call four assistants, who will carry you, very stiff, out of the
hotel room. They will carry you, stretched out in a van, to the apartment where you live with your girlfriend. They will deposit you at her
feet. She will embrace you, kiss you, caress you. Then you will wake
up. You will tell your mother, 'I have committed suicide like my father!
Now that the prediction is fulfilled I will live my own life.' To celebrate,
you will invite your girlfriend, your mother, and the four friends to dine
on tacos made from blue tortillas."

A clairvoyant had predicted to a very fat, childlike man that on his
next birthday he would have a serious accident. The fateful date was
approaching, and he was so preoccupied that he could barely get up in
the morning to go to work. I recommended that he buy one of those
calendars from which one tears off a page for each day. The next day,
in the early morning, he should tear off the pages until he got to the
date of his birthday. Then he should go to a bakery dressed like a child
and buy a multitiered cake covered in cream. He should carry it away
unwrapped, walking down the street. He should purposely stumble and
fall face down onto the cake, burying his face in the cream. He should
scream like a child who believes he has had a major accident. Then he
should go to the seer's house with the crushed cake and smear it on him.

A woman was obsessed because a doctor had told her it was likely
that she would have ovarian cancer. She felt sterile. To eliminate this
negative prediction, I advised her to insert two fresh dove eggs into
her vagina and keep them there for one whole night in order that they
might confer their germinative strength. Then she should bury them in
fertile soil, planting two large flowers there to symbolize her fulfilled
ovaries.

A young woman was worried because all the women in her family tree were only children and had been widowed. She wanted to find

a husband who would not die. I advised her to fulfill the prediction, since she was not currently living with a partner, by dressing in black and having business cards printed with her name on them, followed by "widow of X." She should also make a human-sized doll representing the dead husband with her own hands, with which she would sleep for seven nights. After that time she should bury it and plant a tree over the "grave."

In order to solve a problem I often make the client aware that, as in dreams, he or she is shifting the image of one person onto another. One woman could not break free from her former husband. Although she hated him, the separation made her suffer. I advised her to obtain a picture of her father's face and a picture of her ex-husband's face. The pictures should be large, life size, on transparent sheets. Then she should place the ex-husband's face over that of the father and tape them to the glass of her bedroom window, preferably where the rising sun shines in, in order to see both images at the same time, superimposed. "Go to visit your father, and without him knowing it, dig in his laundry basket and steal a pair of underpants. Back at your house, cut a piece off the fly and stick it at the bottom of the double picture. When you truly realize that you are suffering not from your ex-husband's lack of understanding but from your father's, due to a repressed incestuous desire from childhood, you can burn the two transparencies and the piece of underwear, dissolve some of the ashes in a glass of wine, and drink it. Then you will accept the divorce with pleasure, knowing that it is a liberation."

A very sensitive woman, Barbara, accused herself of being confrontational and destructive. "Because of this, I have destroyed the lives of my three daughters." She wanted to rid herself of the "shadow" of her maternal grandmother, also confrontational and destructive. "My mother is always telling me that I look like her, that I'm following the same path, that I'm causing the same damage. In spite of all sorts of therapies, I can't get rid of this shadow." I advised her to dress up like her grandmother—underwear, clothes, shoes, wig—and stand next to a large surface covered by white paper, onto which she would cast her shadow with a spotlight. Her mother should draw the outline of the shadow with an indelible pen and then fill in the outline with black paint. After this the client should roll up the metaphorical shadow, go to a river, and facing away from the current, throw in both the shadow and the old costume over her left shoulder, then leave without looking back.

Sometimes these psychological shifts result in a dead relative possessing us without our realizing it, prompting us to seek reparation. In these cases, instead of struggling against those urges that we feel to be alien, we should submit to them. One man, with a face as inexpressive as if carved in stone, was deserted by his wife, who left him after giving birth to their daughter and returned to her parental home after one year of marriage. Her mother had done the same thing: right after giving birth, she had abandoned her husband and returned to the parental home. The man was suffering because he loved his wife and wanted her back. He thought that his wife had gotten bored of him because of his taciturn nature. I advised him to hire a band of mariachis and go to serenade his wife in the Mexican style. When his wife's mother had returned to her parents, her proud husband had never gone looking for her. What she was asking for was proof of love. "Your wife is possessed by her mother and is repeating her act, hoping that finally her husband will behave like a man in love. You should also go dressed in traditional mariachi costume. It's not really about you seducing your wife; it's about her father seducing her mother."

When a problem seems to have no solution because the client admits that he or she is the culprit and, out of repentance, feeling unable to repair the fault, brings about an illness, an economic or emotional failure, or a suicidal obsession, I turn to the concept that the "crimes" can be paid for. During the uprising against foreigners in Algeria, a son of French parents who had settled there watched from his bedroom window as his father and mother left the house, started their car, and were blown up by a bomb placed there by the revolutionaries. Instead of suffering, he began to laugh, feeling liberated from these narcissistic, intolerant, cold parents. Years later he came to see me, overwhelmed by guilt. He could not accept that he had felt so inhumane about the beings that had given him life. I did not allow myself to excuse his action by telling him that the person who had laughed was his badly mistreated inner child. Instead, I affirmed his guilt. Then I advised him to make a financial sacrifice by buying two very expensive jewels, traveling to Algeria, and burying the precious gems exactly at the spot where the car had exploded, without letting anyone see. Thus the emotional debt would be paid.

Sometimes an unjust feeling of guilt can lead to a neurosis of failure. One woman had been told too many times by her parents, "When you were born, you created a problem for us: we were poor. Your arrival plunged us even further into financial difficulties." I recommended that she exchange a five-hundred-franc note for the same amount in five-centime coins. Carrying this heavy weight in a bag at the level of her belly, she should walk along a main street scattering handfuls of coins as if they were seeds while thinking to herself, "I am giving wealth to the world."

Another technique is to transfer the painful feeling to an object and then "give" it to whoever has done the damage. One woman consulted me because she felt she had a symbiotic relationship with her sister, who unceasingly gave her orders, taking control of her will. Although this sister had died of breast cancer, my client still felt owned by her and wanted to be released. I advised her to put a steel ball, such as those used for playing boules, into a leather bag and wear it around her neck day and night. "Resist that weight as much as possible, because it symbolizes your sister, and when you can no longer support it, go to see your mother and give her the ball, saying, "This object is not mine, it's yours. I am giving it back to you. It would be good if you would bury it." I explained that competitive relationships between siblings are caused by the instability of the parents.

A lesbian woman suffered because she did not feel at ease with her lover. She had been sexually repressed and often lacked sexual energy, although sex had worked well with her lover until her desire ceased because her lover constantly asked her to be perfect, as her mother had done before her. I advised her to steal some of her mother's dirty clothes, dress her lover in them, lie in bed with her, and during sexual relations tear up these garments with rage while shouting, "I'm not perfect, and you're not my mother!" Then she should give her lover a massage with rose-scented oil. After this, she should wrap the shredded clothes in white paper and tie up the package with a blue ribbon. In another package of black paper tied with a pink ribbon, she should wrap up a new dress. She should send both packages to her mother with a letter saying, "I do not know if you will understand this: I have destroyed your old dress to return it to you changed into a new one. Thank you."

Another woman, very distressed, said that she was having terrible problems with her period. She felt as if she would never stop bleeding. After analyzing her family tree, I told her, "You are suffering the anguish of your mother. You are bleeding because of the kicks in the belly that your maternal grandfather gave to his wife when he found out she was pregnant again. She gave birth only to girls. You were supposed to have been a boy. You must return these kicks to your grandfather. Go to his grave with a calf fetus and a liter of artificial blood. Throw this cadaver on the slab and pour on the blood. Then kick the grave ferociously. Expel your grandmother's rage from yourself. Then bury the calf fetus nearby and plant a beautiful plant with red flowers there."

A person can be freed from a problem by breaking a record. To a woman who suffered from being twenty kilos overweight I recommended going into a butcher shop, buying twenty kilos of meat and bones, loading the package on her shoulders and walking twenty kilometers, ending up at a river where she would throw the package in. To a bank teller who had lost his will to live, I recommended traversing all of Italy, from one end to the other, on roller skates. To an old lady, an inconsolable widow, I advised going hang gliding accompanied by an instructor.

The problem of perfectionism can be cured by showing yourself as more imperfect than you are to whoever demands the perfection. A very young client, a student in film school, suffered because she demanded too much of herself. "As a child, I was never happy with what I did. This desire for perfection paralyzes me." I advised her to make a short film, as short as possible. It should be badly directed, with poor cinematography, bad interpretation, and a stupid storyline told in absurd form. Then she should gather her family, show them this horror, and demand to be applauded and praised by all.

A man consulted me because he had made up his mind that no woman would love him if he were not perfect. He had a girlfriend whom he decided not to marry because of this. Despite all her demonstrations of affection, he believed that she was faking it because "how can it be possible for her to love such an imperfect man?" I advised him to study with a jeweler and learn to make rings, after which he should try to make the ugliest wedding ring in the world: if she consented to wear it on her finger, he would finally feel loved because his imperfection would be accepted.

If one is lacking a quality that one wants, one can imitate it. This reminds me of the story of a man who was desperate because his stubborn donkey refused to drink. Neither prayers nor blows could convince it. If this went on, the animal would die of thirst. His good neighbor offered to help him. The neighbor brought his own donkey, stood it next to the nondrinker, and gave it a bucketful of water, which the animal drank up with pleasure. Seeing this, the stubborn donkey, in the spirit of imitation, also began to drink. A young woman who had stopped having periods several years earlier due to emotional problems asked me what she should do. I advised her to buy artificial blood (such as is used in films), to inject it into her vagina once a month for three or four days, to use the appropriate hygiene products, and to continue imitating periods in this manner. Soon her real menstruation would return. This same phenomenon often occurs when a woman who cannot have children adopts a child. Thanks to the "imitation" of motherhood, to her surprise, she soon becomes pregnant.

For depressed people—besides asking, "If laws did not exist and anything was allowed, who would you kill and how?" and allowing them to commit their crimes in a metaphorical fashion—it is also very useful to recommend trying something that they have never done or that they have not even imagined doing. For example, taking a balloon ride and throwing seven kilos of seeds down onto the earth, painting a self-portrait with menstrual blood, or going to Mass dressed as a parrot. Or, for someone very masculine, taking Arabian-style belly dancing classes. Or offering a flower to the first bald man you see on the street and asking for permission to kiss his bare head. Or dressing up as a poor person and going out to beg. For a woman who had never played during childhood because she had weak, childish parents who made it necessary for her to act as an adult and take care of them, I advised going to the Dauville casino, buying five thousand francs worth of chips, and playing to lose.

"And if I win?"

"Keep playing, days, weeks, months, years, until you end up losing it all."

Sometimes very simple advice leads to a good result. I drew one woman out of depression by advising her to go to a tea shop and eat an éclair (a pastry with a phallic shape) with coffee-cream filling every morning before breakfast for twenty-eight days in a row.

The film *The Wizard of Oz* provided inspiration for advice I gave to clients with social neuroses. The Tin Man wants to have feelings, so the psychomagician places a heart-shaped watch on his chest. The Scarecrow wants to be intelligent, so the psychomagician gives him a university diploma. The Cowardly Lion wants to be brave, so the psychomagician gives him a medal. The subconscious takes the symbols for realities! In traditional Chinese culture if one burns fake bills on the graves of one's ancestors, one feels that one has made an important sacrifice. A voodoo priest who spits out clouds of rum that evaporate feels that his spirit is ascending to the gods with them. For a doctor whose brother was a tennis champion and who could not get enough patients because he felt anonymous, I recommended placing a photograph of himself with his brother in his waiting room. But using a clever trick, he should switch the heads so that the tennis champion's head was on his body and his head was on his brother's body.

In some cases, the archetype that causes the client's frustration is the mother, backed up by the grandmother and great-grandmother. This coalition is the most powerful of all and can only be overcome by an archetype of divine character. The only one that is psychologically stronger than the mother is the Virgin Mary (assuming the client is Catholic, of course). Often, motivated simply by the desire to help, I have used places that are exalted in popular culture and, at the risk of being branded sacrilegious, elements of sacred ceremonies. An example is a woman from a Protestant background, one of eight siblings, who wanted to start a family but an irrational fear prevented her from marrying. I explained to her that when a family tree has mothers, grandmothers, and great-grandmothers burdened by a large number of children, there is a fear of semen as a diabolical substance that causes unwanted pregnancies as punishment for pleasure. I proposed an act that would make her lose her fear of sperm, giving it its true dimension: a divine substance. "First, make love with your boyfriend, asking him to ejaculate into a glass at the bottom of which there will be a host. After that, fill the glass with melted wax and put in a wick. After the wax has hardened, bring the candle to the crypt dedicated to the Virgin at Lourdes, and place it at her feet. Then light the wick, kneel, and pray nine Our Fathers, one for your father and eight for your eight siblings."

As my students increased in number, I took on broader problems. Santiago Pando, one of the directors of the advertising campaign for President Fox of Mexico, had attended my seminars in Guadalajara and had applied the principles of psychomagic in his successful campaign. Pando asked me, "If we consider that our country has suffered for seventy-five years from a disease called PRI,* could you propose psy-

---

*[*Partido Revolucionario Institucional,* the Institutional Revolutionary Party, which held power in Mexico prior to Fox's victory. —*Trans.*]

chomagical advice to cure it?" I suggested, first of all, to celebrate collectively at the national level: at the moment when power was handed over, the new president would shout, "Mexico is rising!" and millions of helium-filled balloons (made of biodegradable material), in the three colors of the country's flag, would be released into the sky.

Secondly, an Internet site called Virtual Mexico would be launched where all citizens would collaborate, ideally to convert Mexico into Eden. The virtual country would serve as a model for the real country.

I considered it of vital importance to change the appearance of the currency. The bills, which had become symbols of corruption and exploitation, imbued with the suffering of the people, had to recover their dignity and become positive talismans. I advised them to print bills with images from popular faith, such as the Virgin of Guadalupe, Saint Simon, Santa Muerte, Saint Paschal Baylon, and María Sabina.

I also suggested covering the entire Pyramid of the Sun with a thin layer of gold leaf and covering the entire Pyramid of the Moon with silver leaf. At the top of the masculine (gold) pyramid, a silver-plated statue of the goddess Coatlicue should be placed. At the top of the female (silver) pyramid, there should be a gold-plated Aztec solar calendar. This phenomenal act would attract millions of tourists. With the money raised, the lake that had been so absurdly dried up, turning the region into a dusty valley, could be restored.

NINE

From Psychomagic to Psychoshamanism

Psychomagic is about saving time, accelerating the gaining of awareness. Just as a disease can announce itself suddenly, healing can also arrive in an instant. A sudden illness is called unfortunate, while a sudden healing is called a miracle. However, both take part in the same essence: they are forms of the language of the subconscious. Thanks to rapid detection through tarology, a deep understanding gained by studying the repeating patterns in the family tree, and psychomagical actions, we can come closer to the inner peace that is a product of the discovery of our true identity, which allows us to live with joy and die without anguish, knowing that we have not squandered our time in this dream called "reality." However, valuable as these interventions are, if the client does not put in as much effort as the therapist, no mental mutation will be achieved; all the work will do nothing more than calm the symptoms, seeming to eliminate the pain but leaving unhealed the wound that invades the entire individual with its distressing shadow. The client, at the same time that he or she is seeking help, rejects it. The therapeutic act is a strange fight: we struggle mightily to help someone who puts up all possible barriers and tries to steer the healing toward failure. In a way, the healer is the hope of salvation for the sick person, but at the same time an enemy. He who suffers, fearing that the source of his ill health will be revealed to him, wants to be put to sleep, wants to be made insensible to pain, but wants in no way to change, in no way to be shown that his problems are the protesting of a soul locked in the cell of a false identity. Many clients have come to see me because, despite having achieved what they wanted to achieve—success in love, in material life, in social events—for no apparent reason, they want to die. Some triumphant people die in senseless accidents; others, apparently healthy, succumb to chronic diseases. Astute businessmen are ruined every day. Tranquil beings, surrounded by loving families, commit suicide. Why? When a mother, consciously or not, wants to get rid of the fetus for some powerful reason (because the couple has economic or emotional problems, because the father has fled or died, because the woman became pregnant by accident, because ancestors have died in childbirth, or for many other anxiety-related reasons), then this desire for elimination, for death, is embedded in the intra-uterine memory of the new being and acts as an order during his or her earthly life. Without realizing it rationally, the individual feels that she is an intruder who has no right to live. Even if the woman becomes the best of mothers after the birth, the damage is already done. Her son or daughter, even if everything that others consider happiness is at his or her disposal, will have to battle against incessant desires to die.

Moreover, even if the mother joyously accepts the pregnancy, she may not want a real child but an imaginary one who will carry out the family's plans, even if those plans have nothing to do with the child's true nature. The offspring is expected to be equal to his progenitor, or to achieve something that the adult could not achieve, or else the mother—whose father, having unresolved homosexual desires, has made her into a failed man, forcing her to suppress her femininity and develop masculine characteristics—dreams of giving birth to a perfect boy whose phallus she will take control of, satisfying her father's wish. In such cases, it is common for the mother to be single, so that her child is given the surname of the maternal grandfather, metaphorically carrying out the father-daughter incest. Because humans are warm-blooded mammals, in the depths of their animal nature they carry the need to be protected, nurtured, and sheltered from cold by the bodies of their fathers and mothers. If this contact is lacking, the offspring is doomed to perish. A human being's greatest fear is to be unloved by his or her mother, father, or both. If this happens, the soul is marked by a wound that never stops festering. The brain, having not found its true, bright center that would keep it in continuous ecstasy, lives in anguish. Unable to find true pleasure, which is nothing other than being oneself rather than being an imposed mask, it seeks out the less painful situations. I had a French friend who when asked, "Hello, how are you?" would reply with a smirk, "Not too bad." Between two evils, the brain chooses the lesser one. Since the greatest evil is not being loved, the individual does not recognize this lack of love, and rather than enduring the atrocious pain of becoming conscious of it, prefers to be depressed, to create a disease, to be ruined, to fail. Because of these unbearable symptoms, the client starts therapy. If the healer wants to heal the wound at its core, a wide range of defenses must be deployed.

A great Italian theater and film actor came to consult me, accompanied by his wife. He had suffered depression in a cyclical form for many years. He was a handsome old man, very tall, robust, with an impressive voice. However, despite his radiant personality, I realized that in his heart he was still a docile child. His wife, a small brunette with a tremendous personality, exercised a virile authority over him. Exploring the actor's family tree, I saw that his mother, due to the absence of the father, had developed an extremely possessive character, making him into her faithful servant. The famous man did not like acting at all; it was not his vocation. However, wanting to please his mother, who insisted that he must succeed on the stage and screen, he had dedicated most of his life to this. And, of course, becoming an internationally renowned star, racking up one triumph after another without taking any pleasure in it because this was the maternal ideal and not his own, he suffered from one depression after another. He felt that he was not himself, but an individual living a foreign destiny. His wife, who admired him greatly, was in a way a copy of his mother, now deceased. I proposed a psycho-magical act: the obedient child should rebel against both his mother and his wife. To assert his independence, he should go to visit his mother's grave, carrying a rooster. Standing on the slab, he should slit the animal's throat, let the blood fall on his penis and testicles, and with his crotch thus bloodied, he should return home and have intercourse with his wife, without any prior foreplay, with intense movements, while shouting to release his anger, which up until then had been repressed.

The man was not surprised or frightened. He simply said, "I'm sorry, Alejandro, I cannot do that. I'm . . ." (He pronounced his famous name with emphasis and a touch of desperation). "If I were an unknown person, I would probably do it."

How could I explain what he at all costs did not want to see? If his mother had made him into this famous person against his will it was because she had never loved him; she had only loved herself, or perhaps her own father. The act that would have overthrown his dependency, and perhaps would have prolonged his life (he died a couple of years after this consultation), could not be carried out because he was a prisoner of an image of himself, all the more painful because he knew it was false, but yet respected it, as a turtle respects its shell, because it had completely replaced his essence. Without it he would have felt empty, nonexistent. This defensive system caused any attempt at real healing to fail.

The human brain reacts like an animal, defending its territory, which it identifies with its life. The brain delineates this space with its urine and feces. Parents, siblings, spouses, co-workers, and above all, the body are all part of this space. The one who is in charge has limitations that correspond to his or her level of consciousness. The higher the level of consciousness, the greater the freedom, but to reach this level—where the territory is not just a few square meters or a small group of people, but the entire planet and all of humanity, and indeed the entire universe and all living beings—it is first necessary to heal the wound and get rid of the fetal conditioning, then the family conditioning, and finally the social conditioning. In order to reach this mutation in which he abandons the orders he has been given and lives in gratitude for the miracle of being alive, the client must be made aware of his defensive mechanisms. These are mechanisms that all animals use to escape their predatory enemies. They know how to shut themselves off and how to play dead. They roll up, they cover themselves with chitinous shells, they bury themselves in the mud, and they shut down their breathing and heartbeat. The human being does the same thing: she becomes paralyzed, encloses herself in a repetitive system of gestures, desires, emotions, and thoughts, and veg-etates within these narrow limits, rejecting all new information, mired in an endless repetition of the past. To avoid sinking into the depths, she lives floating in a net of superficial sensations, anesthetized most of the time. Animals know how to camouflage themselves, to make themselves similar to the environment in which they live. The chameleon changes color, some insects look like tree leaves, and certain mammals have skin that resembles the terrain that they inhabit. Likewise, a great many human beings, discarding their natural uniqueness, make themselves the same as the world that surrounds them. They forbid themselves the slightest trace of originality, they eat what everyone else eats, they dress according to the latest fad, they speak with accents and idioms that indi-cate that they indubitably belong to some social group, and they form part of the masses that march along all brandishing the same red book, making the same salute with an outstretched arm, or wearing the same uniform. They depend entirely on appearances, relegating their true being to the darkness of their dreams. When animals feel attacked, they can fight back. The fear of knowing oneself, coupled with the fear of being deprived of what one believes oneself to possess, including one's way of life—which would involve a painful encounter with the essential wound—can turn humans into murderers. In other animal species, before attack the primary defense is flight. According to the ancient Chinese treatise the *Thirty-Six Stratagems,* "Flight is supreme poli-tics. To keep one's forces intact, avoiding confrontation, is not defeat." These people do not want to know anything of themselves, they aban-don treatment halfway through, they constantly justify themselves, they struggle to always be right and to prove that others are wrong, they succumb to vices, and they develop infatuations and obsessions; sometimes, they move to a foreign country in order to not confront their problems, using distance as a painkiller. Flight is sometimes accompanied by self-mutilation: the lizard escapes by detaching its tail. My friend G. K., a great French science-fiction writer, was disappointed in love at the height of his literary success: the woman of his dreams married somebody else. G. K. decided to stop writing forever. In a metaphorical sense, he was castrated. Van Gogh cut off his ear. Rimbaud expelled poetry from his life. Some people turn away from their loved ones or their favorite things, others mutilate themselves through cosmetic surgery, squandering their fortunes . . .

In a consultation, the defenses begin as soon as the Tarot reading starts. "I already knew that." In saying this, the client believes he is denying importance to something that he knows but keeps in his subconscious regions. As soon as the reading is over, the client forgets what he saw clearly, in the same way that we forget our dreams when we wake up in the morning. Sometimes, although he speaks clearly and distinctly, he seems not to hear; this is psychological deafness. If he is shown a painful point in the structure of his family tree, he will appear not to see it; this is psychological blindness. If you propose an act, he will haggle as much as he can. Sometimes it seems too difficult, sometimes too long, too expensive, or he will ask to change the details or be afraid of the others' reactions: "If I do this my father might die, my mother will go mad." Once he does decide to carry out the psychomagical act, he will put it off. He might wait for years. Or he may declare that during the time of waiting, he has been cured: he no longer needs a solution because there is no problem! Suddenly, a word offends him or a revelation brings on an attack of vomiting, crying, or shaking, requiring the therapist to calm him, thus diverting the therapy from its objective. If asked to provide useful information, he will start telling interminable anecdotes, or will speak much faster than usual, as if fleeing from his own words, or else will lie, or will be stubbornly silent about important memories, or will appear to be collaborating but will make mistakes with dates and names. Finally, trying by all means possible to be the therapist's friend, he will fall in love with the latter, making sexual advances, offering gifts, invitations to dinner, and will end up disappointed, feeling betrayed, and speaking ill of the therapy.

Ejo Takata said, "For a chicken to be born, the hen should peck at the eggshell from the outside, while the chick pecks at it from within." However, in many cases, however well-intentioned the client may be, his unconscious defenses are so great that he cannot collaborate on his healing. No word, no advice, can break through the barriers of his false identity, no attempt at bringing awareness can separate him from his childlike point of view, and his negative feelings dominate him, driving him away from the path that could lead to self-discovery. When this happens, in order to release the client from his problems, we must treat him as a patient.

For the primitive healer death is always a disease, an injury, caused by envy of others. The patient is invaded by a foreign entity, and instead of being cured she must be liberated, expelling what has been sent from her soul and body. To this end, as we have seen, the charlatans of the city turn to cleansing rituals or the imitation of surgery. In these cases of powerlessness (in which the person creates a tumor, a persistent physical pain, a paralysis, or a depression in order to avoid confronting the cause of her suffering, which might be a family secret, incest, social shame, embarrassing diseases, etc.), no success will be achieved through oral language, analysis, the recommendation of an act, or the gaining of awareness. The only possibility for relief is to eliminate the symptom. However, most of the symptoms are manifested by the body, which is the dumping ground for unresolved problems, so the therapist comes in to expel the problems, treating the patient as "possessed." In the Gospels, we are told that the first thing Jesus Christ did after spending forty days fasting in the desert was to enter a temple and with loud cries expel the demons from a possessed person . . .

A machi with a branch of cinnamon, a sacred tree for the Mapuche.
Photo: George Munro.

On my trip to Temuco, a city in Chile a thousand kilometers from the capital, I had the opportunity to accompany a kind ethnologist on the muddy roads that wind through the mountains. We traveled in a powerful Jeep loaded with "needs"—commodities that these poor people lack such as coffee, fruits, soft drinks, flour, cookies, and so forth—that would allow us to be well received by a Mapuche healer. In a tiny valley between three peaks we found a modest hut surrounded by a garden with small trees and medicinal plants, where pigs, chickens, three dogs, and four children roamed about. Very near the door was a *rehue,* a sacred altar about two meters tall made from the trunk of a tree, with seven steps cut into it and surrounded by cinnamon sticks. In a manner of speaking, the rehue is a vertical altar on which the machi stands. Using it as a base, the machi utters her incantations in a language that comes from the depths of time. Thanks to the shipment of "needs," we were kindly received. The woman, who was pregnant, wore a simple skirt and sweater vest. Over these humble clothes she wore a long silver necklace and spiked silver bracelets on her wrists. Despite her wrinkled face, she was no more than thirty years old.

The ethnologist had told me that this woman, married very young to a man who was a heavy drinker, had dreamed one night that a white serpent came to her and gave her the power to heal. She woke up distraught, feeling ignorant, too burdened by the weight of her husband and children to deal with the ills of so many people. But her body started to become paralyzed, and she found it more and more difficult to breathe, until she was at the point of dying in atrocious pain. The white serpent came to her in a dream again, and this time she told it that she would agree to be a machi. The snake immediately gave her the power to recognize the healing value of plants and taught her to heal using ancestral rites. She awoke speaking the mysterious language of the machis, and the first thing she did was to cure her husband of his vices and make him her assistant.

She allowed us to attend a healing session in a small, very clean room decorated with fabrics woven in geometric patterns and a photo of her with her husband, their children, and their dogs. She received a sick man covered with a wool blanket who was carried in the arms of his wife and his mother. He was pale, with fever and pain in his stomach and liver, and his legs were so weak that he was unable to walk.

"An envious man, we'll soon see who, has paid a sorcerer to send you this ill. I will chase it off of you," the machi said to him as she laid him down on his back on a small rectangular table, with his feet flat on the dirt floor on each side. She struck the *kultrung*, a small drum with cosmic significance, and while hitting it began an incantation to each of the four cardinal points. Then, apparently in a trance, she flogged the air around the sick man with a handful of herbs, as if banishing invisible entities. "Evil spirits, leave this place! Leave this poor man alone!" Then, in a resounding voice she said, "Bring me the white hen!" Her husband, a broad-chested, short-legged man, his face embellished by respectful love, brought her the bird. The healer tied its legs and folded its wings so that it could not flutter or escape. She put the hen on the patient's chest. "Look well, poor man. The life you see in those eyes is your life. The heart that beats is your heart. Those lungs that breathe are your lungs. Do not blink; do not stop looking at her." She struck the drum rhythmically, crying with surprising authority, "Get out, bad bile! Get out, devil fever! Get out, stomach pain! Set free this good man, this brave man, this handsome man." Then, gently, she took the white hen and showed it to the sick man and his family, who trembled in surprise. The hen was dead!

"The evil in your husband, your son, passed into this hen. She died so that you might live. You are healed. Go to the yard, gather dry wood, and burn her."

Seeing that his illness had passed to the hen, the sick man's imagination allowed him to believe that he was healthy. His fever and pains vanished. He got up without any help, went smiling out to the garden, gathered dry twigs, skillfully lit a fire, and burned the bird. For my part, I imagined several ways in which the machi could have managed to kill the bird surreptitiously. Perhaps she thrust one of the spikes on her bracelet into its neck, pressed on a nerve center, or, in complicity with her husband, poisoned it beforehand. What did it matter? The point was that she was able to affect the patient's mind, making him believe that his illness had been removed. Are all diseases a manifestation of the imagination, a kind of organic dream?

Some time later in a course that I taught to doctors and therapists in Sanary, in the south of France, I applied this primitive concept to the removal of evil from the body, coming closer to what I call "psychoshamanism," taking a few minutes to cure a woman of a tic that she had had for forty years. Constantly, every two or three seconds, in a broken rhythm, she would shake her head from side to side. I called her up in front of a hundred students and proceeded to interrogate her, using a friendly voice that instantly made me a paternal archetype for her. Applying Pachita's technique, despite her forty-eight years, I spoke to her like a child. "Tell me, little girl, how old are you?" She fell into a trance and replied in a childlike voice, "Eight years old."

"Tell me, little one, who are you saying no to all the time with your head?"

"The priest!"

"What did this priest do to you?"

"When I went to confess to prepare for my first communion, he asked me if had sinned mortally. Since I did not know what a mortal sin was, I said no. He insisted, asking me if I had touched myself between my legs. I had done it without knowing it was wrong. It gave me great shame, and I lied with a resounding 'No.' He kept on insisting, and I kept denying it. I left there and received the sacred host feeling that I was a liar, in a state of mortal sin, condemned forever."

"My poor child, you have kept on denying for forty years. You have to understand that this priest was sick, that you did not have to feel guilty: it is normal for children to investigate their bodies and touch themselves; the sex organs are not the seat of evil. I will remove the useless 'No!' from your head . . ."

I had the woman write "NO!" on masking tape with a black marker and stuck it to her forehead. I asked her to lie on her back on a table and shook my outstretched hands all around her body as if severing invisible bonds, shouting, "Go away, you stupid priest; leave this innocent child alone! Out! Out!" Then, acting as if it was a great effort, I began to tear the tape with the "NO!" off her forehead. I pretended that it was very difficult. I exclaimed, "It has deep roots! Push! Push it out! Help me, girl!" She began to push, screaming in pain. Finally, I triumphantly pulled off the masking tape. She covered her face with her hands and burst into tears. When she raised her head, she no longer had the tic. I told her to go out to the garden and burn the "NO!" I told her to take some of the ashes, dissolve them in honey, and swallow it. She did. Her head shaking never returned.

This successful "operation" opened up a vast field of experimentation. I came to the conclusion that everything that Pachita, machis, Filipino doctors, quacks, and shamans achieve in a primitive, superstitious setting could also be achieved, without deception or illusory effects, with patients born into a rational culture. Just as the subconscious accepts symbolic acts as realities, the body also accepts as real the metaphorical operations to which it is submitted, even if reason rejects them.

My experiences with what I had called "initiatory massage" served as a basis. When I began studying the body, considering it as a terrain in which the subconscious manifests, I saw that to a certain degree some people moved with gestures that I perceived as "shining." By contrast, the depressed people, entrenched in their problems, lacking projection, made gestures that were "opaque." It occurred to me that the past, with its painful memories and the principal fears of being, of loving, of creating, of living, accumulated like a crust covering the skin. I remembered the Mexican "cleansings," in which the witch would rub the client's body with a handful of herbs to purge him of his misfortune. I thought that an even more profound psychological effect could be achieved if, instead of lightly rubbing the skin, I scraped it, just as one does with a piece of metal in order to remove the oxidized layer. I acquired a synthetic bone spatula, about twenty centimeters long and two wide, the kind that is used to fold paper, and began to scrape my naked client. This went on for three hours. After being entirely scraped, people felt reborn; many of the old fears that they had carried stuck to their skin dissolved away. But, although it is true that this technique made the patient "shine," it must be admitted that after a while new sediments accumulated that gradually brought back the "opacity." However, some progress had been made. The person with feelings of abandonment that caused so many unresolved problems now received physical contact, an indispensable complement to the mental and emotional contact that a psychoanalyst provides.

In the early 1970s I lived in Mexico City, where trains rolled along the broad Avenida Chapultepec. One morning I saw a group of curious people surrounding one of these vehicles. They were motionless, expressionless, staring transfixed at the front wheels. I made my way through the crowd: the vehicle had trapped a man. It was impossible to remove him manually. A wheel had pinned him at the waist. He was pale, strangely calm. He had abandoned all hope, given himself over to the designs of Providence, awaiting the capricious Red Cross, which could take hours to arrive. What could we do? A crane would be needed to move the heavy train. I felt an immense compassion for the poor man, but then I was overtaken by a peace that I will dare to call, in a good way, abnormal. It was like falling into the ocean of time, where the seconds were like eternity. I knelt beside the injured man, staining my pants with his blood, and took his hand gently, so that he would feel that he had company. He looked at me with gratitude, and we remained there tranquilly, I do not know how long, until the nurses, firefighters, police, and the crane arrived. Before I let go, he squeezed my hand, speaking a thousand silent words with that contact. I could do no more for him. I walked away slowly. When I was a child and cried terrified in the darkness, desperately calling for my parents, who had gone out to the cinema, all I wanted was a loving touch to keep me company. That would have allowed me to accept being devoured by the shadow. The simple company of another, in adverse situations, is as necessary as life itself . . .

When Bernadette died in the plane crash and our son Brontis came to see me after identifying the remains of his mother in the morgue, I could not find words to comfort him. All I could do was to take him in my arms and put his right ear over my heart so that he could hear it beating. He stayed there, I do not know if it was for an hour or two or three . . . These sad events taught me to keep the patient company, to give all of my time in a limited time, to put my heart into the task, knowing that its beats are mediators between the human and the divine.

Once the person was scraped, the past removed, and the vital energies recovered—the energies that would drive him or her to embrace the present—I followed up with a session of skin stretching. The deviant, egotistic individual "I" tends to separate from the world and lives under the skin. And in its zeal for possession, it makes that skin into a defensive border. Feeling insecure, afraid of emptiness, it unwittingly draws the skin inward, making it into a corset. In the old days infants were wrapped up, perhaps with the secret fear that their uncontrolled movements would cause them to "spill out." I felt that I had to teach the skin to expand itself, restoring its elasticity in order to unite it with humanity and the cosmos. I started grabbing parts of skin and stretching them as much as possible. The skin of the back was elastic and stretched surprisingly well; likewise the skin of the chest and abdomen. I stretched the eyelids, cheeks, forehead, scalp, the skin of the neck, arms, legs, feet, hands. The scrotum could be opened up like a fan, sometimes stretching almost as far as the navel. Stretching the outer labia of the vulva, removing them for a few moments from their desire to be absorbed, produced an intense state of freedom. At the end of the session, the patient was no longer separated from the world, knowing that his or her limits were out beyond the stars.

The next step was to massage the bones. We have a tendency to forget our bone structure: the skeleton reminds us of death. It appears impersonal to us, macabre, inanimate. However, it is a living and responsive structure. In contrast with stroking the skin or putting pressure on the muscles to loosen them up, this involved kneading the bones, exploring their forms, their interstices, their corners. Every phalanx was taken into account, every vertebra, every rib, the long bones, the joints, the different parts of the skull, the orbits of the eyes, the structure of the pelvis. At the end of the massage the patient would stand up and dance, moving like a cheerful skeleton.

From there I went on to conquer the flesh, muscles, and viscera. Using high quality oil I began with continuous rubbing with both hands, giving a touch without beginning or end. The body ceases to have individual parts; it becomes a whole, a path that does not desire to arrive at any point, only to extend. The hands pass over and over, taking different directions every time, and the body loses its limits and feels infinite. After this, the massager begins to "open." The hands, on a given region of the body, are placed together, side by side, and then pressed strongly apart from each other, transmitting the idea to the patient that she is being opened up. Accumulated sufferings, withheld love, anger, and resentment all flow out through this metaphorical opening. The entire body is a memory. I remember a woman who began to whimper when I opened her left knee: there she carried the pain of her mother, who had lost her leg in a car crash. Screams and rage arise when the chest is opened. From the back, resentment against betrayals emerges. When the pubis is opened, a mother's hatred of men might come out, or guilt over an abortion, the anguish of frustrated homosexuality, and so forth. When I opened the soles and heels of an old man he wept, letting out his sorrow at having been taken away from his native village at age six, losing the landscape and his friends forever. A woman whose heart I opened began trembling as if having a seizure. Without reasoning, driven by a strange impulse, I took off her wedding ring and instantly she calmed down. She had been forced to marry because of an unintended pregnancy.

For a few years I continued investigating every type of massage that could raise the level of consciousness. Marie Thérèse, one of my students, was a nurse. At that time she was working for a Jewish husband and Christian wife whose only son, as a baby, had fallen into a coma for unknown reasons. He lay in a bed in Necker, a children's hospital in Paris. The boy had kept on living there for five years, motionless as a vegetable. They had opened his skull and closed it again, without remedying the problem at all. Marie Thérèse asked me to do something for him. I refused outright: if the best doctors in France had not been able to do anything, how could I? If I gave the slightest hope to the parents, I would be a charlatan. My student told me that she had an intuition that my massage techniques might be beneficial. I saw such sincere faith in her eyes that I agreed to visit the child, in total secrecy, in the presence of his father and mother but hidden from the doctors and nurses at the hospital. I asked her not to promise anything, to say only that I was willing to try a new therapeutic method. At noon, the hour at which the French religiously suspend their activities to go and have lunch, Marie Thérèse brought me through a service door, and we entered the child's room as stealthily as thieves. The mother and father were no more than thirty years old. He was dressed in black in the manner of religious Israelis, and she had dyed-blond hair, typical of the French middle class. The five-year-old child, his shaved head showing his scars, lay on the iron bed, wearing a large diaper like a baby. On the wall behind his head hung a framed photograph of an old religious man. I asked the father who this man was, and he answered, "He is the rabbi of New York. He works miracles."

"Did you visit him to heal your son?"

"Certainly, but the holy man refused to see him or pray for him; because the boy has a Catholic mother he cannot be considered Jewish."

"What? Are you telling me that your son is lying beneath the picture of someone who rejected him, which is equivalent to a curse? If you want me to try to do something for him, take that picture down right away and hide it!"

My anger was not feigned. I realized that I was in the middle of a racial and religious problem between two families, in which the child was being used as a scapegoat. The man obeyed, shutting the rabbi's image in a closet. I asked the mother, "Have you ever nursed the boy?"

"Never," she replied. I asked her to put the nipple of her left breast into her child's mouth. She did so. I then asked the father to suck on the big toe of each of the child's feet. I thought that in this way, the sleeping body would be informed of how to suck. After ten minutes of this activity, much to everyone's surprise, the boy's mouth moved and he sucked lightly. Marie Thérèse was moved and shed a few tears. The parents did not. I became hopeful. The following Wednesday, as usual, I gave a lecture attended by between three hundred and four hundred people, told them about the case, and asked for couples to volunteer to give the boy two-hour massages in shifts so that he would be massaged continuously for twelve hours a day, every day for a week. Many benevolent spectators, all students from my seminars, volunteered to do this; Marie Thérèse introduced them into the hospital, and they gave their efforts freely to heal the child.

After a week, he began to move. I remember Marie Thérèse coming to see me, euphoric, hugging me and saying one word: "Awake!" Three months later, with a sad expression, she invited me to come and see the child. He was now in a private clinic. I found him sitting in a crib, playing with a stuffed animal and manipulating a radio at the same time. "He hears perfectly. Now he is learning to see," Marie Thérèse said. "Everything is going well; the boy is cured!"

"Why are you so sad?" I asked her.

"His parents almost never come to visit him; they have left him completely in my care. And what's more, they refuse to talk to you. They say you're a despot, that you treated them badly; indeed they hate you."

I was not surprised to receive no thanks. A vegetative child was useful to them for capturing their family curses. The living child obliged them to tackle the issue of their marriage, which was repudiated by each of their family trees. Now, for having healed him, it was my turn to be the scapegoat.

A much more pleasant experience was what I achieved with Moebius. After watching him work for four years, drawing *The Incal,* I noticed that he was tired at the beginning of the fifth volume. To give him new energy I suggested that he draw his family tree, and when he had finished I realized that each person in our comic corresponded to one of his family members. For example, the Metabaron was his deaf grandfather, elevated to mythic proportions. I believed that the supreme emotional fulfillment of an individual consisted of being loved unconditionally by the members of his or her family tree, from parents to the great-grandparents. Receiving this affection would heal the scars left by previous suffering. These scars can eventually accumulate and form a depressive weight that makes the artist unable to enjoy creating. I visualized Moebius naked in the midst of his family members, also naked, receiving an affectionate massage from all of them. After my friend accepted this idea, I summoned twenty of my best students from my initiatory massage courses and convened them in my library. These men and women, of various ages, agreed to carry out this experience for free. What a luxury: a massage from forty hands! When I asked Moebius to relate the memories he had of this event, he sent me the following testimony:

"Having attended a number of your Wednesday lectures, I decided to accept your proposal to analyze my family tree. Since I was your friend and collaborator, you offered at the end of the analysis to organize a massage tailored to my history. Despite my perplexity, I agreed without voicing doubts. Some days later, entering your library, I found myself surrounded by about twenty people (I recognized some of them from your lectures), smiling politely and waiting for me. With the air of cheerful gravity that characterizes you, you introduced me to my massage group, and then you added sardonically, before vanishing, 'They embody the members of your family tree: give them roles and make them live.'

"Overcoming my shyness, I began to choose carefully who my father, my mother, my grandfathers, my brothers, my aunts, and uncles should be. All of them, loved or unknown, near or far, were gradually embodied by these strangers. They were truly professional, knew the process of identification very well, and soon, without the least doubt, my family was there. After immersing the room in semi-darkness we all undressed and began the massage. Many hands were placed on my body, gentle, strong, hesitant, affectionate. I was touched with luminous and tender attention. I felt the contact that all the children in the world dream of:

the vigilant love of the adult for the innocent. Suddenly, through these people, who became a channel, my real family was present; the spirit of my ancestors was there. The emotion that possessed me was so intense that I felt myself projected into the region of impassivity. From there I saw myself cry and laugh at myself.

"Next, ecstatic at this new consciousness, protected by my family from the assaults of darkness, I decided to take advantage of that window of power. I became the central organizer: I had to rebuild the group into what every family really is, a wonderful space-time-ship sailing the infinite ocean of life in search of the promised Father. I was the captain of that ship! I distributed the roles without hesitation, and they all happily took their places. One was the indefatigable engine, another was the protective hull, another was the radar, another the control panel, and so forth. This fantastic voyage across the universe was a unique experience insomuch as our collective imagination was freed, for a few moments, from the comfortable and illusory rational prison, entering into a marvelous dimension, so subtle, so true, so perfect, that in the end, upon returning to our habitual reality, we rejoiced with the excitement of a crew that has successfully completed an important mission.

"The years have passed, and this moment, far from being forgotten, continues to be a source of inspiration and allows me to remain absolutely certain of the incredible power of love and imagination when they are thus mixed in the crucible of bodily sensation."

Moebius drew volumes five and six of *The Incal* with superhuman creative enthusiasm. Making the most of my collaborator's experience, I had written an adventure in which the main characters, forming a family, combined themselves into a spatial-temporal ship and crossed the universe to find Orh, the Supreme Father.

It seemed important to me to give the same attention to the feet that is given to the hands. These extremities, driven to insensibility by spending most of their time imprisoned in shoes, are keepers of important information by virtue of their receiving the weight of the entire body.

With massage the patient can be led to completely experience the consciousness of her feet, made to penetrate deeper and deeper into them with the sensation of touch until she feels her soul. The heel is strengthened in order to prevent retreating from life. The toes are stretched toward the infinite future. The entire surfaces of the feet are tenderly kissed in order to release the child that is a prisoner in them.

Despite these investigations, and many others (for example, massaging not only the body but also its shadow and the objects the shadow touches, such as the floor, furniture, other objects, or another person, treating them all as a unit; experiencing a perfect birth in the arms of a man and a woman, on the "mother's" belly, protected by the "father," covered by a warm damp sheet, feeling oneself emerge into life amidst loving touches, simulating development, growth, and finally birth with ease and joy; or massaging the space that surrounds a body, imagining that it is an aura that belongs to it; etc.), I felt that there was still an essential aspect that had not yet been discovered. I began to ask myself, "Who is massaging?" I realized when observing my students that the patients did not offer objective bodies but images, according to how they felt and conceived themselves. Although it seemed incredible, some of them were living without sex organs, others without backbones or without feet, while others were a head from which a sort of fetal body hung. Most of them perceived themselves as their relatives had perceived them. Moreover, the massagers were not massaging with their whole being. Sometimes they would act seductively, sometimes like cold doctors, sometimes like sadistic children, and so on. Their frustrations, complexes, insecurities, and interests slipped into every movement. I concluded that I was not working with beings with a single body, but with many. The vision of one's body changes according to the "I" that is dominant at the moment.

Recalling my youthful experiences, I began to work on massage teaching the imitation of holiness. The greatest desire of a patient in search of consolation is to be taken in the arms of a saint or a Buddha. However, one who surrenders to such contact must be cleansed, like a sacrificial animal, of all egotism. Someone who can give everything is powerless before someone who can receive nothing. In many cases, the patient suffers from inhibitions or irrational antipathies. Then he or she must be touched like a son or a daughter. That is the secret of the Christlike laying on of hands. If it is difficult to give and the person pushes us away with her hands, we love those hands and start our massage by caressing them. We must respect the defenses and advance with parental love, starting at the fingertips, millimeter by millimeter, with extreme delicacy and total attention, into the heart of the other person, dissolving the tension muscle by muscle, giving sturdy support to each limb so that the patient will never have the impression that a part of her is being neglected, however small that part may be. In order to massage in this way, one must breathe deeply and calmly; one must be at the service of the other person, completely attentive. One must act as an empty vessel with nothing to seek and nothing to impose. One must be a refuge without limits, an infinite and eternal companion, not invasive but discreet, a companion who becomes invisible at the slightest movement of rejection.

However, although this massage is effective at calming, it does not heal the essential wound. In the depths, the patient guards his suffering like a treasure. I thought to myself, "It isn't fair to abandon someone who can't receive. As a society, we are all responsible for their ills. Not only the tree is sick, but the entire forest. This string of diseases, this reproduction of harm from generation to generation, has to stop someday. There must be a way to make those without eyes see, to make those without ears hear, to communicate love to those whose hearts are closed."

Just at the moment when I was in need of some valuable new information, dancing reality put a book into my hands by psychotherapist Catherine Lemaire titled *Membres fantómes* (Phantom Limbs, published in 1998), with a preface by Gérald Rancurel, a professor of neurology at the hospital of Salpêtrière. The subject of this book is one of the most fascinating mysteries of clinical neurology: the "phantom limb," a phenomenon whereby the patient continues to perceive the presence of a limb that has been lost. However imaginary it may seem, the phantom limb is very real, practically flesh, insofar as it can be felt and described.

Even if it does not exist, it can cause pain. Even an amputated limb imposes itself on the consciousness, continuously or intermittently, for many years in some cases. The subject feels his or her leg or arm as if it were actually there. The eyes see through the phantom, but in the dark it is there again, sometimes larger than ever. Touching it is impossible. The missing part is there, perceived but invisible and untouchable. Not only legs and arms produce phantoms, but also the breasts, nose, penis, tongue, jaw, and anus. Jean-Martin Charcot observed a patient who felt not only the phantom of his hand but also the wedding ring on his finger. Some people who were born without certain limbs, and therefore have no sensory experience of them, also develop phantoms. How? I found the answer in another phenomenon observed by neurologists: some people, when they relax their muscles and lie still with their eyes closed, sometimes feel an immaterial limb in a position different from that of the physical limb. Phantom limbs can exist without amputation!

It appeared to me that the scientists spoke mostly of phantom parts of the body, such as limbs, and never of a whole phantom body. I allowed myself to consider that we might have a whole phantom body: an immaterial body veiled by the flesh that exists before any amputation takes place and that has sensations. The experimenters had also encountered blind patients who saw phantom sights and deaf patients who heard phantom sounds.

Some amputees feel excruciating pain in their absent limbs. The neurologists, thinking that the perceived but intangible body parts were not real, could not alleviate these pains, even though they performed operations, desensitizing the cutaneous areas over the stump and also on the torso, where they believed the topological sensations creating the phantom limb originated. I wondered, "What if we were to accept the phantom limb as real and soothe its pain by operating on it? If the limb can feel the presence of a ring or a watch, could it not feel the touch of a scalpel?" I understood the aspect that was missing from my initiatory massages: we do not perceive the body as it is; we are only aware of a material representation of it that is adulterated by the views of others.

We do not *feel* everything we feel, we do not *see* everything we see, and we do not *hear* everything we hear; there are tastes and odors that are captured by the tongue and sense of smell but not by the consciousness. With the initiatory massage, I had dedicated myself to cleansing the tangible body without acting on the phantom body. I concluded that Pachita and other witches, when they operated, did not do so on the material body, but acted on the intangible phantom body. Except that with their tricks, they added visible elements such as blood, entrails, and so on, so that the patients would believe that they were operating on their "real" bodies.

I decided to eliminate everything that was intended to deceive the primitive, superstitious spirit and to proceed to operate in all honesty without any kind of gimmick. In the same way that a state of mind changes the body's attitude, a bodily attitude modifies the state of mind. Moreover, just as what happens to the material body affects the phantom body, what is done to the phantom body affects the material body. Based on this belief, I imagined a psychoshamanic ritual. The shaman acts in his medium, using his surroundings, plants, and animals as elements of power. But the psychoshaman, not imitating that which he is not and which belongs to a different culture, uses the elements provided by his environment, namely the city. A mobile phone, a vacuum cleaner, a car, or supermarket products are as magical as a snake, a fan of feathers, or a mushroom. The psychoshaman does not wear exotic clothes, necklaces, or other ornaments. A typical suit, preferably black for neutrality, will suffice. He does not operate in the shadows, lit by a single candle. He appropriates the words of the poet Arthur Cravan: "mystery in broad daylight." And, since the act is metaphorical, he does not wield any knife; if it is necessary to symbolize one, a wooden ruler suffices. He never operates in his own name, an attitude consistent with psychoanalysis. Lacan told his students, "You can be Lacanians, I must be a Freudian." Pachita operated in the name of Cuauhtémoc, Carlos Said in the name of Doña Paz. Every shaman is inhabited by mythical allies, and a psychoshaman can choose his allies from his own familiar urban mythology: He can operate in the name of a famous singer, a film star, a boxing champion, a prominent politician, a dead relative, or a children's character such as Pinocchio, Popeye, or Mandrake the Magician. He can choose to be assisted by a person of his religion such as Jesus Christ, the Virgin Mary, the Pope, Stalin, Gandhi, Moses, Allah, and so forth. To create a magical setting, it is enough for the psychoshaman to simply pass his palm over the floor drawing an invisible circle and then, indicating the four cardinal points, the nadir, and the zenith with precise gestures, to say, "There is the north, there is the south, there is the east, there is the west, there is the upper world, there is the lower world, we are in the middle. All paths arrive here, and all paths depart from here."

After having the patient stand barefoot in the middle of this imaginary circle, he proceeds to fortify it. Witches rub the body with an egg or two, sometimes three, because eggs are considered to be seeds that contain great power. The psychoshaman, bending his thumb inward and enclosing it with the other four fingers, makes a fist symbolizing the seed, a hand position that can be observed in the human fetus. He rubs the patient with this fist, giving him or her energy. Then the patient lies down, prone or supine, on a table, on a cot, or on the floor. Some patients can be operated on while sitting or standing. With an open hand held rigid, wielded like a knife, the psychoshaman slices the air around the patient, cutting away hostile influences.

(To prepare our spirits for the intensity of the operations, my son Cristóbal—who worked with me on many occasions—decided that we should recite in our minds, "There is no being here and now, because here is all space, now is all time, and being is all consciousness. Being, space, and time are the same thing.")

Thus, without any decorative objects, without any conjurer's tricks, with the patient aware that it is her phantom body that is being operated on and not her material body, aware that we are undertaking metaphorical actions, and aware that as psychoshamans we do not have supernatural powers but are imitating such powers in a form of sacred theater, we can achieve the "miracles" performed by Pachita and all manner of saints and primitive healers. We can metaphorically extract tumors, cut bones, implant new limbs, cleanse the heart of its sorrows, change the negative ideas in a brain, purify the blood, and so on.

I applied this new technique in my psychomagic courses, and amazing healings took place. As usual, I began cautiously with small operations. Then, as they became complicated during the last three years I enlisted the help of my son Cristóbal, who put his youthful energy at the service of psychoshamanism.

Knowing how anxious sick people can be to find quick solutions, we never operated in a professional manner and never charged fees. All the examples given below were performed during courses for therapists who proposed to their patients that they try these experiments.

The first operation was practiced on an Algerian woman of about forty years old who was suffering from eye pain for which doctors had been unable to find any organic cause, and thus had been unable to find a cure. After the ceremonies described above, I had her close her eyes. I put a small bandage over each eyelid. With a voice full of authority I said, "These are the terrible things that you have seen and that have damaged your eyes. I am going to remove them forever." Acting as if it took a great effort, I peeled the bandages off. She surprised me by screaming with intense pain, as if something glued to her body were really being ripped off. Then, with great care, I pressed my fingers into her eye sockets and, with calculated pressure, gave her the impression that I was holding her eyeballs. "Now I'm going to take out your eyes, wash them, and put them back." I pretended that it took a great effort to take her eyes out, and she cried again, in real pain. I stuck my fingers in a glass of water and made a noise as if I were washing her eyeballs. Then, with wet hands, I pretended to return her eyes to their sockets. "Now you can lift the eyelids. Your view is clear, finally free of your painful memories." She opened her eyes and wept: the pain that had tortured her for so many years had ceased.

On another occasion I was introduced to a young man with a stutter. His family tree revealed his father to be indifferent, selfish, childish, capricious, and unjust. The boy, not being loved by him, felt that he had no virile strength. I told him to take down his pants and sit on the edge of a chair. "I'm going to inject the energy of the Father. Breathe deeply." Then, with my right hand, I took his testicles, and without squeezing but exerting a very solid contact, I made him feel that I was injecting an immense paternal strength. I imitated this injection with my lips narrowed, blowing out a long and intense jet of air. Without releasing him, I said with complete conviction, "You are cured. Breathe deeply, relax, think of your voice coming from your powerful testicles, and speak." The young man spoke correctly. His stutter was gone.

With Cristóbal's aid, I then began to perform more complex operations. Our years of theatrical practice were essential: the psychoshaman must use a voice that is never for an instant tinged with doubt or weakness. The feigned certainty must be total. To exorcise a "possessed" person, the cries must be impressive. It is very helpful to imagine a mythical ally acting through us. Whenever we encounter an invading spirit, we imitate the authority of Jesus Christ in Mark 9:25: "When Jesus saw that the people came running together, he rebuked the foul spirit, saying unto him, Thou dumb and deaf spirit, I charge thee, come out of him, and enter no more into him."

A thirty-five-year-old woman who suffered because she was six kilos overweight showed us her thighs, affected by cellulite. For fifteen years, despite all sorts of treatments, she had not been able to get rid of it. Examining her family tree, we understood that this affliction of the cellular tissues symbolized her possessive mother. The woman felt that her mother, with her hatred of men, had prevented her from having a satisfactory sex life. We propose to operate to remove these six kilos of material and also to liberate her from her mother. We proceeded to wrap each thigh in a large sheet of paper, which symbolized the cellulite. Then we told her to choose a woman to represent her mother from among the course participants. She chose one. We asked the chosen woman to cling to the patient's body and put up as much resistance as possible. We began to give orders, demanding that the impure spirit leave the body of her daughter. We tried to detach her, and she clung tight. Finally we tore her off the patient, who during this theatrical scene had wept, shouted insults at her mother, and let out her anger. Once liberated, she calmed down. We then had her lie down, simulated the opening of a channel in her thighs, and with great effort, tore off the paper that surrounded them. The woman screamed with authentic pain. We gave her the paper, crumpled into a ball. "Here's your cellulite. Go to the bathroom, burn it, throw the ashes in the toilet, and flush it." She did. Four months later, I received a letter from her telling me that she had entirely lost those six kilos.

In some operations in which a patient felt devalued or not accepted by his or her parents—for example, because the parents wanted a child of the opposite sex or told their child that he or she was ugly—we used a special powder to color the patient's entire body gold or silver after the operation. We would then ask the person to go home, painted like this, for others to see. It changed the patients' perceptions of themselves and made them feel worthy of admiration.

For a woman whose lover had left her and who could not stop suffering because of it, we ripped a piece of paper off her chest on which the man's name was written, then simulated sinking our hands deep into her and exchanging her heart for a new one. While we were simulating pulling out the old heart with enormous strength, she cried from immense sadness combined with physical pain, which was alleviated as soon as we pretended to put in the new heart. Before closing the imaginary wound, we told her that we were going to tattoo a word on her new heart. Poking her chest with a finger dipped in gold paint, we wrote "Love." She felt relieved and now had the energy to resume her love life.

For a fifty-year-old man who had undergone a surgical intervention to remove a tumor from his left ear and who now needed surgery on his right ear because it had also developed a tumor, we tried a psychoshamanic operation to see if we could bring about healing without the intervention of surgeons. We symbolized the growth with a ball of cotton soaked in condensed milk, which we inserted into his ear canal. Then we seated the patient on a chamber pot. Next, twelve women lined up on his right-hand side. One by one, they put their lips to his ear and whispered in a sweet voice, "My son . . . I love you." When they had all spoken these words they gathered around him, and while Cristóbal extracted the symbolic tumor with a pair of tweezers, pretending that it took great effort, the women sang a lullaby. Some time later we received a letter of thanks: the tumor had disappeared.

A sixty-year-old man had a sore right knee that gave him a limp. X-rays had not revealed any anomalies. Thinking that the right leg could be associated with the father and noting that the French word for knee is *genou,* a word that can sound the same as *je-nous* ("I-us"), we asked him what kind of relationship he had with his father. The patient was deeply moved. His father had always rejected him, staying shut away in his problems. Only when he was in the hospital, suffering from a terminal illness, did the father consent to call his son in order that they might disconnect him from the machines and thus finally let him die. Our patient felt obligated to comply with his father's wish. It was for this reason that he carried the guilt of having killed his father, which caused him to feel a rage that he repressed. This was when the pain in his knee began. Before operating on him we stuck several layers of tape onto his knee to symbolize the knee bone. We laid him down on his back, placing a participant whom the patient had previously chosen to symbolize his father on all fours on the floor on his right side, with a cushion on his back to protect him. While we "opened" the flesh and "extracted" the bone, acting as if it took a great effort to tear off the mass of tape, we asked him to express his anger by hitting his "father" on the back. He did, and amid cries of pain from the operation and insults shouted at his progenitor, he let loose his fury while dealing tremendous blows to the cushion. I put in a "new" bone and painted the knee gold. After the operation, the patient went to the participant who had received the beating and, weeping, embraced him for several emotional minutes. From that moment on, his pain was gone.

A young man was attending the course along with his wife. He loved her deeply, but had a problem: when they made love, his penis only became semierect, halfway between hard and soft. This defect was ruining the couple's sex life. Luckily, the man's father and mother were also attending the course. Looking at the family tree, we saw that all the men were childish and committed the sin of being absent and that the women were invasively possessive and considered sexuality sinful because of the religious prejudices of their upbringing. We also saw that there was tension between the man's wife and his mother: the wife thought that the mother had not loved her son, causing him to be stuck at a childish level and, as her husband, to be dependent on her. The four participants, in a genuine search for a balanced life, let down their defenses and became conscious of the root of the problem. We then proceeded with the operation: the man lay down on a table, naked, on his back. I held one leg, Cristóbal held the other, and two other participants held his arms; his mother lay on top of him, clinging to his body. Outside the room, behind a closed door, his father waited. His wife, leaning near to his left ear, whispered constantly, over and over again, "I love you." The patient's task was to try to shake his mother off, but the people holding his arms and legs would not let him move. Then he was to shout for his father to get help. The father struck the door with great violence, then opened it, rushed at the mother, and after simulating an intense struggle, removed her. The mother then had to blow as if inflating a balloon, with all her affection, on the region of her son's heart, and the father had to blow similarly on his perineum, to breathe new manly strength into him. Meanwhile I pretended to cut off his sex organs, placing my fingers around the penis and testicles. I held the sex organs and gave the impression of pulling them off. I then implanted new imaginary sex organs. After the procedure we sprinkled the operated area with holy water, then had the father and mother take their son and place him in his wife's arms. At that moment, the four of them burst into tears and embraced each other in relief and affection. The next day the couple happily came to tell us that the erection was now perfect.

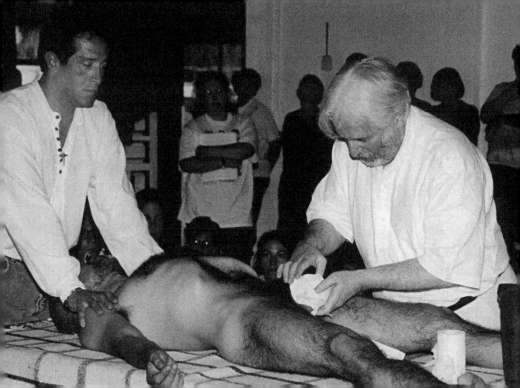

An older woman had lumps of fat on many parts of her body. Upon studying her family tree we observed that her maternal grandmother had suffered from the death of a pair of twins during childbirth, a girl and a boy. She had never recovered. Our patient's mother had watched her own mother being consumed by inconsolable sorrow for many years. When our patient was born, her mother had given her the name of the dead female twin, unconsciously wishing to relieve the grandmother's suffering. Her grandmother had effectively raised her, but in an atmosphere of sadness: the male twin had never been replaced. When we told her that the lumps of fat were the representation of the dead child within her she said, "I always thought I had a twin brother somewhere." We proceeded with the operation. We pretended to push all the lumps into one location, in the belly. Then, as if they were all in a single packet, we pushed them up toward her throat and, with implacable authority, we ordered, "Vomit the twin! You do not need him in order to be loved!" I put a plastic bag under her mouth. She retched strongly and began vomiting. When finished, we tied the bag shut and told her to go with her mother to bury it by her grandmother's grave. In a letter, she told us that she had done this and that her lumps of fat had begun to disappear. But she wondered if it was because of the operation or because she was following a strict diet . . . How difficult it is to be grateful!

A young man, twenty-five years old, asked us for help because he felt incapable of loving. He had come to the course accompanied by his mother. We had asked him to do so because he had a symbiotic relationship with her. His father, a weak man and an alcoholic, had been expelled from the home, and the son, very young at the time, had taken on his role. He and the mother had been in Lacanian psychoanalysis for five years, which had enabled them to become aware of their Oedipal bond but not to solve the problem. We told the mother to wrap a thick red silk cord around the man's neck seven times, as we knew that he had been born with the umbilical cord wrapped seven times around his neck. We had him write on a piece of paper, "Mama, you are the only woman I will ever love in my life. Yours forever . . ." and his signature.

We slathered this contract with gum arabic, slid it under his shirt, and stuck it over his heart. We wrapped him from head to toe in a wet sheet and tied him up with the remainder of the red silk cord, wrapping it around him. Then we gave his mother a pair of tailor's scissors and told her to start by cutting the red silk, saying "Free!" with each cut, louder every time. Then we tore off the sheet, as if removing a noxious aura, and removed him from the cocoon. The man, almost motionless, in a kind of trance, let himself be carried. Simulating a huge effort, we removed the sticky contract. He shouted with physical and mental pain and wept like a child. Then we asked his mother to cut the seven rings of silk that were wrapped around his neck, saying, "Ring one: for you, my son, pure love and love of life. Ring two: for you, my son, love of the mother and love of the father. Ring three: for you, my son, love of yourself and love of another. Ring four: for you, my son, love of the family and love of humanity. Ring five: for you, my son, love of all living beings and love of the planet. Ring six: for you, my son, love of the stars and love of the universe. Ring seven: for you, my son, love of all creation and love of the Creative Consciousness." When she had finished reciting these words, which we had been whispering in his ear, the mother and son fell into each other's arms, sobbing and forgiving one another. After a while, they separated, happy, both feeling liberated.

A couple asked us for help. They quarreled continuously over futile causes, but once they started, they could not stop: they kept on intensifying their insults and raising their voices. He was exasperated with her because she would not stop shouting until he started to strangle her. He was afraid he would kill her someday. She felt attached to him and, despite the danger, could not leave. Studying their family trees, the wife mentioned that her three brothers had raped her when she was twelve years old. To stop her from protesting, they had held her down, strangling her. The husband recalled having seen his father strangle his mother during their fights. Now he had to struggle against his own desire to strangle women, while his wife had to struggle against her desire to be strangled. We proceeded with the operation. We asked her to choose three men from among the attendees to represent her brothers. We explained to her that after the rape, she had remained possessed by them. The three men clung to her, holding her by the neck. All the women in the course, about twenty of them, had to make them release their prey by shouting insults and ordering them to leave this "girl" alone. The men pretended to resist, then finally let her go. The victim's sobs were convulsive. We laid her down and proceeded, metaphorically, to remove her vagina and replace it with another one. We painted her outer labia and pubic hair bright silver. For her husband, who said that he felt he had the hands of a murderer, ten men and ten women "detached" his "father" and "mother" from him, then "cut off" the hands that he so detested and put on "new" hands, painting them gold. From their letter of thanks, we learned that their fights had ceased.

These operations, due to their extremely unusual nature, produce a state of attention so intense that therapists, patients, and observers enter a psychological dimension in which their sensations of time and space change, as was the case with Pachita. They are entirely "there," in the "moment." The actions and reactions are intertwined in a perfect form, and because all are a product of this intense moment, there is no possibility of error. The world is concentrated on the operation. One can compare this to moments that occur in a traditional bullfight. In that deadly ceremony, at a given moment the bullfighter and the bull enter the ring, they merge, they join, the charge and the deception become a single thing, and this dance becomes a magnet that irresistibly attracts the attention of the public. The healer's hands are rooted in the world. It is not an individual who operates; it is all of humanity. It is not the bullfighter that makes passes; it is the very audience. In one case, life is given, in the other, death. The essence of that similarity must be discovered.

Fundamentally, every illness is a lack of consciousness saturated with fear. This unconsciousness is rooted in a prohibition imposed without prior conviction, which the victims must accept without understanding. It requires the child to be what she is not. If she disobeys, she is punished. The greatest punishment is not being loved.

The psychoshaman, like the primitive healer, should operate by circumventing not only the patient's defenses but also his or her fears. Purely rational education prohibits us from using the body to its full extent, making the skin the limit of our being, making us believe that it is normal to live in a reduced space. This education strips sex of its creative power, giving us the illusion that we live only for a short time, denying our eternal essence. By means of a devaluing philosophy, sublime sentiments are extirpated from our emotional center. We are instilled with a fear of change, and we maintain an infantile level of consciousness in which we venerate toxic security and detest healthy uncertainty. By all means possible, supported by political, moral, and religious doctrines, we are made ignorant of our mental power.

If reality is like a dream, we must act in it without suffering from it, as we do in lucid dreams, knowing that the world is what we think it is. Our thoughts attract their equivalents. The truth is what is useful, not only for us but also for others. All the systems that are necessary in a given moment will later become arbitrary. We have the freedom to change systems. Society is the result of what it believes itself to be and what we believe it is. We can begin to change the world by changing our thoughts.

The skin is not our barrier: there are no limits. The only definite limits are those that we need, momentarily, in order to individualize ourselves while at the same time knowing that everything is connected. Separation is a useful illusion, as when the healer places a loop of rope around the patient's neck in order to tell him to take responsibility for his disease and not propagate it. Miraculous healing is possible, but depends on the patient's faith. The psychoshaman must subtly guide the patient to believe in what he or she believes in. If the therapist does not believe, no healing is possible.

Life is a source of health, but this energy comes forth only where we concentrate our attention. This attention must be not only mental but also emotional, sexual, and corporeal. The power does not lie in the past or in the future, which are the seats of illness. Health is found here

382   From Psychomagic to Psychoshamanism

and now. Toxic habits can be abandoned instantaneously if we cease to identify ourselves with the past. The power of the "now" grows with the sensory attention. The patient must be led to explore the present moment, to become aware of colors, lines, volumes, sizes, shadows, spaces between objects. One should feel every part of one's body in order then to unite the parts into a whole; breathing should become pleasure, and one should capture its warmth and energy flowing in and out and understand that to love is to be happy with what one is and with what others are. Love grows to the extent that criticism decreases. Everything is alive, awake, and responding. Everything gains power if the patient bestows it . . . A mother using a phytotherapeutic treatment to heal her baby, in which she had to give him water to drink with forty drops of a mixture of essential oils added, found that the disease continued. I told her, "What is happening is that you do not believe in this medicine. Since your religion is Catholicism, say the Lord's Prayer every time you give him the drops to drink." She did this, and the boy was quickly cured. If we do not give spiritual power to medicine, it does not act.

Here, it is necessary to emphasize the importance of imagination. In a certain way, I have undertaken an exercise of imaginary autobiography in this book. This was not in the "fictional" sense, since all the characters, places, and events are real, but by virtue of the fact that the profound history of my life is a constant effort to expand the imagination and widen its boundaries in order to grasp its therapeutic and transformative potential. Along with intellectual imagination are emotional imagination, sexual imagination, physical imagination, sensory imagination, and economic, mystical, scientific, and poetic imaginations. It acts in all areas of our lives, even those considered "rational." It is for this reason that one cannot tackle reality without developing the imagination from multiple angles. Normally, we visualize everything according to the narrow limits of our conditioned beliefs. We perceive nothing more of the mysterious reality, so vast and unpredictable, than what is filtered through our limited point of view. *Active imagination* is the key to a broad vision: it permits us to focus on life from angles that are not our

Alejandro Jodorowsky, age 72. Photo: Roger Favin

own, *imagining* other levels of consciousness that are higher than ours. If I were a mountain, or the planet, or the universe, what would I say? What would a great teacher say? And what if God spoke through my mouth, what would the message be? And what if I were Death? The Death that revealed a dog to me that deposited a white stone at my feet, that separated me from my illusory "I," that made me flee Chile, that drove me to search with desperation for a meaning in life—that Death has changed from a dreadful enemy to my amiable companion.

To conclude this book, I would like to return to my youth, sitting once again on the branch of a tree next to my poet friend, and, as on that memorable occasion, deduce from the many things that we do not know what precious little we do know:

> *I do not know where I'm going, but I know who I am going with.*
>
> *I do not know where I am, but I know that I am in myself.*
>
> *I do not know what God is, but God knows what I am.*
>
> *I do not know what the world is, but I know it is mine.*
>
> *I do not know what I'm worth, but I know not to compare myself.*
>
> *I do not know what love is, but I know that I rejoice at its existence.*
>
> *I cannot avoid blows, but I know how to resist them.*
>
> *I cannot deny violence, but I can deny cruelty.*
>
> *I cannot change the world, but I can change myself.*
>
> *I do not know what I make, but I know that what I make makes me.*
>
> *I do not know who I am, but I know that I am not the one who does not know.*

Psychomagical Acts

Transcribed by Marianne Costa

1. A young man would like to work in the tourism industry, going to Hong Kong and other legendary cities. But this professional desire seems impossible. He doubts himself. After questioning him, A.J. found that the client's mother had died and that during childhood his brother had captured all the maternal love.

Response: On one side of a can of sardines stick a picture of your mother, and on the other side, a picture of your brother. Walk along the right-hand side of Champs-Élysées, from the Obelisk of Luxor to the Arc de Triomphe, kicking the can along in front of you until you reach the Tomb of the Unknown Soldier. Then leave without looking back.

2. After this young man, a young woman came in to consult. She is his girlfriend, but their relationship has not gone beyond the platonic. She also doubts her professional abilities, and her psychological problems are similar to those of her boyfriend: an older sister favored by the parents, a distant and perhaps incestuous father.

Response: Do the same thing your boyfriend was advised to do, but instead of a can of sardines buy a fake phallus in a sex shop. To avoid being bothered by the police wrap it in a bag, along with a picture of your father. Walk with your boyfriend, each of you kicking your own item along. Face each other before leaving the Arc de

Triomphe, with your faces an inch apart, and roar in anger until you are exhausted.

3. An Algerian woman is possessed by great sadness. The Tarot shows that this pain is that of her mother, who died in exile, separated from her homeland.

Response: Since you cannot go there, have someone in Algeria send you a bag containing seven kilos of earth from the village where your mother lived. Go to the cemetery and deposit this soil on her grave. Then, to celebrate this event, go to the Grand Mosque and drink seven cups of mint tea.

4. Another sad woman; she does not know the joy of living. When her mother was six months pregnant with her, her father left to go and live with another woman.

Response: Go to see your father, disguised as if you were six months pregnant. Ask him to kneel before your belly and ask forgiveness from the fetus he abandoned.

5. The client, a vegetarian pacifist, admits to having such rage against his mother that he wants to kill her.

Response: How can you realize your desire without killing an animal? Buy two watermelons to symbolize your mother's breasts and destroy them with your fists. Put the pieces of watermelon in a flesh-colored sack that you will make yourself. At midnight, throw the sack into the Seine and leave without looking back.

6. A young man who is professionally disoriented says he does not know what profession he should go into. When questioned, he confesses that he studied law and political science at a good school but failed to get his diploma.

Response: Fabricate a diploma identical to what you would have received, but thirty centimeters larger in width and length. Frame it, hang it on the wall of your bedroom, and put a boxing champion's cup under it. Then go find the job you want.

7. A thirty-year-old woman doubts herself. She is greedy, materially and emotionally.

Response: If you live insecurely asking for things, it is because your parents, blinded by their own projections, did not see you as you truly were. Buy two nice red apples. Keep one in your bag and carry the other in your hand. Take the metro and observe the passengers. If a person, man, woman, or child, awakens in you the desire to give them the apple, do so. Keep riding the metro until you get that urge, even if it takes several days. When you have given someone the apple, leave the subway and walk along the street savoring the other apple, which you have kept in your bag. Thus you will understand that to give is to receive.

8. A thirty-year-old man cannot achieve success as a musician. As a child he studied piano, but his father, a garage mechanic, made fun of his hobby, considering it gay. He has a sister who lives symbiotically with their mother, both of them hating men. The two worlds, masculine and feminine, are separated by an abyss in their home.

Response: You must take on your feminine sensibility in order to express yourself artistically. Cover your body with auto grease and play the piano naked, dirty like your father. Of course you will get grease on the keys. Furiously play all the melodies that you fancy then clean the keys. After this massage the piano as if it were a woman, for exactly one hour. Stick a picture of your mother on the sole of your left foot, one of your sister on your right foot, and start playing again. You will see the anger converted into creative pleasure. To thank me, bring me a white rose.

9. A fifty-year-old man cannot bear the process of divorce from his wife. Three months earlier, after living with him for eight years, his wife expressed her deep desire to become pregnant. He rejected the proposition outright. She thought it over, then suggested divorce, which he

accepted calmly. But after three months he suddenly repented and proposed to his wife that they have the desired child. She was inflexible and told him she would have it with someone else. The Tarot reveals that this man has a twin brother. When asked how his relationship is with this brother, he stammers a bit and answers laconically, "Okay."

Response: Call your wife and tell her you do not want one child, but two. That being a twin, you could not imagine having an only child, and that was the reason why you refused to get her pregnant when she asked for "a" child. This will require you to consider: would you really want to be a father of two children? If you want that, call her. She is very likely to accept.

10. A brunette woman with large black eyes, about forty years old, has a very conflicted relationship with a coworker in the office where she works. He refuses to resolve the conflict, despite the pacifying efforts she makes.

Response: We see in the Tarot that your relationship with your older brother was disastrous. You project this original conflict, which is very much part of you, onto your colleague. You need him to hate you, to reproduce your childhood love/hate relationship. He, in turn, must project his sister onto you. You must destabilize his view. If you see yourself differently, you will not be the object of his rage. You must go to the office as soon as possible with a different appearance: a new haircut, dyed blond, with contact lenses that make your eyes light, and a different style of clothing.

11. A woman who has moved to a new house does not feel good in her new territory; it seems alien to her. What should she do?

Response: Put your urine in a bowl, fill a dropper with it, and put a drop in every corner of the new house.

12. A forty-year-old therapist is in a passionate but troubled relationship with a woman who feels a great aggressiveness toward men due to

her having seen her father kill her mother with a hunting rifle that had been given to him by his grandfather. How to calm this hatred of men that she constantly projects onto him?

Response: Go to see your partner carrying a hunting rifle loaded with blanks and ask her to shoot at your chest. Keep a plastic bag filled with artificial blood hidden there. When she fires, break the bag to spill the blood. Before this, you will have told her that the bullets are blanks, but will have kept the blood effect secret. You'll see, she will burst into tears and embrace you. From that time on the relationship will improve.

13. A twenty-year-old woman consults the Tarot to see how relations are going with her lover. It seems that nothing is wrong; he has agreed to marry her and have children. But she suffers from not knowing what she wants, what she likes, what she truly feels. The Tarot reveals the strong influence of her mother, who she feels is like a vampire. How can she tell if it is really she who is seeing and thinking, or if it is her mother taking over her mind?

Response: Enlarge a picture of your mother's face to actual size. Cut holes in the eyes and make it into a Venetian-style mask on a stick. When you find yourself in a situation where you want to dissociate your view from that of your mother, put the mask over your face and become aware that you see and feel like her. Then take the mask off and observe how you see and how you feel things as yourself.

14. A thirty-year-old woman is still suffering as an adult from her father's rejection of her as a child. This attitude was the result of her younger brother's dying three weeks after being born. The father, who wanted to pass on his name, considered it unfair that his son died and not his daughter.

Response: When your brother died, he must have weighed about three kilos. Buy a calf's head and, if necessary, some meat and bone to make it up to three kilos. Put this in a waterproof, airtight bag and then into a black backpack, which you will wear on your back for three full days (symbolizing the three weeks for which the boy lived). Then go to your father's house, without him knowing, and bury your burden in the garden. Afterward, offer your father a sausage, watch him eat a few slices, and ask him to give you a box of chocolates.

15. A well-dressed lady, sixty years old, cannot get over her deep resentment toward a doctor who misdiagnosed her with Alzheimer's disease and kept her in anguish for two years. During those years, her relationships with her children completely deteriorated. The Tarot reveals that she projects her own paralyzing parents onto this doctor who predicted the paralysis of her mental functions.

Response: You must protest in a childish manner. Put some of your excrement in a cookie tin and mail it to the doctor. The box must be wrapped as a Christmas gift.

16. A young man with a childlike face, voice, and gestures says he has "existential suffering." According to him, the reason he cannot leave childhood and become a man is his mother, who conceived him out of wedlock with a stranger.

Response: You are right. If your mother hates men, you must remain a child in order not to lose her love. Dress as you imagine this father you have never seen would dress. Over these clothes, put on women's clothes, stolen from your mother. Go out and wander the streets dressed like that. As soon as you find a woman whom you like the look of, begin to stare at her while taking off the women's clothes to expose your male suit. When you've made the change, go to the woman and tell her that you like her. She may reject you; she may accept. Experience the situation with pleasure. Later, paint an apple black and wrap your mother's clothing around it, then wrap your "father's" clothes around those. Then bring the package to your mother, giving it to her without explanation, saying only, "I am returning what you gave me." The black apple symbolizes your existential angst.

17. A woman of seventy, who suffers from deafness, comes for a consultation to solve a problem with her forty-eight-year-old daughter, who complains that she has never listened to her.

Response: In the presence of your daughter, wash each ear seven times with rose-scented soap. Then anoint your ear canals with acacia honey, using the middle finger of the right hand for your left ear and the middle finger of the left hand for your right ear. Then ask your daughter to lick the honey while whispering everything that she wants to tell you.

18. An alcoholic woman who is about forty years old complains of being "nothing" and that she "cannot achieve." She was raised Catholic and now practices Buddhism. When I ask her what her favorite drink is, she replies "red Bordeaux wine."

Response: Buy a bottle of red Bordeaux wine. Go to church with it, sit on a bench, put it in front of you, and pray to it as if it were a saint. Then go to your Buddhist temple and meditate with the bottle between your legs to consecrate it. Then make a small altar in your home with flowers, incense sticks, and two lamps, one obtained from the church, the other from the temple. Thus you will have your own sanctuary in your home, and wine will become a magical elixir. At night, before going to sleep, rub your chest with it. This sacred wine will protect and heal you.

19. A very fat woman wants to lose weight. "My mother began to gain weight after giving birth to me. I carry with me the responsibility for her incessant diets, her 'body drama.' I weigh ten kilos more than she does."

Response: Buy any object that weighs ten kilos, for example a TV, a vacuum cleaner, a collection of pots, and so forth. Put a picture of yourself on the package, naked and sad, and offer it to your mother, saying: "This is yours. I'm returning your gift to you."

20. A painter of fifty years old who is a well-known artist confesses with shame that he hates his younger brother, born late to his parents. The baby came when he was twenty-two years old and "stole" his mother's love.

   Response: Buy a wooden bassinet, a life saver, and a large melon. Put the melon in the bassinet and the bassinet on top of the life raft. With an automatic pistol, shoot the fruit twenty-two times. Then pour a bottle of gasoline over its remains, set fire to it, and send the flaming melon and bassinet floating down a river on the life-raft. Then, to change the rage into acceptance, give twenty-two white roses to your brother.

21. A woman dressed in Hindu garments has spent twelve years in an ashram. Her guru, Muktananda, baptized her daughter with the name Krishna. There is something about this that makes her feel bad. In light of the Tarot, she realizes that this act reveals her unconscious desire to sleep with her teacher, elevated to the status of God the Father, in order to create a Christ (a Krishna), a perfect child.

   Response: Buy a plaster figurine of Jesus Christ and paint it entirely blue to transform it into the god Krishna, who is of that color. Tie several orange balloons (Muktananda's color) to the figurine's feet and release it to the sky. Carry out this ceremony accompanied by your husband and daughter. When you see the Jesus figurine disappear, give the girl a Western name. Thus you will free her from the obligation to be a demigod and will restore her identity and her femininity.

Brief Psychomagical Correspondence

I. STEALING TO HEAL

When people say they cannot love, it is not because they have empty hearts. The anesthetized feelings build up like ice in a freezer. In this psychomagical act, instead of trying to give what is desired, a succession of dangerous situations provokes the awakening of the fundamental positive feeling: the love of life itself.

I wrote to you from Chile: "There are days when my vision becomes cloudy and I do nothing but lament being alive. I would be infinitely grateful to you if you would prescribe me a psychomagical act in order that I might be able to love without asking for so much in return." You answered me: "Steal a raw heart from a supermarket on the sixth day of every month for a year. Cook the hearts, cut them into pieces, and give them to friends and hungry animals. Then you'll be able to love." From April 1997 to March 1998, I stole one heart each month from a different supermarket in Santiago. I was never caught, and each time completed the task of cooking it and then distributing it among friends and to animals. (It was hard to find hungry animals in my neighborhood, so I went out walking and generally gave them to the first dogs I saw.) Since the date indicated was the sixth (I suppose because card VI of the Tarot is the Lover), I was very nervous, terrified, at the beginning of every month. I used various strategies to steal the hearts: hiding them in my jacket pocket, in my underwear, under my cap, and so forth. During the summer it was even harder, because the weather was too hot for me to wear a jacket. Fortunately by then I was well experienced at shoplifting in supermarkets, so I was always highly successful. Another difficulty was that not all those large stores sell hearts. I had to visit several different ones to find them. As for the friends with whom I was supposed to share the cooked pieces, I mostly shared them with my family. Once in a while I shared them with someone I knew who happened to be in my house. In the last month, with the last heart, I invited a group of young neighbors. This social communion was a way of celebrating the fact that I had completed my task and had done well. Soon after, an uncle died, my mother's brother, who I was very close to. The inner strength I had acquired allowed me to act with resolution with my family: this was something that surprised everyone. This strength was not a tough attitude, but rather meant that I had the appropriate attitude for the situation. Now, three months later, I'm learning a form of Brazilian dance that is also a martial art. The energy that I use in this activity, an energy that continues to grow, gives me a self-assurance that I had never experienced. I have just turned twenty-five, and I feel that I have great strength to love without asking for so much in return.

2. SYMBOLIC CONVERSATION

Thanks to symbolic acts one can enter into profound, cathartic relationships without reason intervening.

This was my question: "My brother hanged himself on the day of his twenty-eighth birthday. In a certain manner, I have carried the burden of my mother's guilty suffering for this brutal death. How can

I rid myself of it?" You answered me: "Carry a bocce ball that you have painted black in a white bag on your back for twenty-eight days. Afterward, offer it to your mother, saying, "This ball is yours, I am returning it to you."

I went to see my mother, and just before I took out the ball and gave it to her, she said to me, "I'd like to make you a black shirt," and began to take the measurements. I was very surprised, I let her measure me and then gave her the ball. She looked at it, scratched it with a fingernail and smiling, said, "The paint comes off easily." I answered her, "The black goes away, but the weight remains." She began to cry. I held her in my arms for a long while. Today I am breathing much better.

3. THE LOST COLOR

A tiny painful detail hinders overall development. I have often compared a problem that is considered small to a nail in the shoe. Although small in size, it affects one's whole gait. This is the testimony of José Zaragoza, a Mexican poet living in Paris.

Knowing the work of A.J., I went to have him read the Tarot cards for me. At that time I was obsessed with the idea that I caused fear in people, an idea reinforced by the fact of my being a foreigner. Without further ado Mr. J. said, "The devil should be dressed in red," and advised me to get dressed from head to toe in clothes of that color. I simply refused, because I had a strong fear of the ridiculous. But the next day, out of pride rather than conviction, I decided to carry out the prescribed treatment, adding on a scarf in the style of the Tarahumara people, which, as we know, is red and is worn on the forehead. The experience was terrible. At the corner by my house I encountered a group of people who looked at me, surprised. "I'm going to a costume party," I stammered. In the metro things became almost unbearable. Everyone stared at me, from head to toe. I felt bad because I have always wanted to pass unnoticed, and this was impossible for me under such circumstances. Back at home I felt extremely tired and dirty. I took a shower and felt better. The next day I noticed that my perception had changed significantly. I felt as if I had taken a dose of medicine. I saw red as orange, orange as yellow, and so forth. I went out into the street and found that indeed my perception had changed and that I must be getting used to seeing the whole range of warm colors differently. Although this situation was somewhat embarrassing, I did not feel at all bad, and was able to perform my normal activities. Dressed in red, I went to all the places I normally go, saw all the people I usually see. A week later I had integrated myself into the prescribed color. It was then that I remembered a definite event in my childhood: one day, my mother had ferociously reprimanded me for a small fault saying, "You're a devil." This irritated me profoundly and made me blush. She insisted: "You see, now you've even turned red!" I then had a fit of inexpressible anger; once this passed over, I became extremely sad: I realized that my mother did not like the color red. From that moment on I removed it from my clothes and, as is obvious from my appearance, got rid of the smallest details relating to red, even though it was my favorite color. When I got that color back, thanks to the act of psychomagic, I regained the world. My trouble was resolved.

4. MILK IN THE EYES

Some physical diseases can be cured with symbolic elements.

The day after my mother died, my eyes began to hurt. The pain lasted eight years and no medicine could alleviate it. You gave me the following advice: "Go to your garden on a moonlit night accompanied by your husband and boil a liter of milk. Let it cool down, bathed in the moonlight. Then repeatedly rinse your eyes with the milk, until dawn." I did this. The pain disappeared.

5. A DEVOURER OF DENIALS

The whole is present in every part. More often than not, when we get angry it is for reasons other than what we think, and what we demand is not what we really want.

I came to consult you because my son was having fits of anger, demanding things, kicking and screaming. You advised me to give in to his demands, but to satisfy them partially, not completely: "If he wants chocolates, give him one. If he wants cake, give him a small piece, and so on." I wondered how this could make the child stop throwing one fit after another. Well, for the first few days it was the same as always: he ate up the first chocolate then howled for the second. One day he ate a whole packet of chocolates and ate five gumballs (which I had badly hidden) in one bite. And of course, as usual, he had a fit of rage.

Then, little by little, I realized one thing you'd suggested to me in the reading: I was impatiently saying "no" to him all day. Very few "nos" were because of actual danger, and a great many "nos" were because his demands were disrupting my habitual activities. That is, I only noticed him when he bothered me. For this reason he did everything he could to bother me, especially out of the house where he was not at risk of violence from me. Now, for a month, not a single "no" has escaped my mouth. For a month, whenever we have been together, I have given him my complete attention. His tantrums have ceased. We get along very well. But now I realize that I am lacking a husband, and he a father.

6. ASPIRING TO BALDNESS

Sometimes the daughter's disease is only the mother's disease.

This is what I told you: "I pluck out my hairs one by one and chew them between my teeth. I feel this has something to do with my relationship with my mother. I do not know how to stop this habit." You replied: "You are pulverizing your lover with your teeth. Every hair you pluck out and chew brings you closer to baldness and therefore further away from men. Your mother, abandoned while she was pregnant, has given you a terrible image of your father. You see men through her gaze. You feel too much in this world. When you go to bed, pull out a hair and give it to your mother to chew. While she munches on it, she should stay very close to you and sing you a lullaby. The next morning she should wash your hair and then comb it gently." I carried out everything that you advised. Strangely, my mother, always so taciturn and cold, collaborated in the act with her entire soul. While combing my hair she began to cry, asking for forgiveness. I no longer pluck out my hair, and my relationship with my mother has improved.

7. METAPHORICAL REALIZATION OF LESBIAN INCEST

Certain neuroses of failure come from a prohibition of sexual pleasure. Most diseases are caused by a lack of freedom. When the client's way of getting sexual pleasure is not criticized, when she feels she has been given "permission," then she ceases to unconsciously attach herself to her incestuous desire and allows her dreams to be realized.

My greatly deteriorated relationship with my mother was affecting my femininity. Despite my intense desire, for years I had not been able to have children. When a pregnancy occurred, I always miscarried. Psychoanalysis made me aware of a great lesbian psychological tie with my mother, who was so absent and so desired before being so hated. Knowing that my mother has lived in the Antilles for fifteen years, and I have almost no contact with her, you proposed that I make a huge salad of fresh exotic fruits to eat in the company of a woman, any woman, without giving her any explanation. At work I have a colleague my age who, like me, is called Catalina, and has a little daughter. The ideal person! We often eat a sandwich together in the coffee shop. That day she was very pleasantly surprised when I invited her to share an abundant exotic fruit salad. We ate zealously. In the following months I gave birth to a boy, conceived with awareness and loved. His name is Ángel. His father was born and raised in the Ivory Coast amid exotic fruits such as those I shared with my colleague.

8. REPENTANT PROSTITUTE

According to magical thinking, a person's clothes are the extension of that person. For this reason, witches do to the clothes what they would like to do to the person.

I came to see you because, having found the love of my life, I had tortured myself by believing that, out of economic necessity, I had to prostitute myself (something recommended by my mother, a woman who had completely erased my father, burning photographs of him and keeping his identity secret; sometimes I think I may be the daughter of my grandfather). Faced with my partner's moral purity, I felt dirty, despicable. You asked me if I had kept some of the clothes that had been used to attract customers. I told you I kept them all in a trunk. You told me to put them all on, however many they might be; one outfit over the other. Then I should lie down on my mother's bed (I live with her) at 3:00 in the afternoon and stay there until midnight. Then I should get up, and in the garden by the light of the full moon, after being sprayed with seven liters of holy water I should wash all the clothes in a tub, without soap, which would require me to wring and rub them forcefully. After washing, according to your instructions, I set up three strings in my room and hung up the wet clothes. Then I placed containers under them to collect the dripping water. The next morning I gathered the clothes, dug a hole in the garden, buried them there, and planted a tree that I watered with the water collected in the containers. Then I performed a second act: you told me to buy a life-size plaster statue of Christ, place it in my room, and cover it with all the whips that I had used to lash masochists. It had to stay there, starting on the twenty-second day of the month, for a period of twenty-two days. Every night before bed I had to observe this statue and meditate, connecting my old work to spirituality. In a way, the whips became sacred objects. You had told me that, according to legend, the spear that wounded Christ later began to grow roses from its tip, the petals of which cured blindness. You remarked: "In contact with the divine, even the most vile object becomes sacred." The result: I have left my mother's home, and without remorse, I live with the man I love. We have decided to stop using birth control.

9. LETTER TO THE ABSENT PARENT

We are united with the collective unconscious. Whenever we commit an act, even if it is anonymous, the world responds. What we do to others, we do to ourselves.

During the consultation you spoke to me about an unconscious contract that I had made with my father when I was a girl ("I will love only you"), which prevented me from fulfilling myself emotionally. My father went out one day to buy matches and never returned. You advised me to free myself from this bond by writing him a letter telling him everything I felt about our relationship and insulting him for having fled in such an irresponsible manner. I should also write "I will love only you" on a piece of paper, sign it with a drop of blood, then tear it to pieces and put them in the envelope with the letter. I was to address the envelope as follows:

Mr. Absent Father
Unconscious Street
City of Myself
Universal Consciousness

I wrote the letter and put it in the mail with several stamps on it and no return address. I cried, feeling rage invade me, burning the inside of my chest. But then I was overtaken by a peace that I had never felt before. The following week, to my immense surprise, the mailman deposited the letter I had sent in my mailbox. How did the post office know that I had sent it? Certainly not from the postmark on the stamps, because I did not mail it in my neighborhood; I do not believe in miracles, there must be some mysterious explanation. But I remember that in one of your lectures, you told this story: a student asked the great mystic Ramakrishna, "If I throw a stone into the infinite, where does it land?" The enlightened man replied, "It lands in your hand." In any case, I sincerely thank you for this act, which has led me to make progress. Especially because something has happened that seems related to that letter: without any inquiry on my part, an association has offered me a job as a teacher in a poor neighborhood. They use very comprehensive methods in which the parents, who are skillfully advised by pediatricians, heal their relationships with their children.

10. THE FALSE INVALID

To see yourself, you must realize how others see you. The essential being is imprisoned in a psychological cage built from others' gazes.

My first sexual experience was traumatic. I immediately got pregnant and secretly had an abortion. I was ill for several months. From then on, I only met men who did not function well sexually. I was married for twenty years to a premature ejaculator. I asked you what to do. You answered: "You must understand that these men are prisoners of their egotism and none of them have seen you as you feel yourself to be. Because of your sensual appearance, they think you are a passionate woman, when in fact you are living as a sexual invalid. We must do everything possible to make them see you as you really are. I advise you to have someone push you around public places in a wheelchair for six

days in a row. The daily ride should last six hours." The next day I found
the specialized store where I could rent the chair, and a friend agreed to
come. As soon as she wheeled me out into the street I burst into tears, I
felt ashamed, I felt like a living corpse exposed to the eyes of the whole
world. Although it was a hot day, my legs went numb, and the fatigue
of more than twenty years of hopeless fighting fell down upon me. I saw
my reflection in a shop window. That was me, that woman dressed in
black, cowering there. I became aware of the self-flagellation that has
been my life. I almost went mad with anger, then became grateful for
this opportunity to plunge into the reality of my feelings, to come out
on the other side of my frustration. The next day I dressed as seductively as possible. We went to have lunch at an Indian restaurant, but I
could not get through to the dining rooms. Two young men, with big
smiles, carried me in my wheelchair. I made no effort to hide the satisfaction on my face. I have lost the fear of desiring and being desired.
After six days, I had expelled twenty years of fears, stagnant desires,
and scorned sexuality. I decided to treat the gazes of men as complicit
sexuality. When I returned the wheelchair I was filled with joy and also
sadness for the woman who, in her denial of existence, had immobilized
herself. For the first time, I felt that I was advancing toward life.

Index

Page numbers in *italics* indicate photos.

mushroom experience of, 266–68
with Pachita, 269, 270–91
painting the Furious's house, 176
seven-day Zen meditation, 196–98
Tarot reading sessions, 303–5
as theatrical advisor, 194–95
touching sacred symbols, 225–27
as unwanted child, 50–52
See also childhood in Tocopilla; lucid
dreaming; youth in Santiago
Jodorowsky, Alejandro (grandfather),
11, 23–24, 50–51
Jodorowsky, Axel Cristóbal (son), *179,*
209, 222–23, 328–29
Jodorowsky, Benjamin (uncle), 37, 51
Jodorowsky, Brontis (son), *179,* 207,
209, 361
Jodorowsky, Denisse (first wife), 207–8
Jodorowsky, Eugenia (daughter),
291–93
Jodorowsky, Jaime (father), *29*
adultery by, 166
Alejandro not wanted by, 50–52
anger after house burned, 165–66
arts despised by, 41–42
business competition by, 14–16
childhood of, 37
circus career, 3, 146
cleaning banknotes, 42–43
cowardice hated by, 44, 51, 81
Cristina criticized by, 236–37
disappointment in his father, 50–51, 54
dream therapy with, 221–22
on giving away the red shoes, 10
God denied by, 26–27
at in-laws' golden anniversary, 88, 89
name taken by, 158
Rebbe pushed on Alejandro by, 11
Santiago shop of, 38, 39–40
scabs peeled by, 18–19
on scratching Gadfly's back, 8
small penis of, 44–46
Stalin mimicked by, 14

stamp collecting by, 18
teaching author to conquer pain,
16–18
toys denied by, 12
worms emptied on bed of, 81–82
Jodorowsky, Raquel (sister), 50, 53–60,
57, 80, 208
Jodorowsky, Sara (mother), *29*
Alejandro's long hair loved by, 27
author's letter to, 210–11
childhood of, 37
corset set free, 166–68
Jaime's discipline supported by, 28, 81
not a virgin at marriage, 52
at parents' golden anniversary, 88
red shoes bought by, 9
seen dying in dream, 208
sleeping with hand on Jaime's penis, 45
socks mended by, 28
violin obtained by, 40–41
worms emptied on bed of, 81–82
Jodorowsky, Teo (son), 172, 208
Jodorowsky, Teresa (grandmother), 207
Joos, Kurt (choreographer), 137
Jung, Carl, 212

Kath center, 259–60, 267

Landru, Bernadette (wife), 206–7, 361
Lefevre, Marie, 239–40
Lemaire, Catherine, 368
Lettuce Clown, 147
Lihn, Enrique (poet friend), *115*
author's first meeting with, 114, 116
carnival inspired by, 168
dance recital suggested by, 140
poetic acts with, 117–26
seen in dream, 208
lions, 3, 4, 146, 201–2, 267
lucid dreaming
accepting and receiving in, 229–30
author's method, 201
author's study of dreams, 200–201

About Jodorowsky and
The *Dance* of *Reality* Film

Alejandro Jodorowsky was born in Tocopilla, Chile, in 1929. During his career as tarologist, therapist, author, actor, theatrical director, and director of cult films (*El Topo, The Holy Mountain,* and *Santa Sangre*) he developed psychomagic and psychogenealogy, two new therapeutic techniques that have revolutionized psychotherapy in many countries. Psychogenealogy served as the background for his novel *Donde mejor canta un pájaro* (Where a Bird Sings Better), and psychomagic was used by Jodorowsky in the novel *El niño del jueves negro* (Black Thursday's Child). Both of these techniques are discussed and explored in his book *Psicomagia* (*Psychomagic*), in his autobiography *La danza de realidad* (*The Dance of Reality*), and in *Métagénéalogie: L'arbre généalogie comme art, thérapie et quète de Soi* (*Metagenealogy: Self-Discovery through Psychomagic and the Family Tree*), written with Marianne Costa. He has also written two books on the therapeutic application of the Tarot: *La vía del Tarot* (*The Way of Tarot*), written with Marianne Costa, and *Yo, el Tarot* (I, the Tarot).

The Dance of Reality, his first film since the 1990 release of *The Rainbow Thief,* was written, produced, and directed by Jodorowsky. An autobiographical film, it was shot in Chile in his childhood village of Tocopilla as well as Santiago and other southern Chile locations, with cameo appearances by the author throughout the film.

The film was shown at the 2013 Cannes Film Festival and received rave reviews. *The Dance of Reality* will have its U.S. preview in 2014 at the South by Southwest Film Festival, its premiere in New York City, and will be shown in select cities throughout the United States.

QUINZAINE
DIRECTORS' FORTNIGHT
CANNES 2013

MICHEL SEYDOUX presents

OFFICIAL SELECTION
SXSW
FILM FESTIVAL
2014

ALEJANDRO JODOROWSKY'S

THE DANCE OF REALITY

WITH BRONTIS JODOROWSKY PAMELA FLORES AND JEREMIAS HERSKOVITS

EDITED BY MARYLINE MONTHIEUX CINEMATOGRAPHY BY JEAN-MARIE DREUJOU A.F.C. COSTUME DESIGN PASCALE MONTANDON-JODOROWSKY MIXING JEAN-PAUL HURIER ORIGINAL MUSIC ADAN JODOROWSKY

ADDITIONAL MUSIC, ARRANGEMENTS AND ORCHESTRATION JON HANDELSMAN EXECUTIVE PRODUCER (AND) PRODUCTION DIRECTOR XAVIER GUERRERO YAMAMOTO

A FRENCH/CHILEAN CO-PRODUCTION CAMERA ONE / LE SOLEIL FILMS WRITTEN AND DIRECTED BY ALEJANDRO JODOROWSKY

PRODUCED BY MICHEL SEYDOUX MOISES COSIO AND ALEJANDRO JODOROWSKY -LEY DE DONACIONES CULTURALES - CHILE

abkco Films

DanceOfRealityMovie.com

"Shut up, you coward, they'll say my son is a queer."

"Tocopilla, this tremor, this scent of stones, this lament of a small town torn to shreds by the sun, these patient streets longing for a drop of water."

"Should I suffer the anguish of the sardines or should I delight in the joy of the gulls?"

"Willpower overcomes pain."

Something is dreaming us

"The darkness is swallowing everything."

"God does not exist."

"All you are going to be, you are already.
What you are looking for is already within you."

THE FILMS OF
ALEJANDRO JODOROWSKY
Available from ABKCO FILMS

The Dance of Reality	The Holy Mountain	El Topo	Fando y Lis
(2013)	(1973)	(1970)	(1968)

From legendary filmmaker Alejandro Jodorowsky comes his first film in over 23 years. *The Dance of Reality* is a surreal, bittersweet ode to the director's childhood that tells the allegorical story (adapted from his autobiography) of the young Jodorowsky's memories of his father's political protests and his mother's attempts to nurture him, with cameos from the filmmaker himself as the narrator of the story.

Blending his personal history with metaphor, mythology, and poetry, *The Dance of Reality* reflects Jodorowsky's philosophy that reality is not objective but rather a "dance" created by our own imaginations.

Also available on ABKCO Films, from the father of the Midnight Movie, is the landmark cult film that started it all, *El Topo,* as well as the scandalous *The Holy Mountain* and the bizarre *Fando y Lis*.

Extras include feature commentaries and on-camera interviews by the director, deleted scenes, original theatrical trailers, original script excerpts, a short about the Tarot, and a photo gallery.